TRUE STORY
SWEAR TO GOD
THIS ONE GOES TO ELEVEN

— *Tom Beland* (signature)

TOM BELAND

SAN FRANCISCO

TRUE STORY SWEAR TO GOD: THIS ONE GOES TO ELEVEN
BY TOM BELAND

PUBLISHED BY
AIT/PLANET LAR
2034 47TH AVENUE
SAN FRANCISCO, CA 94116

FIRST EDITION: MAY 2005

10 9 8 7 6 5 4 3 2 1

COVER ILLUSTRATION BY TOM BELAND

ISBN: 1-932051-34-1

PRINTED AND BOUND IN CANADA BY QUEBECOR PRINTING, INC.

TRUE STORY
SWEAR TO GOD
THIS ONE GOES TO ELEVEN

TOM BELAND

INTRODUCTION

I'M LATE. I'M LATE ON EVERYTHING. I DON'T HAVE TIME TO WRITE THIS.

HOW LATE AM I? I'VE BEEN SICK THE LAST FEW DAYS, I'M FLYING TO NEW ZEALAND FOR TWO WEEKS TOMORROW MORNING -- AND IT'S THEORETICALLY A VACATION, EXCEPT I'M LATE ENOUGH THAT I'M BRINGING ALONG TWO SCRIPTS I HAVE TO WRITE WHILE I'M THERE AND A 1200-PAGE BOOK ON THE HIS-TORY OF THE WORLD I NEED TO READ AS RESEARCH FOR THE NEXT *ARROWSMITH* MINISERIES. AND I'D BETTER FINISH THEM, BECAUSE WHEN I GET BACK, I HAVE TO WRITE A RESEARCH-INTENSIVE SCRIPT RIGHT AWAY OR A NONE-TOO-FAST ARTIST IS GOING TO BE LEFT IDLING ON A PROJECT THAT DOESN'T NEED TO LOSE ANY MORE TIME.

AND LET'S FACE IT, THE ONLY THING YOU GOT OUT OF THAT IS, "HE'S GOING TO NEW ZEALAND! COOL!" FAIR ENOUGH, THAT'S ABOUT HOW I FEEL ABOUT IT TOO.

BUT THE UPSHOT IS THAT I HAVE TO WRITE THIS INTRO AND THEN GO HAVE DINNER WITH AN EDITOR TO WORK OUT ONE OF THE SCRIPTS I'LL BE WRITING AND THEN COME HOME AND PACK AND GET SOME SLEEP BEFORE WE RACE OFF TO THE AIRPORT TOMORROW. SO I'VE GOT NO TIME TO THINK.

IF I'D BEEN SMART, I'D HAVE TOLD TOM I COULDN'T DO IT, BUT THERE WAS NO WAY I WAS GOING TO DO THAT. THIS BOOK IS ONE OF THE COMICS INDUSTRY'S RARE GEMS, AND I'D KICK MYSELF IF I PASSED UP A CHANCE TO BE A PART OF IT. HECK, MY WIFE WOULD KICK ME IF I PASSED IT UP.

SO I HAVE TO RESORT TO ONE OF THE OLD STANDBYS, THE EASY APPROACHES TO WRITING AN INTRO. I CAN TELL YOU HOW I CAME TO DISCOVER AND FALL IN LOVE WITH THIS BOOK. I CAN TELL YOU WHAT I KNOW ABOUT TOM (AND LILY) THAT YOU DON'T. OR I CAN JUST BE FUNNY FOR A COUPLE OF PAGES.

UNFORTUNATELY, THERE ARE PROBLEMS WITH ALL THOSE APPROACHES. HERE, I'LL PROVE IT.

ONE. HOW I CAME TO DISCOVER THIS BOOK

I DON'T HAVE ANYTHING COMPELLING TO TELL YOU. I DISCOVERED IT THE WAY A LOT OF PEOPLE DID, I'D GUESS. I'D SEEN TOM'S "TRUE STORY, SWEAR TO GOD" ONLINE STRIPS HERE AND THERE, AND THOUGHT THEY WERE FUNNY. AND PUBLISHER LARRY YOUNG WOULD DOUBTLESS LIKE ME TO MENTION THAT IF YOU, YES YOU, HAVEN'T READ THE ONLINE STRIPS, YOU CAN FIND A LOT OF THEM IN THE HANDY TRADE PAPER-BACK *TRUE STORY SWEAR TO GOD: 100 STORIES,* SECURABLE FROM WHATEVER FINE EMPORIUM YOU GOT THIS VOLUME FROM, EITHER FROM THEIR SHELVES OR WITH A FRIENDLY SPECIAL ORDER. YOU'RE WELCOME, LARRY.

BUT I LIKED THE STRIPS -- THEY WERE FUNNY ENOUGH TO SEARCH FOR, ONLINE. SO WHEN I SAW THAT THERE WAS AN ACTUAL COMIC BOOK COMING UP BY THE GUY WHO DID THOSE FUNNY *TRUE STORY SWEAR TO GOD* STRIPS ONLINE, I ORDERED IT AS A PART OF MY MONTHLY COMICS ORDER. NO BIG DEAL.

BOY, WAS I WRONG.

BECAUSE THE ONLINE STORIES ARE FUNNY AND CLEVER AND WELL-DRAWN AND ALL, BUT THEY'RE JOKES, OBSERVATIONS ON LIFE -- A QUICK STING OF HUMOR AND RECOGNITION, AND POW!, THEY'RE DONE. I WAS EXPECTING SOMETHING LIKE THAT, NOT A -- NOT A ROMANCE!

AND CERTAINLY NOT A ROMANCE SO WARM AND OPEN AND HONEST AND APPROACHABLE AND TOUCHING THAT IT'D BE THE ONLY COMIC I CONSISTENTLY CHOKE UP WHILE READING.

SO WHEN THAT FIRST ISSUE ARRIVED, IT HIT LIKE A THUNDERBOLT AND I'VE BEEN READING IT EVER SINCE AND TALKING IT UP TO FRIENDS, LIKE PRETTY MUCH EVERYONE ELSE WHO'S READ IT. AND THAT'S REALLY ALL THERE IS TO THAT STORY.

ONE OTHER ADDITION. WHEN I READ THE FIRST ISSUE OF *TRUE STORY* , I GAVE IT TO MY WIFE AND SAID, "YOU OUGHT TO READ THIS, YOU'LL LIKE IT." BIG MISTAKE. NOW, WHENEVER A NEW ISSUE OF *TRUE STORY* COMES IN, I'VE GOT TO READ IT FAST -- AND I MEAN LIKE RIGHT-AWAY FAST -- OR SHE'LL SEE IT AND IT'LL BE GONE AND I MAY NEVER CATCH A GLIMPSE OF IT AGAIN. GUYS, IF YOU CAN'T GET YOUR GIRL-FRIEND-WIFE-WHOMEVER INTERESTED IN READING COMICS ABOUT BURLY GUYS IN SKINTIGHT CLOTHES SMACK-ING EACH OTHER AROUND AS THEY FALL OFF BUILDINGS, TRY THIS. BUT READ THE ISSUES YOURSELF BEFORE YOU MENTION THEM, OR BE PREPARED TO BUY SPARES.

ANYWAY. STORY DONE, NOT MUCH OF AN INTRO THERE.

TWO. WHAT I KNOW ABOUT TOM AND LILY THAT YOU DON'T

NOTHING.

I MEAN, I'VE MET THEM AT CONVENTIONS, A COUPLE OF TIMES. AND TOM'S A FINE GUY, CHEERFUL AND OPEN AND FANNISH, AND DELIGHTED THAT PEOPLE LIKE HIS BOOK AS MUCH AS WE ALL DO. AND LILY IS AS CHARMING AND FRIENDLY AND POISED AS YOU'D EXPECT -- THE BOOK AIN'T CALLED "TRUE STORY" FOR NOTHING -- AND IT'S EASY TO SEE HER AS A POPULAR RADIO PERSONALITY IN PUERTO RICO.

BUT C'MON, FOLKS -- THE BOOK IS ABOUT THEM! IT TAKES YOU INTO THEIR LIVES, THEIR WORK, THEIR MEALS, THEIR BEDROOM -- A COUPLE OF MEETINGS AT CONVENTIONS AREN'T GOING TO TELL ME ANY-THING THE BOOK WON'T TELL YOU. ALMOST EVERYTHING I KNOW ABOUT TOM AND LILY COMES FROM READING THE COMIC.

WHICH IS AS IT SHOULD BE. IF YOU NEEDED AN INTRO TO EXPLAIN SOMETHING ABOUT THE LEAD CHARAC-TERS OF THE BOOK, THE BOOK WOULDN'T BE DOING ITS JOB, WOULD IT?

STILL, EVEN LESS INTRODUCTION FODDER THERE.

THREE. BE FUNNY FOR A COUPLE OF PAGES

NO WAY.

ASIDE FROM THE TROUBLE OF BEING FUNNY UNDER TIME PRESSURE -- AND I SEE THAT I'VE NOW GOT UNDER TEN MINUTES TO FINISH THIS, COPY EDIT IT AND SEND IT OFF TO TOM BEFORE I HAVE TO HOP IN THE CAR AND HEAD OUT FOR THAT DINNER MEETING -- THERE'S THE ISSUE OF COMPETITION. THERE'S LIKE, SEVEN ISSUES OF TRUE STORY SWEAR TO GOD FOLLOWING THIS INTRO! AND IT'S FUNNY AND WARM AND TOUCHING AND RAW AND EMOTIONAL AND HONEST AND THERE'S NO WAY I CAN COMPETE. NOT GONNA HAPPEN.

***

LUCKILY, MY TRUE PURPOSE HERE IS SIMPLE. MY JOB IS TO BE PLEASANT AND READABLE FOR A FEW PAGES, SO LARRY CAN PUT "INTRODUCTION BY KURT BUSIEK" ON THE COVER OR BACK COVER SOMEWHERE, AND THOSE OF YOU WHO DON'T KNOW ABOUT *TRUE STORY* YET, BUT WHO MAY HAVE LIKED *MARVELS* OR *ASTRO CITY* OR *CONAN* OR SOMETHING ELSE I WROTE, WILL PICK UP THE BOOK AND GIVE IT A CHANCE. AND TOM -- WITH THE ABLE ASSISTANCE OF LILY -- WILL DO THE REST.

AND LET'S FACE IT, YOU SAW THIS COMING FROM THE MOMENT I STARTED TALKING ABOUT OLD STAND-BYS AT THE BEGINNING OFF ALL THIS -- I'D TICK OFF EACH STRATEGY, EXPLAIN WHY I WASN'T GOING TO USE IT, AND THEN HEY PRESTO, LOOK, I'M DONE!

AND HEY PRESTO. LOOK.

YEAH YEAH YEAH. ISN'T THERE ANYTHING I CAN TELL YOU, ANY INSIDE INFORMATION, ANY STORY OR BIT OR SOMETHING THAT'LL MAKE THIS INTRODUCTION SEEM LIKE MORE THAN IT IS?

JUST THIS: THIS IS THE SECOND VOLUME COLLECTING THE STORY OF TOM AND LILY'S ROMANCE. THE FIRST VOLUME, *TRUE STORY SWEAR TO GOD: CHANCES ARE...,* IS ALSO AVAILABLE FROM WHATEVER FINE EMPO⬚ RIUM SOLD YOU THIS ONE, EITHER FROM THEIR SHELVES OR BY CONVENIENT SPECIAL ORDER. YOU'RE WEL⬚ COME, LARRY. I SAY THIS BECAUSE I FIGURE MOST OF YOU HAVEN'T READ THE FIRST VOLUME, OR YOU WOULDN'T BE WASTING YOUR TIME ON ME, WHEN THERE'S ALL THAT BELAND WONDERMENT AHEAD.

AS FOR THE REST, YEAH, THIS IS A WONDERFUL COMIC, BY A WONDERFUL GUY, AND YOU'LL LOVE IT. BUT THE PAGES THAT FOLLOW WILL MAKE THAT CASE FAR, FAR BETTER THAN I EVER COULD.

TOM, LILY, SORRY ABOUT THE INTRO. AND PLEASE, PLEASE DON'T HOLD IT AGAINST ME THAT IT'S SORTA KINDA THE SAME SHTICK I USED FOR A *USAGI YOJIMBO* INTRO A FEW YEARS BACK.

THE REST OF YOU, I GIVE YOU TOM BELAND AND LILY GARCIA, AND THEIR CONTINUING TRUE STORY. THEY'LL MORE THAN MAKE UP FOR ME.

KURT BUSIEK
MARCH 2005

RAINY DAYS AND MONDAYS
SO TELL ME AGAIN WHY I SHOULDN'T WORRY...?
BECAUSE IT'S NOT A HURRICANE.
IT'S NOT.
NO.
IT'S A TROPICAL STORM.
AND THAT'S A GOOD THING...
RIGHT...?
PHONE CALLS.
WE LIVE THROUGH THEM... LILY AND I.
AS OFTEN AS POSSIBLE.
PACIFIC BELL OWNS MY SOUL... JUDGING FROM THE SIZE OF MY PHONE BILLS.
WEDNESDAY... SEPTEMBER 16.

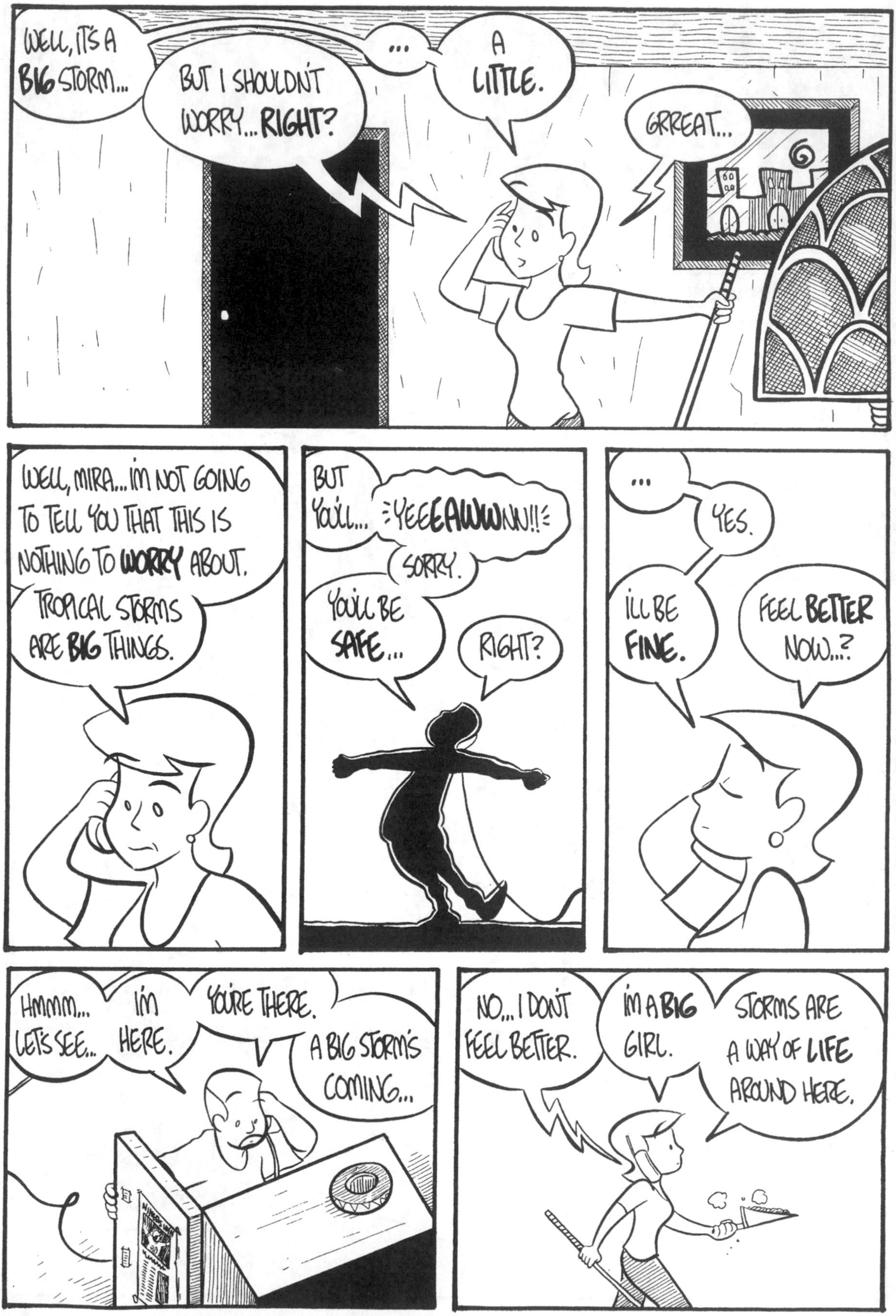
WELL, IT'S A BIG STORM...
BUT I SHOULDN'T WORRY... RIGHT?
...
A LITTLE.
GRREAT...
WELL, MIRA... I'M NOT GOING TO TELL YOU THAT THIS IS NOTHING TO WORRY ABOUT.
TROPICAL STORMS ARE BIG THINGS.
BUT YOU'LL...
YEEEAWWNN!!
SORRY.
YOU'LL BE SAFE...
RIGHT?
...
YES.
I'LL BE FINE.
FEEL BETTER NOW...?
HMMM... LET'S SEE...
I'M HERE.
YOU'RE THERE.
A BIG STORM'S COMING...
NO... I DON'T FEEL BETTER.
I'M A BIG GIRL.
STORMS ARE A WAY OF LIFE AROUND HERE.

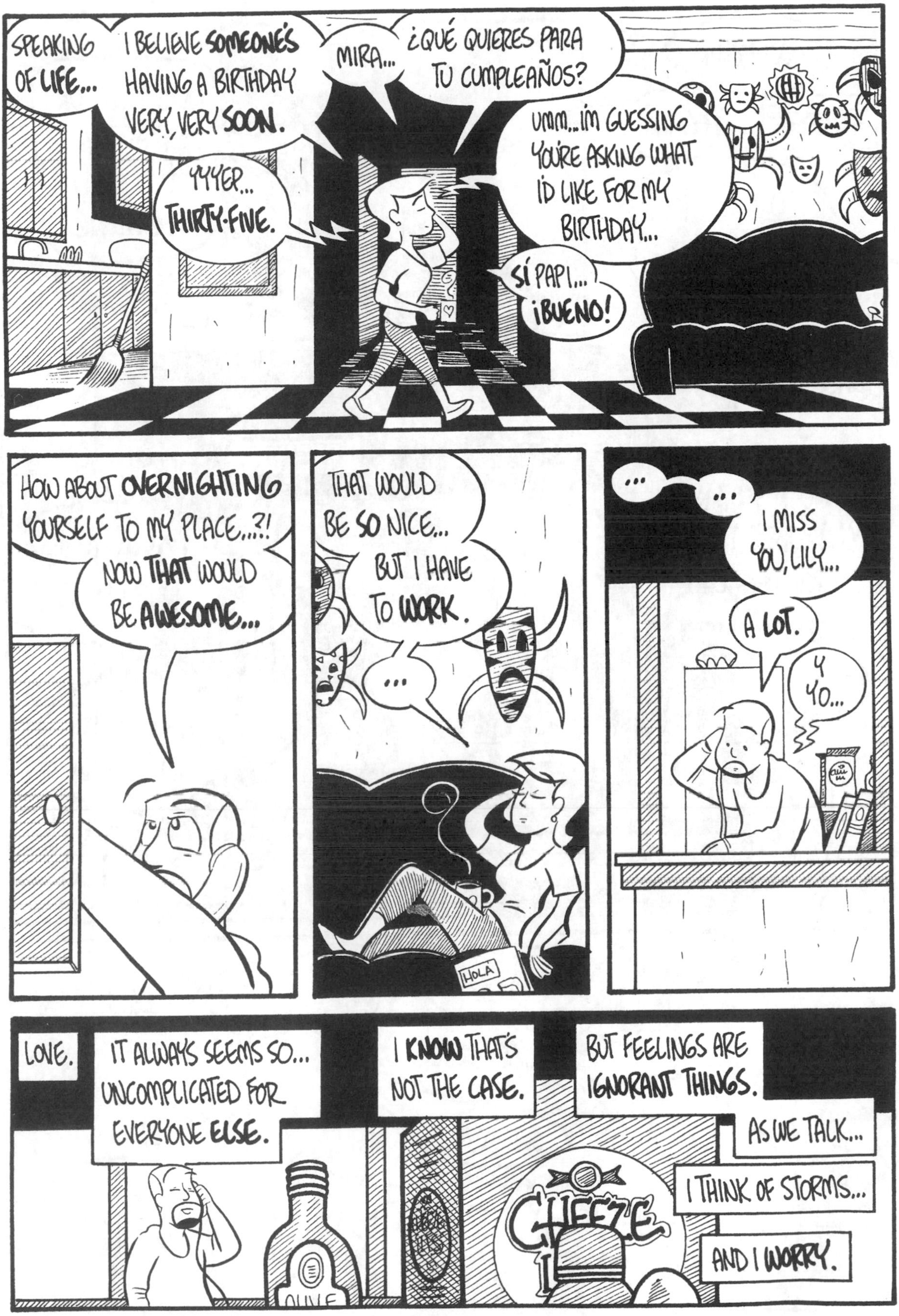

SPEAKING OF LIFE...
I BELIEVE SOMEONE'S HAVING A BIRTHDAY VERY, VERY SOON.
MIRA...
¿QUÉ QUIERES PARA TU CUMPLEAÑOS?
YYYEP... THIRTY-FIVE.
UMM...IM GUESSING YOU'RE ASKING WHAT I'D LIKE FOR MY BIRTHDAY...
SÍ PAPI... ¡BUENO!
HOW ABOUT OVERNIGHTING YOURSELF TO MY PLACE...?!
NOW THAT WOULD BE AWESOME...
THAT WOULD BE SO NICE...
BUT I HAVE TO WORK.
...
HOLA
...
...
I MISS YOU, LILY...
A LOT.
Y YO...
LOVE.
IT ALWAYS SEEMS SO... UNCOMPLICATED FOR EVERYONE ELSE.
I KNOW THAT'S NOT THE CASE.
BUT FEELINGS ARE IGNORANT THINGS.
AS WE TALK...
I THINK OF STORMS...
AND I WORRY.

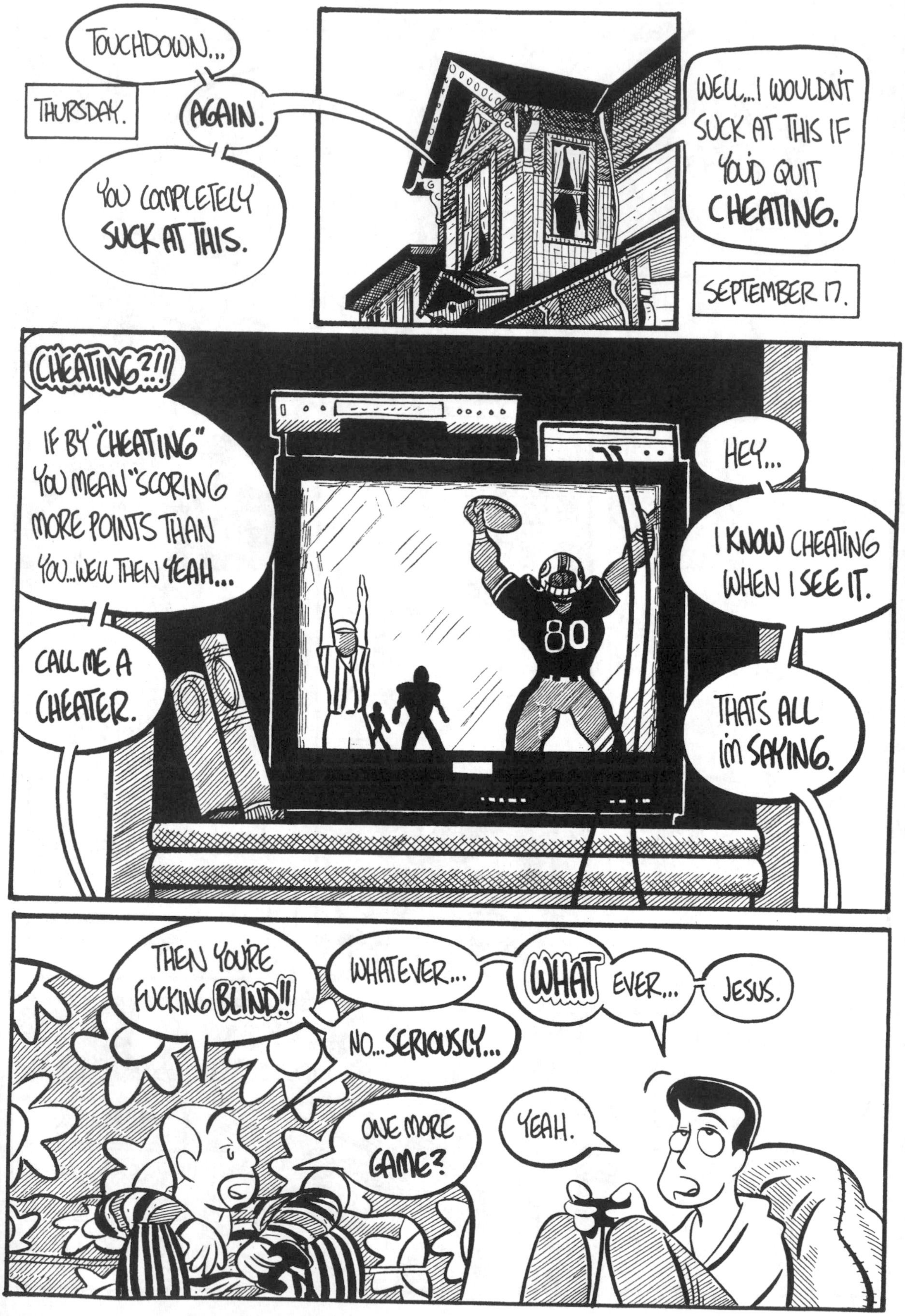
THURSDAY.
TOUCHDOWN...
AGAIN.
YOU COMPLETELY SUCK AT THIS.
WELL...I WOULDN'T SUCK AT THIS IF YOU'D QUIT CHEATING.
SEPTEMBER 17.
CHEATING?!!
IF BY "CHEATING" YOU MEAN "SCORING MORE POINTS THAN YOU...WELL THEN YEAH...
CALL ME A CHEATER.
HEY...
I KNOW CHEATING WHEN I SEE IT.
THAT'S ALL I'M SAYING.
80
THEN YOU'RE FUCKING BLIND!!
WHATEVER...
NO...SERIOUSLY...
WHAT EVER...
JESUS.
ONE MORE GAME?
YEAH.

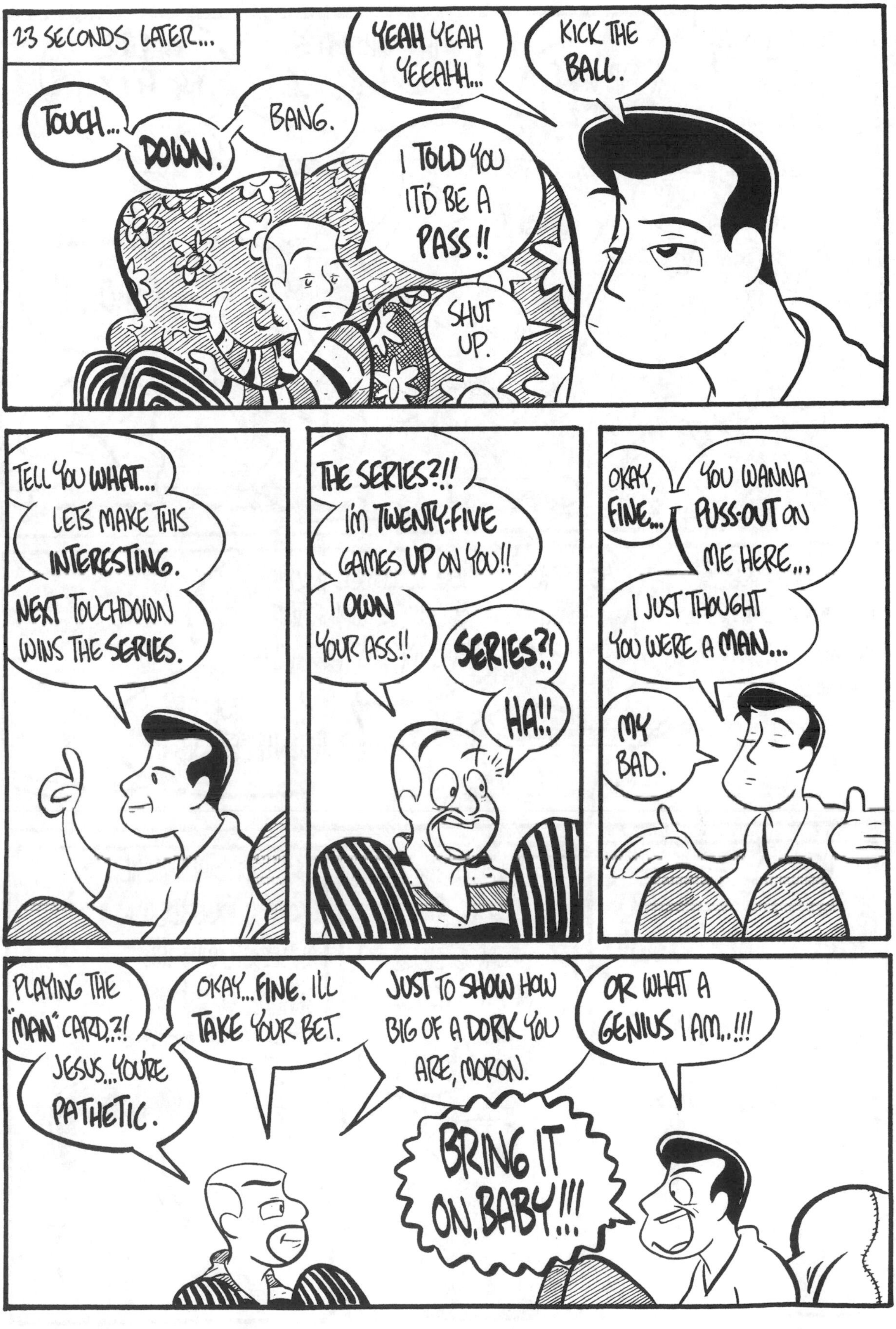
23 SECONDS LATER...
TOUCH... DOWN.
BANG.
YEAH YEAH YEEAHH...
KICK THE BALL.
I TOLD YOU ITD BE A PASS!!
SHUT UP.
TELL YOU WHAT... LETS MAKE THIS INTERESTING.
NEXT TOUCHDOWN WINS THE SERIES.
THE SERIES?!! I'M TWENTY-FIVE GAMES UP ON YOU!!
I OWN YOUR ASS!!
SERIES?! HA!!
OKAY, FINE...
YOU WANNA PUSS-OUT ON ME HERE...
I JUST THOUGHT YOU WERE A MAN...
MY BAD.
PLAYING THE "MAN" CARD?!! JESUS... YOU'RE PATHETIC.
OKAY... FINE. I'LL TAKE YOUR BET.
JUST TO SHOW HOW BIG OF A DORK YOU ARE, MORON.
OR WHAT A GENIUS I AM..!!!
BRING IT ON, BABY!!!

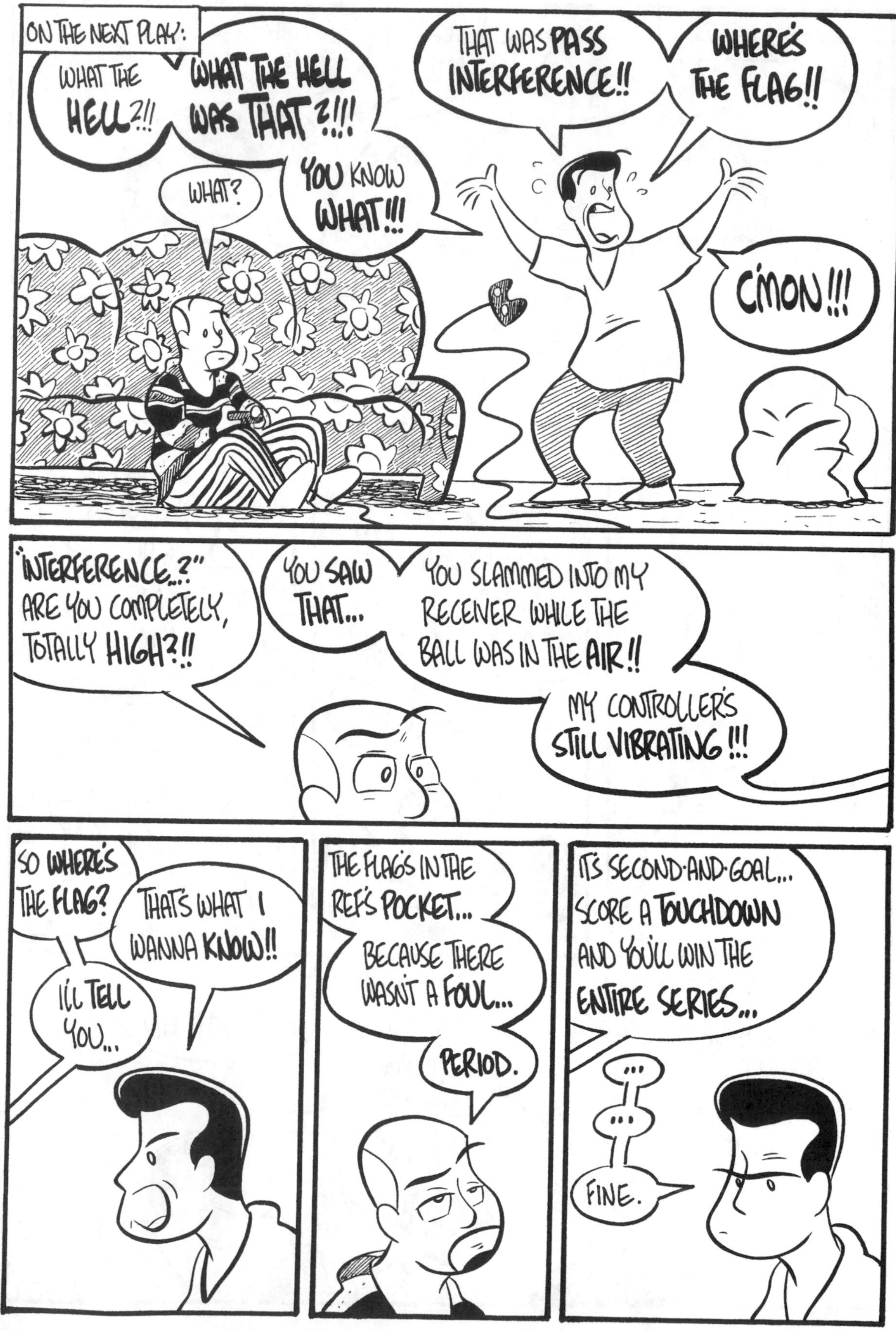
ON THE NEXT PLAY:
WHAT THE HELL?!!
WHAT THE HELL WAS THAT?!!!
THAT WAS PASS INTERFERENCE!!
WHERE'S THE FLAG!!
WHAT?
YOU KNOW WHAT!!!
C'MON!!!
"INTERFERENCE..?" ARE YOU COMPLETELY, TOTALLY HIGH?!!
YOU SAW THAT...
YOU SLAMMED INTO MY RECEIVER WHILE THE BALL WAS IN THE AIR!!
MY CONTROLLER'S STILL VIBRATING!!!
SO WHERE'S THE FLAG?
THAT'S WHAT I WANNA KNOW!!
I'LL TELL YOU...
THE FLAG'S IN THE REF'S POCKET...
BECAUSE THERE WASN'T A FOUL...
PERIOD.
IT'S SECOND-AND-GOAL... SCORE A TOUCHDOWN AND YOU'LL WIN THE ENTIRE SERIES...
...
...
FINE.

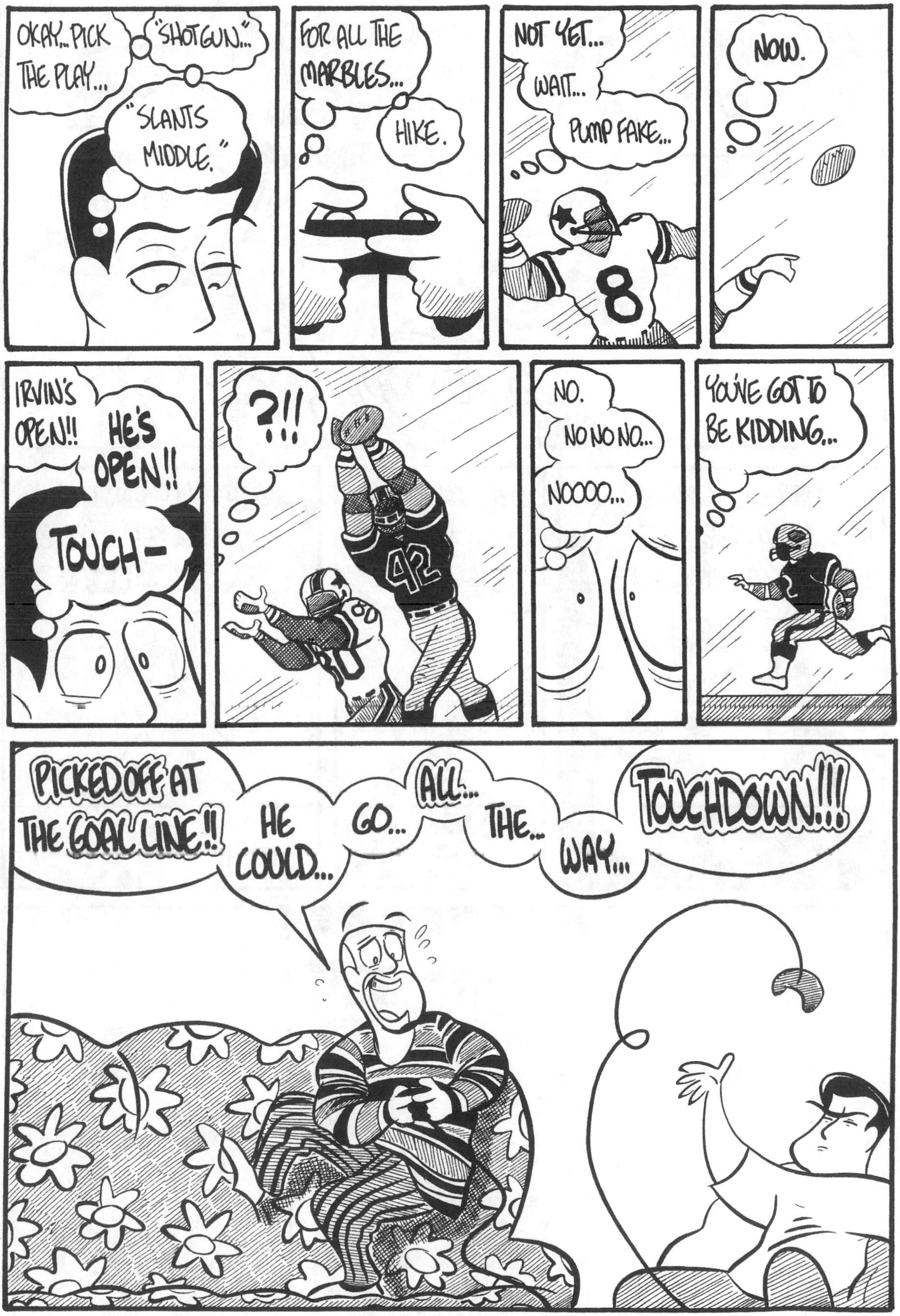

OKAY... PICK THE PLAY...
"SHOTGUN..."
"SLANTS MIDDLE."
FOR ALL THE MARBLES...
HIKE.
NOT YET...
WAIT...
PUMP FAKE...
NOW.
IRVIN'S OPEN!!
HE'S OPEN!!
TOUCH-
?!!
NO.
NO NO NO...
NOOOO...
YOU'VE GOT TO BE KIDDING...
PICKED OFF AT THE GOAL LINE!!
HE COULD...
GO...
ALL...
THE...
WAY...
TOUCHDOWN!!!

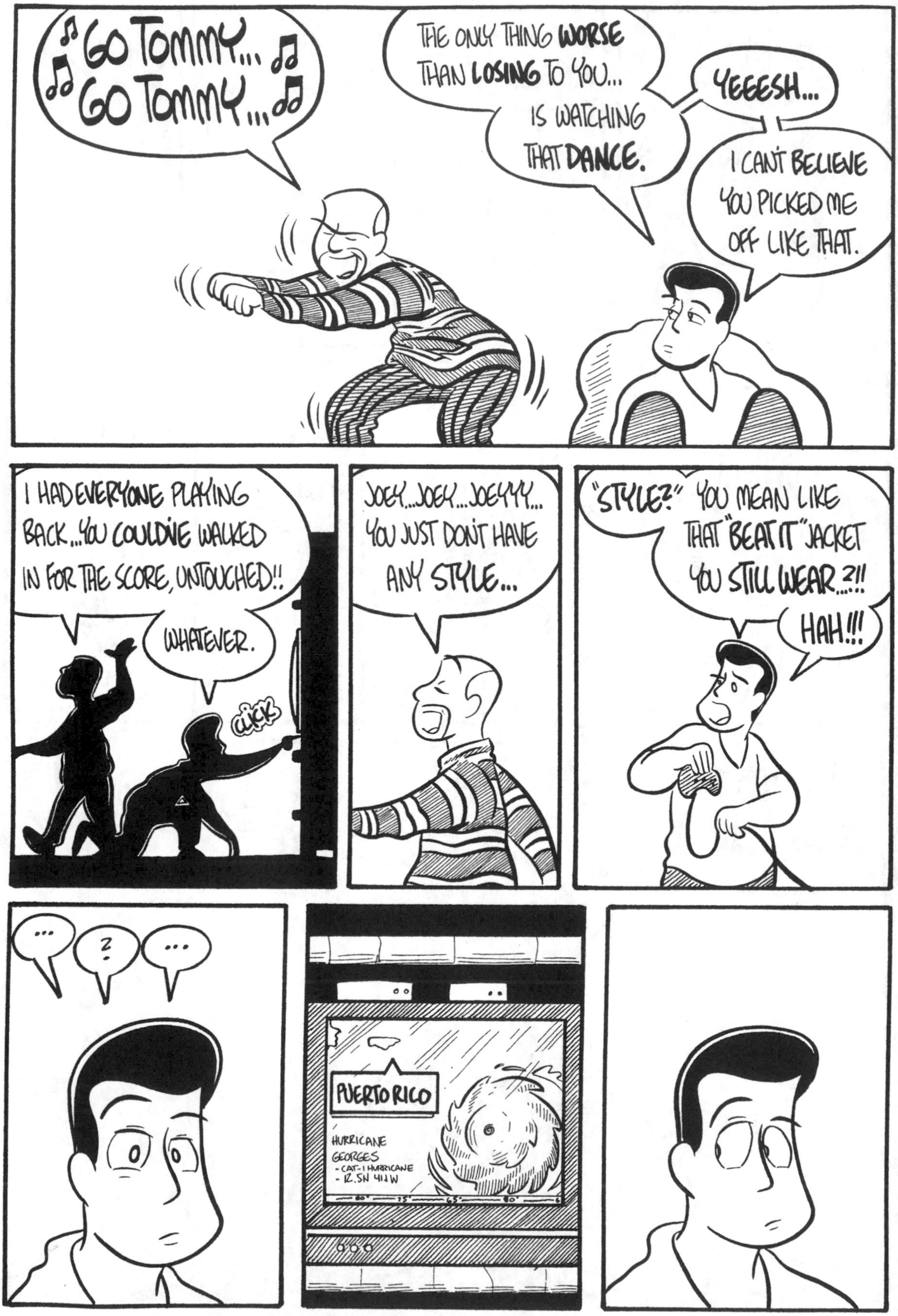
GO TOMMY... GO TOMMY...
THE ONLY THING WORSE THAN LOSING TO YOU...
IS WATCHING THAT DANCE.
YEEESH...
I CAN'T BELIEVE YOU PICKED ME OFF LIKE THAT.
I HAD EVERYONE PLAYING BACK... YOU COULD'VE WALKED IN FOR THE SCORE, UNTOUCHED!!
WHATEVER.
CLICK
JOEY... JOEY... JOEYYY... YOU JUST DON'T HAVE ANY STYLE...
"STYLE?" YOU MEAN LIKE THAT "BEAT IT" JACKET YOU STILL WEAR...?!!
HAH!!!
...
?
...
PUERTO RICO
HURRICANE GEORGES
- CAT-1 HURRICANE

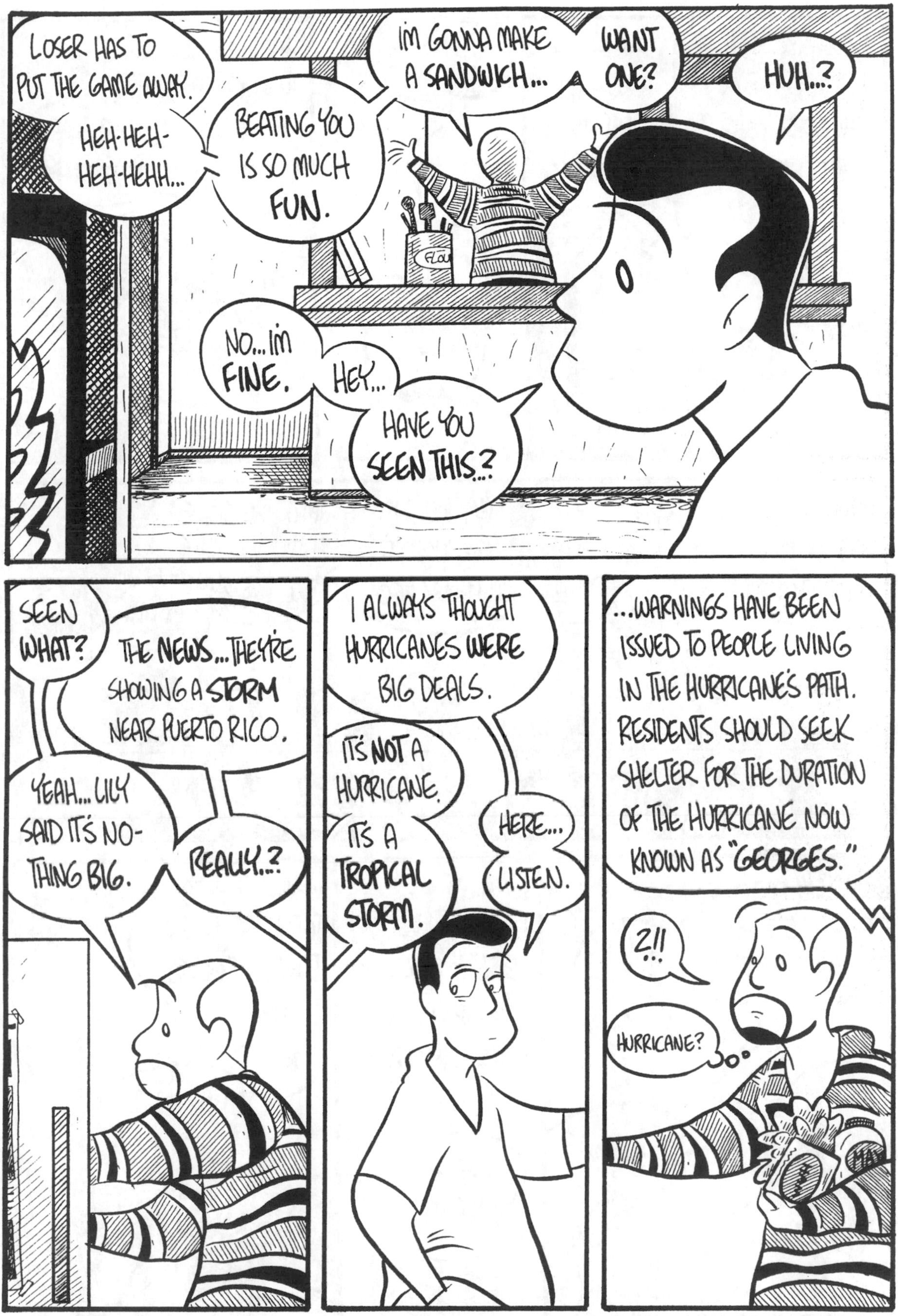
LOSER HAS TO PUT THE GAME AWAY.
HEH-HEH-HEH-HEHH...
BEATING YOU IS SO MUCH FUN.
I'M GONNA MAKE A SANDWICH...
WANT ONE?
HUH...?
NO... I'M FINE.
HEY...
HAVE YOU SEEN THIS...?
SEEN WHAT?
THE NEWS... THEY'RE SHOWING A STORM NEAR PUERTO RICO.
YEAH... LILY SAID IT'S NOTHING BIG.
REALLY...?
I ALWAYS THOUGHT HURRICANES WERE BIG DEALS.
IT'S NOT A HURRICANE.
IT'S A TROPICAL STORM.
HERE...
LISTEN.
...WARNINGS HAVE BEEN ISSUED TO PEOPLE LIVING IN THE HURRICANE'S PATH. RESIDENTS SHOULD SEEK SHELTER FOR THE DURATION OF THE HURRICANE NOW KNOWN AS "GEORGES."
?!!
HURRICANE?

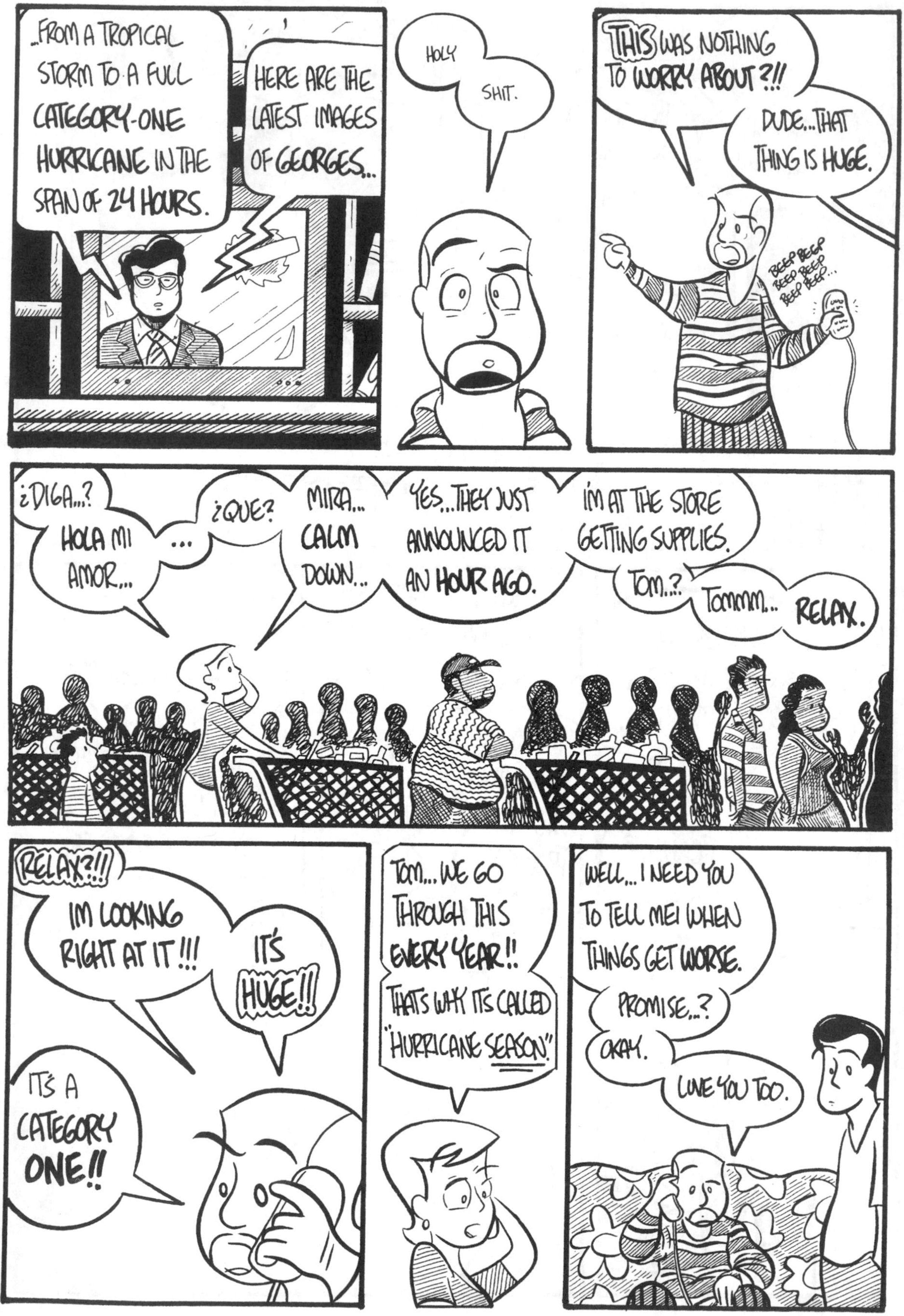

...FROM A TROPICAL STORM TO A FULL CATEGORY-ONE HURRICANE IN THE SPAN OF 24 HOURS.
HERE ARE THE LATEST IMAGES OF GEORGES...
HOLY
SHIT.
THIS WAS NOTHING TO WORRY ABOUT?!!
DUDE...THAT THING IS HUGE.
BEEP BEEP BEEP BEEP BEEP BEEP...
¿DIGA...?
HOLA MI AMOR...
...
¿QUE?
MIRA... CALM DOWN...
YES...THEY JUST ANNOUNCED IT AN HOUR AGO.
I'M AT THE STORE GETTING SUPPLIES.
TOM..?
TOMMM...
RELAX.
RELAX?!!
IM LOOKING RIGHT AT IT!!!
IT'S HUGE!!
IT'S A CATEGORY ONE!!
TOM... WE GO THROUGH THIS EVERY YEAR!!
THATS WHY ITS CALLED "HURRICANE SEASON."
WELL... I NEED YOU TO TELL ME! WHEN THINGS GET WORSE.
PROMISE...?
OKAY.
LOVE YOU TOO.

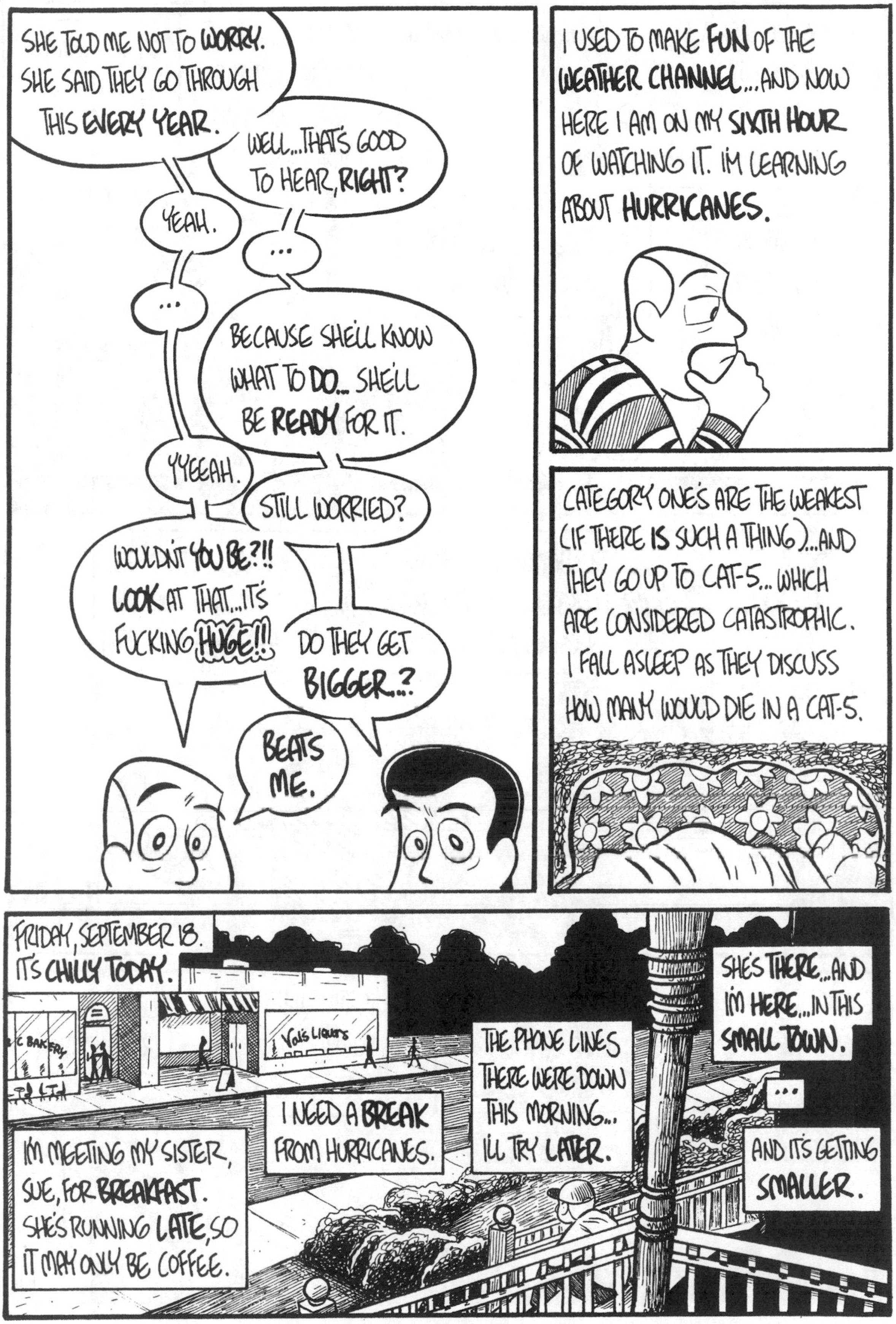

SHE TOLD ME NOT TO WORRY. SHE SAID THEY GO THROUGH THIS EVERY YEAR.
WELL...THAT'S GOOD TO HEAR, RIGHT?
YEAH.
...
...
BECAUSE SHE'LL KNOW WHAT TO DO... SHE'LL BE READY FOR IT.
YYEEAH.
STILL WORRIED?
WOULDN'T YOU BE?!! LOOK AT THAT...IT'S FUCKING HUGE!!
DO THEY GET BIGGER..?
BEATS ME.
I USED TO MAKE FUN OF THE WEATHER CHANNEL...AND NOW HERE I AM ON MY SIXTH HOUR OF WATCHING IT. I'M LEARNING ABOUT HURRICANES.
CATEGORY ONE'S ARE THE WEAKEST (IF THERE IS SUCH A THING)...AND THEY GO UP TO CAT-5... WHICH ARE CONSIDERED CATASTROPHIC. I FALL ASLEEP AS THEY DISCUSS HOW MANY WOULD DIE IN A CAT-5.
FRIDAY, SEPTEMBER 18. IT'S CHILLY TODAY.
I'M MEETING MY SISTER, SUE, FOR BREAKFAST. SHE'S RUNNING LATE, SO IT MAY ONLY BE COFFEE.
Val's Liquors
I NEED A BREAK FROM HURRICANES.
THE PHONE LINES THERE WERE DOWN THIS MORNING... I'LL TRY LATER.
SHE'S THERE...AND I'M HERE...IN THIS SMALL TOWN.
...
AND IT'S GETTING SMALLER.

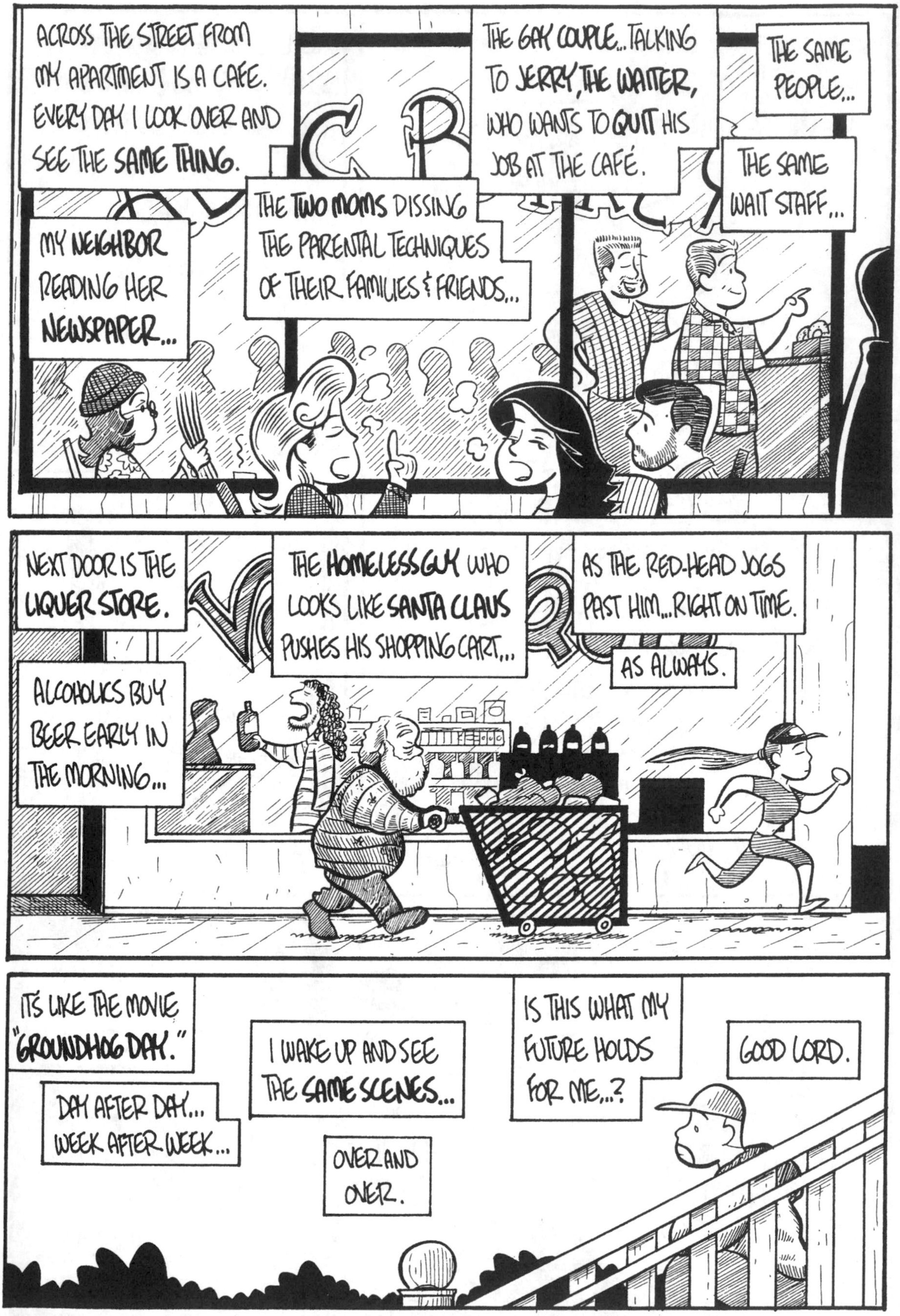
ACROSS THE STREET FROM MY APARTMENT IS A CAFE. EVERY DAY I LOOK OVER AND SEE THE SAME THING.
THE GAY COUPLE... TALKING TO JERRY, THE WAITER, WHO WANTS TO QUIT HIS JOB AT THE CAFÉ.
THE SAME PEOPLE...
THE SAME WAIT STAFF...
THE TWO MOMS DISSING THE PARENTAL TECHNIQUES OF THEIR FAMILIES & FRIENDS...
MY NEIGHBOR READING HER NEWSPAPER...
NEXT DOOR IS THE LIQUER STORE.
THE HOMELESS GUY WHO LOOKS LIKE SANTA CLAUS PUSHES HIS SHOPPING CART...
AS THE RED-HEAD JOGS PAST HIM... RIGHT ON TIME.
AS ALWAYS.
ALCOHOLICS BUY BEER EARLY IN THE MORNING...
IT'S LIKE THE MOVIE "GROUNDHOG DAY."
DAY AFTER DAY... WEEK AFTER WEEK...
I WAKE UP AND SEE THE SAME SCENES...
OVER AND OVER.
IS THIS WHAT MY FUTURE HOLDS FOR ME...?
GOOD LORD.

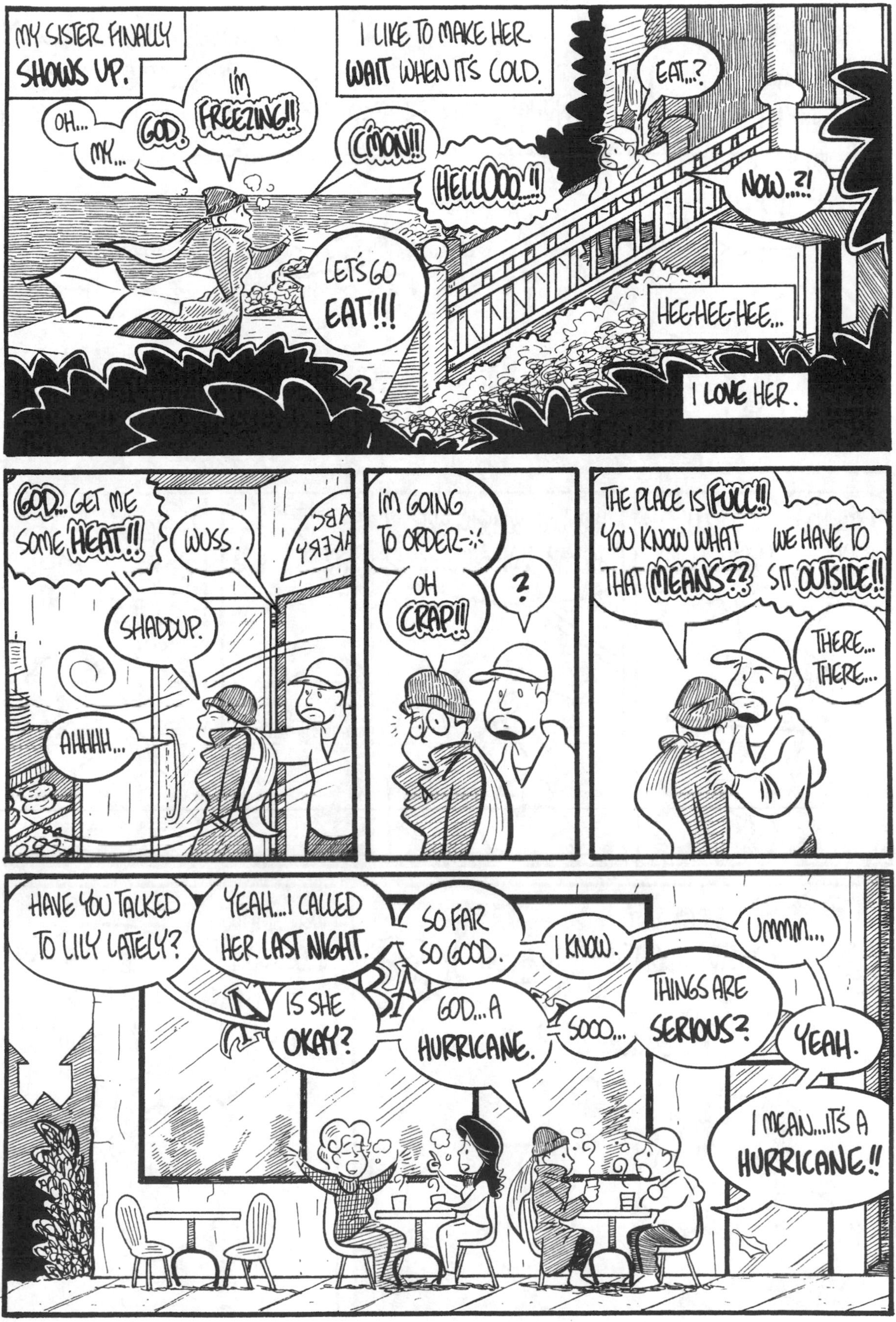
MY SISTER FINALLY SHOWS UP.
OH...
MY...
GOD.
I'M FREEZING!!
I LIKE TO MAKE HER WAIT WHEN IT'S COLD.
C'MON!!
HELLOOO..!!
EAT..?
NOW..?!
LET'S GO EAT!!!
HEE-HEE-HEE...
I LOVE HER.
GOD... GET ME SOME HEAT!!
WUSS.
SHADDUP.
AHHHH...
I'M GOING TO ORDER-
OH CRAP!!
?
THE PLACE IS FULL!! YOU KNOW WHAT THAT MEANS??
WE HAVE TO SIT OUTSIDE!!
THERE... THERE...
HAVE YOU TALKED TO LILY LATELY?
YEAH...I CALLED HER LAST NIGHT.
IS SHE OKAY?
SO FAR SO GOOD.
GOD... A HURRICANE.
I KNOW.
SOOO...
THINGS ARE SERIOUS?
UMMM...
YEAH.
I MEAN...IT'S A HURRICANE!!

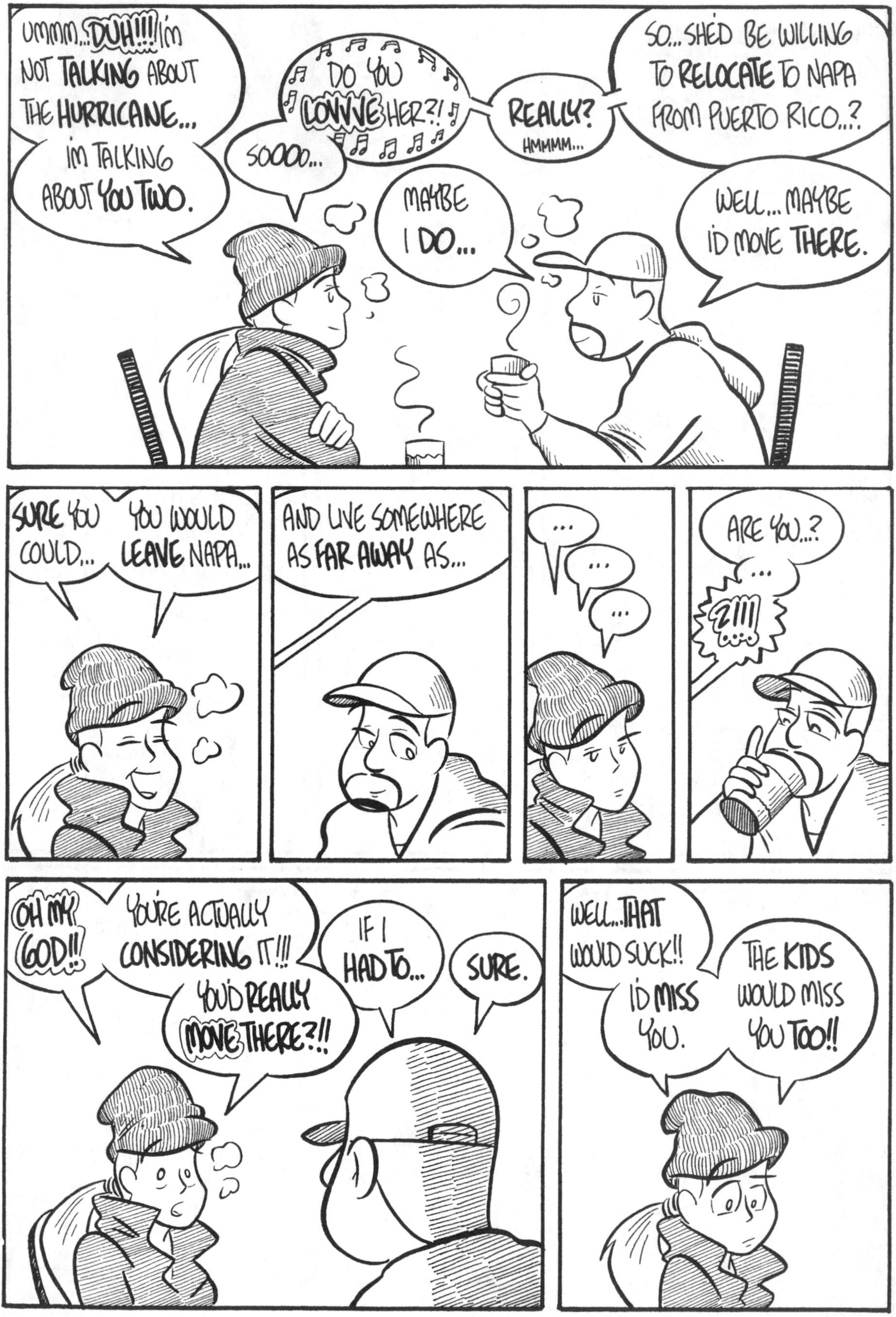
UMMM...DUH!!! I'M NOT TALKING ABOUT THE HURRICANE...
I'M TALKING ABOUT YOU TWO.
SOOOO...
DO YOU LOVVVE HER?!
REALLY? HMMMM...
SO...SHE'D BE WILLING TO RELOCATE TO NAPA FROM PUERTO RICO...?
MAYBE I DO...
WELL... MAYBE I'D MOVE THERE.
SURE YOU COULD...
YOU WOULD LEAVE NAPA...
AND LIVE SOMEWHERE AS FAR AWAY AS...
...
...
...
ARE YOU...?
...
?!!!
OH MY GOD!!
YOU'RE ACTUALLY CONSIDERING IT!!!
YOU'D REALLY MOVE THERE?!!
IF I HAD TO...
SURE.
WELL...THAT WOULD SUCK!!
I'D MISS YOU.
THE KIDS WOULD MISS YOU TOO!!

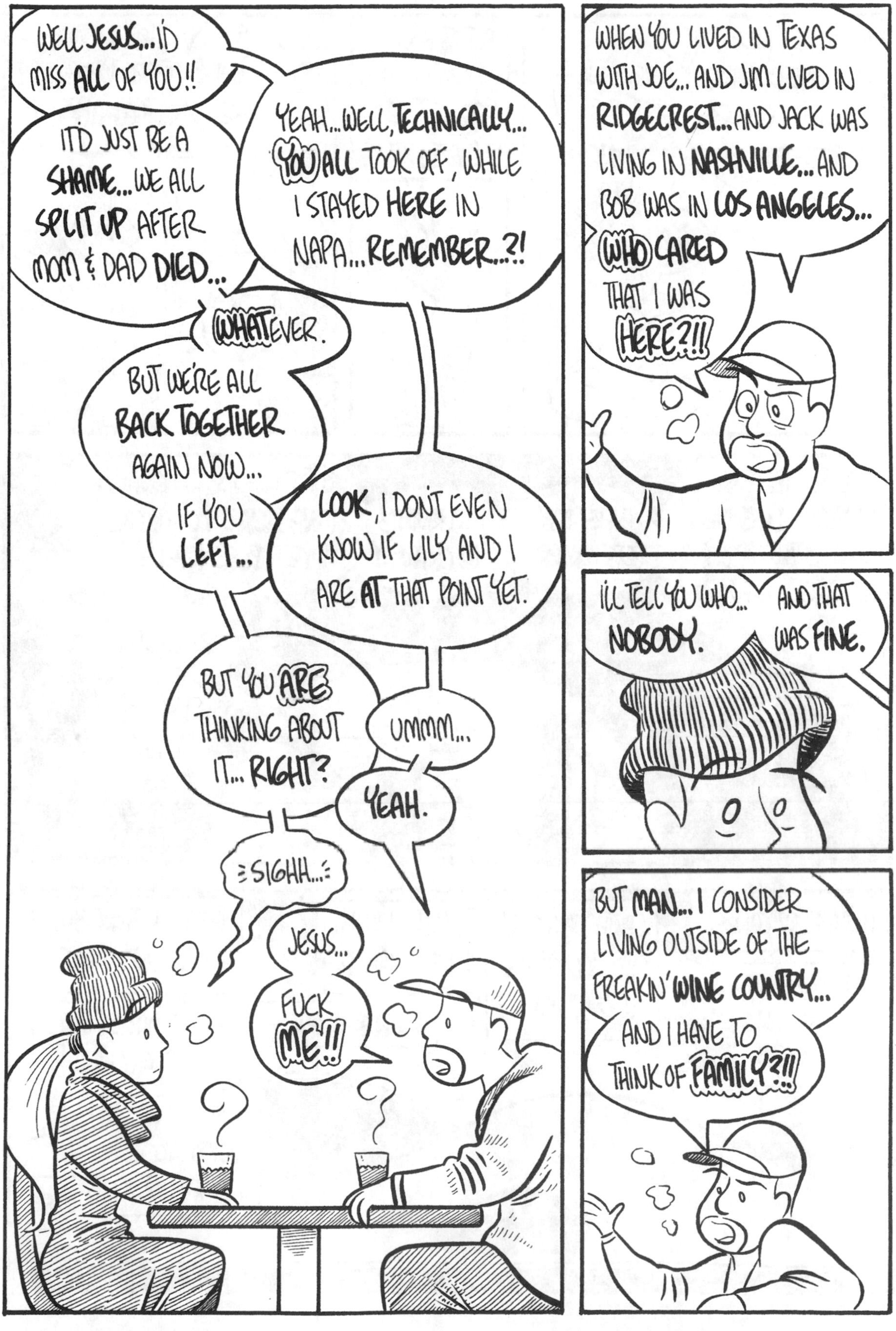
WELL JESUS... I'D MISS ALL OF YOU!!
IT'D JUST BE A SHAME... WE ALL SPLIT UP AFTER MOM & DAD DIED...
YEAH... WELL, TECHNICALLY... YOU ALL TOOK OFF, WHILE I STAYED HERE IN NAPA... REMEMBER...?!
WHATEVER.
BUT WE'RE ALL BACK TOGETHER AGAIN NOW...
IF YOU LEFT...
LOOK, I DON'T EVEN KNOW IF LILY AND I ARE AT THAT POINT YET.
BUT YOU ARE THINKING ABOUT IT... RIGHT?
UMMM...
YEAH.
SIGHH...
JESUS...
FUCK ME!!
WHEN YOU LIVED IN TEXAS WITH JOE... AND JIM LIVED IN RIDGECREST... AND JACK WAS LIVING IN NASHVILLE... AND BOB WAS IN LOS ANGELES...
WHO CARED THAT I WAS HERE?!!
I'LL TELL YOU WHO... NOBODY.
AND THAT WAS FINE.
BUT MAN... I CONSIDER LIVING OUTSIDE OF THE FREAKIN' WINE COUNTRY...
AND I HAVE TO THINK OF FAMILY?!!

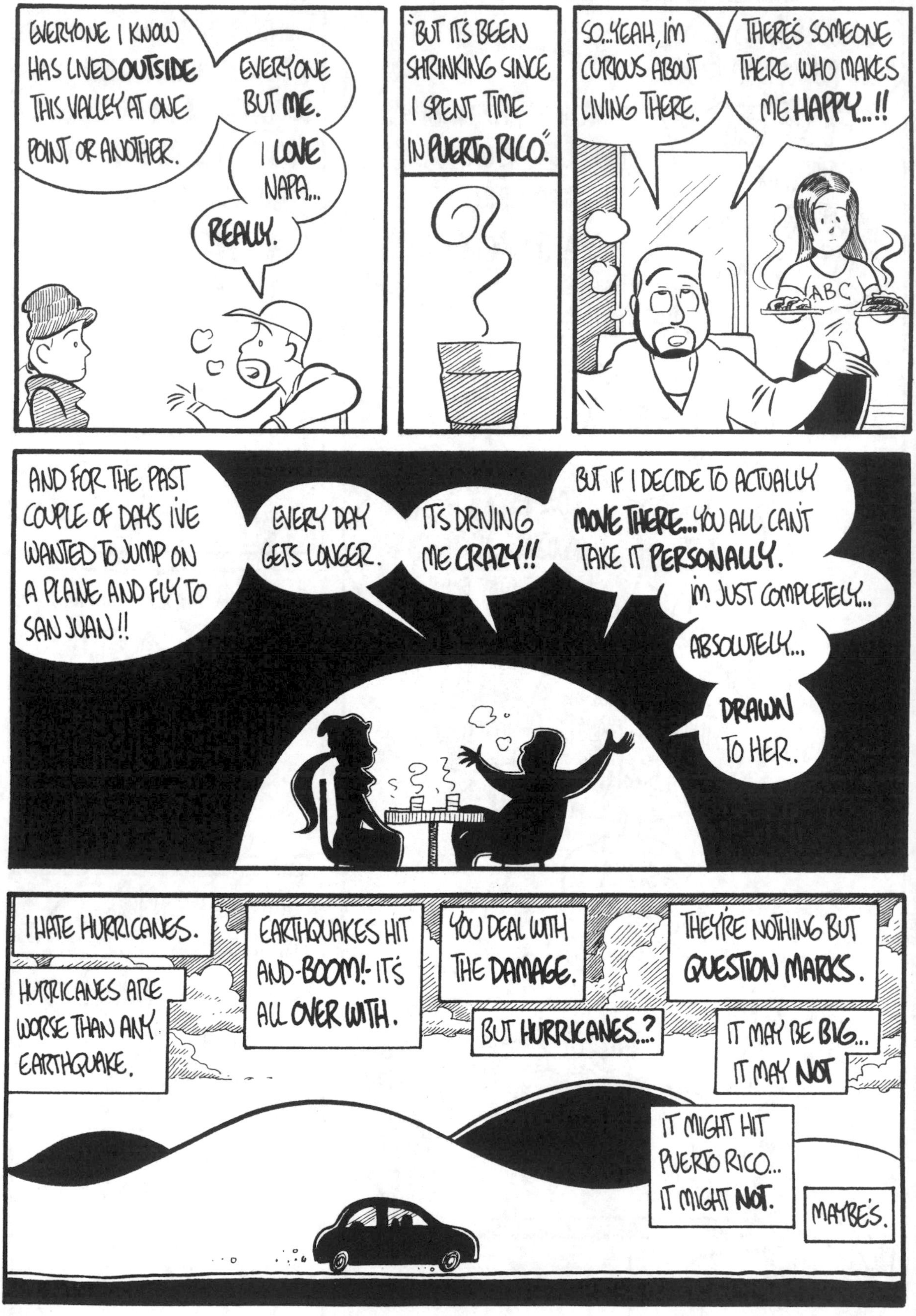
EVERYONE I KNOW HAS LIVED OUTSIDE THIS VALLEY AT ONE POINT OR ANOTHER.
EVERYONE BUT ME.
I LOVE NAPA...
REALLY.
"BUT IT'S BEEN SHRINKING SINCE I SPENT TIME IN PUERTO RICO."
SO...YEAH, I'M CURIOUS ABOUT LIVING THERE.
THERE'S SOMEONE THERE WHO MAKES ME HAPPY...!!
ABC
AND FOR THE PAST COUPLE OF DAYS I'VE WANTED TO JUMP ON A PLANE AND FLY TO SAN JUAN!!
EVERY DAY GETS LONGER.
IT'S DRIVING ME CRAZY!!
BUT IF I DECIDE TO ACTUALLY MOVE THERE...YOU ALL CAN'T TAKE IT PERSONALLY.
I'M JUST COMPLETELY...
ABSOLUTELY...
DRAWN TO HER.
I HATE HURRICANES.
HURRICANES ARE WORSE THAN ANY EARTHQUAKE.
EARTHQUAKES HIT AND-BOOM!- IT'S ALL OVER WITH.
YOU DEAL WITH THE DAMAGE.
BUT HURRICANES..?
THEY'RE NOTHING BUT QUESTION MARKS.
IT MAY BE BIG... IT MAY NOT
IT MIGHT HIT PUERTO RICO... IT MIGHT NOT.
MAYBE'S.

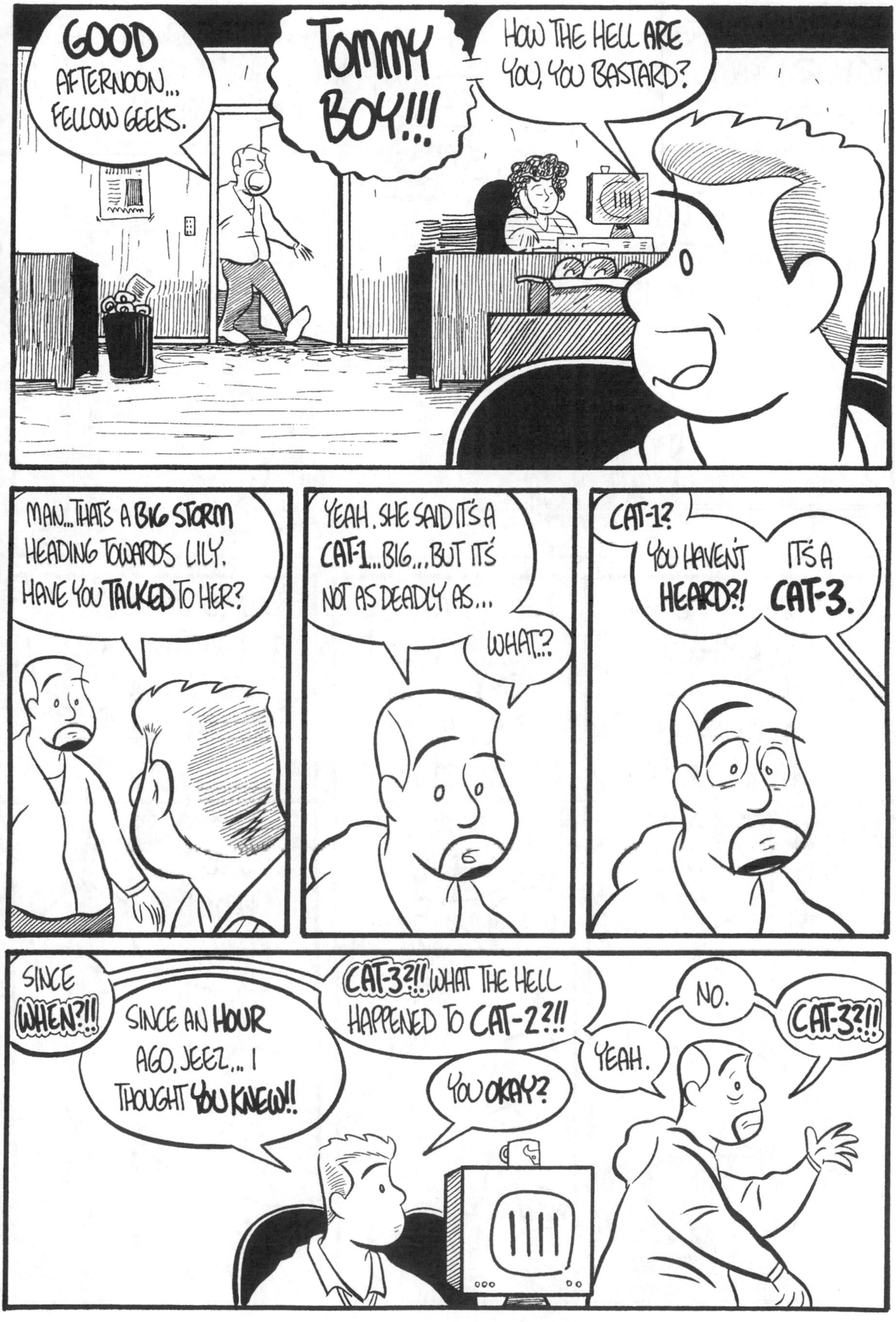
GOOD AFTERNOON... FELLOW GEEKS.
TOMMY BOY!!!
HOW THE HELL ARE YOU, YOU BASTARD?
MAN... THAT'S A BIG STORM HEADING TOWARDS LILY. HAVE YOU TALKED TO HER?
YEAH. SHE SAID IT'S A CAT-1... BIG... BUT IT'S NOT AS DEADLY AS...
WHAT...?
CAT-1?
YOU HAVEN'T HEARD?!
IT'S A CAT-3.
SINCE WHEN?!!
SINCE AN HOUR AGO. JEEZ... I THOUGHT YOU KNEW!!
CAT-3?!! WHAT THE HELL HAPPENED TO CAT-2?!!
YOU OKAY?
YEAH.
NO.
CAT-3?!!

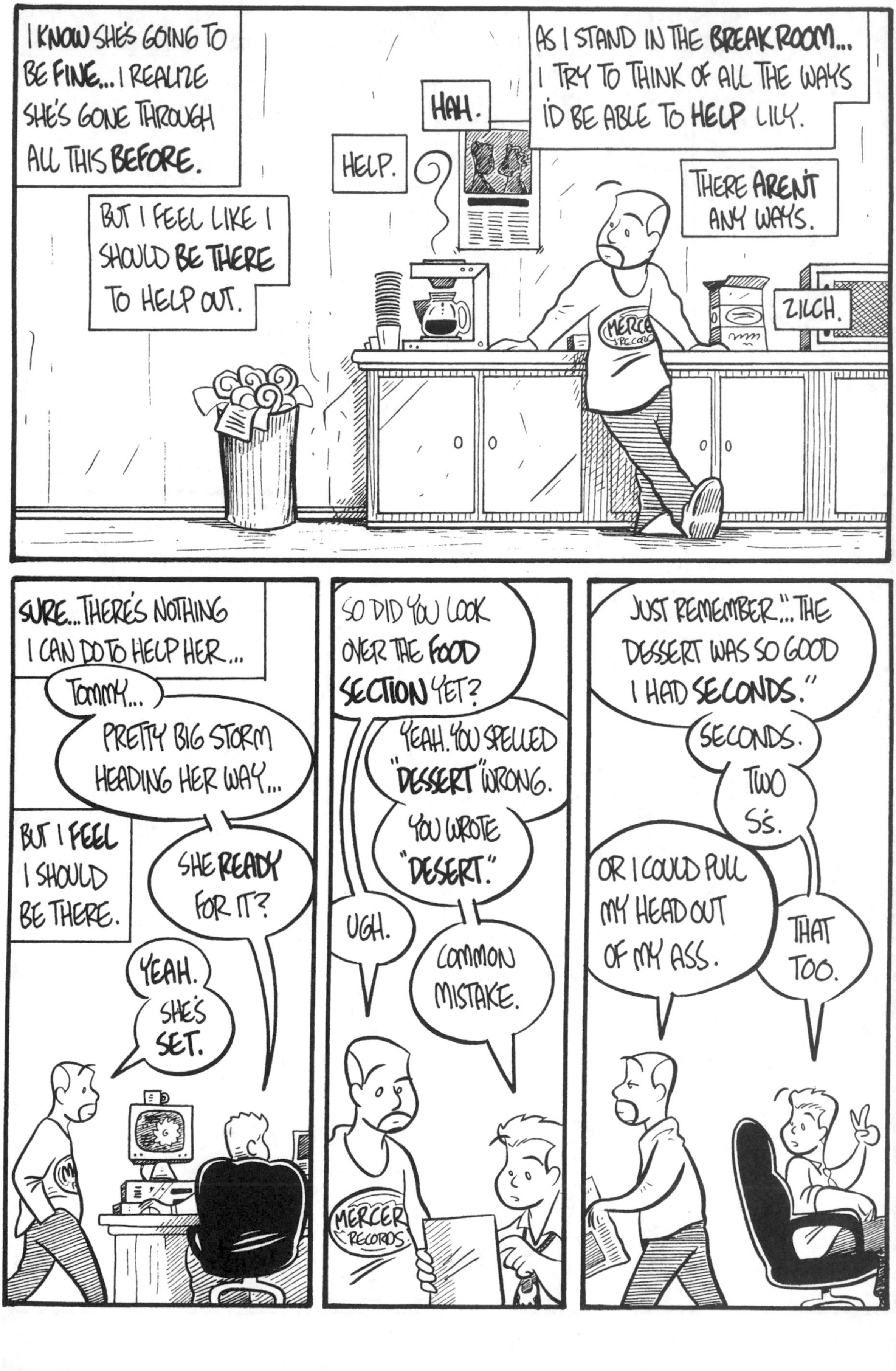
I KNOW SHE'S GOING TO BE FINE... I REALIZE SHE'S GONE THROUGH ALL THIS BEFORE.
BUT I FEEL LIKE I SHOULD BE THERE TO HELP OUT.
HELP.
HAH.
AS I STAND IN THE BREAK ROOM... I TRY TO THINK OF ALL THE WAYS I'D BE ABLE TO HELP LILY.
THERE AREN'T ANY WAYS.
ZILCH.
SURE... THERE'S NOTHING I CAN DO TO HELP HER...
TOMMY...
PRETTY BIG STORM HEADING HER WAY...
BUT I FEEL I SHOULD BE THERE.
SHE READY FOR IT?
YEAH. SHE'S SET.
SO DID YOU LOOK OVER THE FOOD SECTION YET?
YEAH. YOU SPELLED "DESSERT" WRONG.
YOU WROTE "DESERT."
UGH.
COMMON MISTAKE.
JUST REMEMBER: "... THE DESSERT WAS SO GOOD I HAD SECONDS."
SECONDS.
TWO S'S.
OR I COULD PULL MY HEAD OUT OF MY ASS.
THAT TOO.

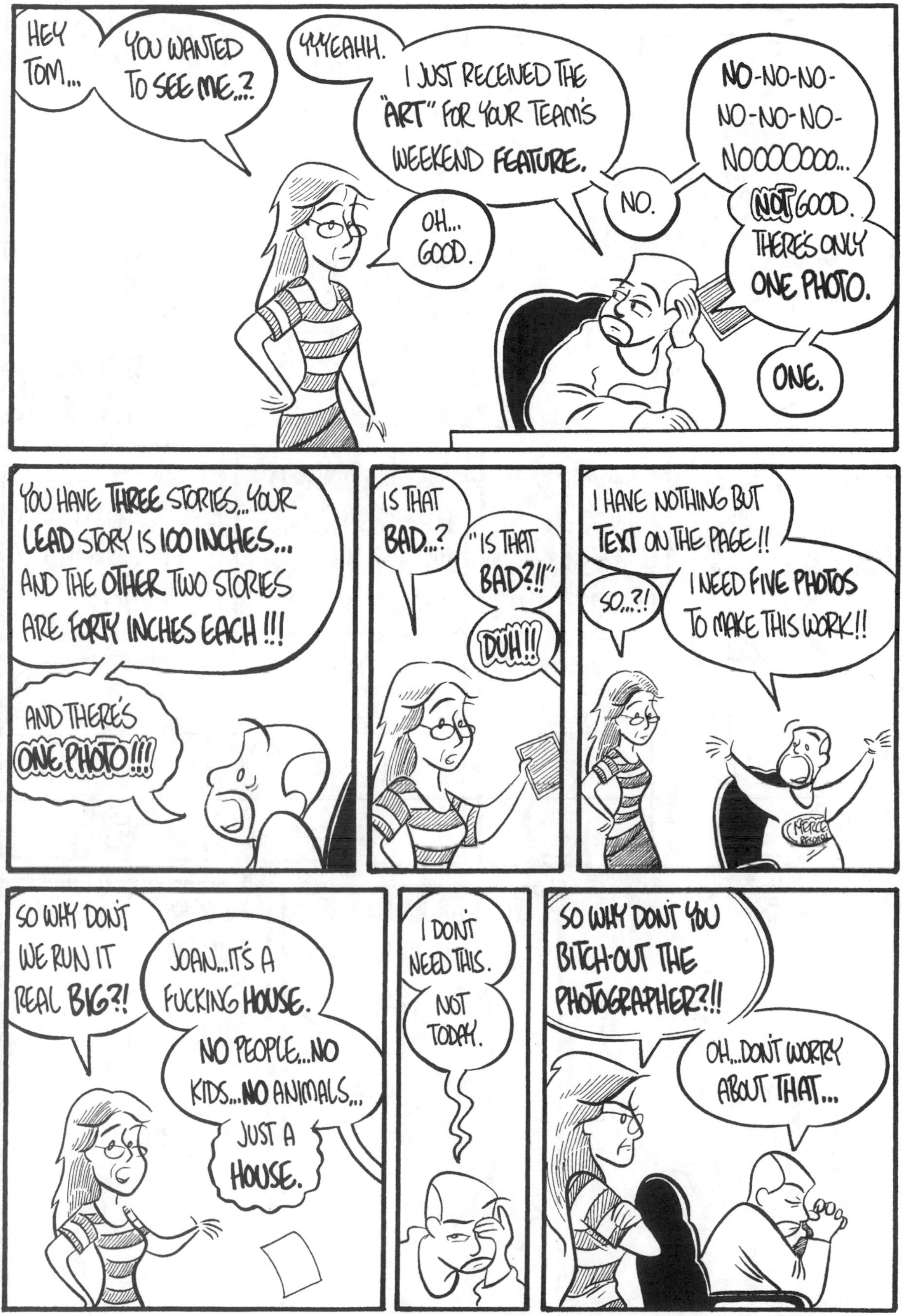
HEY TOM...
YOU WANTED TO SEE ME...?
YYYEAHH.
I JUST RECEIVED THE "ART" FOR YOUR TEAM'S WEEKEND FEATURE.
OH... GOOD.
NO.
NO-NO-NO-NO-NO-NO-NOOOOOOO...
NOT GOOD.
THERE'S ONLY ONE PHOTO.
ONE.
YOU HAVE THREE STORIES... YOUR LEAD STORY IS 100 INCHES... AND THE OTHER TWO STORIES ARE FORTY INCHES EACH !!!
AND THERE'S ONE PHOTO!!!
IS THAT BAD...?
"IS THAT BAD?!!"
DUH!!
I HAVE NOTHING BUT TEXT ON THE PAGE!!
SO...?!
I NEED FIVE PHOTOS TO MAKE THIS WORK!!
SO WHY DON'T WE RUN IT REAL BIG?!
JOAN... IT'S A FUCKING HOUSE.
NO PEOPLE... NO KIDS... NO ANIMALS...
JUST A HOUSE.
I DON'T NEED THIS.
NOT TODAY.
SO WHY DON'T YOU BITCH-OUT THE PHOTOGRAPHER?!!
OH... DON'T WORRY ABOUT THAT...

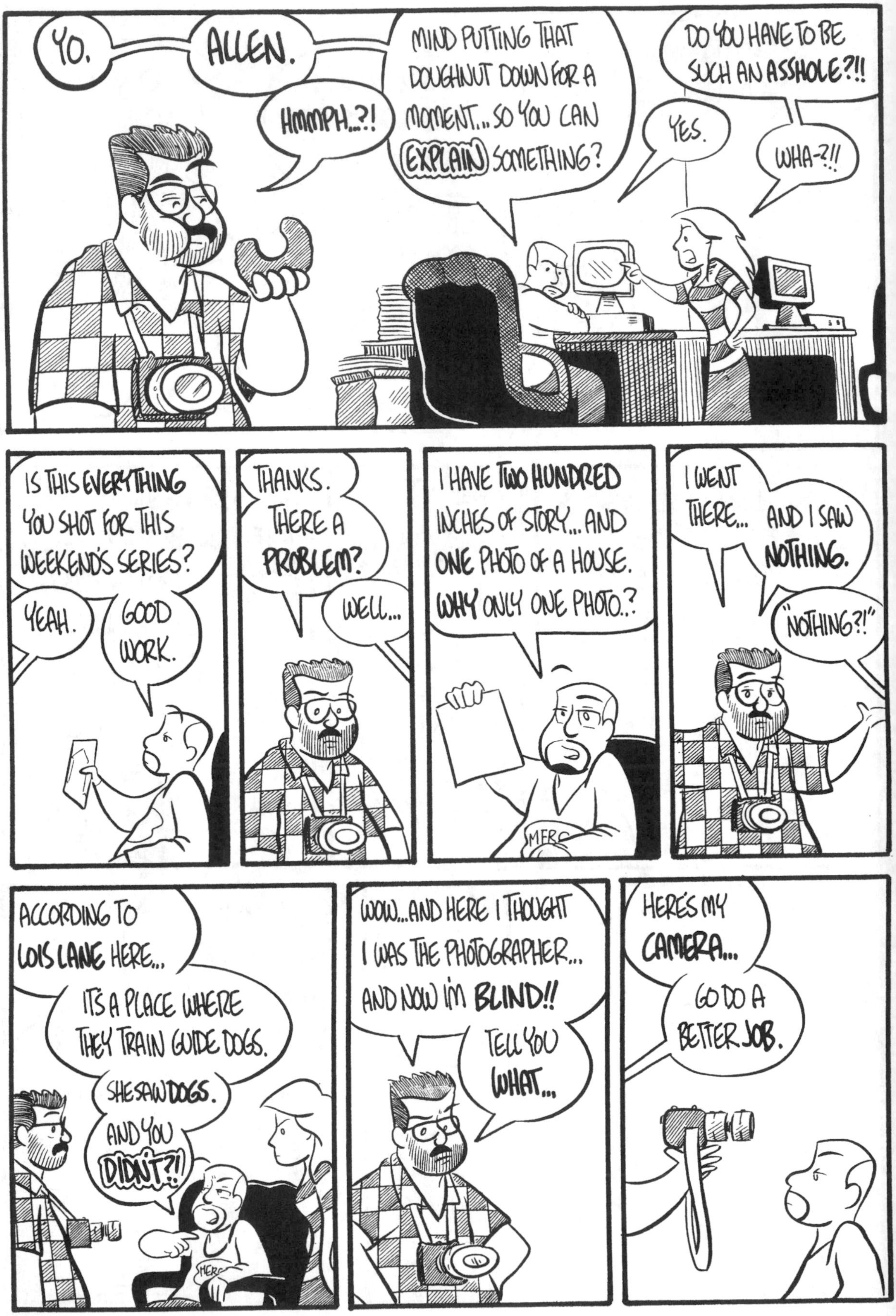

YO.
ALLEN.
HMMPH..?!
MIND PUTTING THAT DOUGHNUT DOWN FOR A MOMENT... SO YOU CAN EXPLAIN SOMETHING?
DO YOU HAVE TO BE SUCH AN ASSHOLE?!!
YES.
WHA-?!!
IS THIS EVERYTHING YOU SHOT FOR THIS WEEKEND'S SERIES?
YEAH.
GOOD WORK.
THANKS.
THERE A PROBLEM?
WELL...
I HAVE TWO HUNDRED INCHES OF STORY... AND ONE PHOTO OF A HOUSE. WHY ONLY ONE PHOTO..?
MERC
I WENT THERE...
AND I SAW NOTHING.
"NOTHING?!"
ACCORDING TO LOIS LANE HERE...
IT'S A PLACE WHERE THEY TRAIN GUIDE DOGS.
SHE SAW DOGS.
AND YOU DIDN'T?!
MERC
WOW... AND HERE I THOUGHT I WAS THE PHOTOGRAPHER... AND NOW I'M BLIND!!
TELL YOU WHAT...
HERE'S MY CAMERA...
GO DO A BETTER JOB.

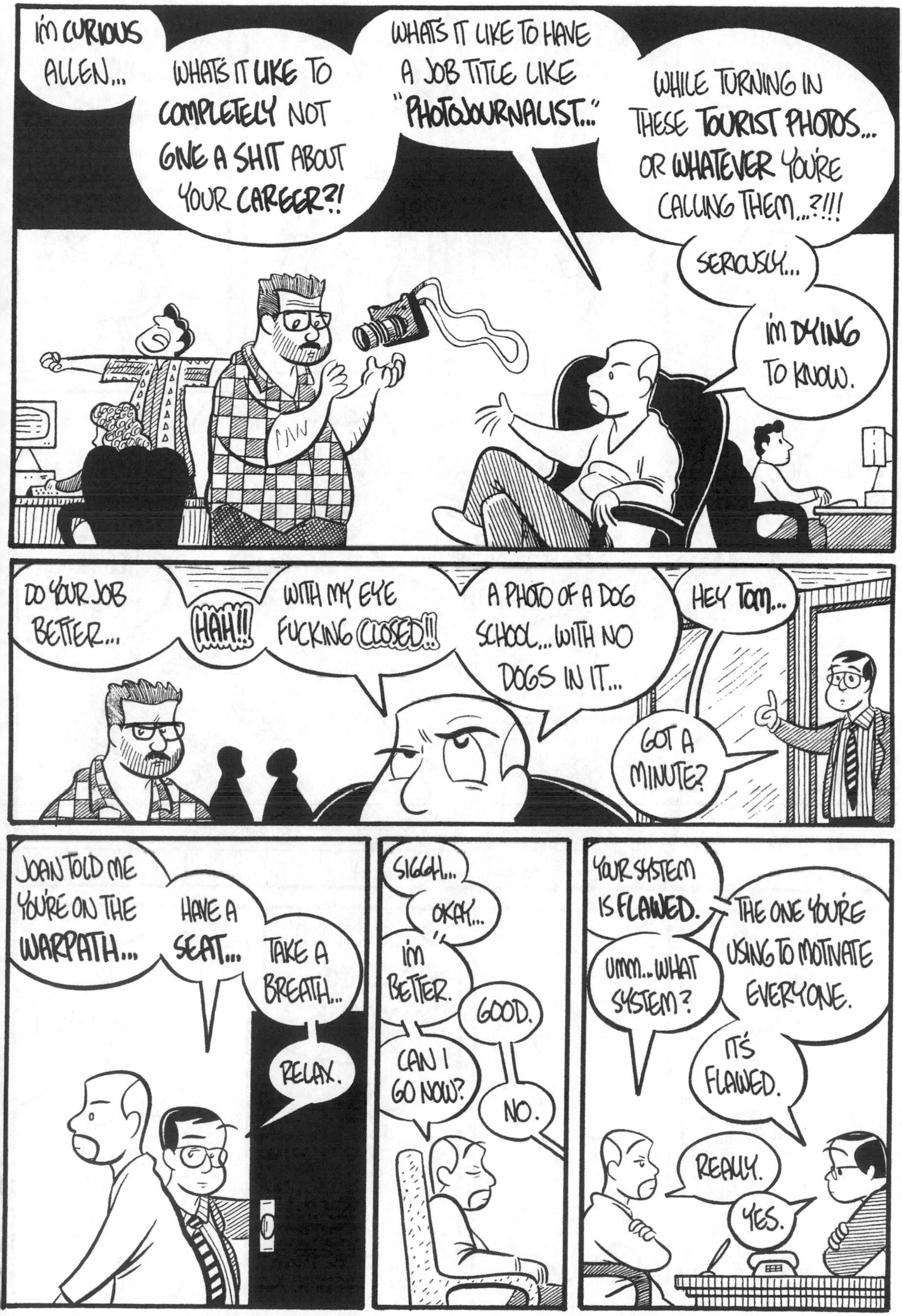
I'M CURIOUS ALLEN...
WHAT'S IT LIKE TO COMPLETELY NOT GIVE A SHIT ABOUT YOUR CAREER?!
WHAT'S IT LIKE TO HAVE A JOB TITLE LIKE "PHOTOJOURNALIST..."
WHILE TURNING IN THESE TOURIST PHOTOS... OR WHATEVER YOU'RE CALLING THEM...?!!!
SERIOUSLY...
I'M DYING TO KNOW.
DO YOUR JOB BETTER...
HAH!!
WITH MY EYE FUCKING CLOSED!!
A PHOTO OF A DOG SCHOOL... WITH NO DOGS IN IT...
HEY TOM...
GOT A MINUTE?
JOAN TOLD ME YOU'RE ON THE WARPATH...
HAVE A SEAT...
TAKE A BREATH...
RELAX.
SIGGH...
OKAY...
I'M BETTER.
GOOD.
CAN I GO NOW?
NO.
YOUR SYSTEM IS FLAWED.
THE ONE YOU'RE USING TO MOTIVATE EVERYONE.
UMM... WHAT SYSTEM?
IT'S FLAWED.
REALLY.
YES.

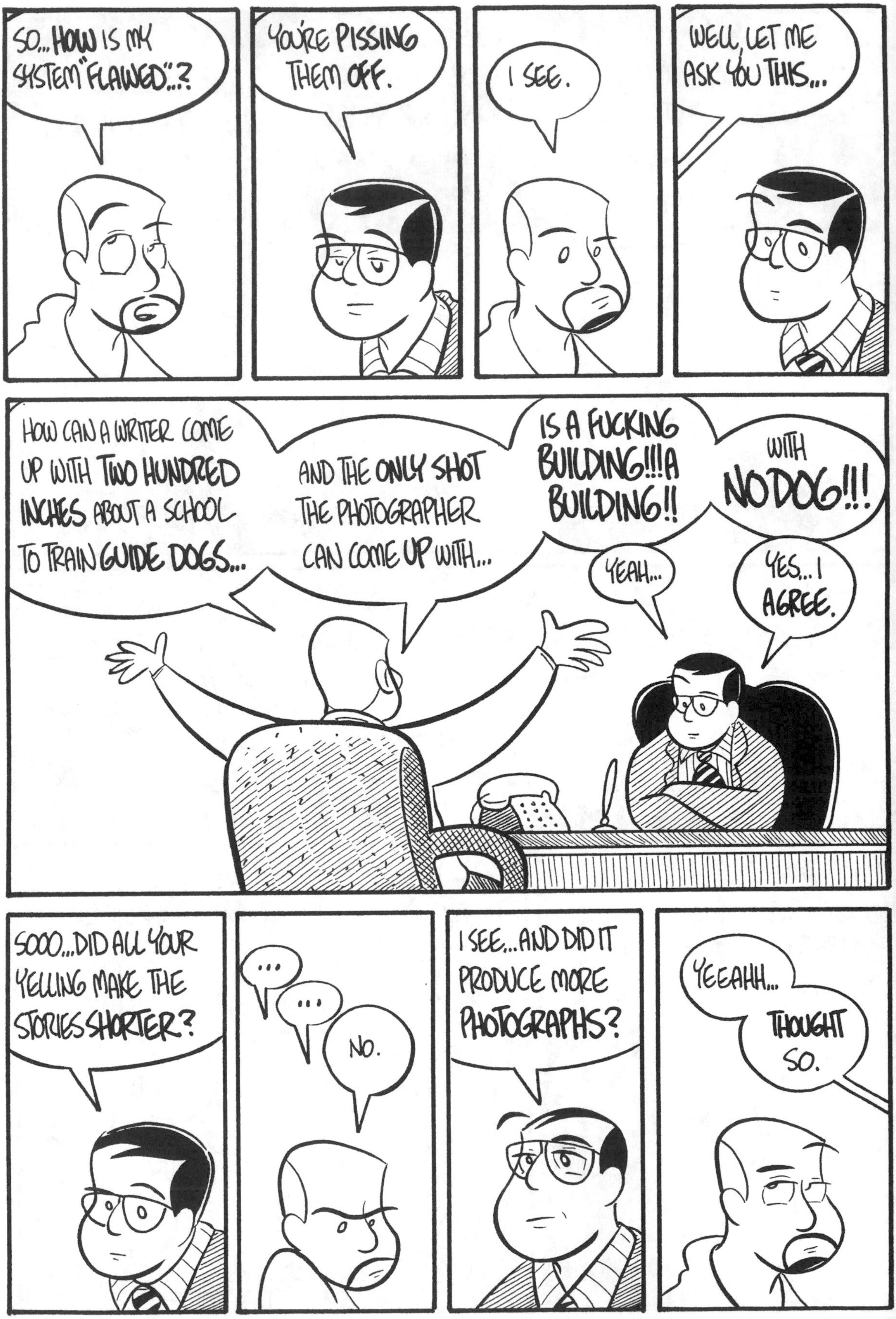
SO...HOW IS MY SYSTEM "FLAWED"...?
YOU'RE PISSING THEM OFF.
I SEE.
WELL, LET ME ASK YOU THIS...
HOW CAN A WRITER COME UP WITH TWO HUNDRED INCHES ABOUT A SCHOOL TO TRAIN GUIDE DOGS...
AND THE ONLY SHOT THE PHOTOGRAPHER CAN COME UP WITH...
IS A FUCKING BUILDING!!! A BUILDING!!
WITH NO DOG!!!
YEAH...
YES... I AGREE.
SOOO...DID ALL YOUR YELLING MAKE THE STORIES SHORTER?
...
...
NO.
I SEE...AND DID IT PRODUCE MORE PHOTOGRAPHS?
YEEAHH... THOUGHT SO.

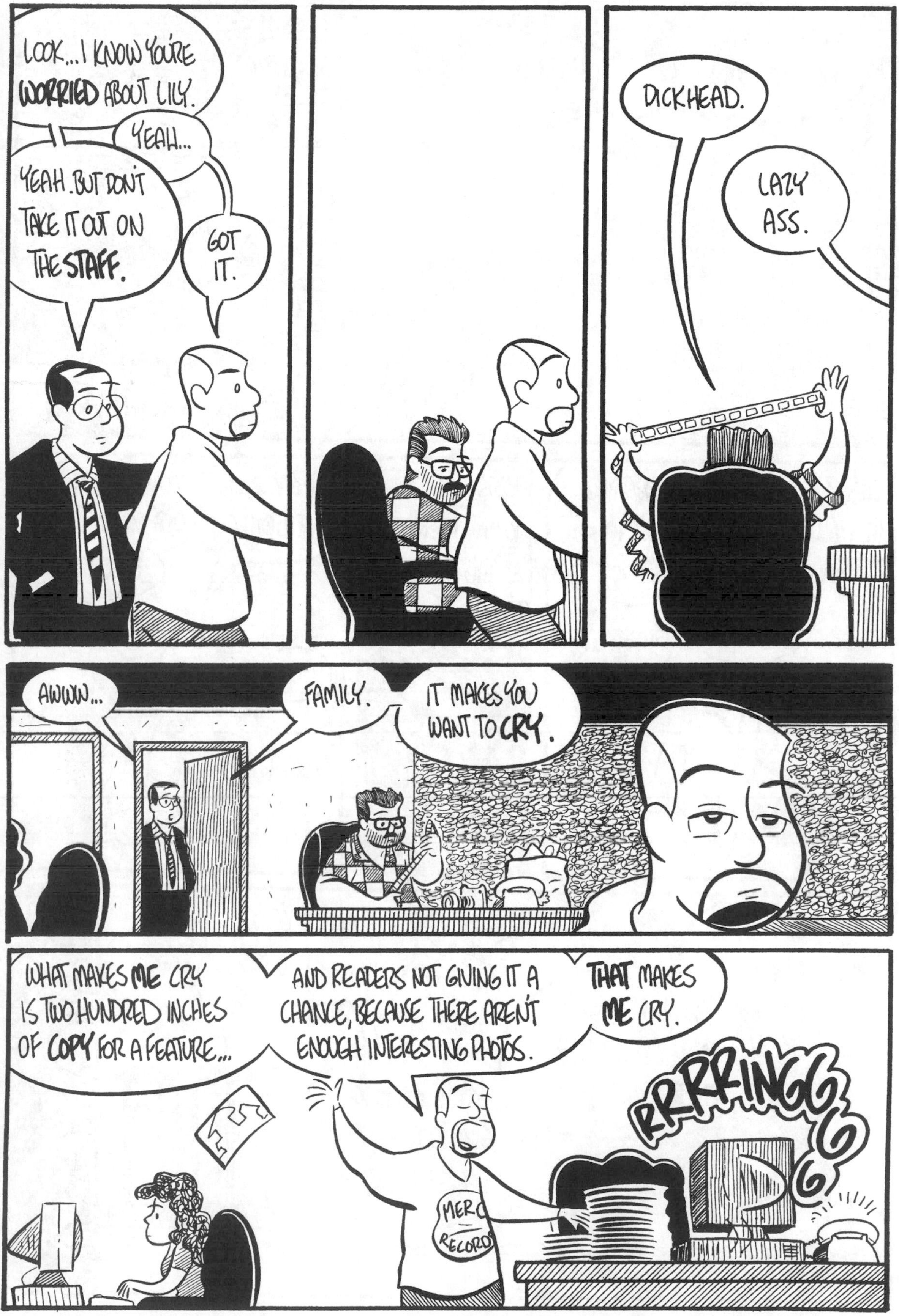
LOOK... I KNOW YOU'RE WORRIED ABOUT LILY.
YEAH...
YEAH. BUT DON'T TAKE IT OUT ON THE STAFF.
GOT IT.
DICKHEAD.
LAZY ASS.
AWWW...
FAMILY.
IT MAKES YOU WANT TO CRY.
WHAT MAKES ME CRY IS TWO HUNDRED INCHES OF COPY FOR A FEATURE...
AND READERS NOT GIVING IT A CHANCE, BECAUSE THERE AREN'T ENOUGH INTERESTING PHOTOS.
THAT MAKES ME CRY.
BRRRINGGGG
MERC
RECORDS

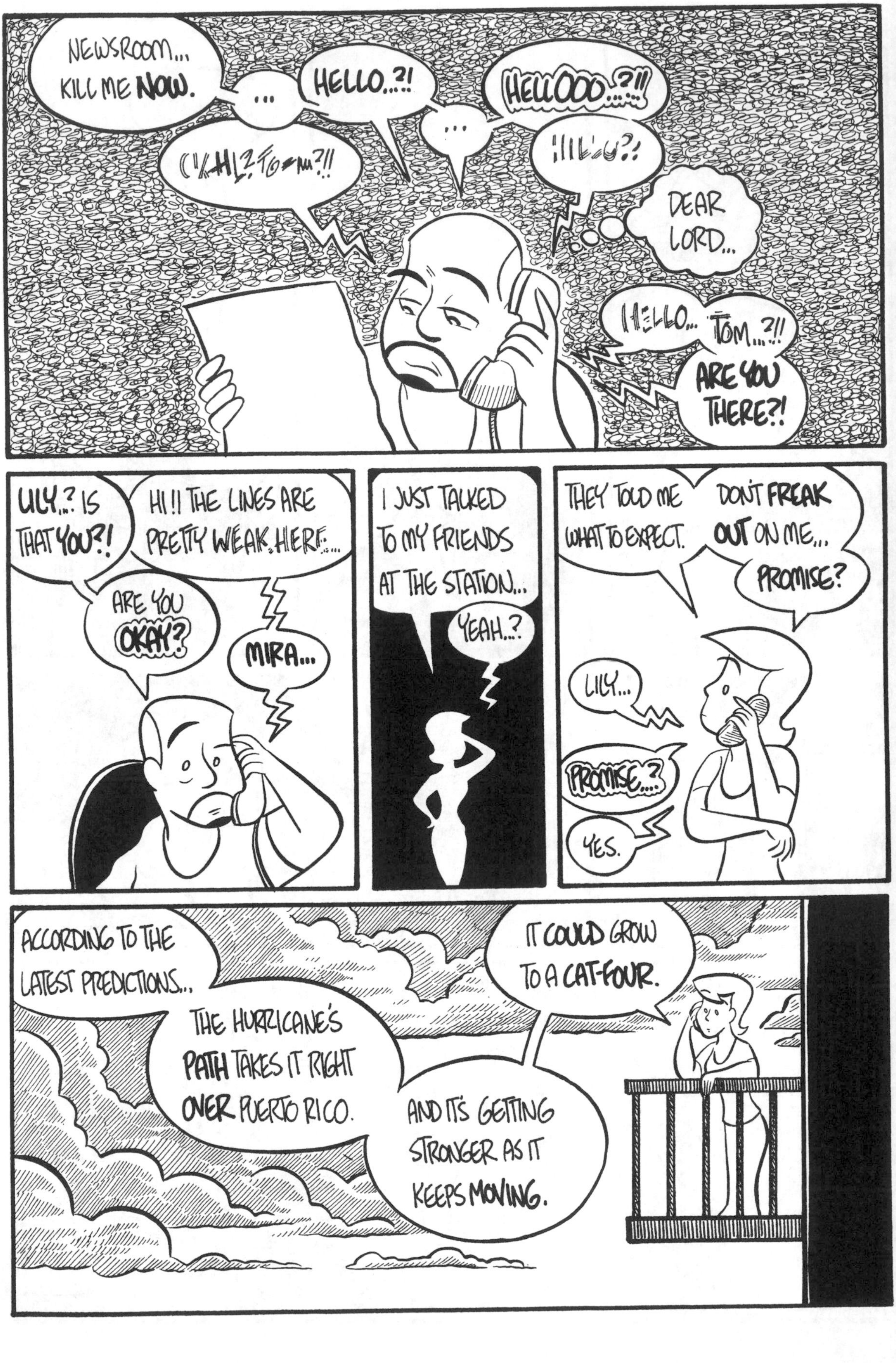
NEWSROOM... KILL ME NOW.
...
HELLO...?!
...
HELLOOO...?!!
DEAR LORD...
HELLO... TOM...?!!
ARE YOU THERE?!
LILY...? IS THAT YOU?!
HI!! THE LINES ARE PRETTY WEAK HERE...
ARE YOU OKAY?
MIRA...
I JUST TALKED TO MY FRIENDS AT THE STATION...
YEAH...?
THEY TOLD ME WHAT TO EXPECT.
DON'T FREAK OUT ON ME... PROMISE?
LILY...
PROMISE...?
YES.
ACCORDING TO THE LATEST PREDICTIONS...
THE HURRICANE'S PATH TAKES IT RIGHT OVER PUERTO RICO.
IT COULD GROW TO A CAT-FOUR.
AND IT'S GETTING STRONGER AS IT KEEPS MOVING.

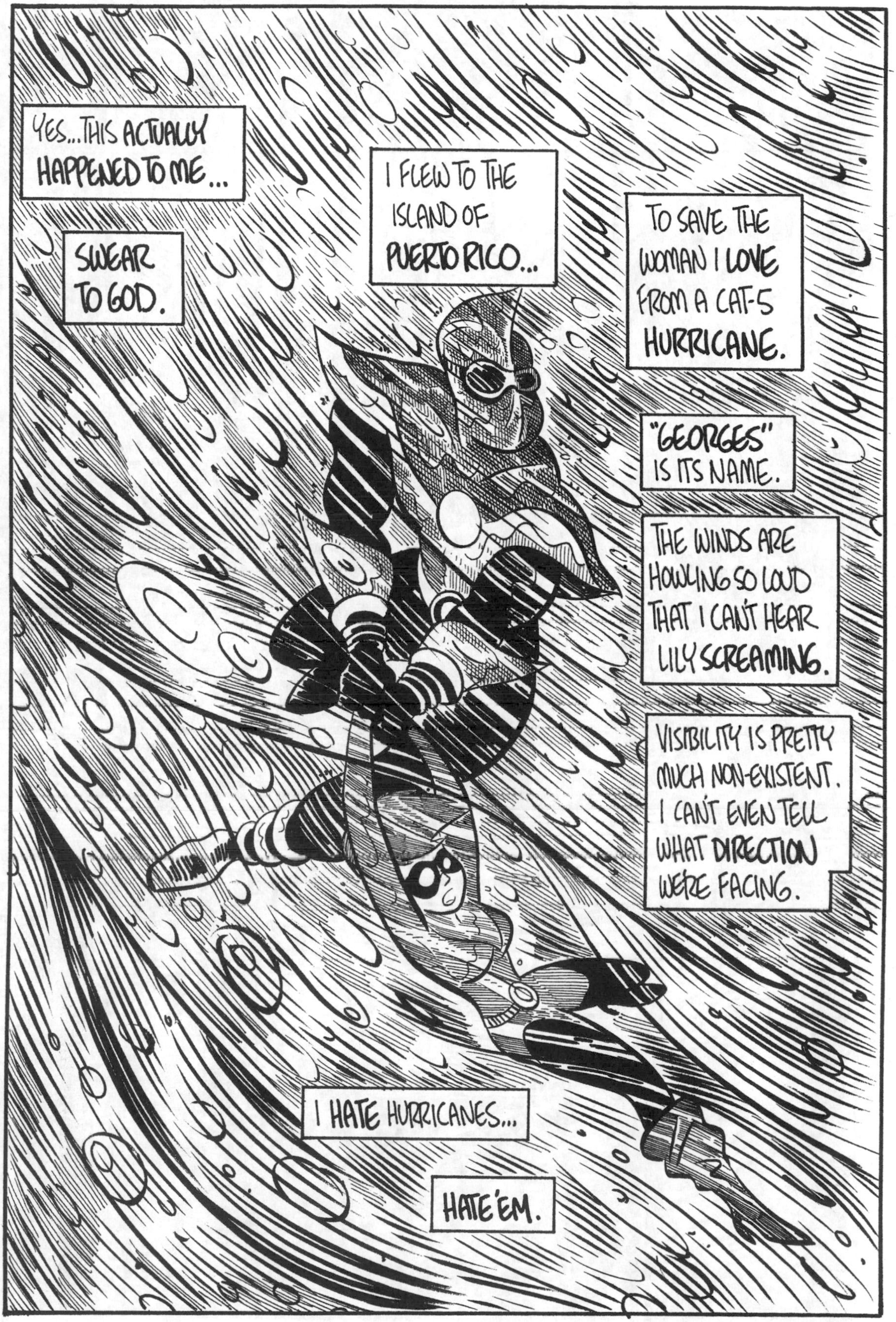
YES...THIS ACTUALLY HAPPENED TO ME...
SWEAR TO GOD.
I FLEW TO THE ISLAND OF PUERTO RICO...
TO SAVE THE WOMAN I LOVE FROM A CAT-5 HURRICANE.
"GEORGES" IS ITS NAME.
THE WINDS ARE HOWLING SO LOUD THAT I CAN'T HEAR LILY SCREAMING.
VISIBILITY IS PRETTY MUCH NON-EXISTENT. I CAN'T EVEN TELL WHAT DIRECTION WE'RE FACING.
I HATE HURRICANES...
HATE 'EM.

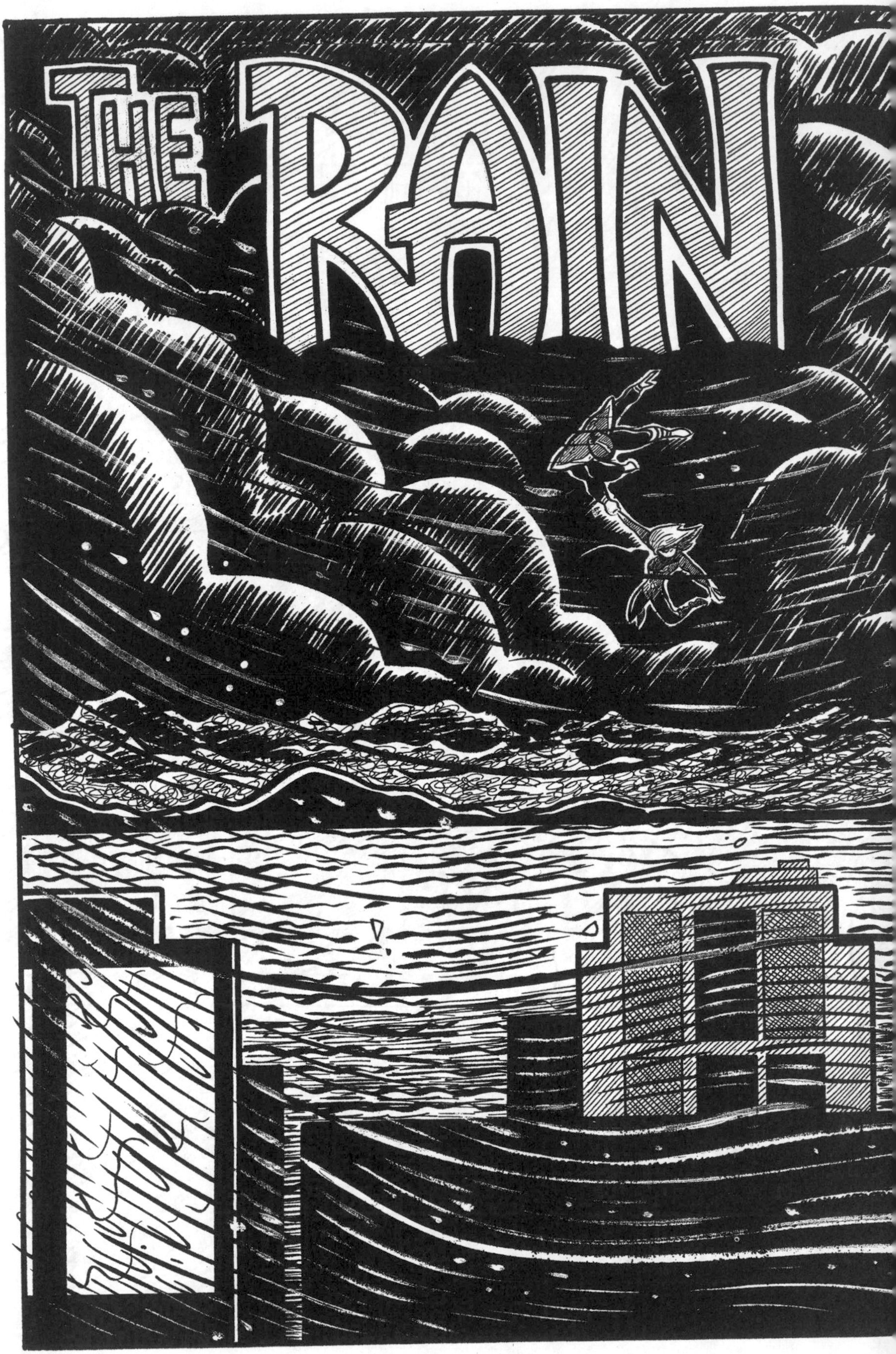
THE RAIN

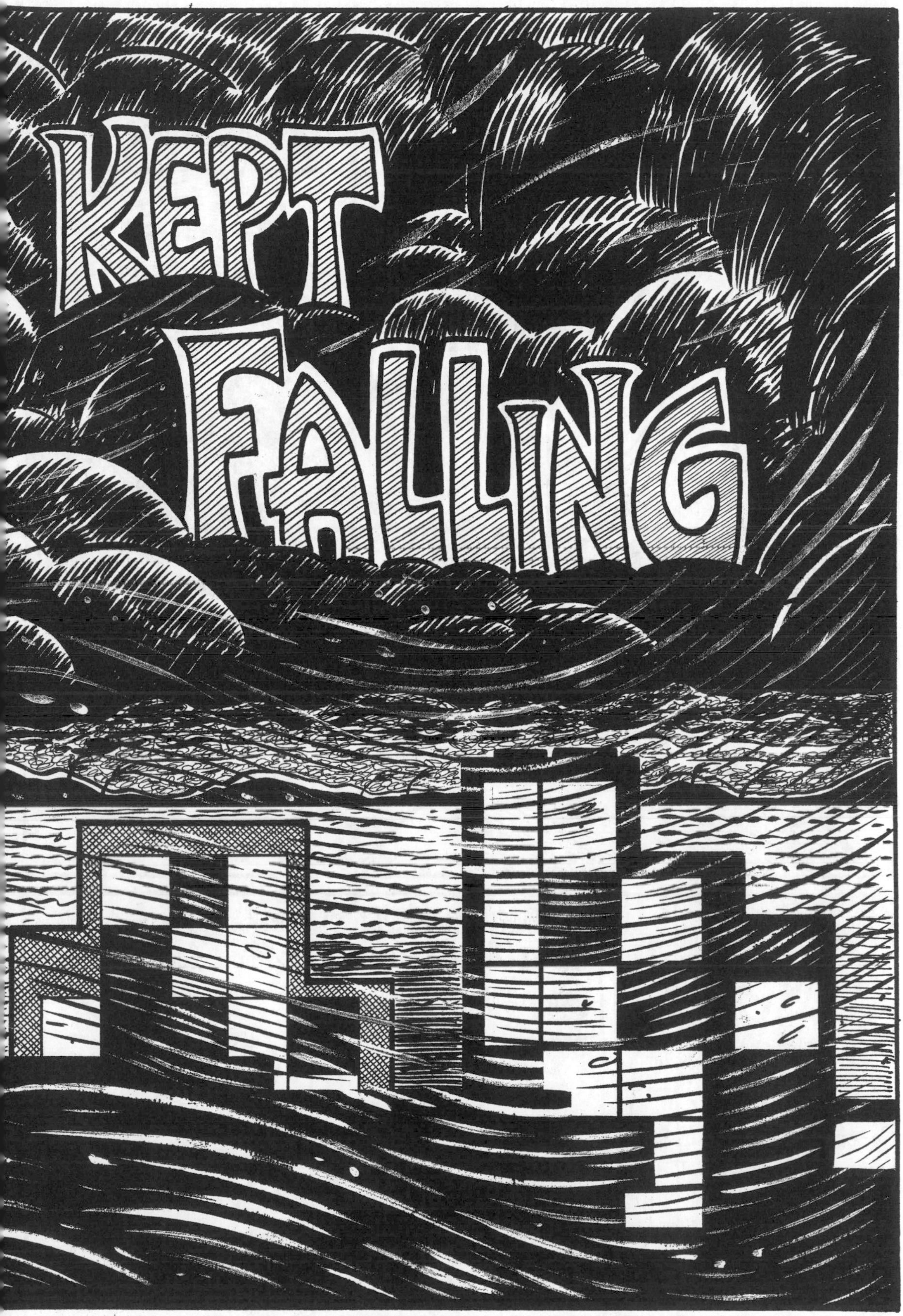
KEPT
FALLING

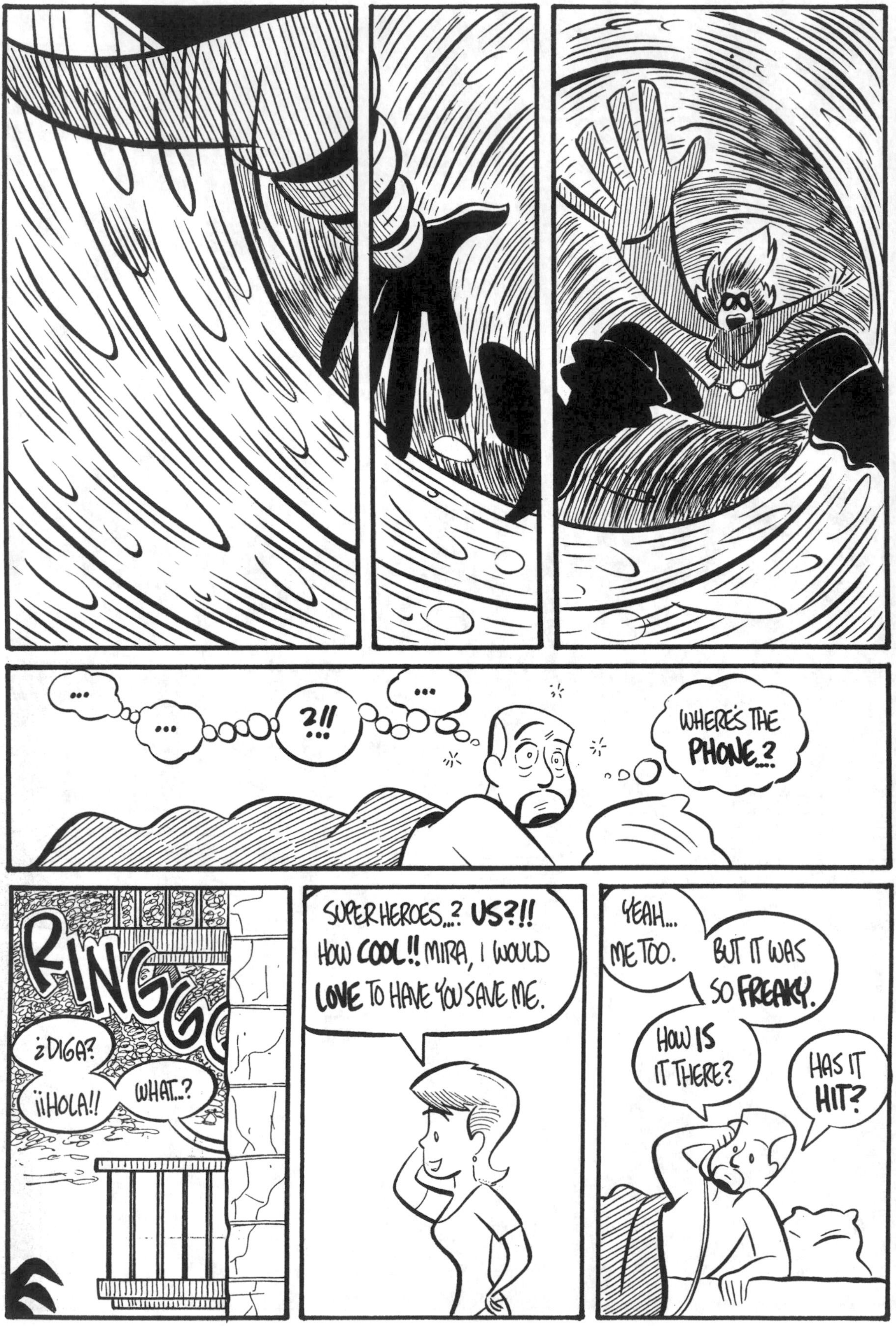
...
...
?!!
...
WHERE'S THE PHONE..?
RINGGG
¿DIGA?
¡¡HOLA!!
WHAT..?
SUPER HEROES...? US?!! HOW COOL!! MIRA, I WOULD LOVE TO HAVE YOU SAVE ME.
YEAH... ME TOO.
BUT IT WAS SO FREAKY.
HOW IS IT THERE?
HAS IT HIT?

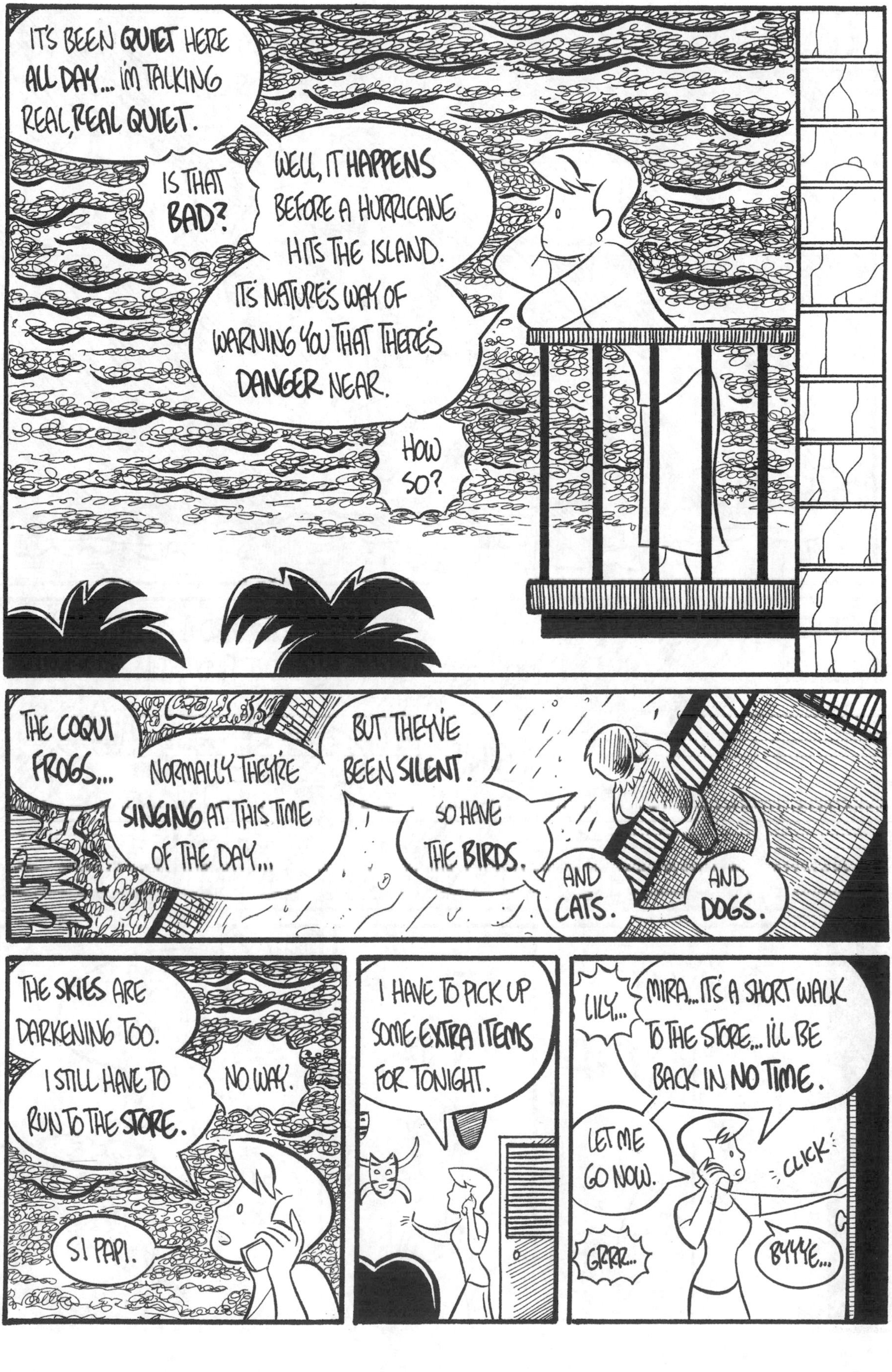
IT'S BEEN QUIET HERE ALL DAY... I'M TALKING REAL, REAL QUIET.
IS THAT BAD?
WELL, IT HAPPENS BEFORE A HURRICANE HITS THE ISLAND.
IT'S NATURE'S WAY OF WARNING YOU THAT THERE'S DANGER NEAR.
HOW SO?
THE COQUI FROGS...
NORMALLY THEY'RE SINGING AT THIS TIME OF THE DAY...
BUT THEY'VE BEEN SILENT.
SO HAVE THE BIRDS.
AND CATS.
AND DOGS.
THE SKIES ARE DARKENING TOO.
I STILL HAVE TO RUN TO THE STORE.
NO WAY.
SI PAPI.
I HAVE TO PICK UP SOME EXTRA ITEMS FOR TONIGHT.
LILY...
MIRA... IT'S A SHORT WALK TO THE STORE... I'LL BE BACK IN NO TIME.
LET ME GO NOW.
CLICK
GRRR...
BYYYE...

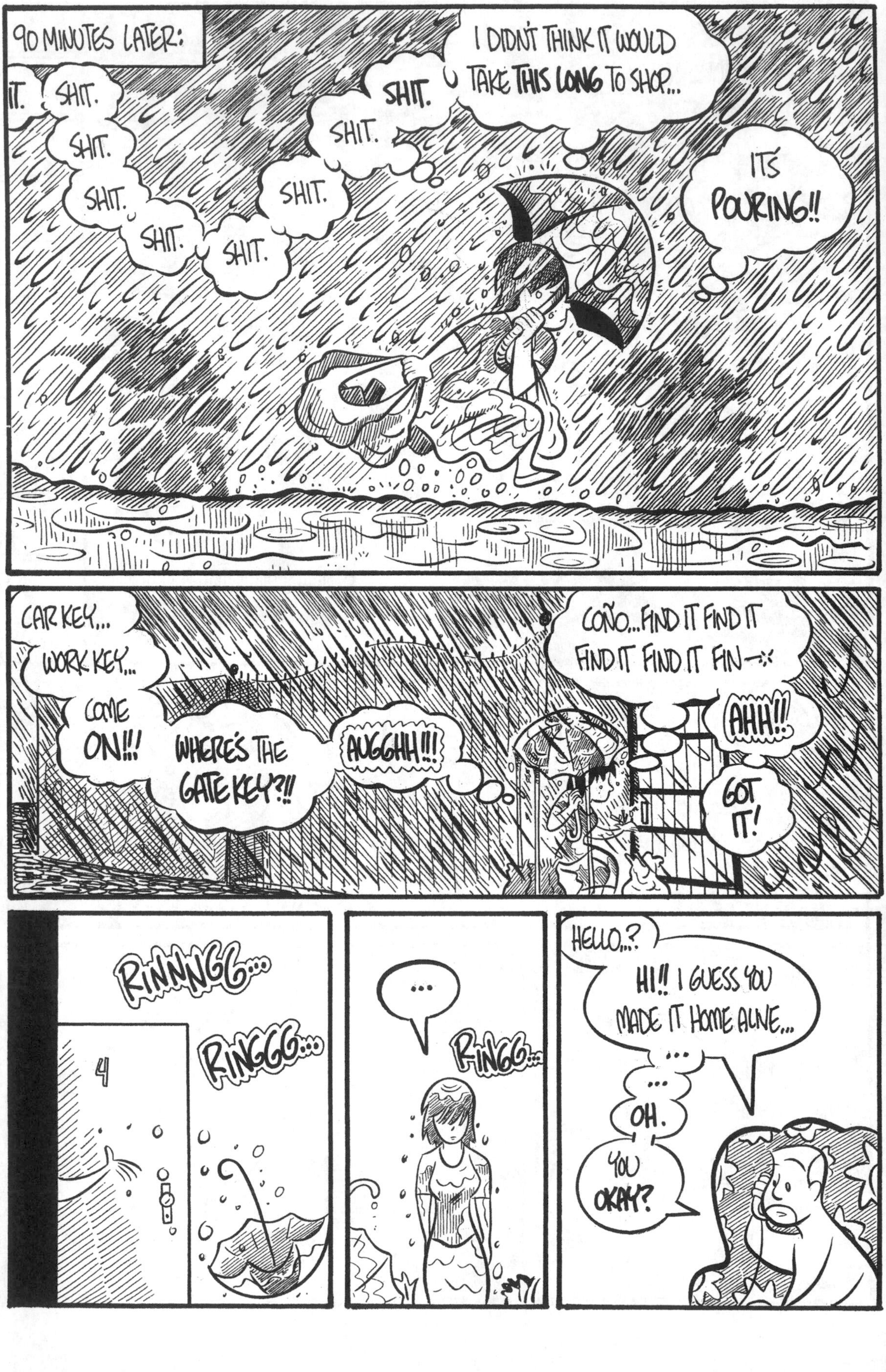

90 MINUTES LATER:
IT.
SHIT.
SHIT.
SHIT.
SHIT.
SHIT.
SHIT.
SHIT.
SHIT.
I DIDN'T THINK IT WOULD TAKE THIS LONG TO SHOP...
IT'S POURING!!
CAR KEY...
WORK KEY...
COME ON!!!
WHERE'S THE GATE KEY?!!
AUGGHH!!!
COÑO...FIND IT FIND IT FIND IT FIND IT FIN—
AHH!!
GOT IT!
RINNNGG...
RINGGG...
4
...
RINGG...
HELLO...?
HI!! I GUESS YOU MADE IT HOME ALNE...
...
...
OH.
YOU OKAY?

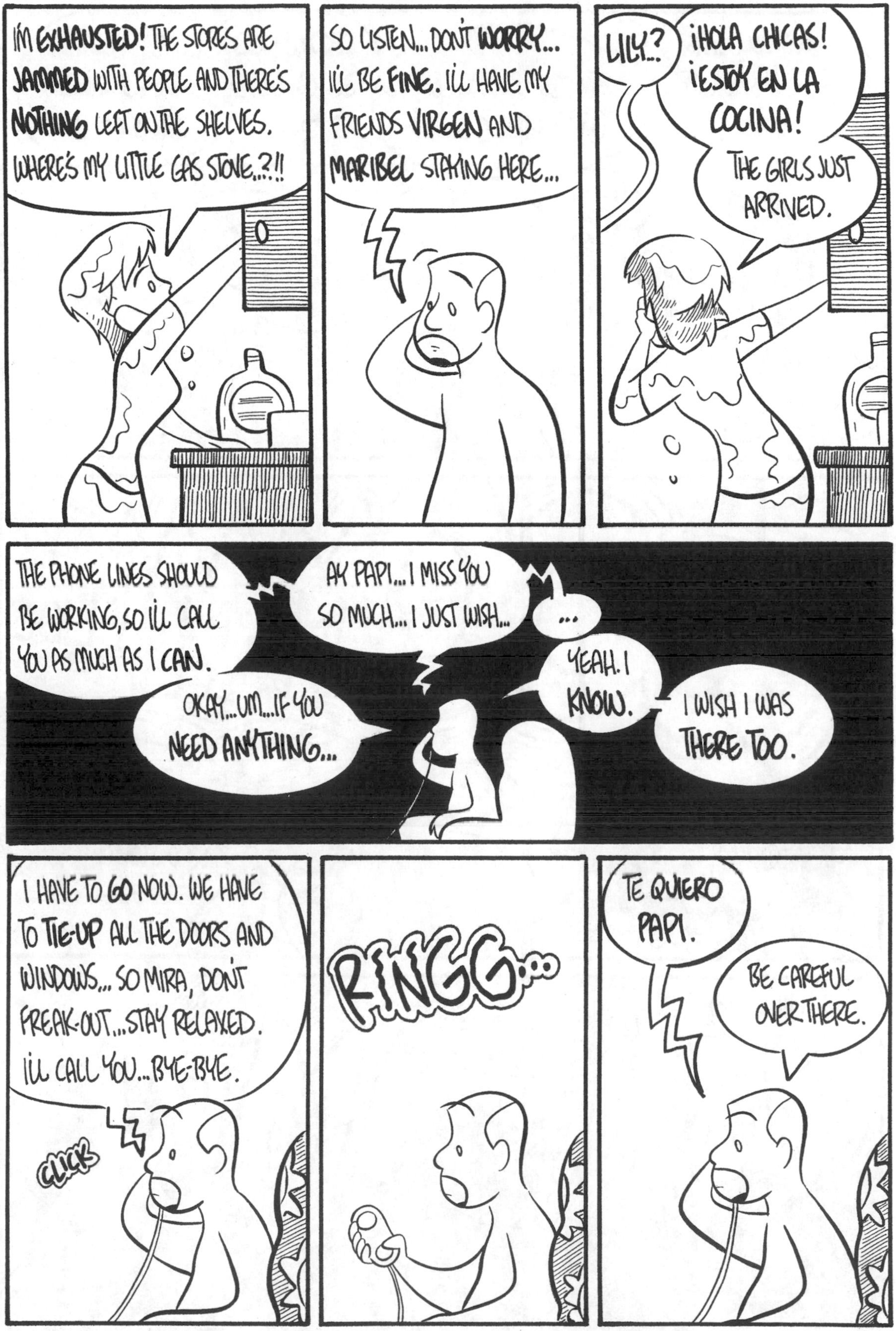
I'M EXHAUSTED! THE STORES ARE JAMMED WITH PEOPLE AND THERE'S NOTHING LEFT ON THE SHELVES. WHERE'S MY LITTLE GAS STOVE..?!!
SO LISTEN... DON'T WORRY... I'LL BE FINE. I'LL HAVE MY FRIENDS VIRGEN AND MARIBEL STAYING HERE...
LILY..?
¡HOLA CHICAS! ¡ESTOY EN LA COCINA!
THE GIRLS JUST ARRIVED.
THE PHONE LINES SHOULD BE WORKING, SO I'LL CALL YOU AS MUCH AS I CAN.
AY PAPI... I MISS YOU SO MUCH... I JUST WISH...
...
OKAY... UM... IF YOU NEED ANYTHING...
YEAH. I KNOW.
I WISH I WAS THERE TOO.
I HAVE TO GO NOW. WE HAVE TO TIE-UP ALL THE DOORS AND WINDOWS... SO MIRA, DON'T FREAK-OUT... STAY RELAXED. I'LL CALL YOU... BYE-BYE.
CLICK
RINGG...
TE QUIERO PAPI.
BE CAREFUL OVER THERE.

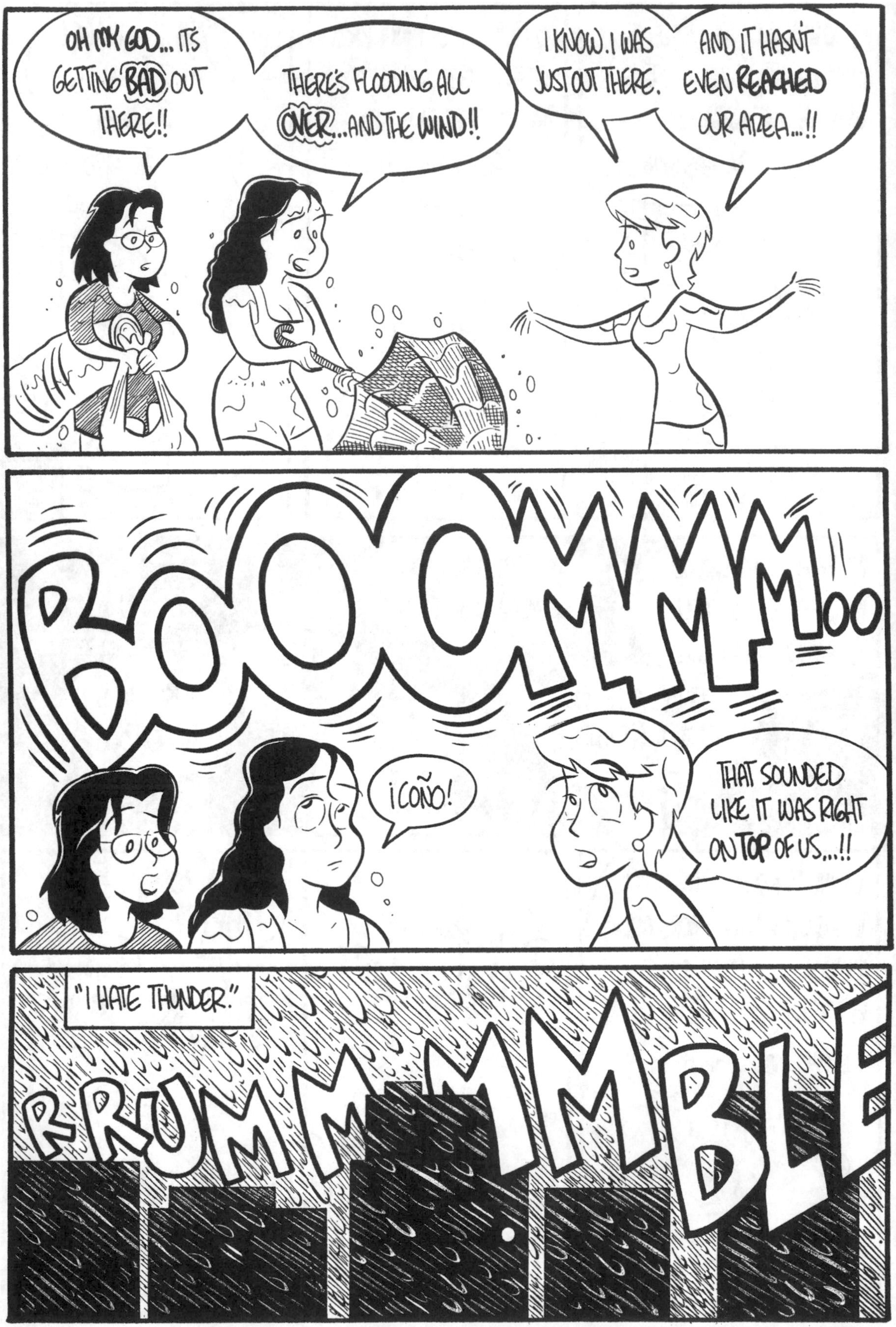
OH MY GOD... IT'S GETTING BAD OUT THERE!!
THERE'S FLOODING ALL OVER...AND THE WIND!!
I KNOW. I WAS JUST OUT THERE.
AND IT HASN'T EVEN REACHED OUR AREA...!!
BOOOMMMMMMOO
¡COÑO!
THAT SOUNDED LIKE IT WAS RIGHT ON TOP OF US...!!
"I HATE THUNDER."
RRUMMMMMMBLE

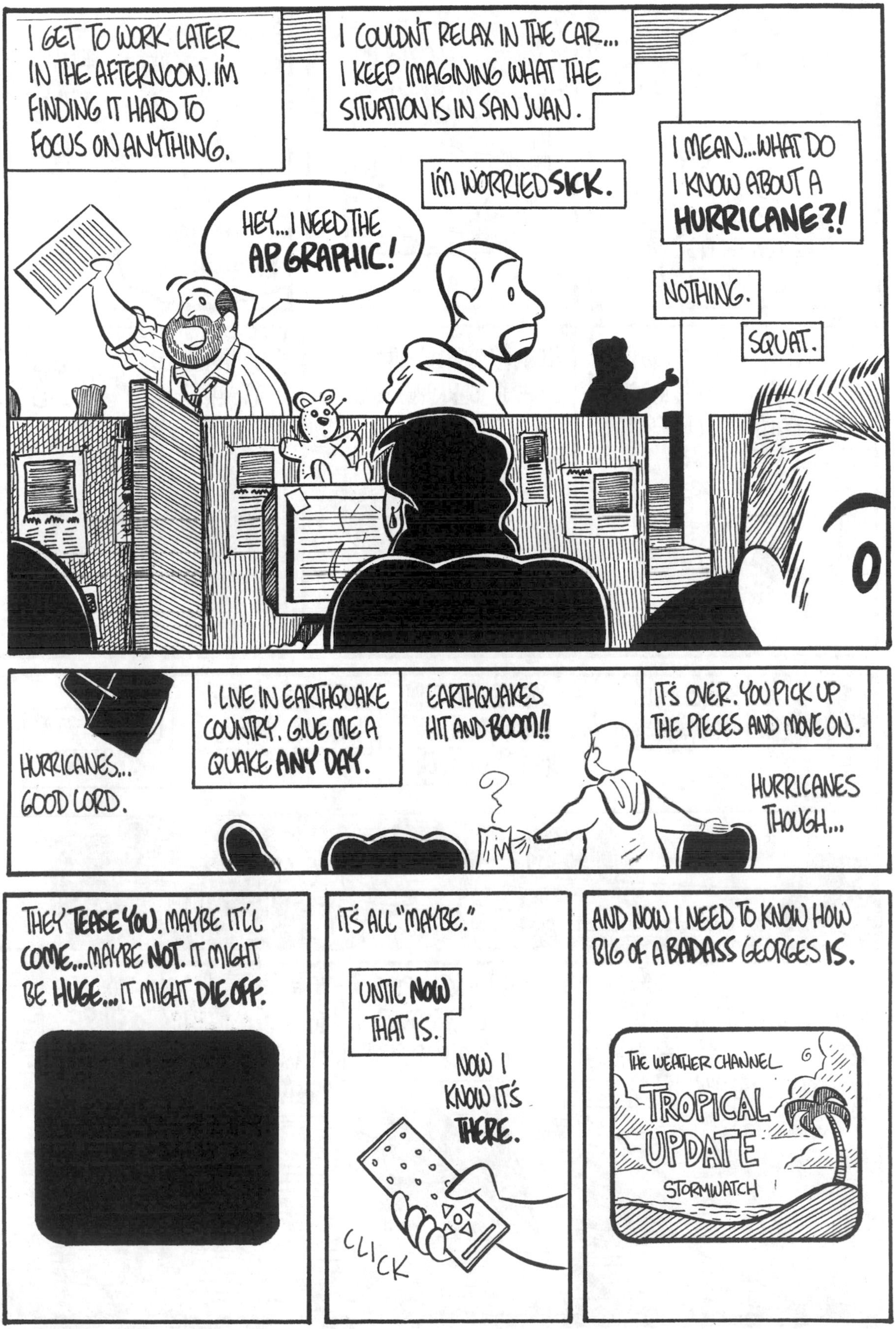
I GET TO WORK LATER IN THE AFTERNOON. I'M FINDING IT HARD TO FOCUS ON ANYTHING.
I COULDN'T RELAX IN THE CAR... I KEEP IMAGINING WHAT THE SITUATION IS IN SAN JUAN.
I'M WORRIED SICK.
I MEAN...WHAT DO I KNOW ABOUT A HURRICANE?!
NOTHING.
SQUAT.
HEY...I NEED THE A.P. GRAPHIC!
HURRICANES... GOOD LORD.
I LIVE IN EARTHQUAKE COUNTRY. GIVE ME A QUAKE ANY DAY.
EARTHQUAKES HIT AND-BOOM!!
IT'S OVER. YOU PICK UP THE PIECES AND MOVE ON.
HURRICANES THOUGH...
THEY TEASE YOU. MAYBE IT'LL COME...MAYBE NOT. IT MIGHT BE HUGE...IT MIGHT DIE OFF.
IT'S ALL "MAYBE."
UNTIL NOW THAT IS.
NOW I KNOW IT'S THERE.
CLICK
AND NOW I NEED TO KNOW HOW BIG OF A BADASS GEORGES IS.
THE WEATHER CHANNEL
TROPICAL UPDATE
STORMWATCH

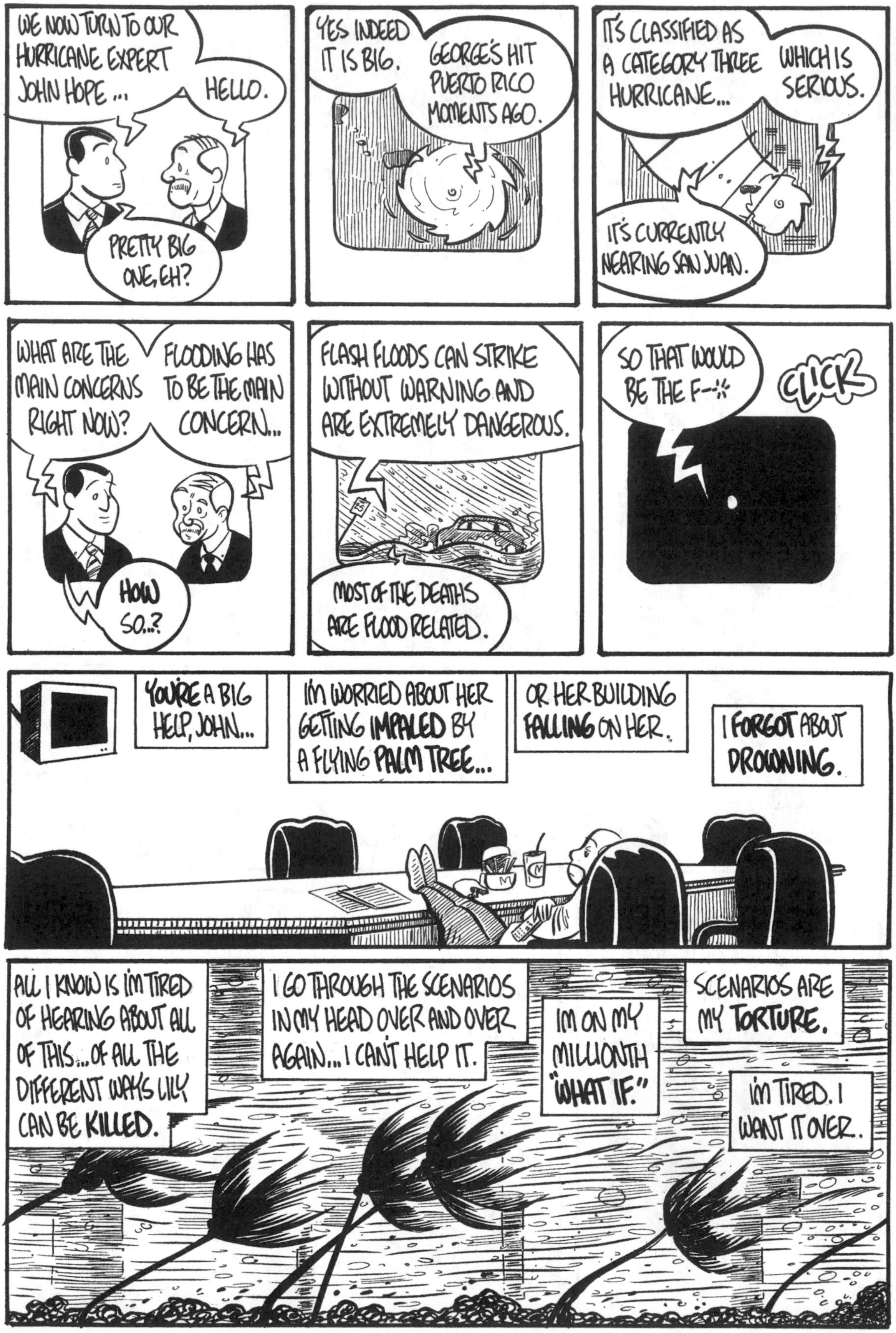

WE NOW TURN TO OUR HURRICANE EXPERT JOHN HOPE ...
HELLO.
PRETTY BIG ONE, EH?
YES INDEED IT IS BIG.
GEORGE'S HIT PUERTO RICO MOMENTS AGO.
IT'S CLASSIFIED AS A CATEGORY THREE HURRICANE...
WHICH IS SERIOUS.
IT'S CURRENTLY NEARING SAN JUAN.
WHAT ARE THE MAIN CONCERNS RIGHT NOW?
FLOODING HAS TO BE THE MAIN CONCERN...
HOW SO..?
FLASH FLOODS CAN STRIKE WITHOUT WARNING AND ARE EXTREMELY DANGEROUS.
MOST OF THE DEATHS ARE FLOOD RELATED.
SO THAT WOULD BE THE F--
CLICK
YOU'RE A BIG HELP, JOHN...
I'M WORRIED ABOUT HER GETTING IMPALED BY A FLYING PALM TREE...
OR HER BUILDING FALLING ON HER.
I FORGOT ABOUT DROWNING.
ALL I KNOW IS I'M TIRED OF HEARING ABOUT ALL OF THIS...OF ALL THE DIFFERENT WAYS LILY CAN BE KILLED.
I GO THROUGH THE SCENARIOS IN MY HEAD OVER AND OVER AGAIN... I CAN'T HELP IT.
I'M ON MY MILLIONTH "WHAT IF."
SCENARIOS ARE MY TORTURE.
I'M TIRED. I WANT IT OVER.

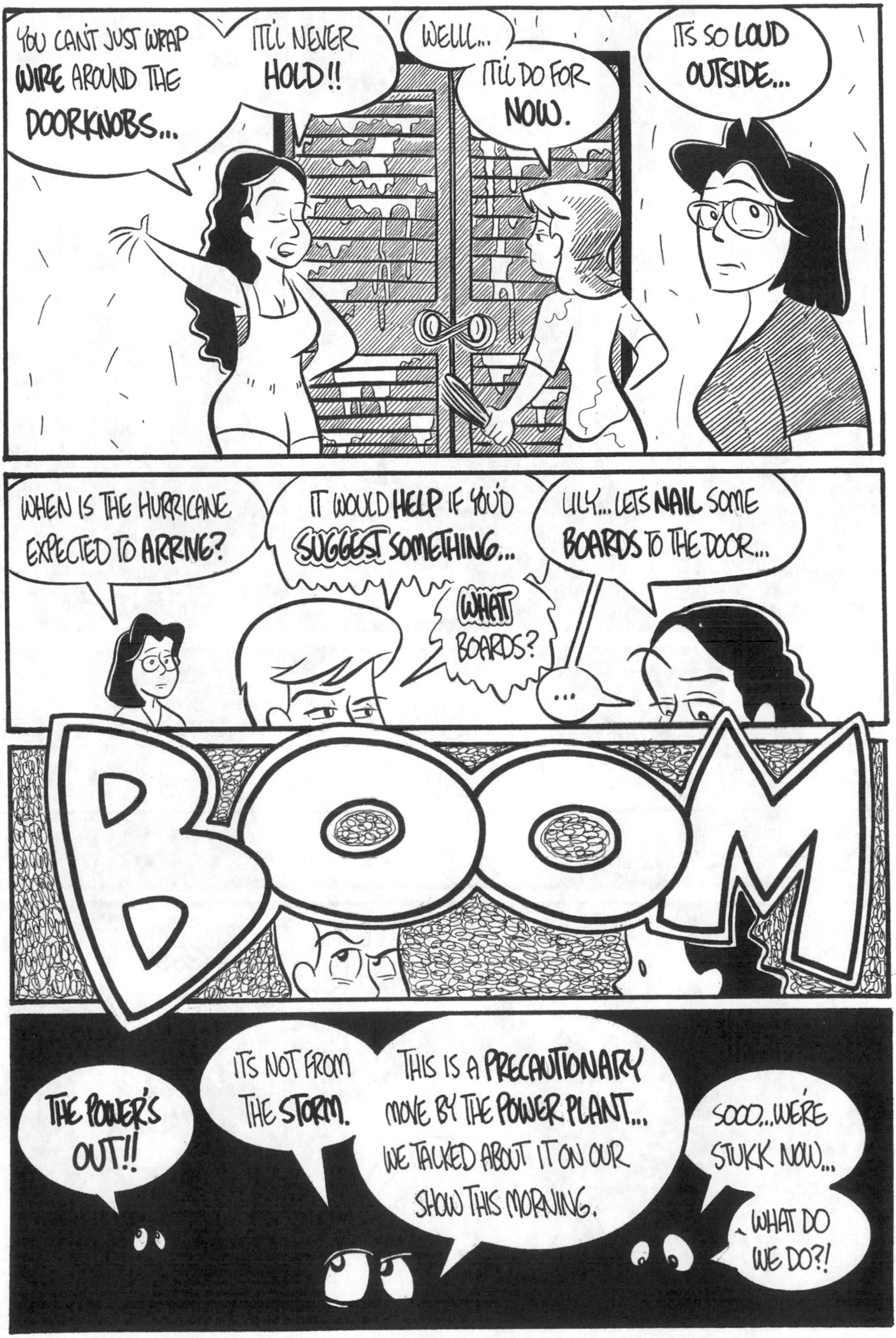
YOU CAN'T JUST WRAP WIRE AROUND THE DOORKNOBS...
IT'LL NEVER HOLD!!
WELLL...
IT'LL DO FOR NOW.
IT'S SO LOUD OUTSIDE...
WHEN IS THE HURRICANE EXPECTED TO ARRIVE?
IT WOULD HELP IF YOU'D SUGGEST SOMETHING...
LILY... LET'S NAIL SOME BOARDS TO THE DOOR...
WHAT BOARDS?
...
BOOM
THE POWER'S OUT!!
IT'S NOT FROM THE STORM.
THIS IS A PRECAUTIONARY MOVE BY THE POWER PLANT... WE TALKED ABOUT IT ON OUR SHOW THIS MORNING.
SOOO... WE'RE STUKK NOW...
WHAT DO WE DO?!

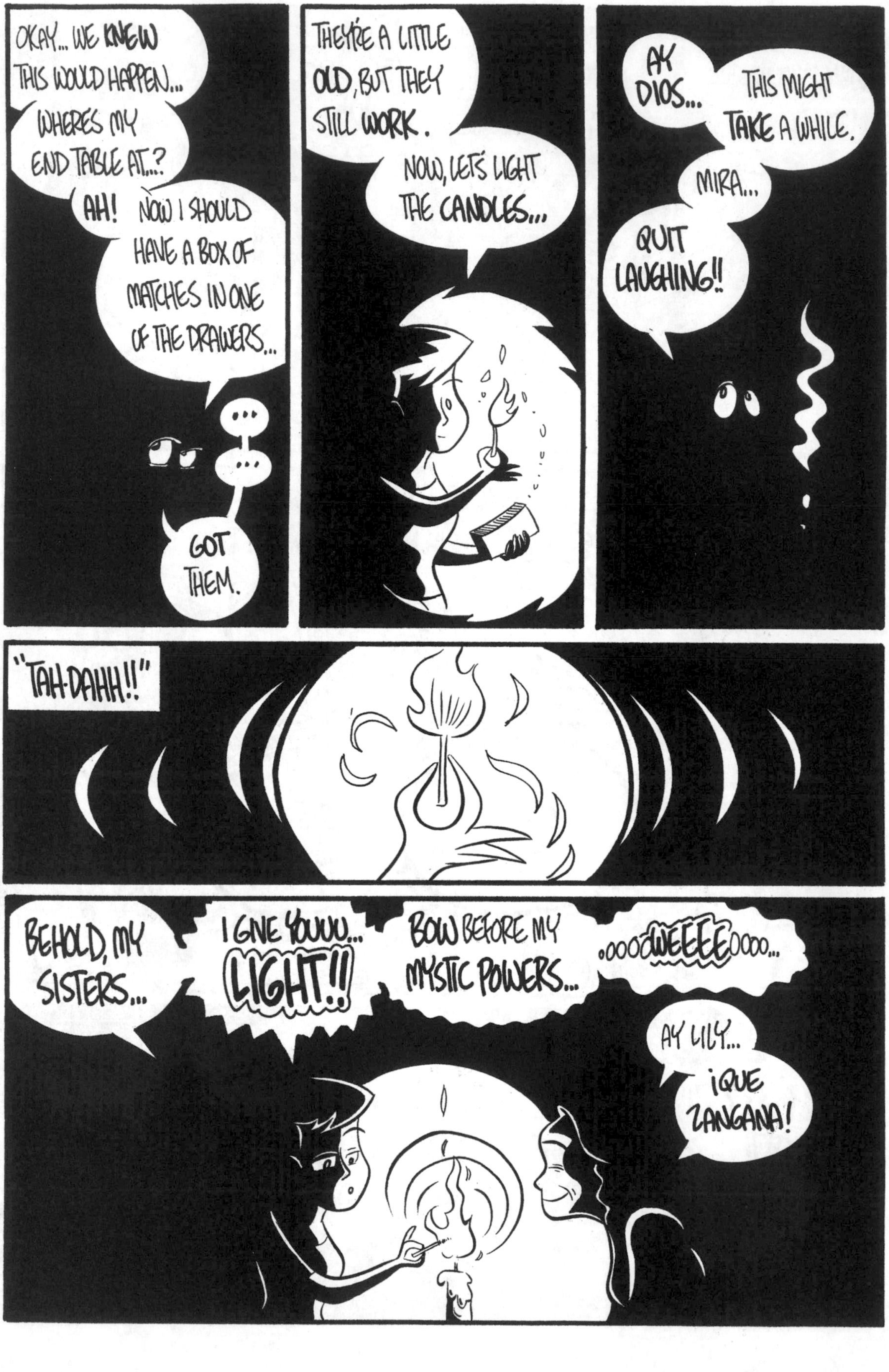

OKAY... WE KNEW THIS WOULD HAPPEN...
WHERES MY END TABLE AT...?
AH!
NOW I SHOULD HAVE A BOX OF MATCHES IN ONE OF THE DRAWERS...
...
...
GOT THEM.
THEY'RE A LITTLE OLD, BUT THEY STILL WORK.
NOW, LET'S LIGHT THE CANDLES...
AY DIOS...
THIS MIGHT TAKE A WHILE.
MIRA...
QUIT LAUGHING!!
"TAH-DAHH!!"
BEHOLD, MY SISTERS...
I GIVE YOUUU... LIGHT!!
BOW BEFORE MY MYSTIC POWERS...
OOOOWEEEEOOOO...
AY LILY...
¡QUE ZANGANA!

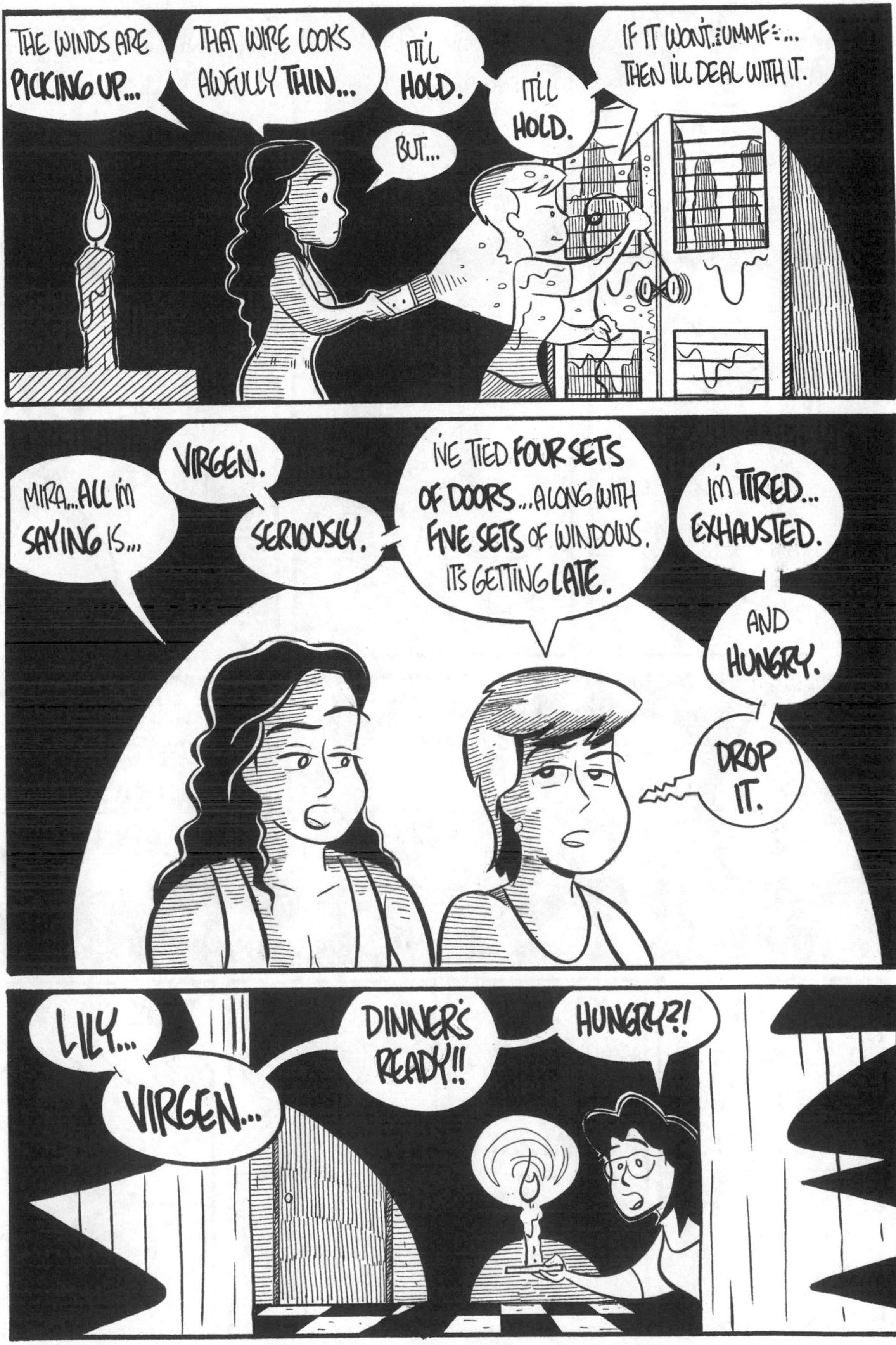
THE WINDS ARE PICKING UP...
THAT WIRE LOOKS AWFULLY THIN...
IT'LL HOLD.
BUT...
IT'LL HOLD.
IF IT WON'T... UMMF... THEN I'LL DEAL WITH IT.
MIRA... ALL I'M SAYING IS...
VIRGEN.
SERIOUSLY.
I'VE TIED FOUR SETS OF DOORS... ALONG WITH FIVE SETS OF WINDOWS. IT'S GETTING LATE.
I'M TIRED... EXHAUSTED.
AND HUNGRY.
DROP IT.
LILY...
VIRGEN...
DINNER'S READY!!
HUNGRY?!

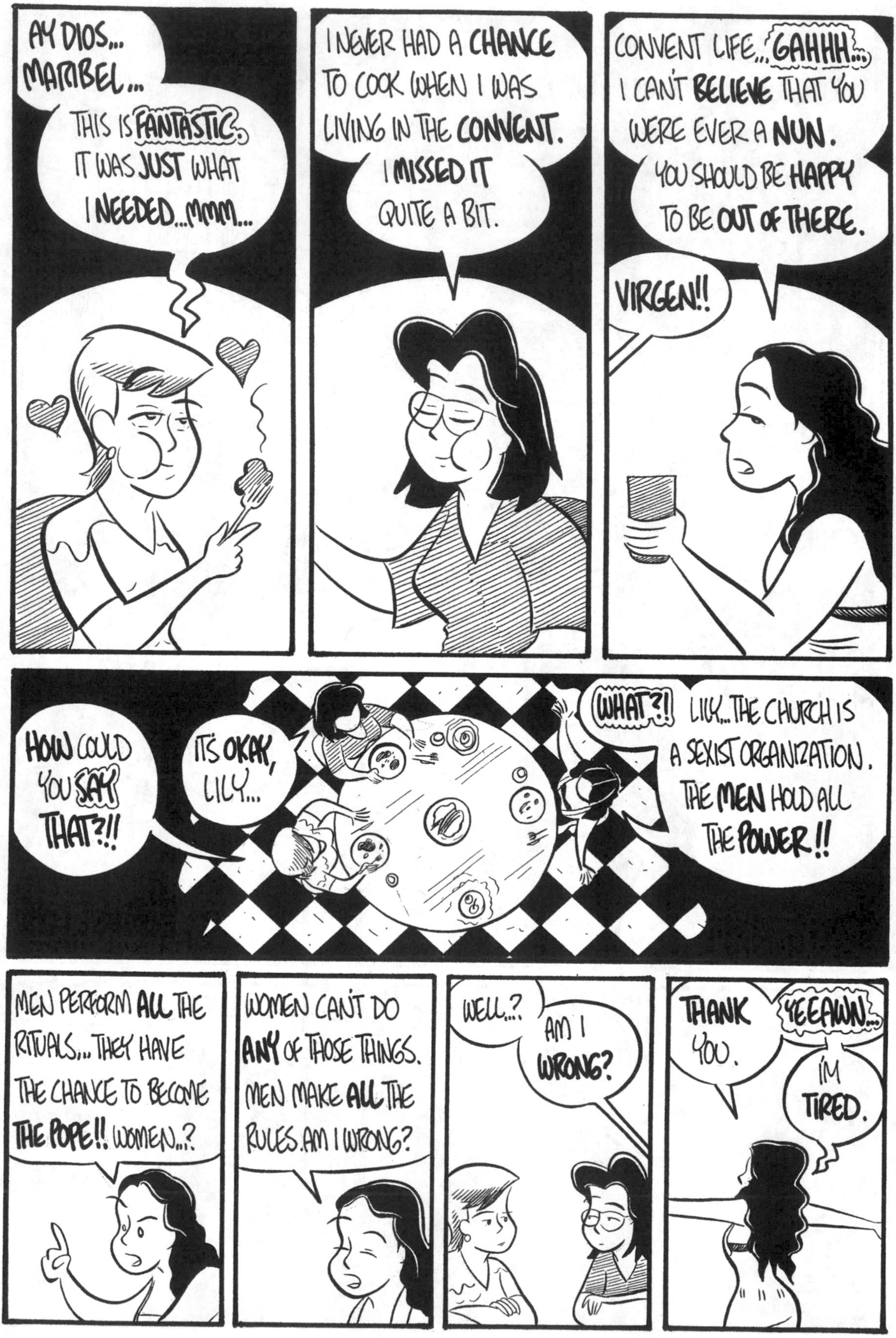
AY DIOS... MARIBEL...
THIS IS FANTASTIC. IT WAS JUST WHAT I NEEDED...MMM...
I NEVER HAD A CHANCE TO COOK WHEN I WAS LIVING IN THE CONVENT.
I MISSED IT QUITE A BIT.
CONVENT LIFE... GAHHH... I CAN'T BELIEVE THAT YOU WERE EVER A NUN.
YOU SHOULD BE HAPPY TO BE OUT OF THERE.
VIRGEN!!
HOW COULD YOU SAY THAT?!!
IT'S OKAY, LILY...
WHAT?!
LILY...THE CHURCH IS A SEXIST ORGANIZATION. THE MEN HOLD ALL THE POWER!!
MEN PERFORM ALL THE RITUALS... THEY HAVE THE CHANCE TO BECOME THE POPE!! WOMEN..?
WOMEN CAN'T DO ANY OF THOSE THINGS. MEN MAKE ALL THE RULES. AM I WRONG?
WELL...?
AM I WRONG?
THANK YOU.
YEEAWN...
I'M TIRED.

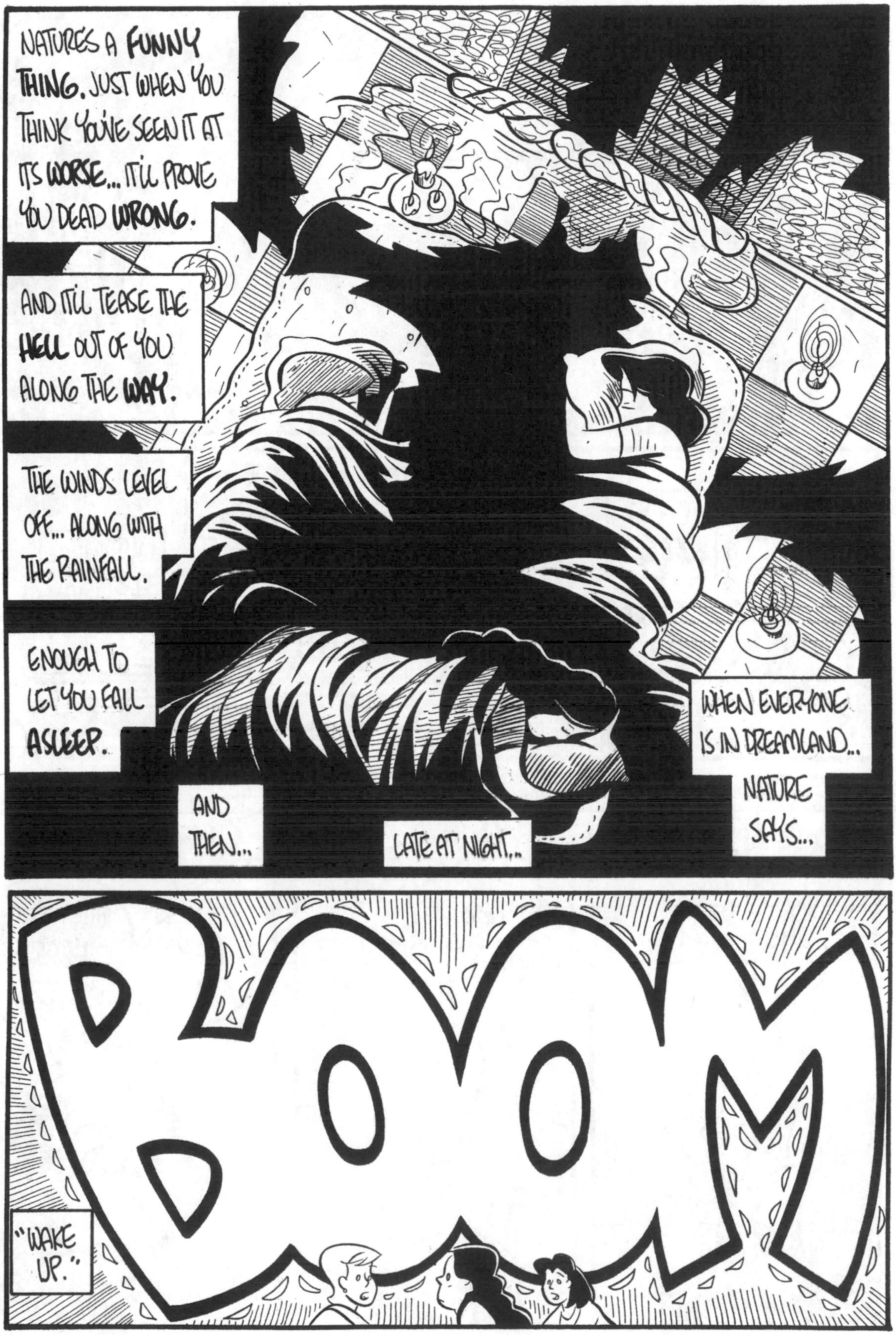
NATURE'S A FUNNY THING. JUST WHEN YOU THINK YOU'VE SEEN IT AT ITS WORSE... IT'LL PROVE YOU DEAD WRONG.
AND IT'LL TEASE THE HELL OUT OF YOU ALONG THE WAY.
THE WINDS LEVEL OFF... ALONG WITH THE RAINFALL.
ENOUGH TO LET YOU FALL ASLEEP.
AND THEN...
LATE AT NIGHT...
WHEN EVERYONE IS IN DREAMLAND... NATURE SAYS...
BOOM
"WAKE UP."

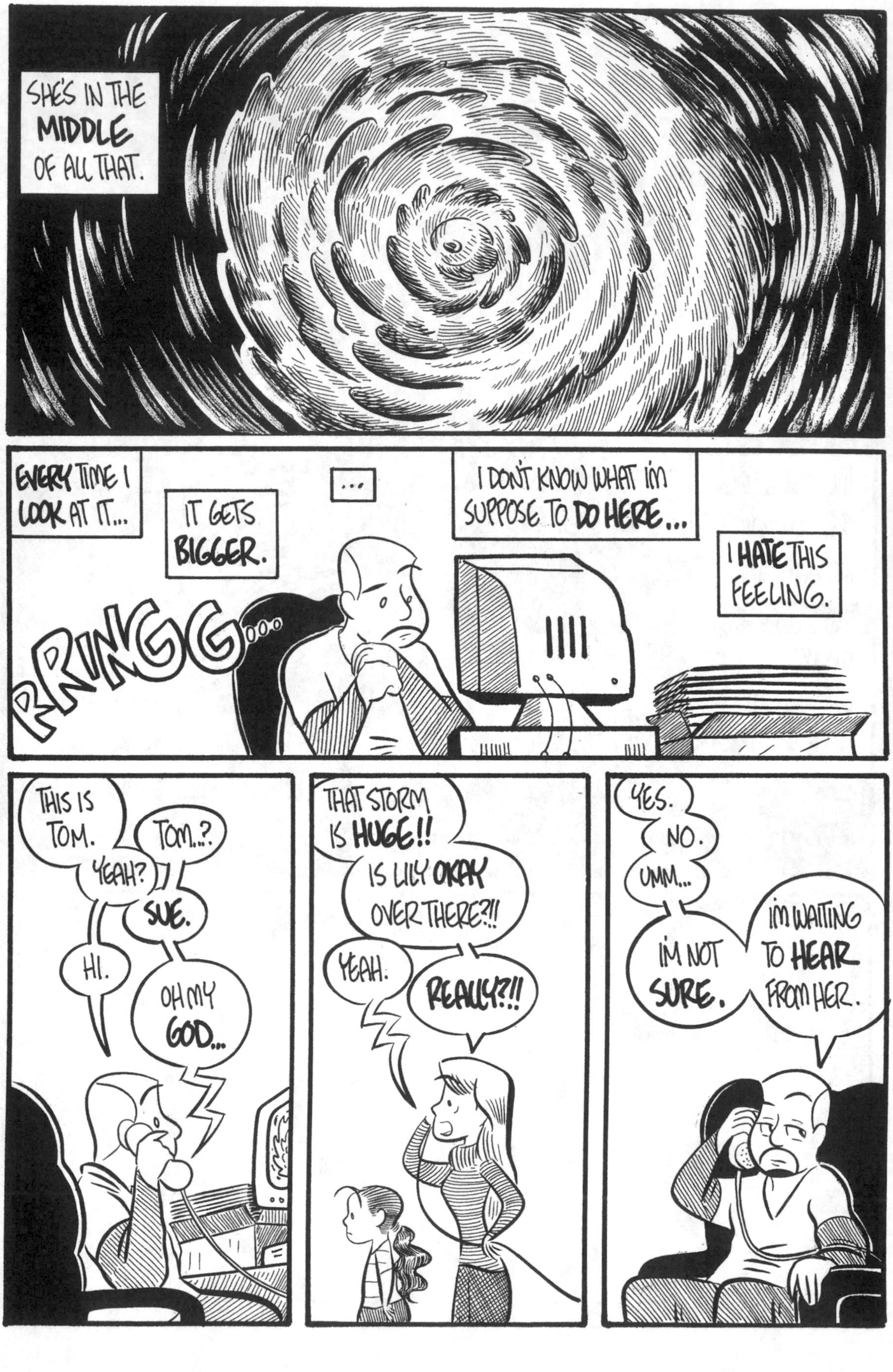
SHE'S IN THE MIDDLE OF ALL THAT.
EVERY TIME I LOOK AT IT...
IT GETS BIGGER.
...
I DON'T KNOW WHAT I'M SUPPOSE TO DO HERE...
I HATE THIS FEELING.
RRINGGooo
THIS IS TOM.
TOM..?
YEAH?
SUE.
HI.
OH MY GOD...
THAT STORM IS HUGE!!
IS LILY OKAY OVER THERE?!!
YEAH.
REALLY?!!
YES.
NO.
UMM...
I'M NOT SURE.
I'M WAITING TO HEAR FROM HER.

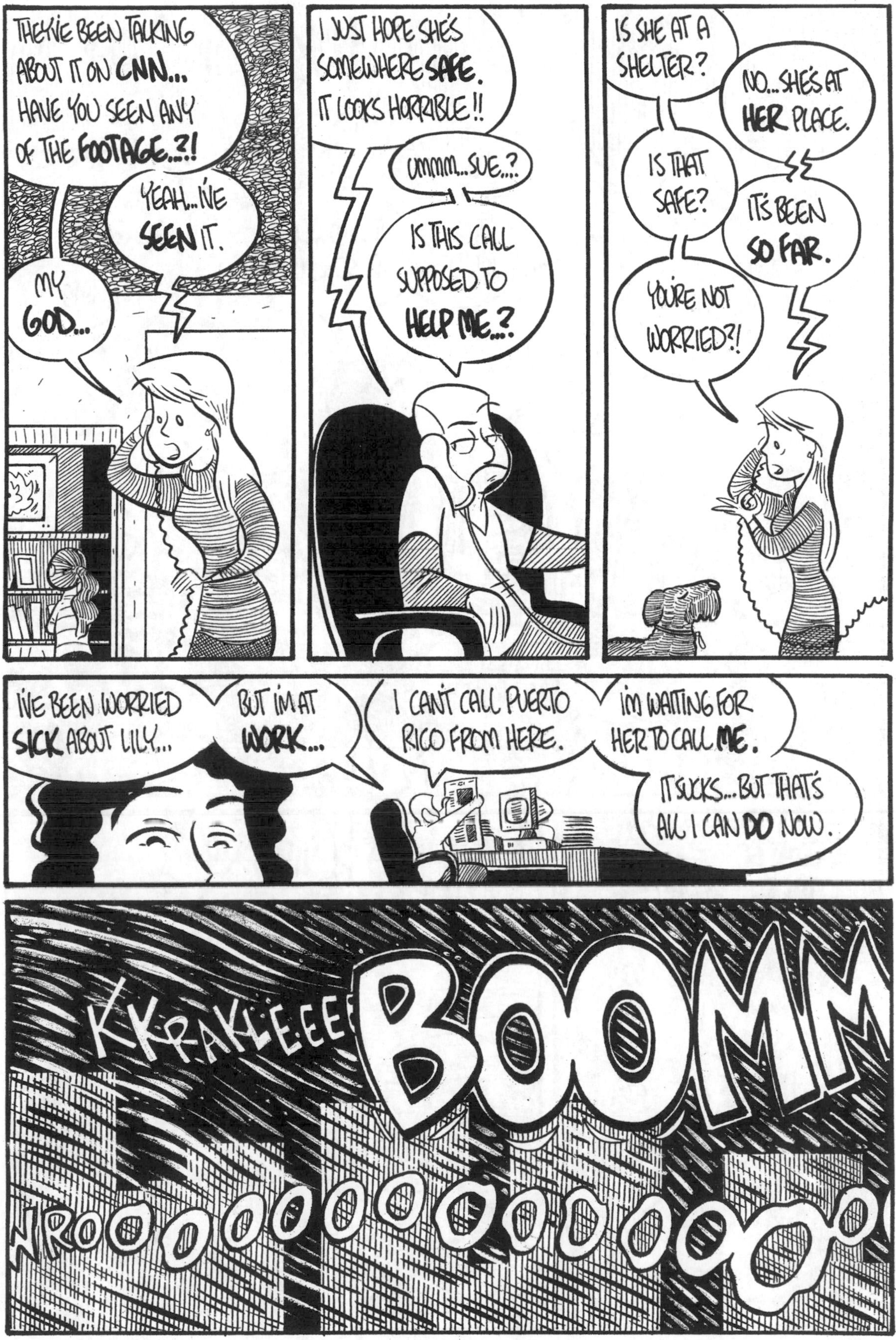
THEY'VE BEEN TALKING ABOUT IT ON CNN... HAVE YOU SEEN ANY OF THE FOOTAGE..?!
YEAH... I'VE SEEN IT.
MY GOD...
I JUST HOPE SHE'S SOMEWHERE SAFE. IT LOOKS HORRIBLE!!
UMMM... SUE...?
IS THIS CALL SUPPOSED TO HELP ME..?
IS SHE AT A SHELTER?
NO... SHE'S AT HER PLACE.
IS THAT SAFE?
IT'S BEEN SO FAR.
YOU'RE NOT WORRIED?!
I'VE BEEN WORRIED SICK ABOUT LILY...
BUT I'M AT WORK...
I CAN'T CALL PUERTO RICO FROM HERE.
I'M WAITING FOR HER TO CALL ME.
IT SUCKS... BUT THAT'S ALL I CAN DO NOW.
KKRAKLEEEE
BOOMM
WROOOOOOOOOOOOOOOO

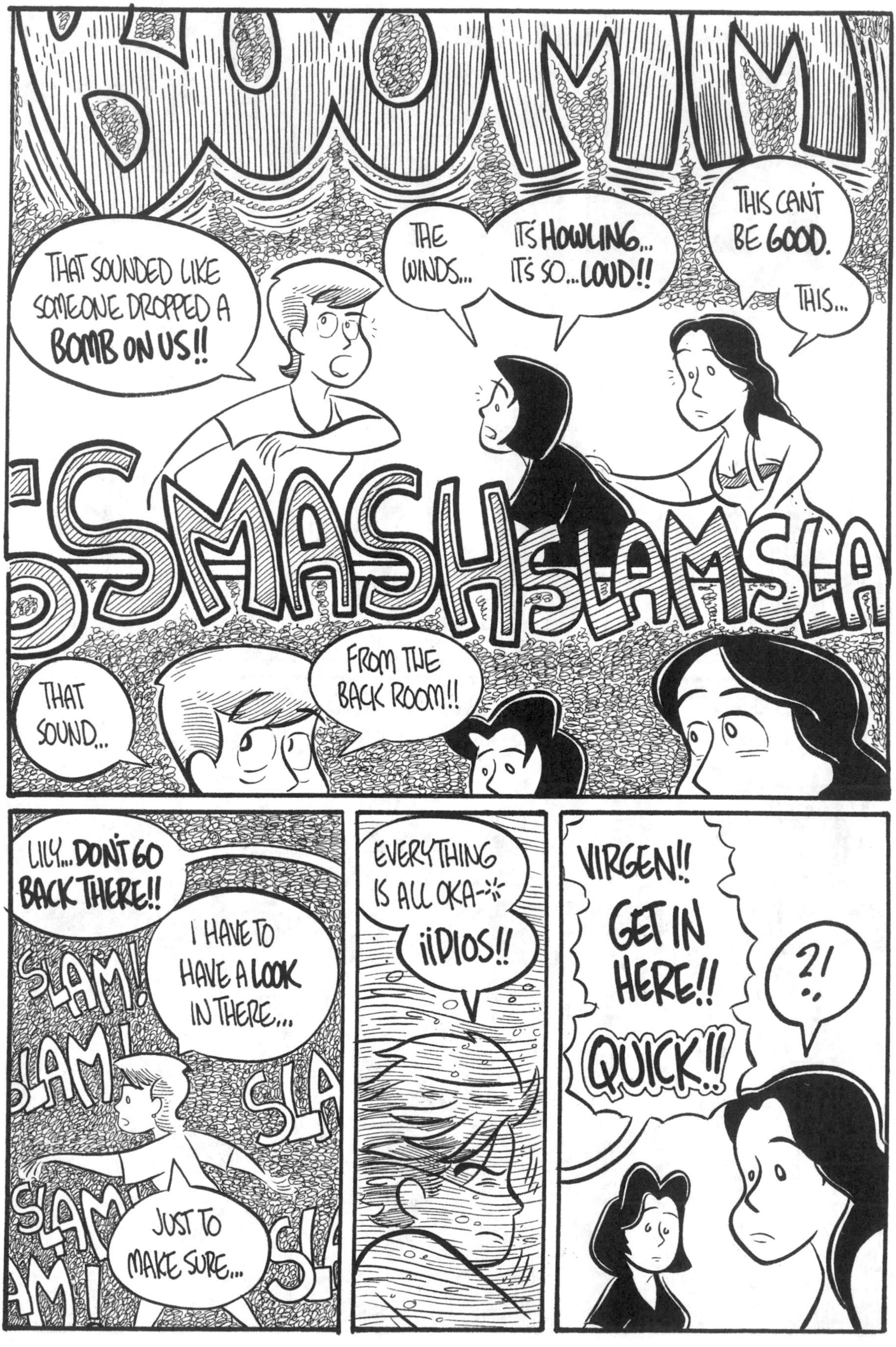
BOOOMMM
THAT SOUNDED LIKE SOMEONE DROPPED A BOMB ON US!!
THE WINDS...
IT'S HOWLING... IT'S SO...LOUD!!
THIS CAN'T BE GOOD.
THIS...
SMASH SLAM SLA
THAT SOUND...
FROM THE BACK ROOM!!
LILY...DON'T GO BACK THERE!!
I HAVE TO HAVE A LOOK IN THERE...
SLAM! SLAM! SLAM! SLAM!
JUST TO MAKE SURE...
EVERYTHING IS ALL OKA-
¡¡DIOS!!
VIRGEN!! GET IN HERE!!
QUICK!!
?!

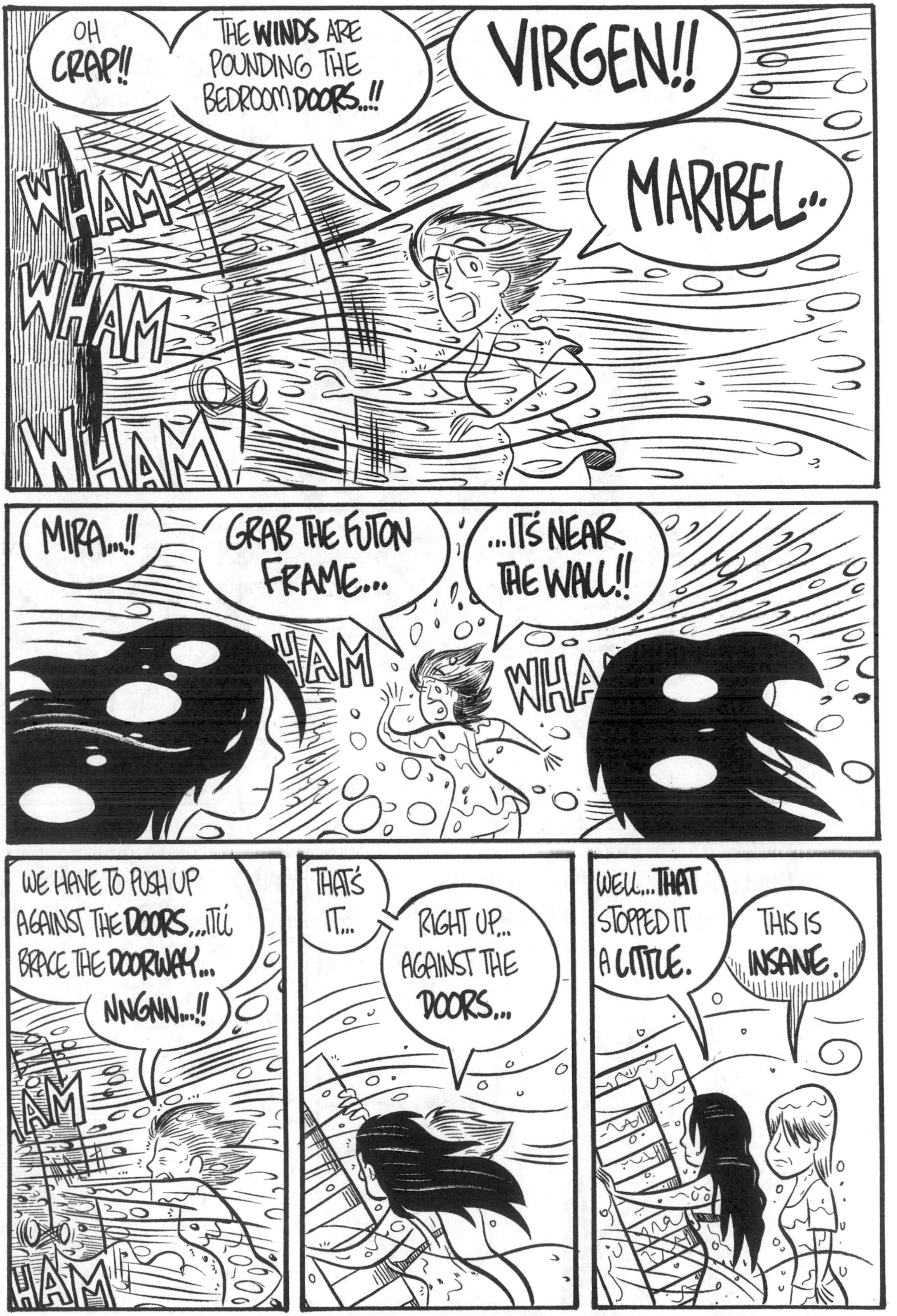
OH CRAP!!
THE WINDS ARE POUNDING THE BEDROOM DOORS...!!
VIRGEN!!
MARIBEL...
WHAM
WHAM
WHAM
MIRA...!!
GRAB THE FUTON FRAME...
...IT'S NEAR THE WALL!!
HAM
WHA
WE HAVE TO PUSH UP AGAINST THE DOORS... IT'LL BRACE THE DOORWAY...
NNGNN...!!
AM
HAM!!
THAT'S IT...
RIGHT UP... AGAINST THE DOORS...
WELL... THAT STOPPED IT A LITTLE.
THIS IS INSANE.

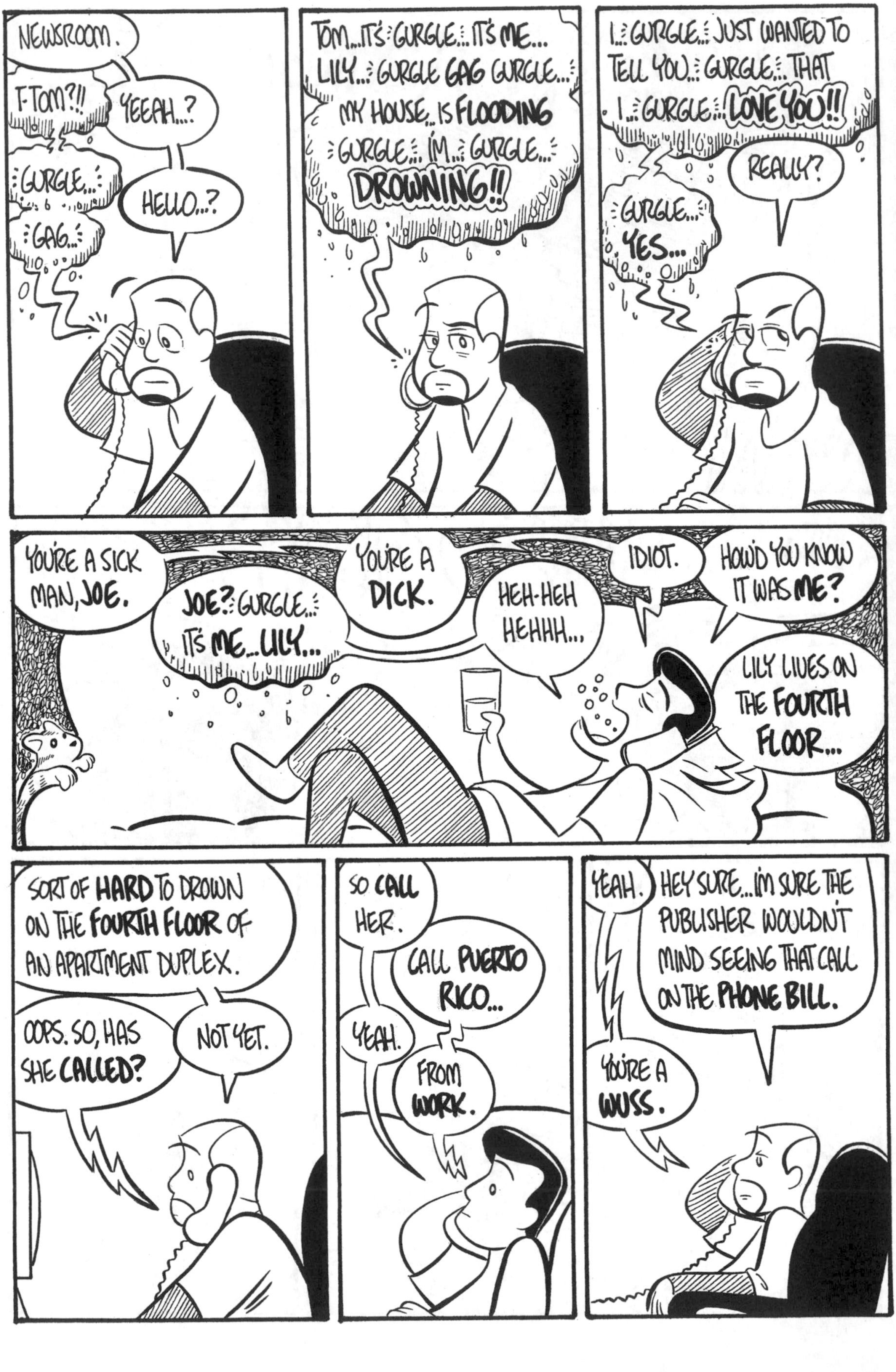
NEWSROOM.
F-TOM?!!
YEEAH...?
GURGLE...
GAG...
HELLO...?
TOM...IT'S GURGLE... IT'S ME... LILY... GURGLE GAG GURGLE... MY HOUSE... IS FLOODING GURGLE... I'M... GURGLE... DROWNING!!
I... GURGLE... JUST WANTED TO TELL YOU... GURGLE... THAT I... GURGLE... LOVE YOU!!
REALLY?
GURGLE... YES...
YOU'RE A SICK MAN, JOE.
JOE? GURGLE... IT'S ME...LILY...
YOU'RE A DICK.
HEH-HEH HEHHH...
IDIOT.
HOW'D YOU KNOW IT WAS ME?
LILY LIVES ON THE FOURTH FLOOR...
SORT OF HARD TO DROWN ON THE FOURTH FLOOR OF AN APARTMENT DUPLEX.
OOPS. SO, HAS SHE CALLED?
NOT YET.
SO CALL HER.
CALL PUERTO RICO...
YEAH.
FROM WORK.
YEAH.
HEY SURE...I'M SURE THE PUBLISHER WOULDN'T MIND SEEING THAT CALL ON THE PHONE BILL.
YOU'RE A WUSS.

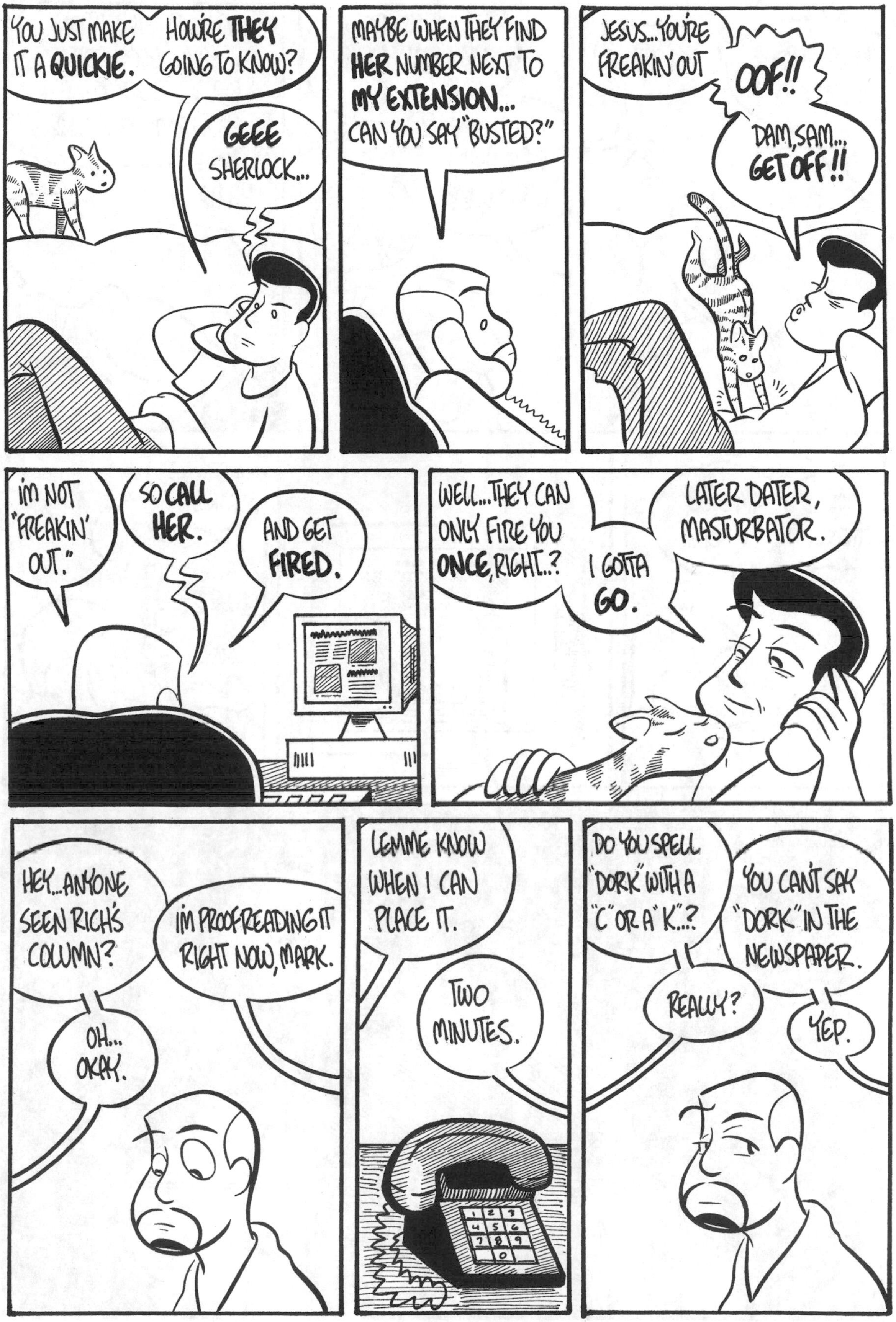

YOU JUST MAKE IT A **QUICKIE.**
HOW'RE **THEY** GOING TO KNOW?
GEEE SHERLOCK...
MAYBE WHEN THEY FIND **HER** NUMBER NEXT TO **MY EXTENSION...** CAN YOU SAY "BUSTED?"
JESUS...YOU'RE FREAKIN' OUT
OOF!!
DAM, SAM... **GET OFF!!**
I'M NOT "FREAKIN' OUT."
SO **CALL HER.**
AND GET **FIRED.**
WELL...THEY CAN ONLY FIRE YOU **ONCE**, RIGHT...?
I GOTTA **GO.**
LATER DATER, MASTURBATOR.
HEY...ANYONE SEEN RICH'S COLUMN?
I'M PROOFREADING IT RIGHT NOW, MARK.
OH... OKAY.
LEMME KNOW WHEN I CAN PLACE IT.
TWO MINUTES.
DO YOU SPELL "DORK" WITH A "C" OR A "K"...?
REALLY?
YOU CAN'T SAY "DORK" IN THE NEWSPAPER.
YEP.

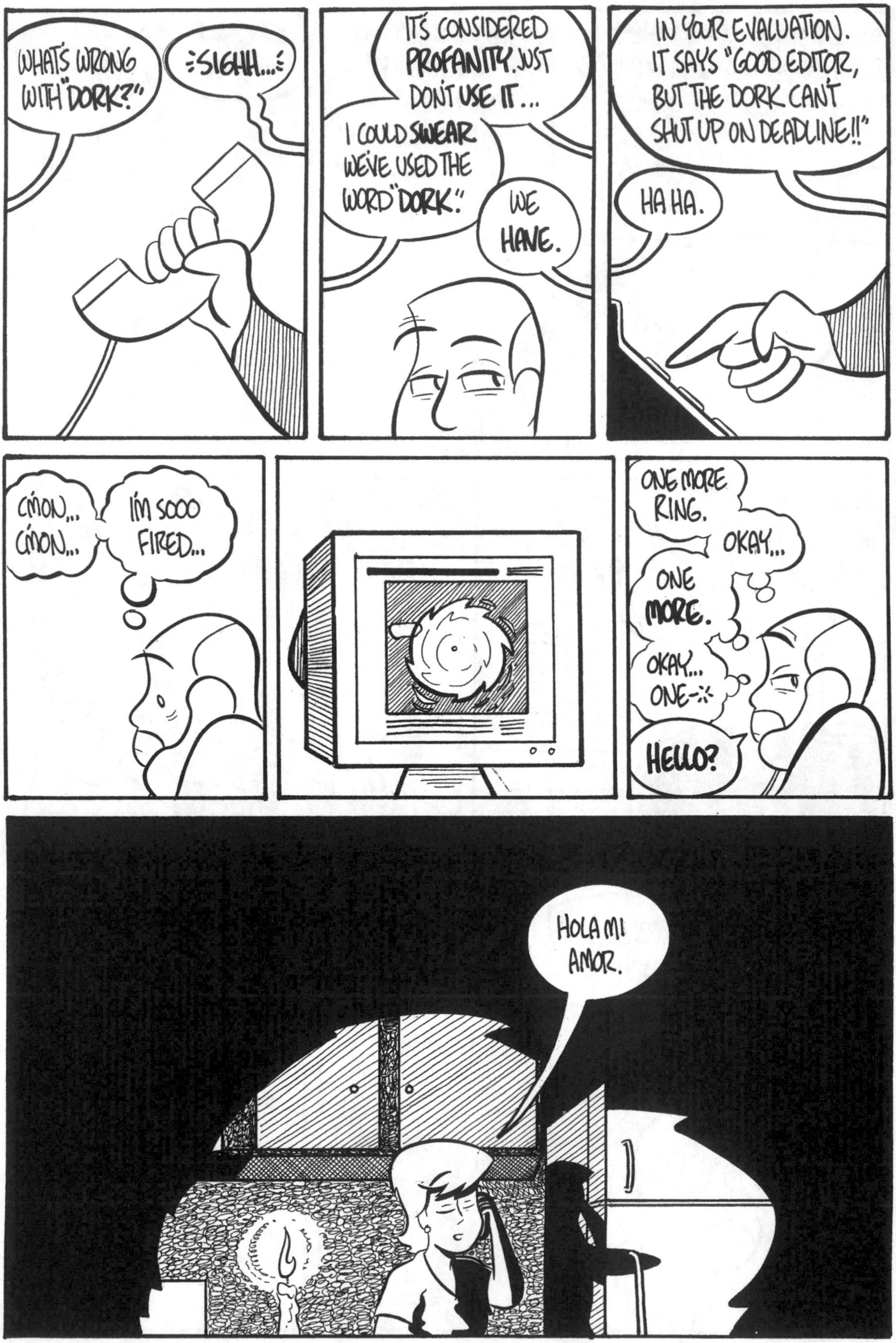
WHAT'S WRONG WITH "DORK?"
SIGHH...
IT'S CONSIDERED PROFANITY. JUST DON'T USE IT...
I COULD SWEAR WE'VE USED THE WORD "DORK."
WE HAVE.
IN YOUR EVALUATION. IT SAYS "GOOD EDITOR, BUT THE DORK CAN'T SHUT UP ON DEADLINE!!"
HA HA.
C'MON... C'MON...
I'M SOOO FIRED...
ONE MORE RING.
OKAY...
ONE MORE.
OKAY... ONE-
HELLO?
HOLA MI AMOR.

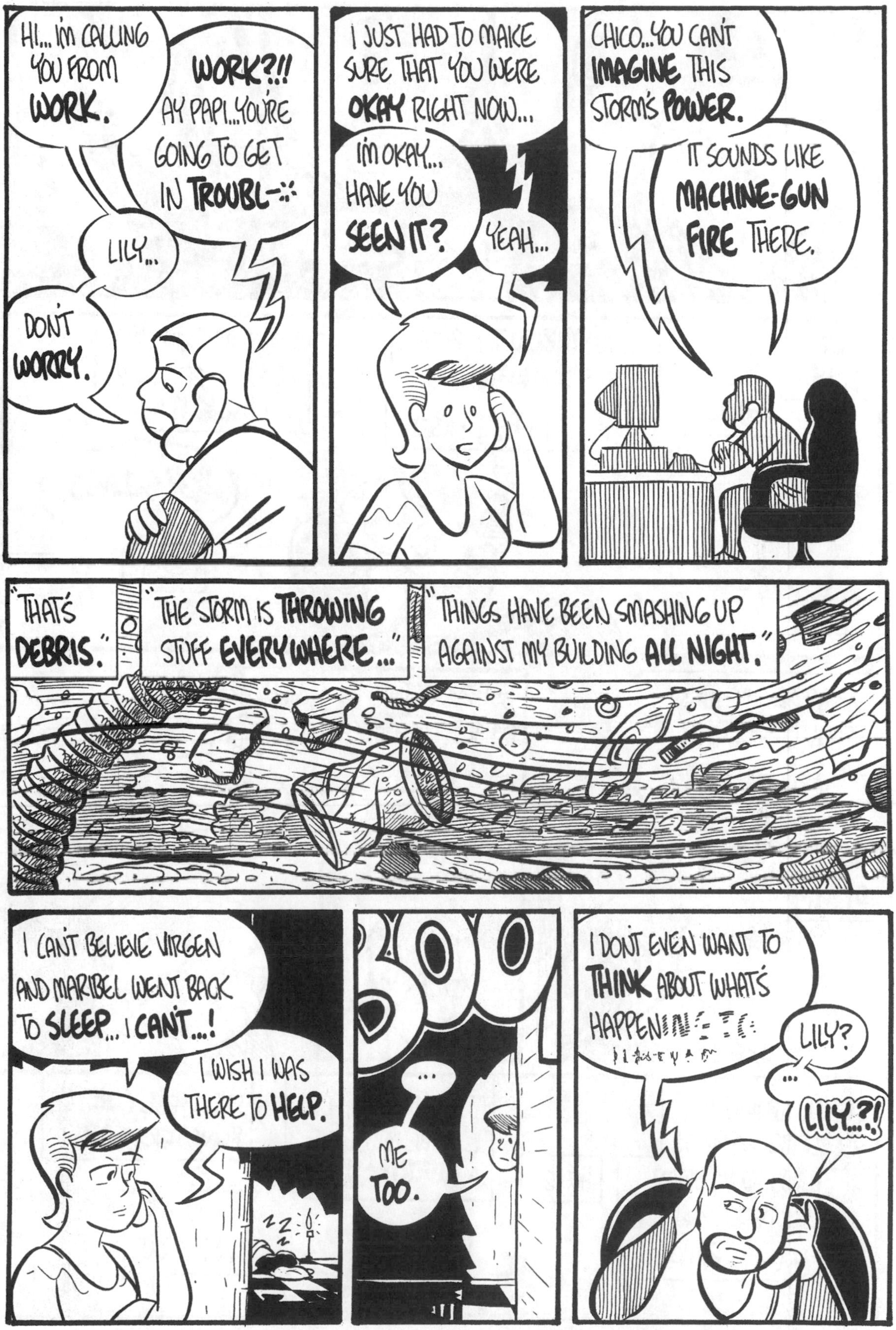
HI... I'M CALLING YOU FROM WORK.
WORK?!! AY PAPI... YOU'RE GOING TO GET IN TROUBL-
LILY...
DON'T WORRY.
I JUST HAD TO MAKE SURE THAT YOU WERE OKAY RIGHT NOW...
I'M OKAY... HAVE YOU SEEN IT?
YEAH...
CHICO... YOU CAN'T IMAGINE THIS STORM'S POWER.
IT SOUNDS LIKE MACHINE-GUN FIRE THERE.
"THAT'S DEBRIS."
"THE STORM IS THROWING STUFF EVERYWHERE..."
"THINGS HAVE BEEN SMASHING UP AGAINST MY BUILDING ALL NIGHT."
I CAN'T BELIEVE VIRGEN AND MARIBEL WENT BACK TO SLEEP... I CAN'T...!
I WISH I WAS THERE TO HELP.
ZZZ
...
ME TOO.
I DON'T EVEN WANT TO THINK ABOUT WHAT'S HAPPENIN
LILY?
...
LILY...?!

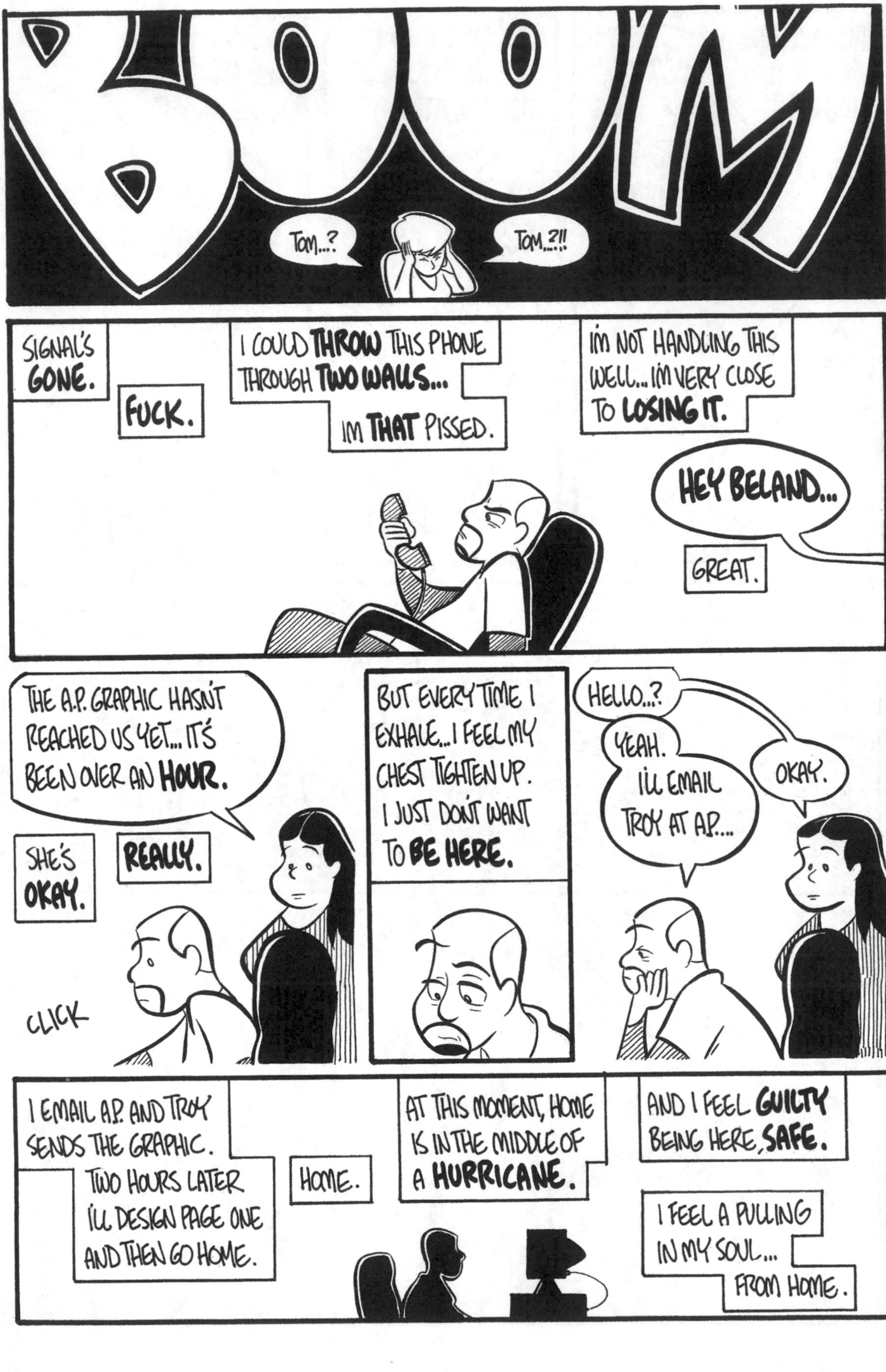
BOOM
TOM...?
TOM..?!!
SIGNAL'S GONE.
FUCK.
I COULD THROW THIS PHONE THROUGH TWO WALLS...
IM THAT PISSED.
IM NOT HANDLING THIS WELL... IM VERY CLOSE TO LOSING IT.
HEY BELAND...
GREAT.
THE A.P. GRAPHIC HASN'T REACHED US YET... IT'S BEEN OVER AN HOUR.
SHE'S OKAY.
REALLY.
CLICK
BUT EVERY TIME I EXHALE... I FEEL MY CHEST TIGHTEN UP. I JUST DON'T WANT TO BE HERE.
HELLO...?
YEAH. I'LL EMAIL TROY AT A.P....
OKAY.
I EMAIL A.P. AND TROY SENDS THE GRAPHIC.
TWO HOURS LATER I'LL DESIGN PAGE ONE AND THEN GO HOME.
HOME.
AT THIS MOMENT, HOME IS IN THE MIDDLE OF A HURRICANE.
AND I FEEL GUILTY BEING HERE, SAFE.
I FEEL A PULLING IN MY SOUL... FROM HOME.

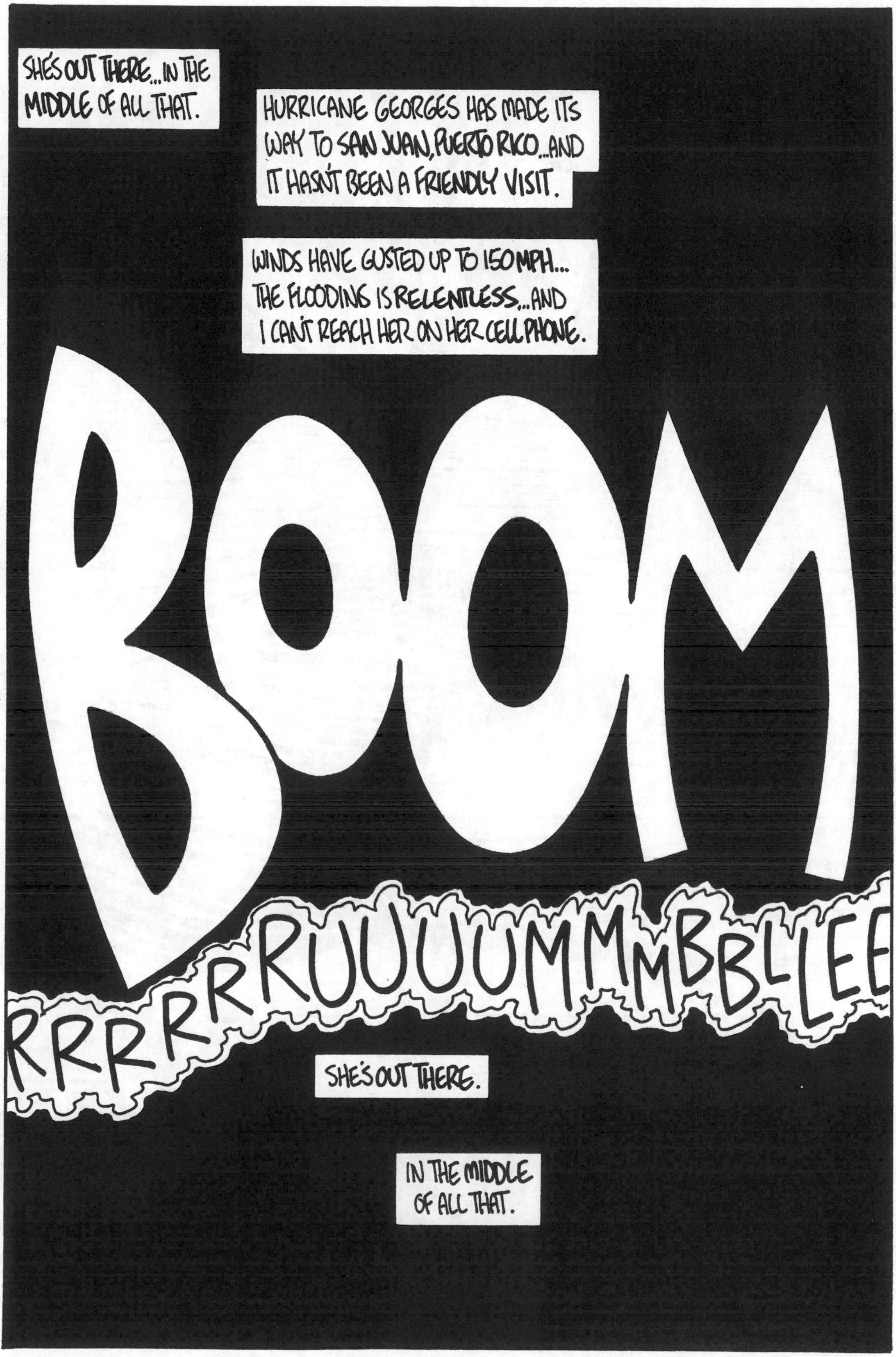
SHE'S OUT THERE... IN THE MIDDLE OF ALL THAT.
HURRICANE GEORGES HAS MADE ITS WAY TO SAN JUAN, PUERTO RICO... AND IT HASN'T BEEN A FRIENDLY VISIT.
WINDS HAVE GUSTED UP TO 150 MPH... THE FLOODING IS RELENTLESS... AND I CAN'T REACH HER ON HER CELL PHONE.
BOOM
RRRRRRUUUUMMMBBLLEE
SHE'S OUT THERE.
IN THE MIDDLE OF ALL THAT.

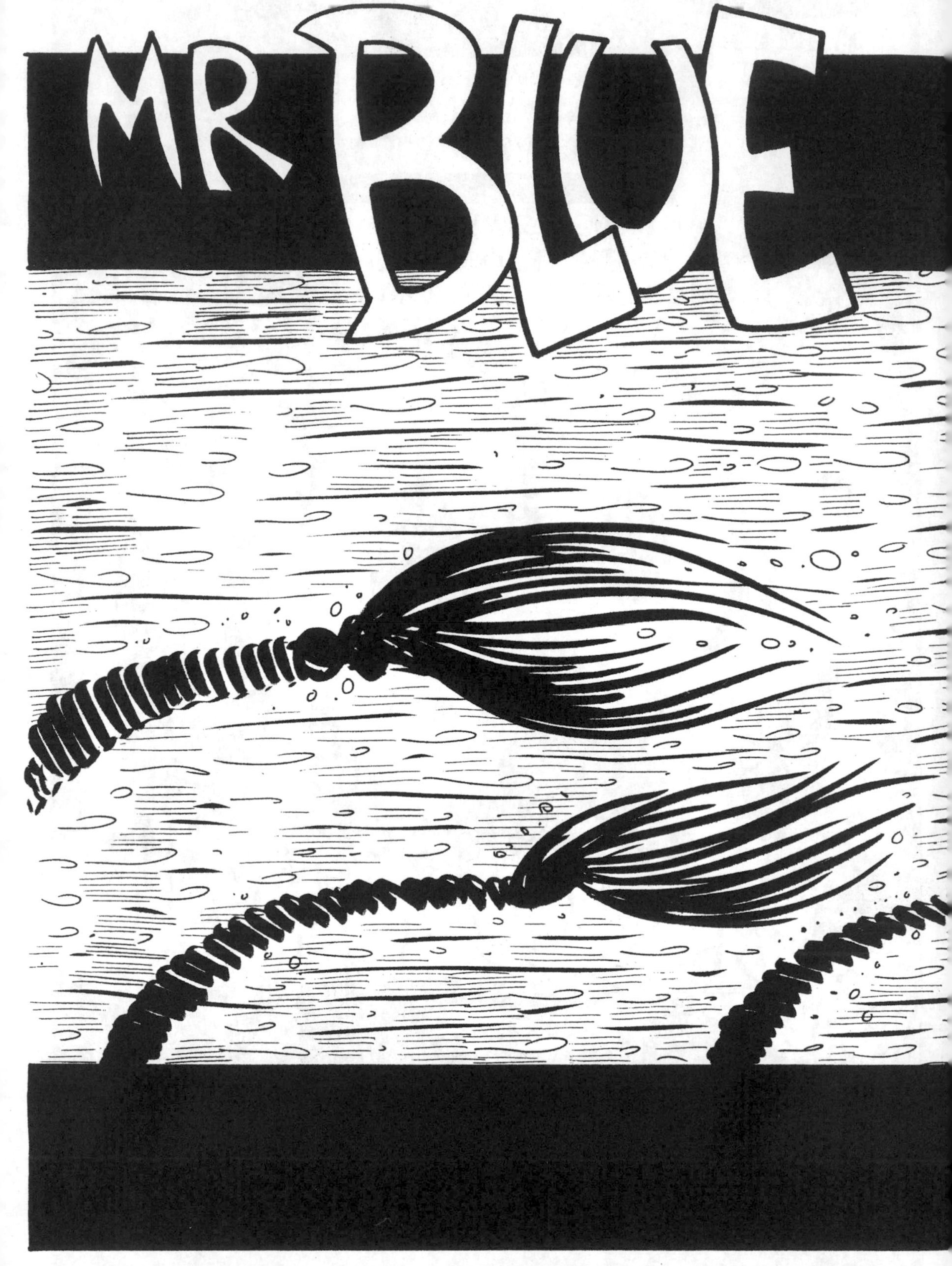
MR BLUE

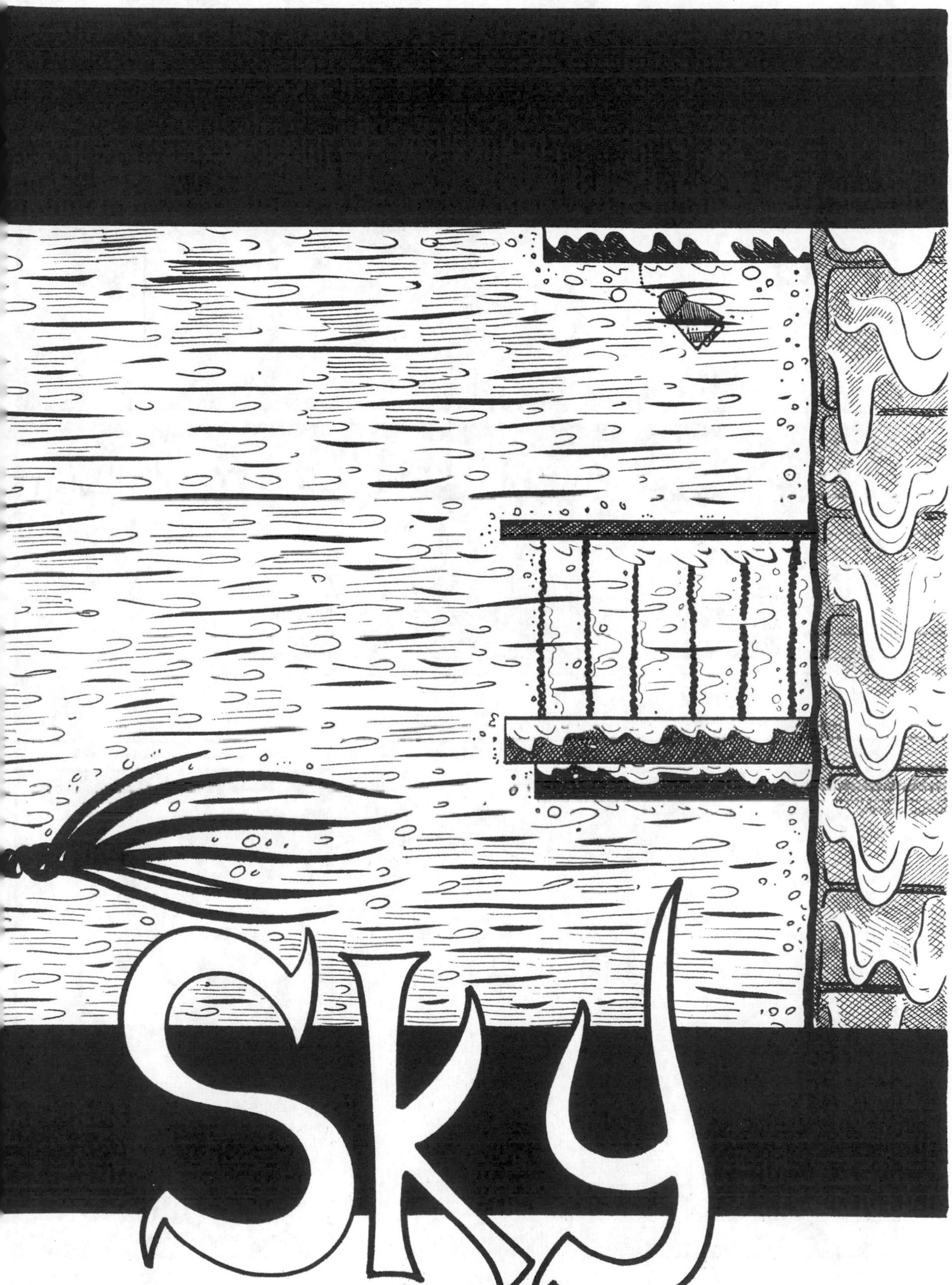
Sky

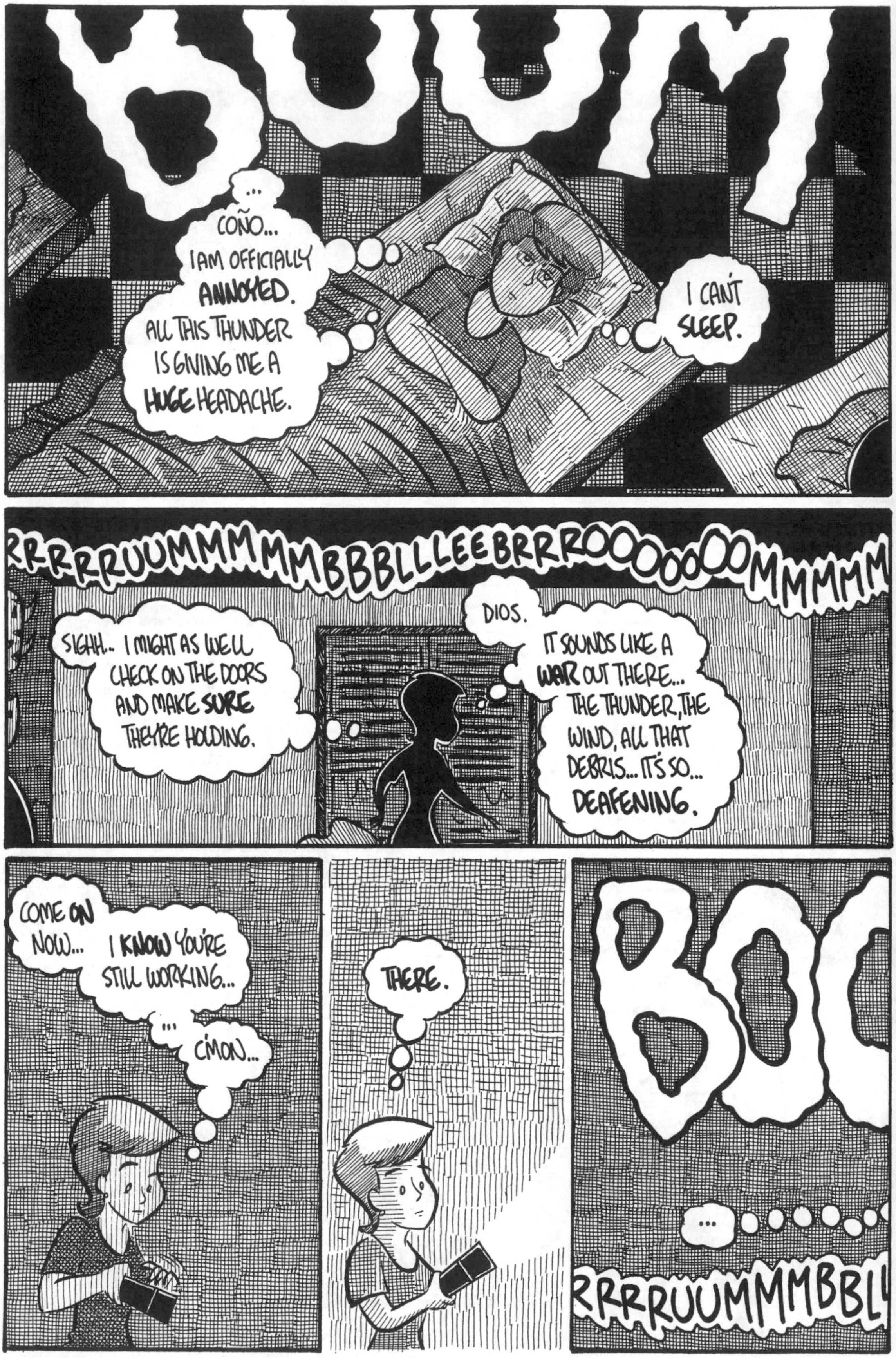
BOOM
...
COÑO...
I AM OFFICIALLY ANNOYED.
ALL THIS THUNDER IS GIVING ME A HUGE HEADACHE.
I CAN'T SLEEP.
RRRRRUUMMMMMMBBBLLLEEBRRROOOOOOOMMMMM
SIGHH.. I MIGHT AS WELL CHECK ON THE DOORS AND MAKE SURE THEY'RE HOLDING.
DIOS.
IT SOUNDS LIKE A WAR OUT THERE... THE THUNDER, THE WIND, ALL THAT DEBRIS... IT'S SO... DEAFENING.
COME ON NOW...
I KNOW YOU'RE STILL WORKING...
...
C'MON...
THERE.
...
RRRRUUMMMBBL

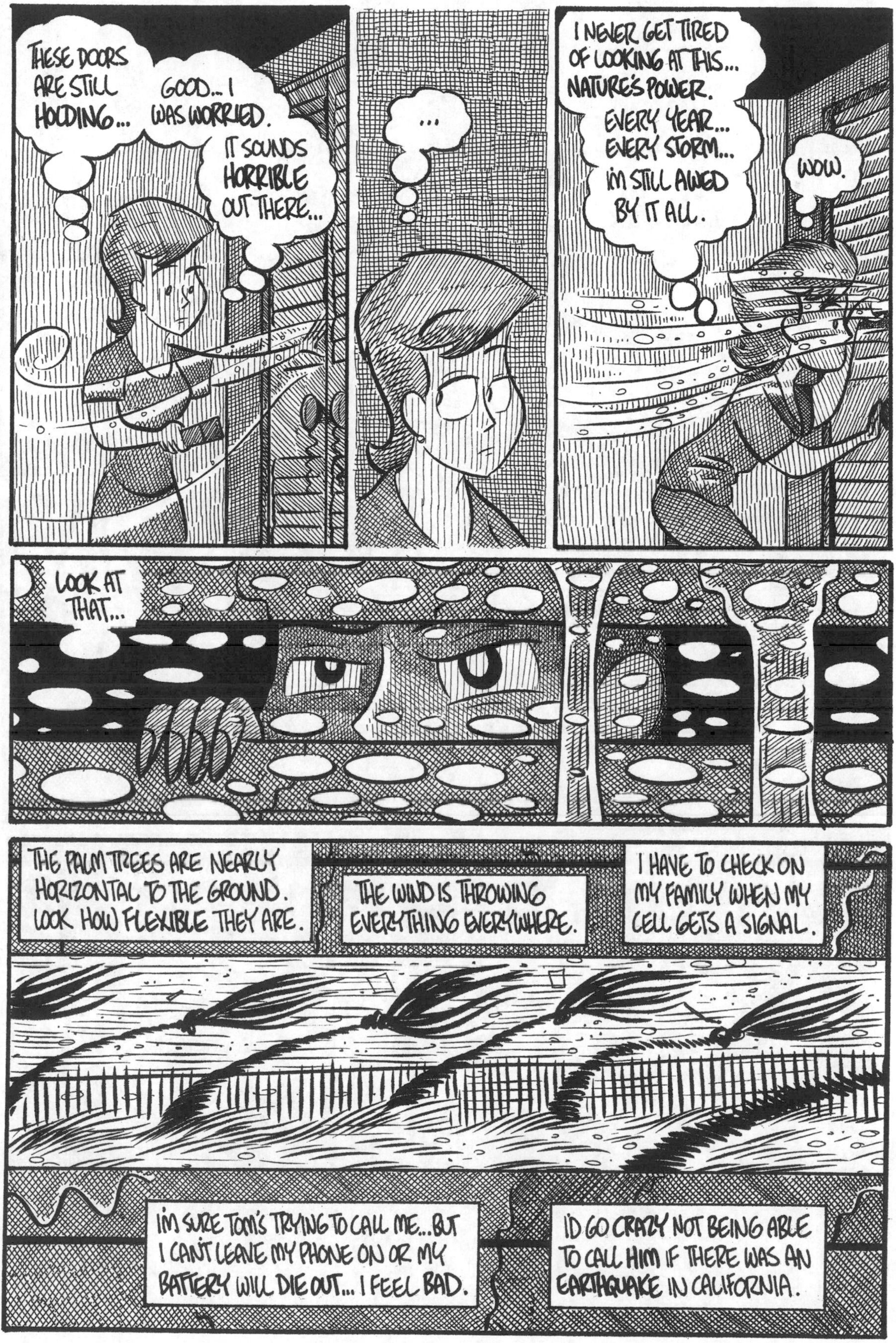
THESE DOORS ARE STILL HOLDING...
GOOD... I WAS WORRIED.
IT SOUNDS HORRIBLE OUT THERE...
...
I NEVER GET TIRED OF LOOKING AT THIS... NATURE'S POWER.
EVERY YEAR... EVERY STORM... I'M STILL AWED BY IT ALL.
WOW.
LOOK AT THAT...
THE PALM TREES ARE NEARLY HORIZONTAL TO THE GROUND. LOOK HOW FLEXIBLE THEY ARE.
THE WIND IS THROWING EVERYTHING EVERYWHERE.
I HAVE TO CHECK ON MY FAMILY WHEN MY CELL GETS A SIGNAL.
I'M SURE TOM'S TRYING TO CALL ME... BUT I CAN'T LEAVE MY PHONE ON OR MY BATTERY WILL DIE OUT... I FEEL BAD.
I'D GO CRAZY NOT BEING ABLE TO CALL HIM IF THERE WAS AN EARTHQUAKE IN CALIFORNIA.

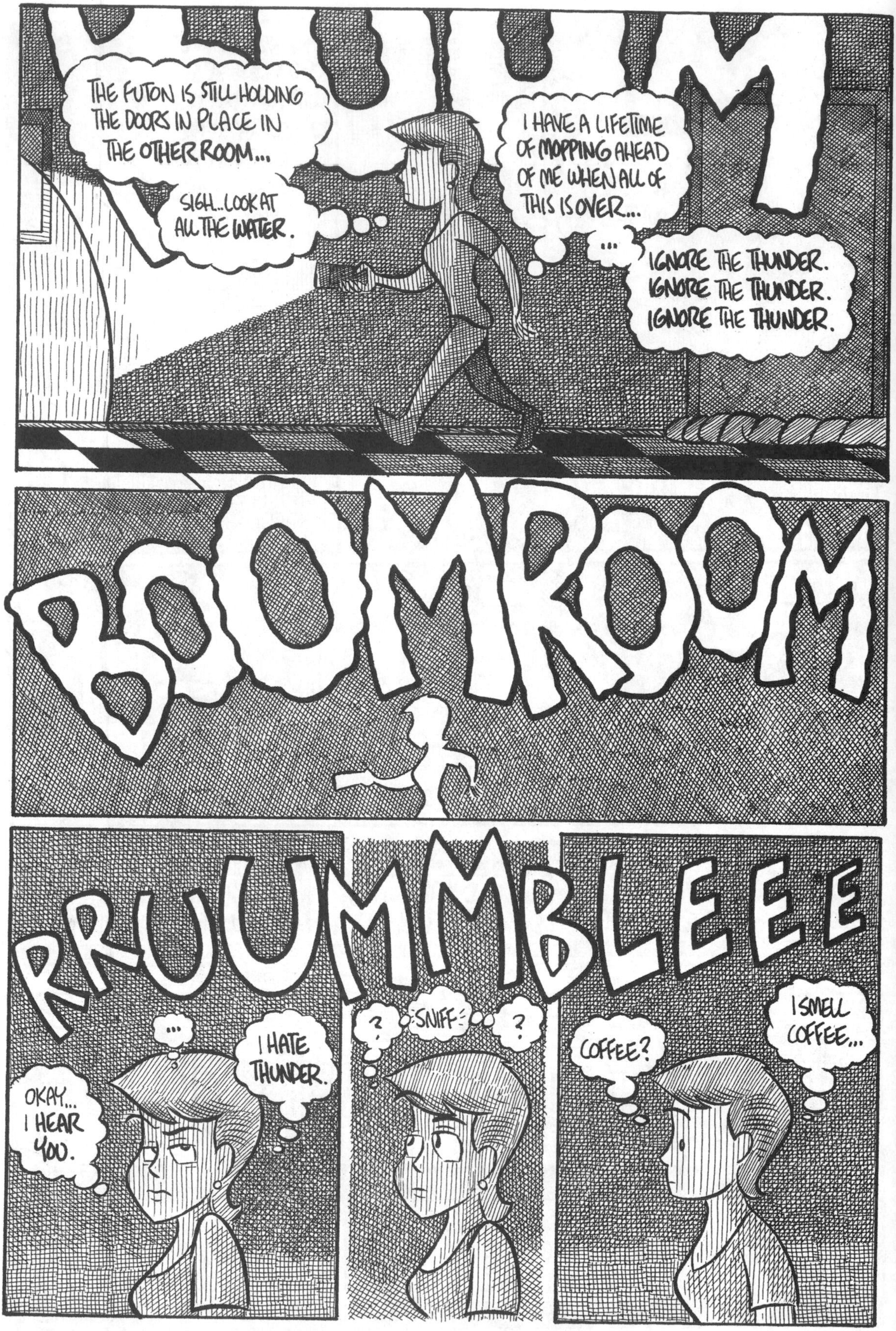
THE FUTON IS STILL HOLDING THE DOORS IN PLACE IN THE OTHER ROOM...
SIGH...LOOK AT ALL THE WATER.
I HAVE A LIFETIME OF MOPPING AHEAD OF ME WHEN ALL OF THIS IS OVER...
...
IGNORE THE THUNDER. IGNORE THE THUNDER. IGNORE THE THUNDER.
BOOMROOM
RRUUMMBLEEE
...
I HATE THUNDER.
OKAY... I HEAR YOU.
?
SNIFF
?
COFFEE?
I SMELL COFFEE...

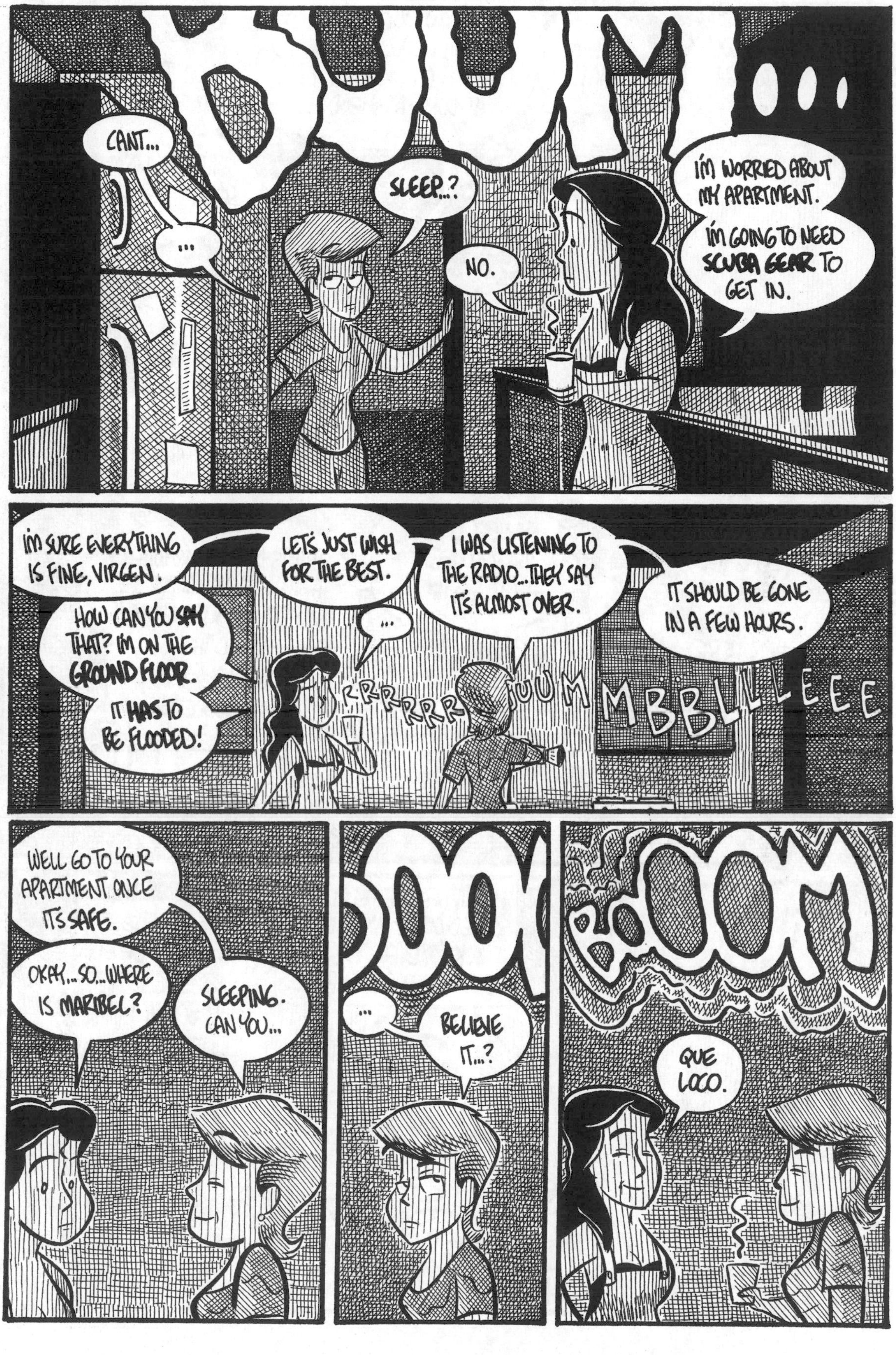BOOM...
CANT...
SLEEP...?
...
NO.
I'M WORRIED ABOUT MY APARTMENT.
I'M GOING TO NEED SCUBA GEAR TO GET IN.
I'M SURE EVERYTHING IS FINE, VIRGEN.
HOW CAN YOU SAY THAT? I'M ON THE GROUND FLOOR.
IT HAS TO BE FLOODED!
LET'S JUST WISH FOR THE BEST.
...
I WAS LISTENING TO THE RADIO... THEY SAY IT'S ALMOST OVER.
IT SHOULD BE GONE IN A FEW HOURS.
RRRRRRRUUMMBBLLLEEE
WELL GO TO YOUR APARTMENT ONCE IT'S SAFE.
OKAY... SO... WHERE IS MARIBEL?
SLEEPING. CAN YOU...
BOOO
...
BELIEVE IT...?
BOOOM
QUE LOCO.

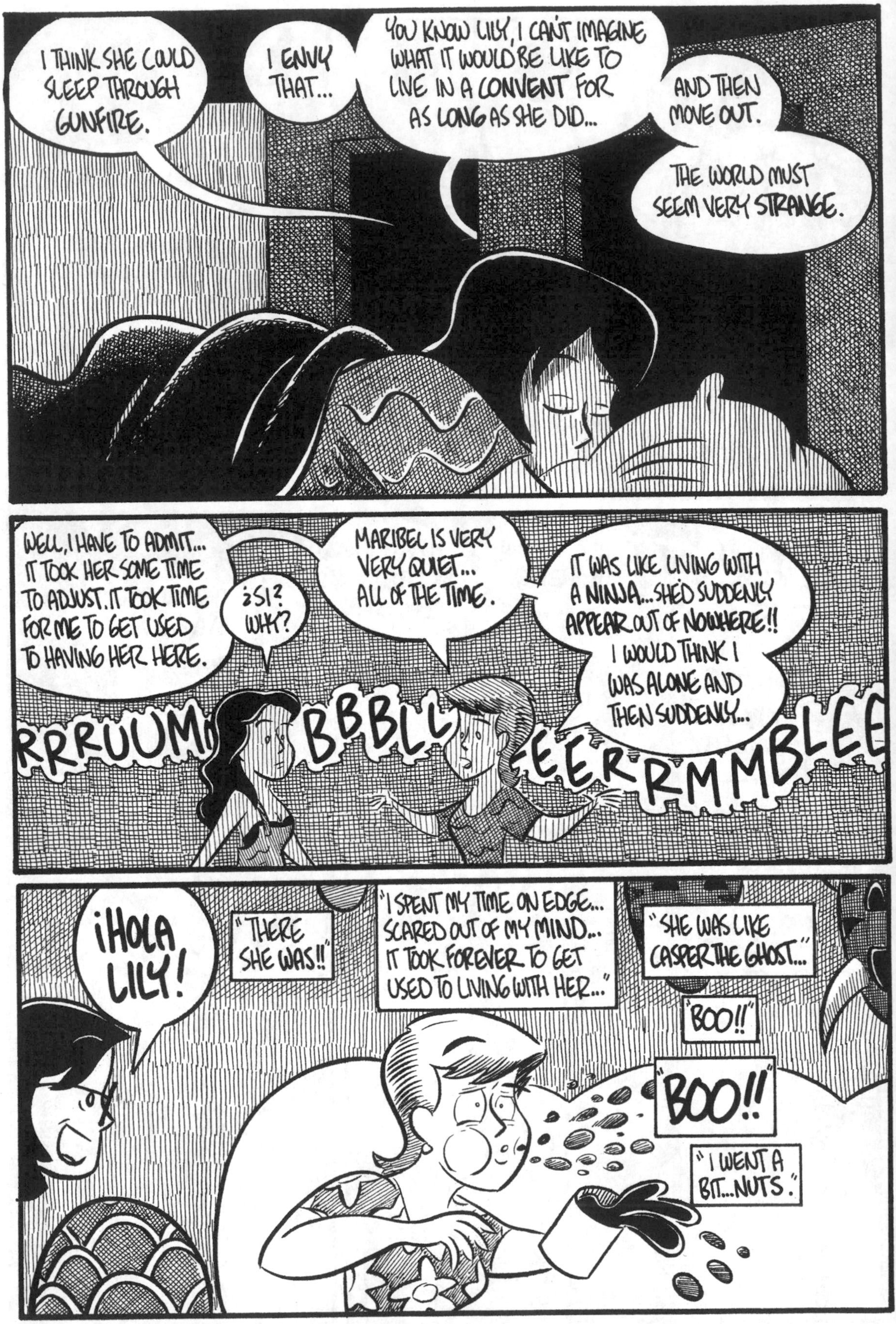
I THINK SHE COULD SLEEP THROUGH GUNFIRE.
I ENVY THAT...
YOU KNOW LILY, I CAN'T IMAGINE WHAT IT WOULD BE LIKE TO LIVE IN A CONVENT FOR AS LONG AS SHE DID...
AND THEN MOVE OUT.
THE WORLD MUST SEEM VERY STRANGE.
WELL, I HAVE TO ADMIT... IT TOOK HER SOME TIME TO ADJUST. IT TOOK TIME FOR ME TO GET USED TO HAVING HER HERE.
¿SI? WHY?
MARIBEL IS VERY VERY QUIET... ALL OF THE TIME.
IT WAS LIKE LIVING WITH A NINJA... SHE'D SUDDENLY APPEAR OUT OF NOWHERE!! I WOULD THINK I WAS ALONE AND THEN SUDDENLY...
RRRUUMBBBLLEERRMMBLEE
¡HOLA LILY!
"THERE SHE WAS!!"
"I SPENT MY TIME ON EDGE... SCARED OUT OF MY MIND... IT TOOK FOREVER TO GET USED TO LIVING WITH HER..."
"SHE WAS LIKE CASPER THE GHOST..."
"BOO!!"
"BOO!!"
"I WENT A BIT...NUTS."

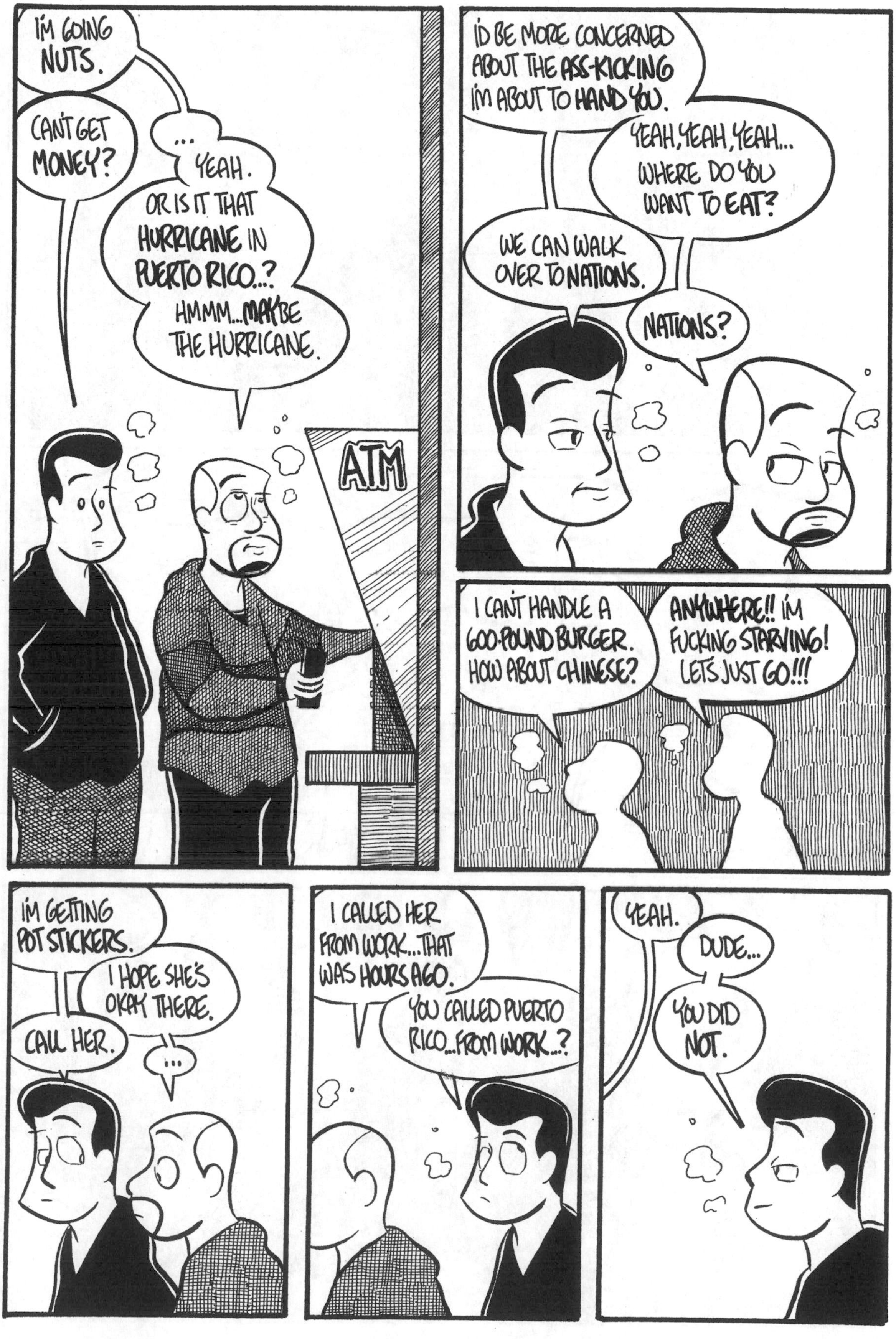
I'M GOING NUTS.
CAN'T GET MONEY?
... YEAH.
OR IS IT THAT HURRICANE IN PUERTO RICO...?
HMMM...MAYBE THE HURRICANE.
ATM
I'D BE MORE CONCERNED ABOUT THE ASS-KICKING I'M ABOUT TO HAND YOU.
YEAH, YEAH, YEAH... WHERE DO YOU WANT TO EAT?
WE CAN WALK OVER TO NATIONS.
NATIONS?
I CAN'T HANDLE A 600-POUND BURGER. HOW ABOUT CHINESE?
ANYWHERE!! I'M FUCKING STARVING! LET'S JUST GO!!!
I'M GETTING POT STICKERS.
I HOPE SHE'S OKAY THERE.
CALL HER.
...
I CALLED HER FROM WORK...THAT WAS HOURS AGO.
YOU CALLED PUERTO RICO...FROM WORK...?
YEAH.
DUDE...
YOU DID NOT.

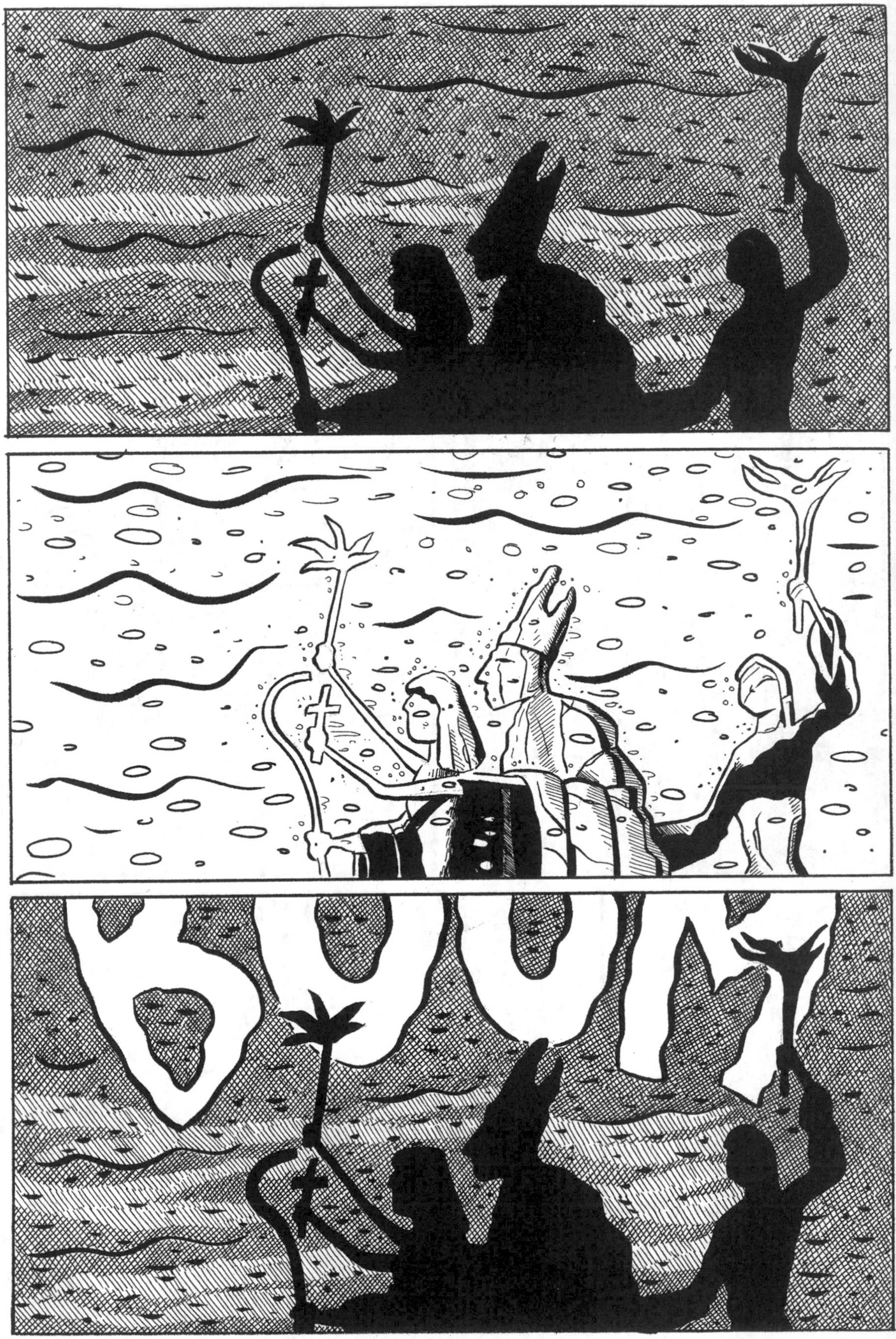

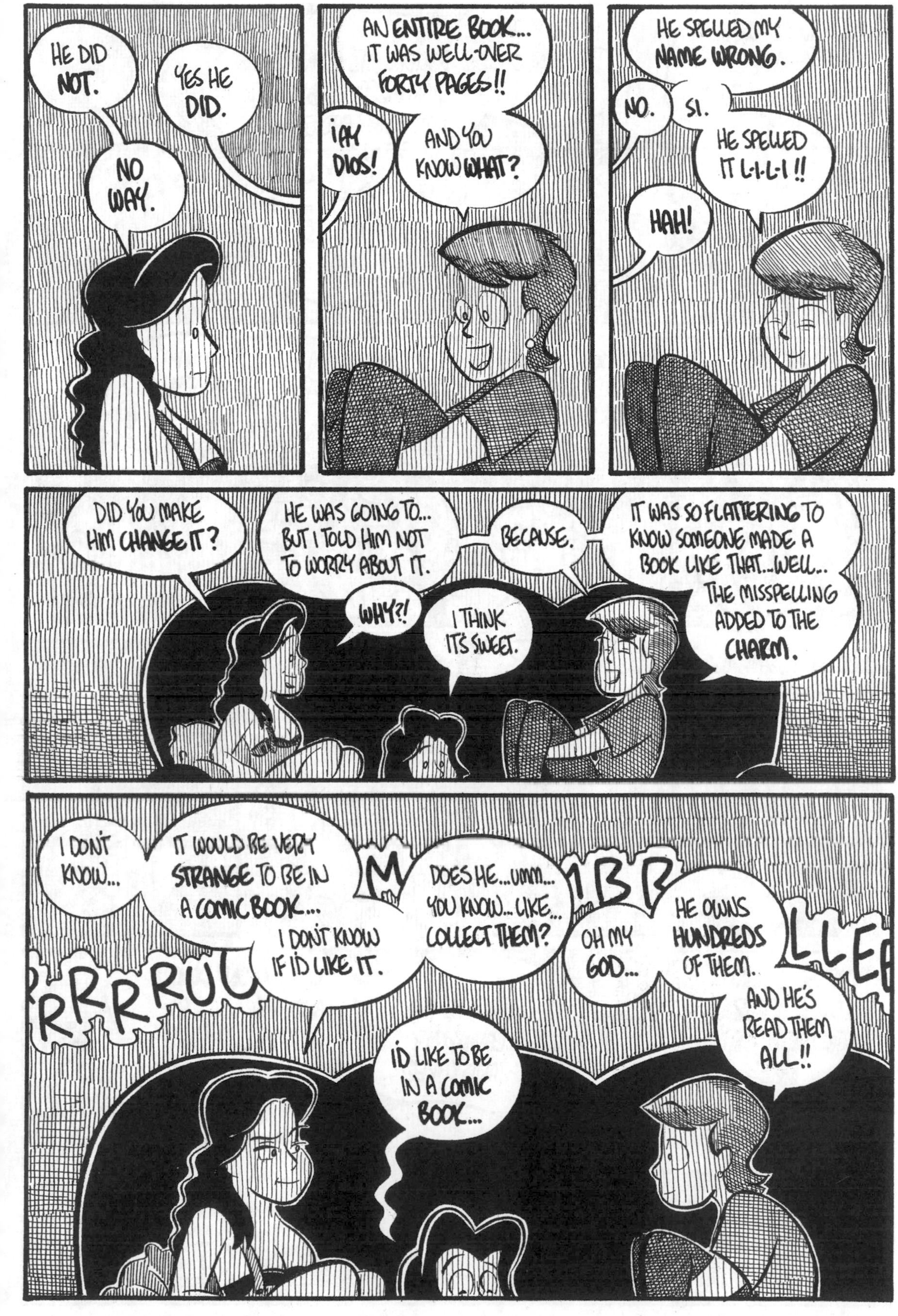
HE DID NOT.
NO WAY.
YES HE DID.
AN ENTIRE BOOK... IT WAS WELL-OVER FORTY PAGES!!
¡AY DIOS!
AND YOU KNOW WHAT?
HE SPELLED MY NAME WRONG.
NO.
SI.
HE SPELLED IT L-I-L-I!!
HAH!
DID YOU MAKE HIM CHANGE IT?
HE WAS GOING TO... BUT I TOLD HIM NOT TO WORRY ABOUT IT.
WHY?!
BECAUSE.
IT WAS SO FLATTERING TO KNOW SOMEONE MADE A BOOK LIKE THAT...WELL... THE MISSPELLING ADDED TO THE CHARM.
I THINK IT'S SWEET.
I DON'T KNOW...
IT WOULD BE VERY STRANGE TO BE IN A COMIC BOOK...
I DON'T KNOW IF I'D LIKE IT.
DOES HE...UMM... YOU KNOW... LIKE... COLLECT THEM?
OH MY GOD...
HE OWNS HUNDREDS OF THEM.
AND HE'S READ THEM ALL!!
I'D LIKE TO BE IN A COMIC BOOK...

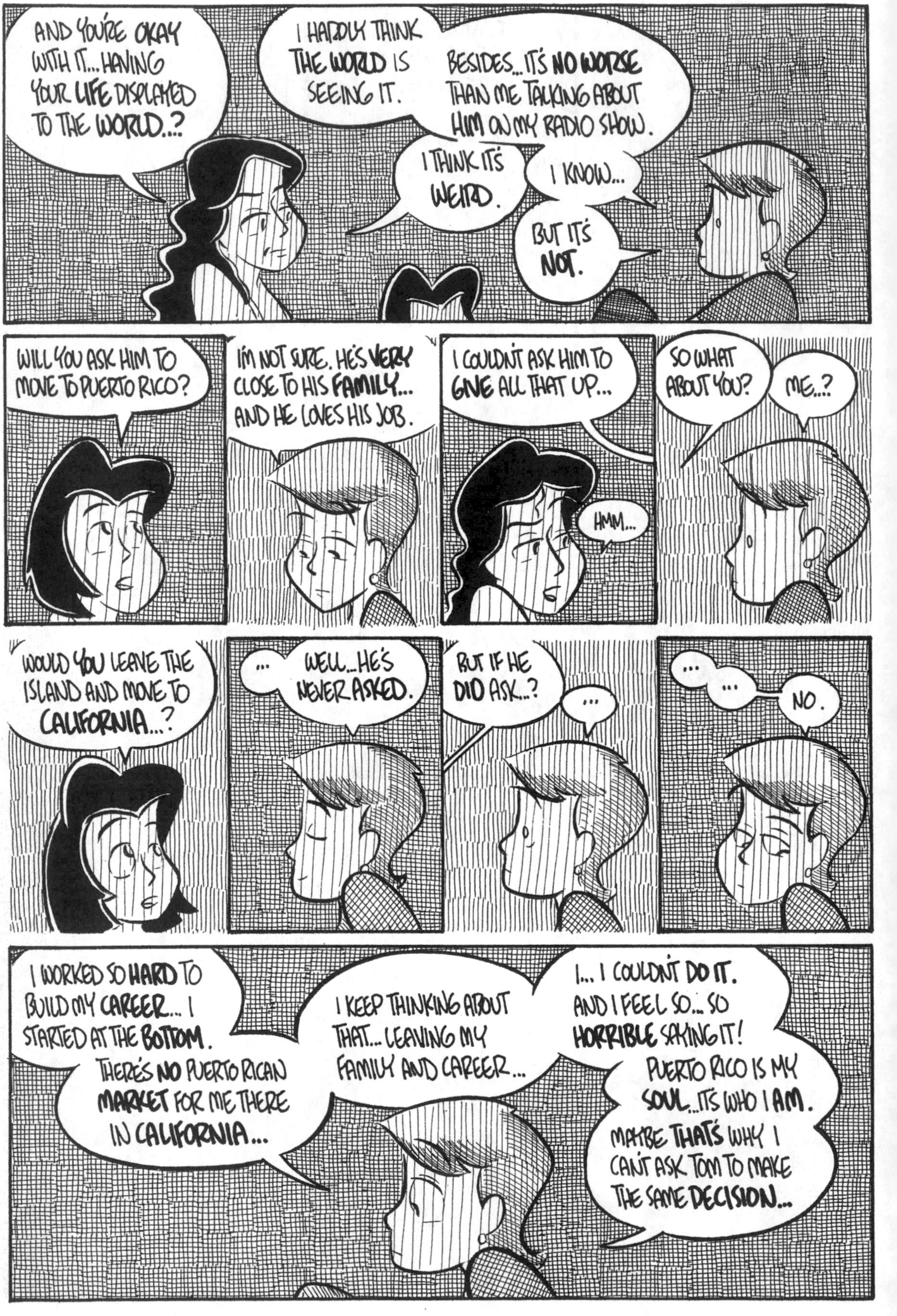
AND YOU'RE OKAY WITH IT... HAVING YOUR LIFE DISPLAYED TO THE WORLD..?
I HARDLY THINK THE WORLD IS SEEING IT.
BESIDES... IT'S NO WORSE THAN ME TALKING ABOUT HIM ON MY RADIO SHOW.
I THINK IT'S WEIRD.
I KNOW...
BUT IT'S NOT.
WILL YOU ASK HIM TO MOVE TO PUERTO RICO?
I'M NOT SURE. HE'S VERY CLOSE TO HIS FAMILY... AND HE LOVES HIS JOB.
I COULDN'T ASK HIM TO GIVE ALL THAT UP...
HMM...
SO WHAT ABOUT YOU?
ME..?
WOULD YOU LEAVE THE ISLAND AND MOVE TO CALIFORNIA...?
...
WELL... HE'S NEVER ASKED.
BUT IF HE DID ASK..?
...
...
...
NO.
I WORKED SO HARD TO BUILD MY CAREER... I STARTED AT THE BOTTOM.
THERE'S NO PUERTO RICAN MARKET FOR ME THERE IN CALIFORNIA...
I KEEP THINKING ABOUT THAT... LEAVING MY FAMILY AND CAREER...
I... I COULDN'T DO IT. AND I FEEL SO... SO HORRIBLE SAYING IT!
PUERTO RICO IS MY SOUL... IT'S WHO I AM.
MAYBE THAT'S WHY I CAN'T ASK TOM TO MAKE THE SAME DECISION...

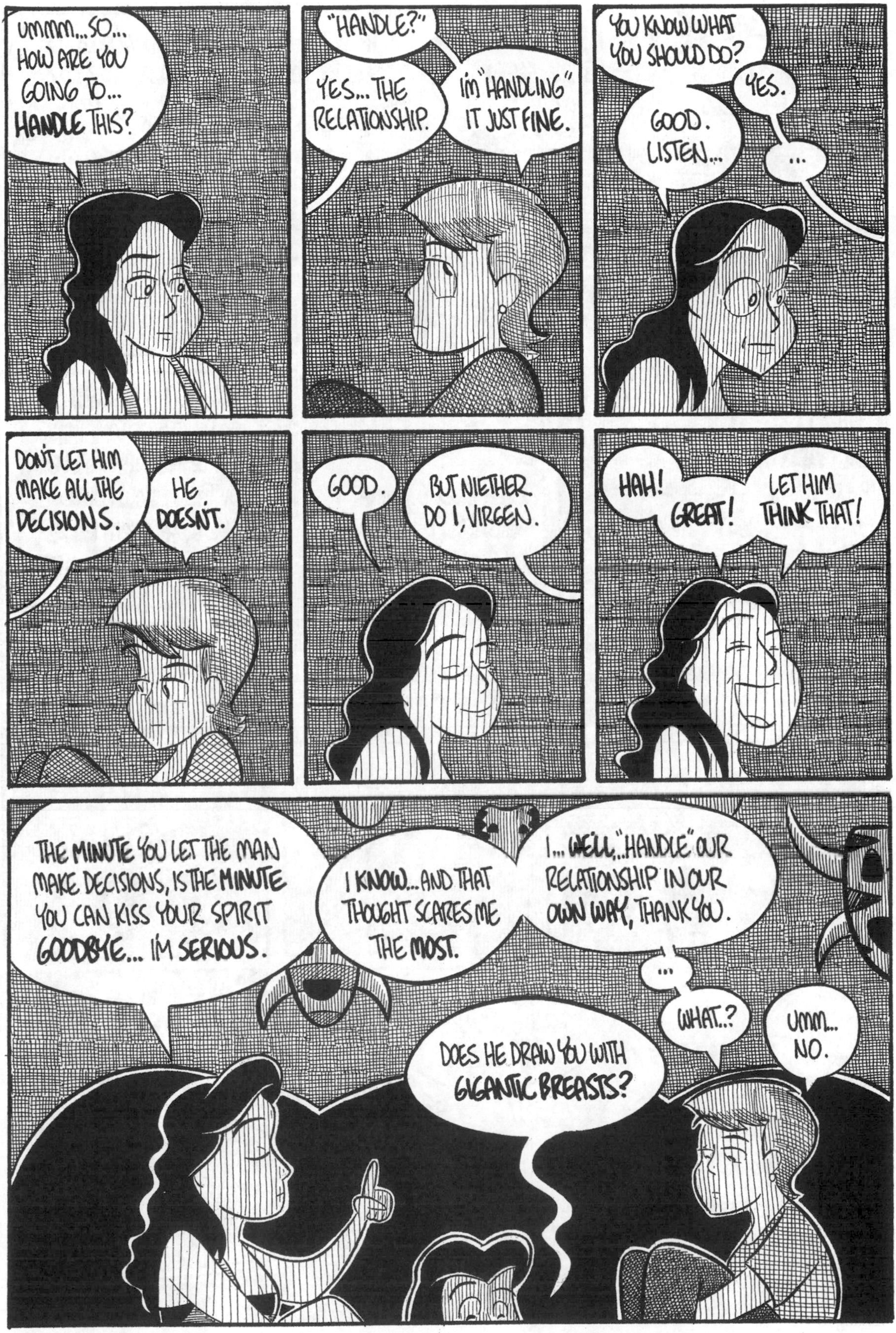
UMMM... SO... HOW ARE YOU GOING TO... HANDLE THIS?
"HANDLE?"
YES... THE RELATIONSHIP.
I'M "HANDLING" IT JUST FINE.
YOU KNOW WHAT YOU SHOULD DO?
YES.
GOOD. LISTEN...
...
DON'T LET HIM MAKE ALL THE DECISIONS.
HE DOESN'T.
GOOD.
BUT NIETHER DO I, VIRGEN.
HAH!
GREAT!
LET HIM THINK THAT!
THE MINUTE YOU LET THE MAN MAKE DECISIONS, IS THE MINUTE YOU CAN KISS YOUR SPIRIT GOODBYE... I'M SERIOUS.
I KNOW... AND THAT THOUGHT SCARES ME THE MOST.
I... WELL, "HANDLE" OUR RELATIONSHIP IN OUR OWN WAY, THANK YOU.
...
WHAT..?
UMM... NO.
DOES HE DRAW YOU WITH GIGANTIC BREASTS?

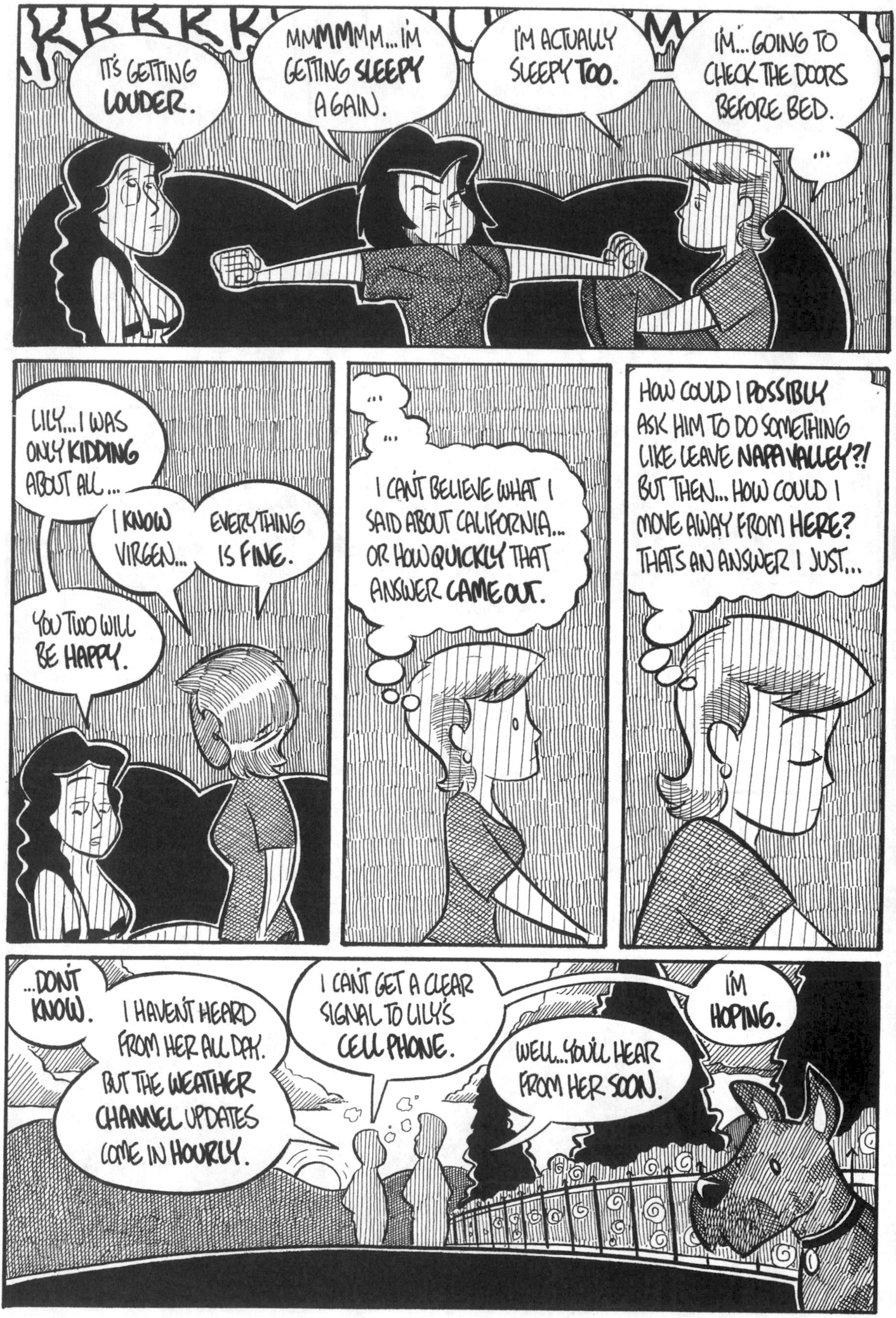
IT'S GETTING LOUDER.
MMMMMM... I'M GETTING SLEEPY AGAIN.
I'M ACTUALLY SLEEPY TOO.
I'M... GOING TO CHECK THE DOORS BEFORE BED.
...
LILY... I WAS ONLY KIDDING ABOUT ALL...
I KNOW VIRGEN...
EVERYTHING IS FINE.
YOU TWO WILL BE HAPPY.
...
...
I CAN'T BELIEVE WHAT I SAID ABOUT CALIFORNIA... OR HOW QUICKLY THAT ANSWER CAME OUT.
HOW COULD I POSSIBLY ASK HIM TO DO SOMETHING LIKE LEAVE NAPA VALLEY?! BUT THEN... HOW COULD I MOVE AWAY FROM HERE? THAT'S AN ANSWER I JUST...
...DON'T KNOW.
I HAVEN'T HEARD FROM HER ALL DAY. BUT THE WEATHER CHANNEL UPDATES COME IN HOURLY.
I CAN'T GET A CLEAR SIGNAL TO LILY'S CELL PHONE.
WELL... YOU'LL HEAR FROM HER SOON.
I'M HOPING.

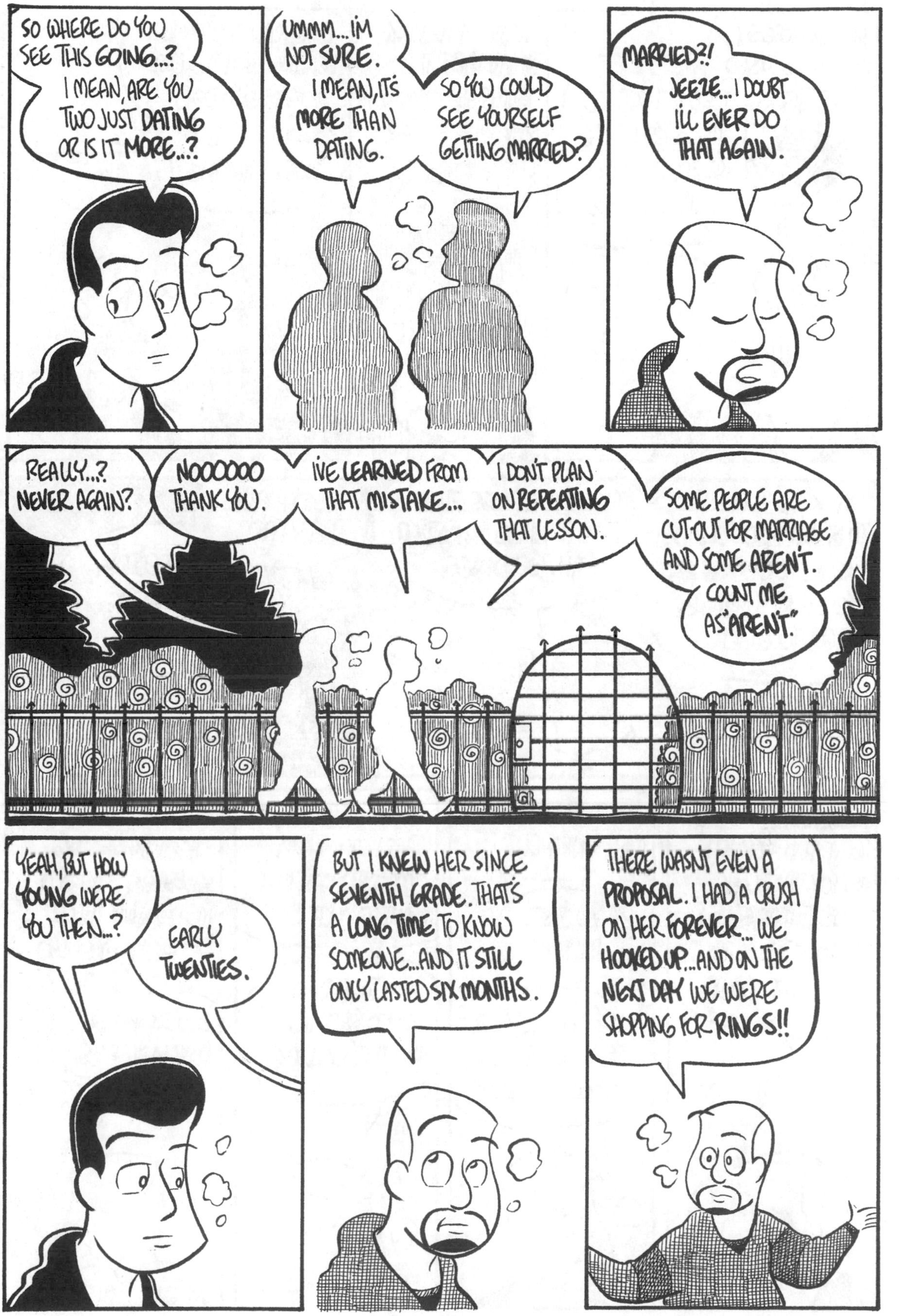
SO WHERE DO YOU SEE THIS GOING...? I MEAN, ARE YOU TWO JUST DATING OR IS IT MORE...?
UMMM... I'M NOT SURE. I MEAN, IT'S MORE THAN DATING.
SO YOU COULD SEE YOURSELF GETTING MARRIED?
MARRIED?! JEEZE... I DOUBT I'LL EVER DO THAT AGAIN.
REALLY...? NEVER AGAIN?
NOOOOOO THANK YOU.
I'VE LEARNED FROM THAT MISTAKE...
I DON'T PLAN ON REPEATING THAT LESSON.
SOME PEOPLE ARE CUT-OUT FOR MARRIAGE AND SOME AREN'T. COUNT ME AS "AREN'T."
YEAH, BUT HOW YOUNG WERE YOU THEN...?
EARLY TWENTIES.
BUT I KNEW HER SINCE SEVENTH GRADE. THAT'S A LONG TIME TO KNOW SOMEONE... AND IT STILL ONLY LASTED SIX MONTHS.
THERE WASN'T EVEN A PROPOSAL. I HAD A CRUSH ON HER FOREVER... WE HOOKED UP... AND ON THE NEXT DAY WE WERE SHOPPING FOR RINGS!!

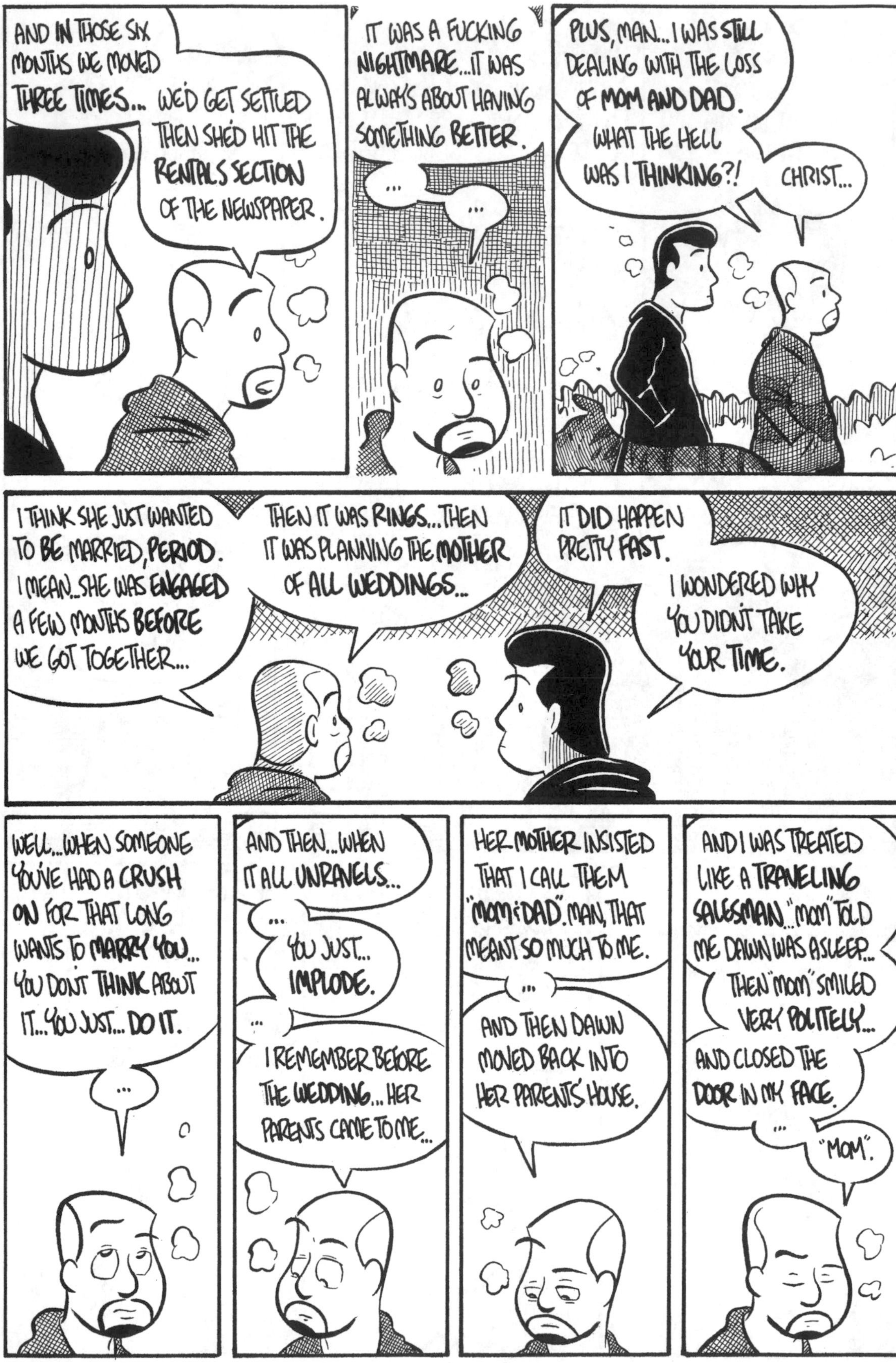
AND IN THOSE SIX MONTHS WE MOVED THREE TIMES...
WE'D GET SETTLED THEN SHE'D HIT THE RENTALS SECTION OF THE NEWSPAPER.
IT WAS A FUCKING NIGHTMARE... IT WAS ALWAYS ABOUT HAVING SOMETHING BETTER.
...
...
PLUS, MAN... I WAS STILL DEALING WITH THE LOSS OF MOM AND DAD.
WHAT THE HELL WAS I THINKING?!
CHRIST...
I THINK SHE JUST WANTED TO BE MARRIED, PERIOD. I MEAN... SHE WAS ENGAGED A FEW MONTHS BEFORE WE GOT TOGETHER...
THEN IT WAS RINGS... THEN IT WAS PLANNING THE MOTHER OF ALL WEDDINGS...
IT DID HAPPEN PRETTY FAST.
I WONDERED WHY YOU DIDN'T TAKE YOUR TIME.
WELL... WHEN SOMEONE YOU'VE HAD A CRUSH ON FOR THAT LONG WANTS TO MARRY YOU... YOU DON'T THINK ABOUT IT... YOU JUST... DO IT.
...
AND THEN... WHEN IT ALL UNRAVELS...
...
YOU JUST... IMPLODE.
...
I REMEMBER BEFORE THE WEDDING... HER PARENTS CAME TO ME...
HER MOTHER INSISTED THAT I CALL THEM "MOM & DAD". MAN, THAT MEANT SO MUCH TO ME.
...
AND THEN DAWN MOVED BACK INTO HER PARENTS' HOUSE.
AND I WAS TREATED LIKE A TRAVELING SALESMAN... "MOM" TOLD ME DAWN WAS ASLEEP...
THEN "MOM" SMILED VERY POLITELY...
AND CLOSED THE DOOR IN MY FACE.
...
"MOM".

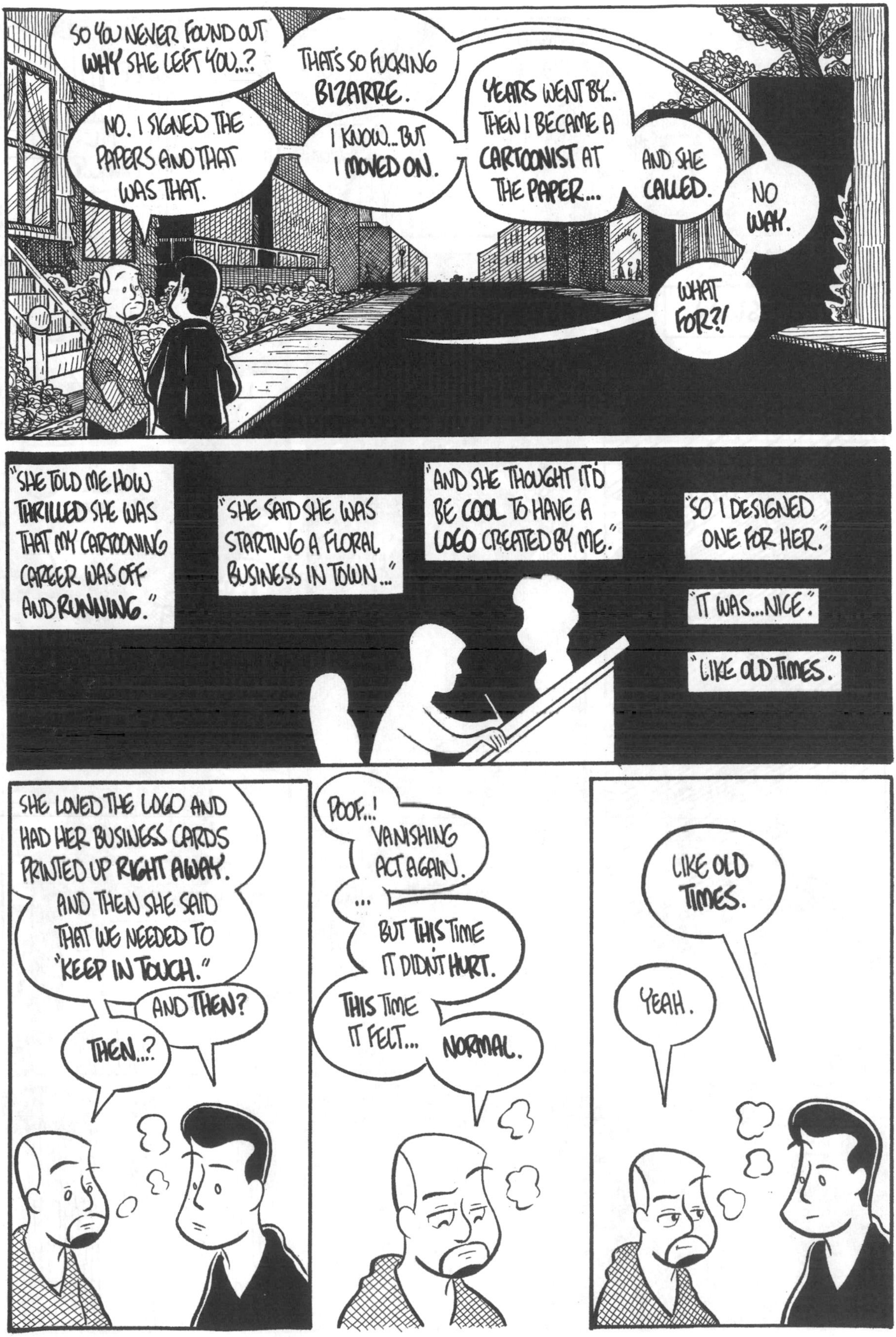
SO YOU NEVER FOUND OUT WHY SHE LEFT YOU...?
NO. I SIGNED THE PAPERS AND THAT WAS THAT.
THAT'S SO FUCKING BIZARRE.
I KNOW... BUT I MOVED ON.
YEARS WENT BY... THEN I BECAME A CARTOONIST AT THE PAPER...
AND SHE CALLED.
NO WAY.
WHAT FOR?!
"SHE TOLD ME HOW THRILLED SHE WAS THAT MY CARTOONING CAREER WAS OFF AND RUNNING."
"SHE SAID SHE WAS STARTING A FLORAL BUSINESS IN TOWN..."
"AND SHE THOUGHT IT'D BE COOL TO HAVE A LOGO CREATED BY ME."
"SO I DESIGNED ONE FOR HER."
"IT WAS... NICE."
"LIKE OLD TIMES."
SHE LOVED THE LOGO AND HAD HER BUSINESS CARDS PRINTED UP RIGHT AWAY.
AND THEN SHE SAID THAT WE NEEDED TO "KEEP IN TOUCH."
AND THEN?
THEN...?
POOF...!
VANISHING ACT AGAIN.
...
BUT THIS TIME IT DIDN'T HURT.
THIS TIME IT FELT...
NORMAL.
LIKE OLD TIMES.
YEAH.

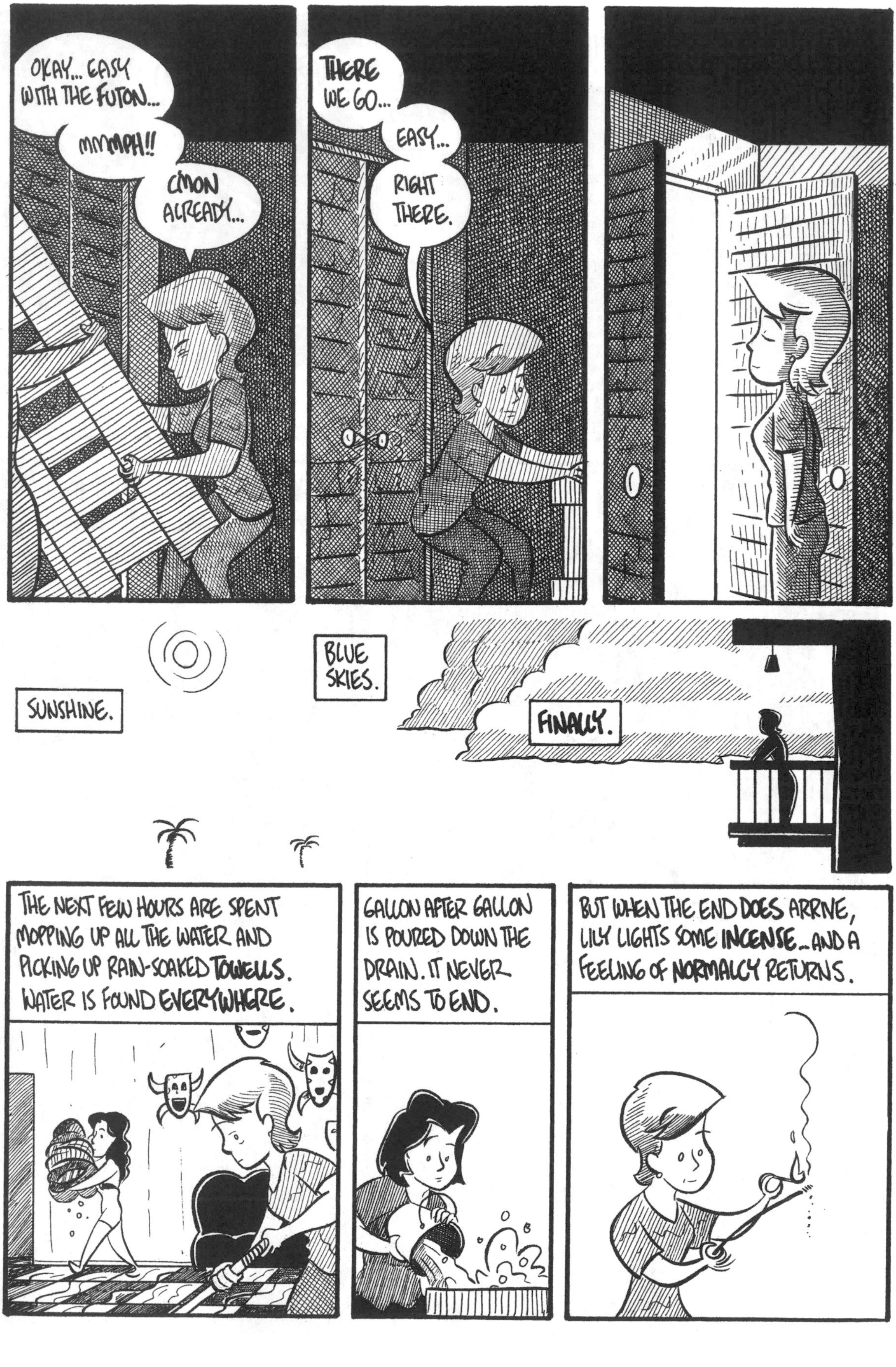
OKAY... EASY WITH THE FUTON...
MMMPH!!
C'MON ALREADY...
THERE WE GO...
EASY...
RIGHT THERE.
SUNSHINE.
BLUE SKIES.
FINALLY.
THE NEXT FEW HOURS ARE SPENT MOPPING UP ALL THE WATER AND PICKING UP RAIN-SOAKED TOWELLS. WATER IS FOUND EVERYWHERE.
GALLON AFTER GALLON IS POURED DOWN THE DRAIN. IT NEVER SEEMS TO END.
BUT WHEN THE END DOES ARRIVE, LILY LIGHTS SOME INCENSE... AND A FEELING OF NORMALCY RETURNS.

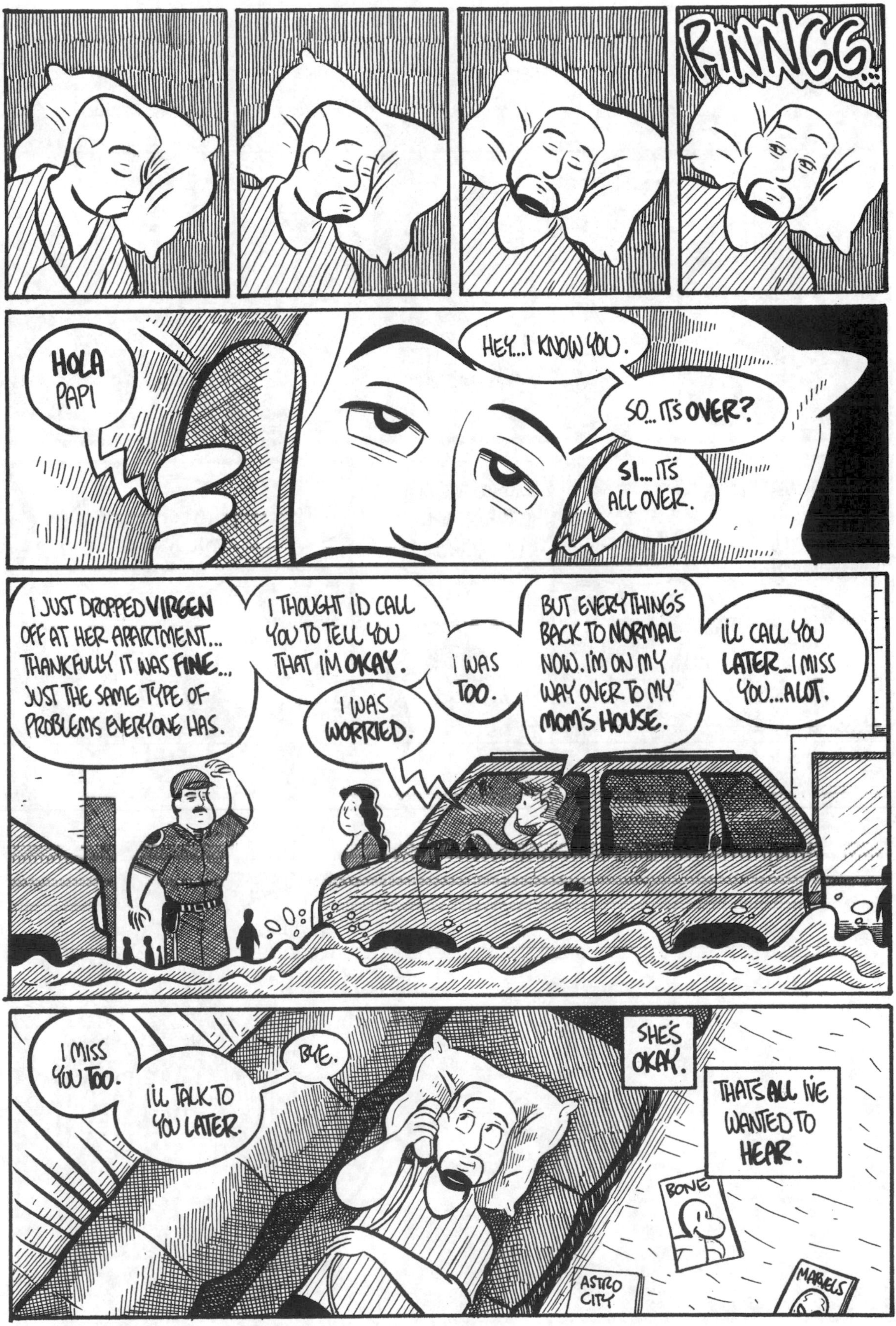
RINNGG...
HOLA PAPI
HEY... I KNOW YOU.
SO... IT'S OVER?
SI... IT'S ALL OVER.
I JUST DROPPED VIRGEN OFF AT HER APARTMENT... THANKFULLY IT WAS FINE... JUST THE SAME TYPE OF PROBLEMS EVERYONE HAS.
I THOUGHT I'D CALL YOU TO TELL YOU THAT I'M OKAY.
I WAS WORRIED.
I WAS TOO.
BUT EVERYTHING'S BACK TO NORMAL NOW. I'M ON MY WAY OVER TO MY MOM'S HOUSE.
I'LL CALL YOU LATER... I MISS YOU... A LOT.
I MISS YOU TOO.
I'LL TALK TO YOU LATER.
BYE.
SHE'S OKAY.
THAT'S ALL I'VE WANTED TO HEAR.
BONE
ASTRO CITY
MARVELS

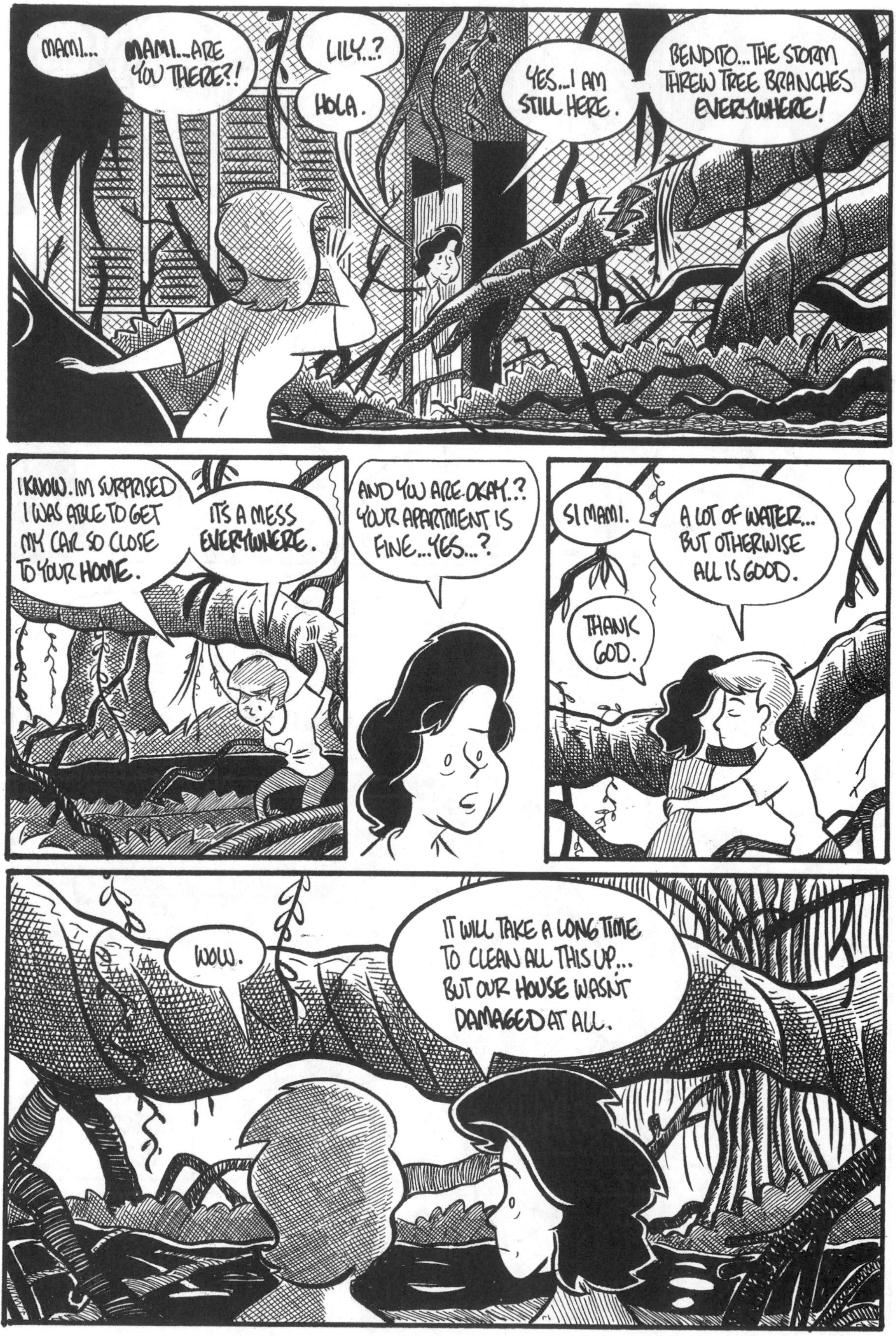
MAMI...
MAMI...ARE YOU THERE?!
LILY..?
HOLA.
YES...I AM STILL HERE.
BENDITO...THE STORM THREW TREE BRANCHES EVERYWHERE!
I KNOW. IM SURPRISED I WAS ABLE TO GET MY CAR SO CLOSE TO YOUR HOME.
IT'S A MESS EVERYWHERE.
AND YOU ARE OKAY..? YOUR APARTMENT IS FINE...YES...?
SI MAMI.
A LOT OF WATER... BUT OTHERWISE ALL IS GOOD.
THANK GOD.
WOW.
IT WILL TAKE A LONG TIME TO CLEAN ALL THIS UP... BUT OUR HOUSE WASN'T DAMAGED AT ALL.

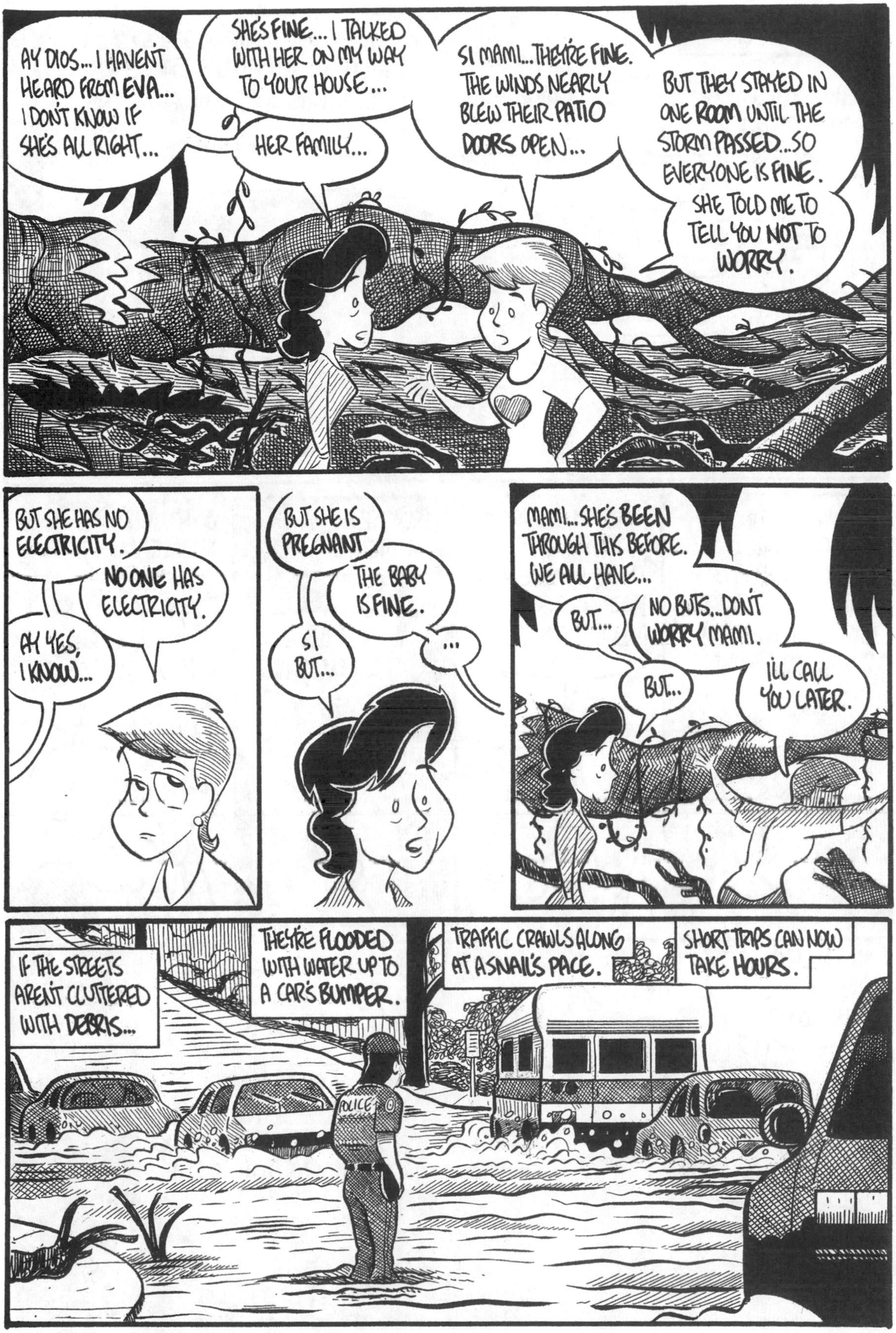
AY DIOS... I HAVEN'T HEARD FROM EVA... I DON'T KNOW IF SHE'S ALL RIGHT...
SHE'S FINE... I TALKED WITH HER ON MY WAY TO YOUR HOUSE...
HER FAMILY...
SI MAMI... THEY'RE FINE. THE WINDS NEARLY BLEW THEIR PATIO DOORS OPEN...
BUT THEY STAYED IN ONE ROOM UNTIL THE STORM PASSED... SO EVERYONE IS FINE.
SHE TOLD ME TO TELL YOU NOT TO WORRY.
BUT SHE HAS NO ELECTRICITY.
NO ONE HAS ELECTRICITY.
AY YES, I KNOW...
BUT SHE IS PREGNANT
THE BABY IS FINE.
SI BUT...
...
MAMI... SHE'S BEEN THROUGH THIS BEFORE. WE ALL HAVE...
BUT...
NO BUTS... DON'T WORRY MAMI.
BUT...
I'LL CALL YOU LATER.
IF THE STREETS AREN'T CLUTTERED WITH DEBRIS...
THEY'RE FLOODED WITH WATER UP TO A CAR'S BUMPER.
TRAFFIC CRAWLS ALONG AT A SNAIL'S PACE.
SHORT TRIPS CAN NOW TAKE HOURS.
POLICE

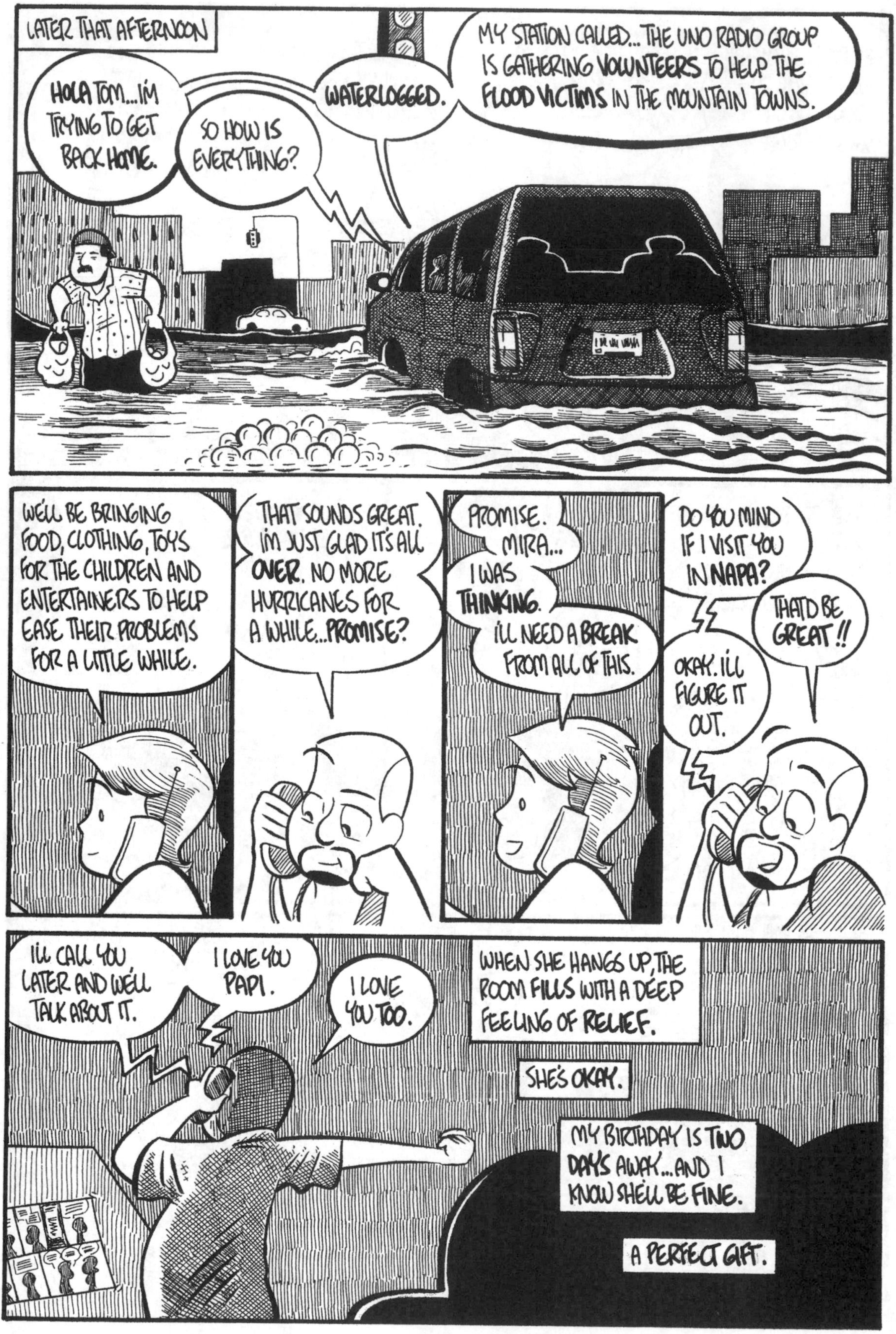
LATER THAT AFTERNOON
HOLA TOM...I'M TRYING TO GET BACK HOME.
SO HOW IS EVERYTHING?
WATERLOGGED.
MY STATION CALLED... THE UNO RADIO GROUP IS GATHERING VOLUNTEERS TO HELP THE FLOOD VICTIMS IN THE MOUNTAIN TOWNS.
WE'LL BE BRINGING FOOD, CLOTHING, TOYS FOR THE CHILDREN AND ENTERTAINERS TO HELP EASE THEIR PROBLEMS FOR A LITTLE WHILE.
THAT SOUNDS GREAT. I'M JUST GLAD IT'S ALL OVER. NO MORE HURRICANES FOR A WHILE...PROMISE?
PROMISE.
MIRA...
I WAS THINKING.
I'LL NEED A BREAK FROM ALL OF THIS.
DO YOU MIND IF I VISIT YOU IN NAPA?
THAT'D BE GREAT!!
OKAY. I'LL FIGURE IT OUT.
I'LL CALL YOU LATER AND WE'LL TALK ABOUT IT.
I LOVE YOU PAPI.
I LOVE YOU TOO.
WHEN SHE HANGS UP, THE ROOM FILLS WITH A DEEP FEELING OF RELIEF.
SHE'S OKAY.
MY BIRTHDAY IS TWO DAYS AWAY...AND I KNOW SHE'LL BE FINE.
A PERFECT GIFT.

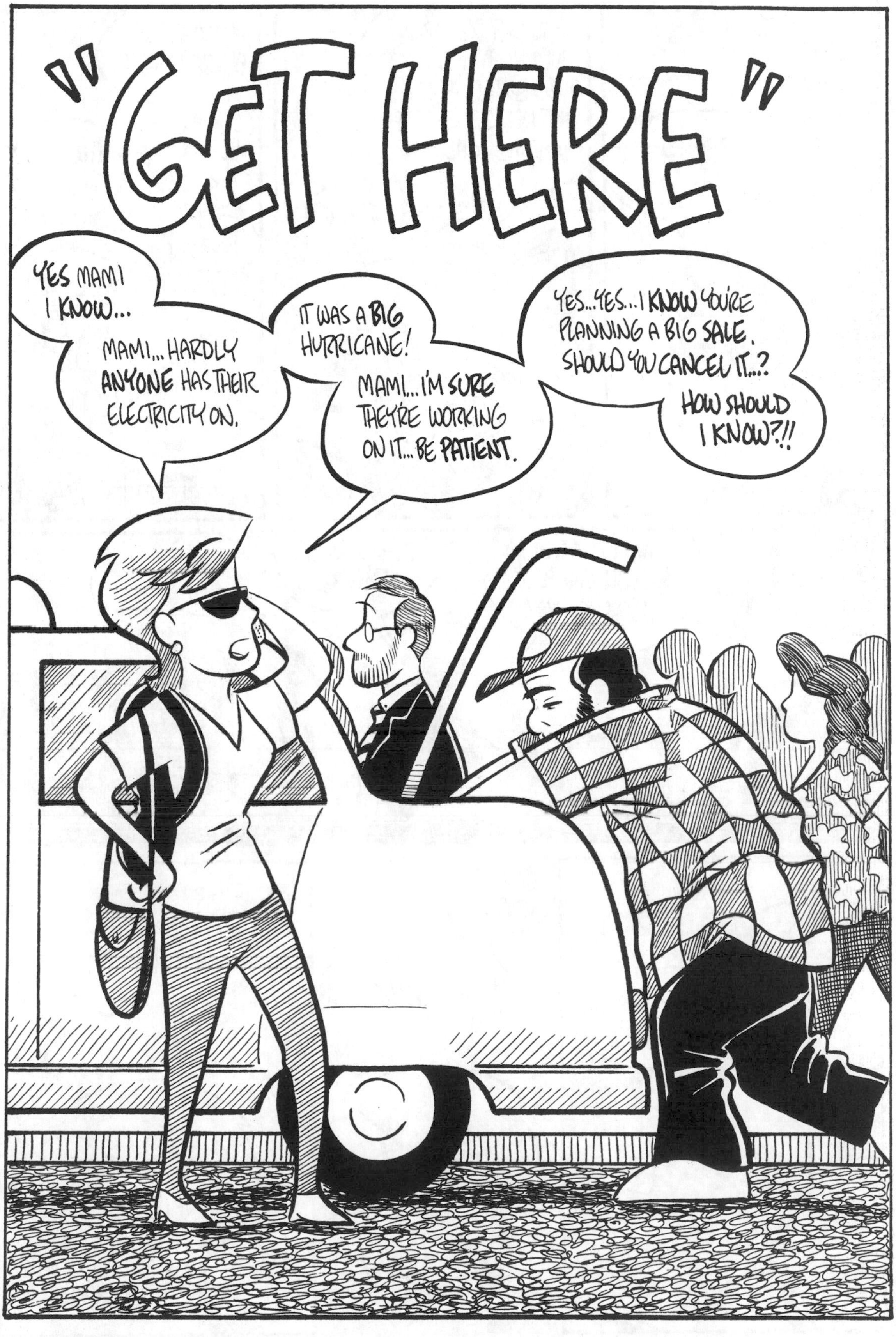
"GET HERE"
YES MAMI I KNOW...
MAMI... HARDLY ANYONE HAS THEIR ELECTRICITY ON.
IT WAS A BIG HURRICANE!
MAMI... I'M SURE THEY'RE WORKING ON IT... BE PATIENT.
YES... YES... I KNOW YOU'RE PLANNING A BIG SALE. SHOULD YOU CANCEL IT...?
HOW SHOULD I KNOW?!!

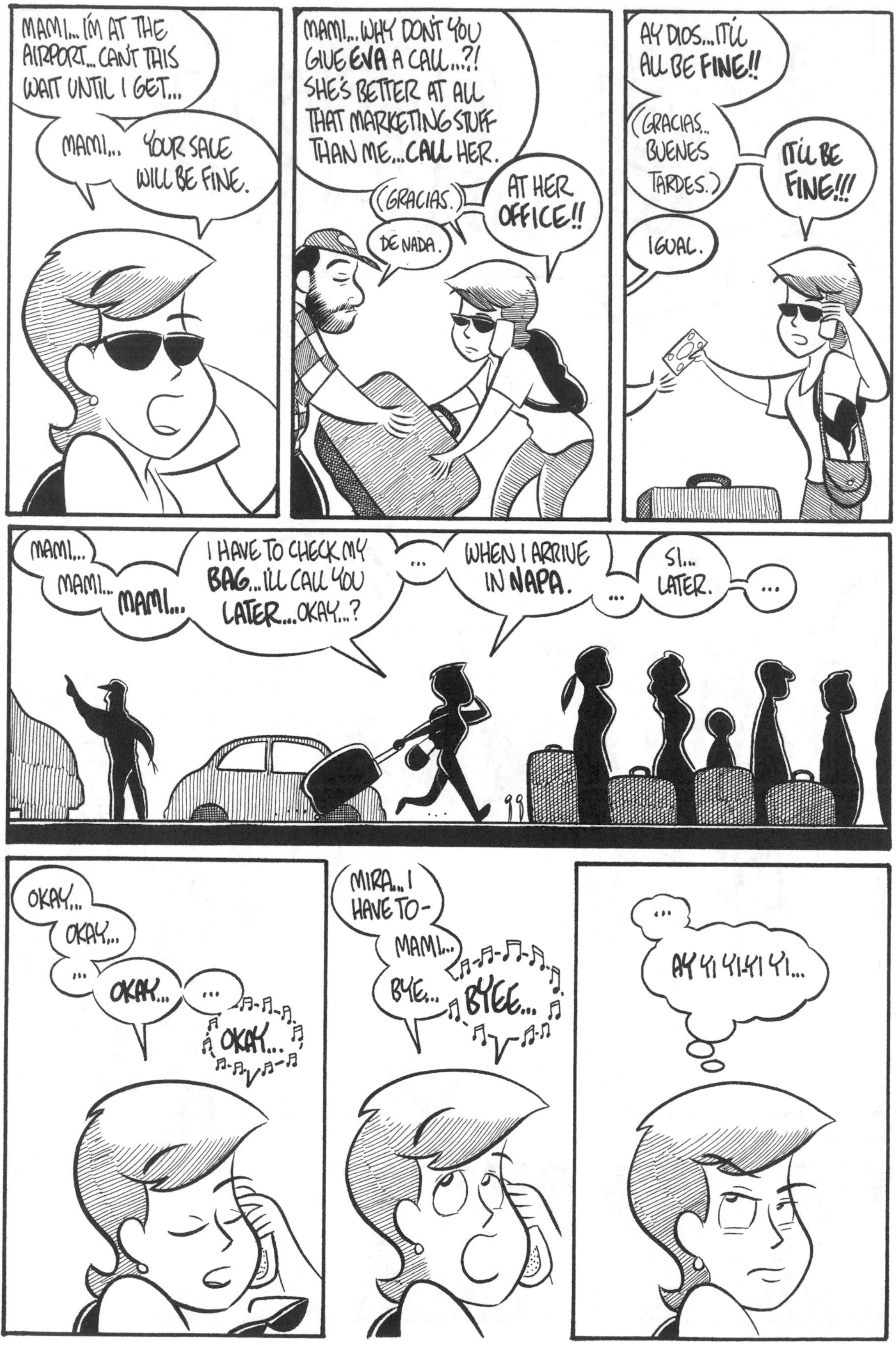
MAMI... I'M AT THE AIRPORT... CAN'T THIS WAIT UNTIL I GET...
MAMI...
YOUR SALE WILL BE FINE.
MAMI... WHY DON'T YOU GIVE EVA A CALL...?! SHE'S BETTER AT ALL THAT MARKETING STUFF THAN ME... CALL HER.
(GRACIAS.)
DE NADA.
AT HER OFFICE!!
AY DIOS... IT'LL ALL BE FINE!!
(GRACIAS.. BUENES TARDES.)
IT'LL BE FINE!!!
IGUAL.
MAMI...
MAMI...
MAMI...
I HAVE TO CHECK MY BAG... I'LL CALL YOU LATER... OKAY...?
...
WHEN I ARRIVE IN NAPA.
...
SI... LATER.
...
OKAY...
OKAY...
...
OKAY...
...
OKAY...
MIRA... I HAVE TO-
MAMI...
BYE...
BYEE...
...
AY YI YI-YI YI...

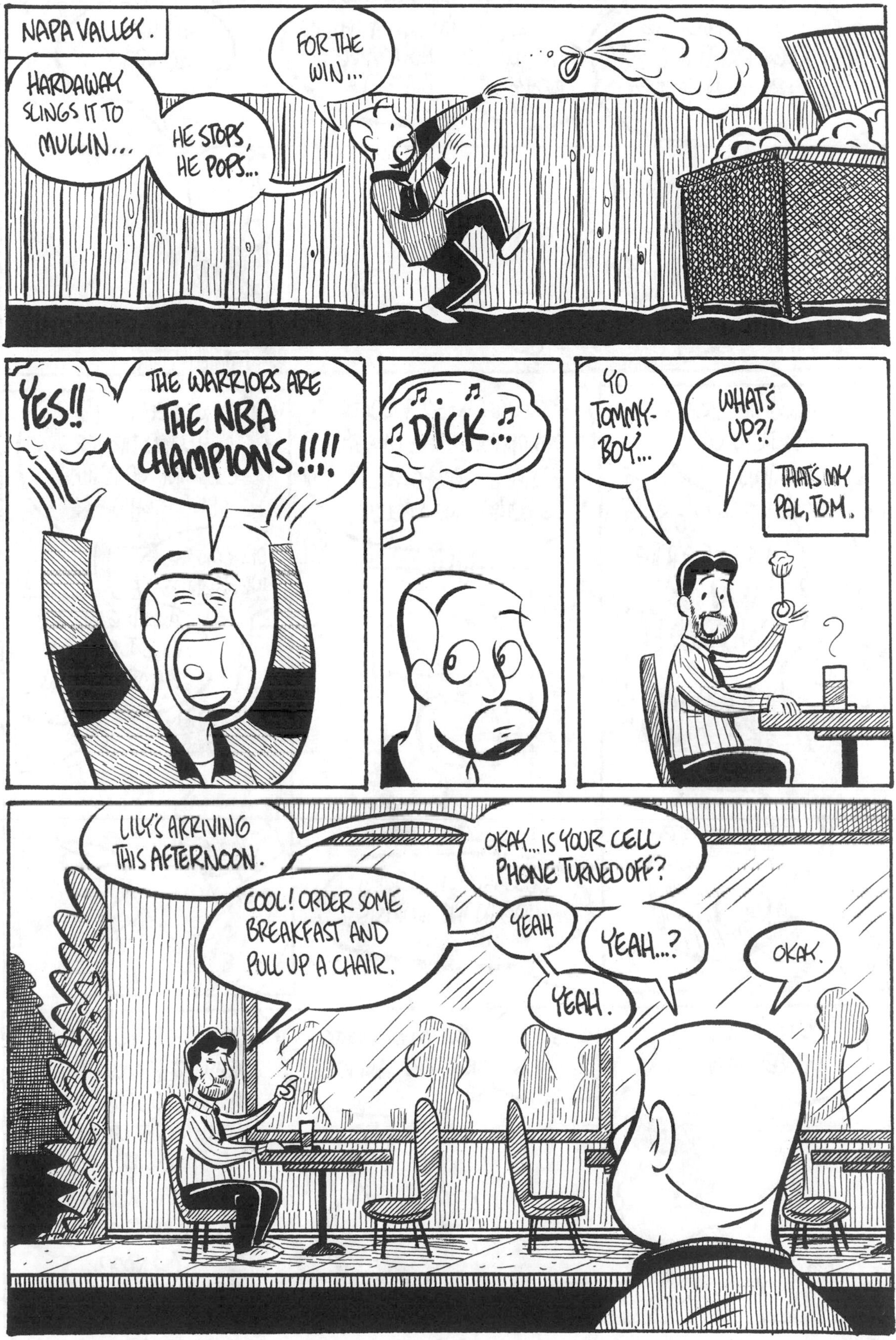
NAPA VALLEY.
HARDAWAY SLINGS IT TO MULLIN...
HE STOPS, HE POPS...
FOR THE WIN...
YES!!
THE WARRIORS ARE THE NBA CHAMPIONS!!!!
♫ DICK...♫
YO TOMMY-BOY...
WHAT'S UP?!
THAT'S MY PAL, TOM.
LILY'S ARRIVING THIS AFTERNOON.
COOL! ORDER SOME BREAKFAST AND PULL UP A CHAIR.
OKAY... IS YOUR CELL PHONE TURNED OFF?
YEAH
YEAH.
YEAH...?
OKAY.

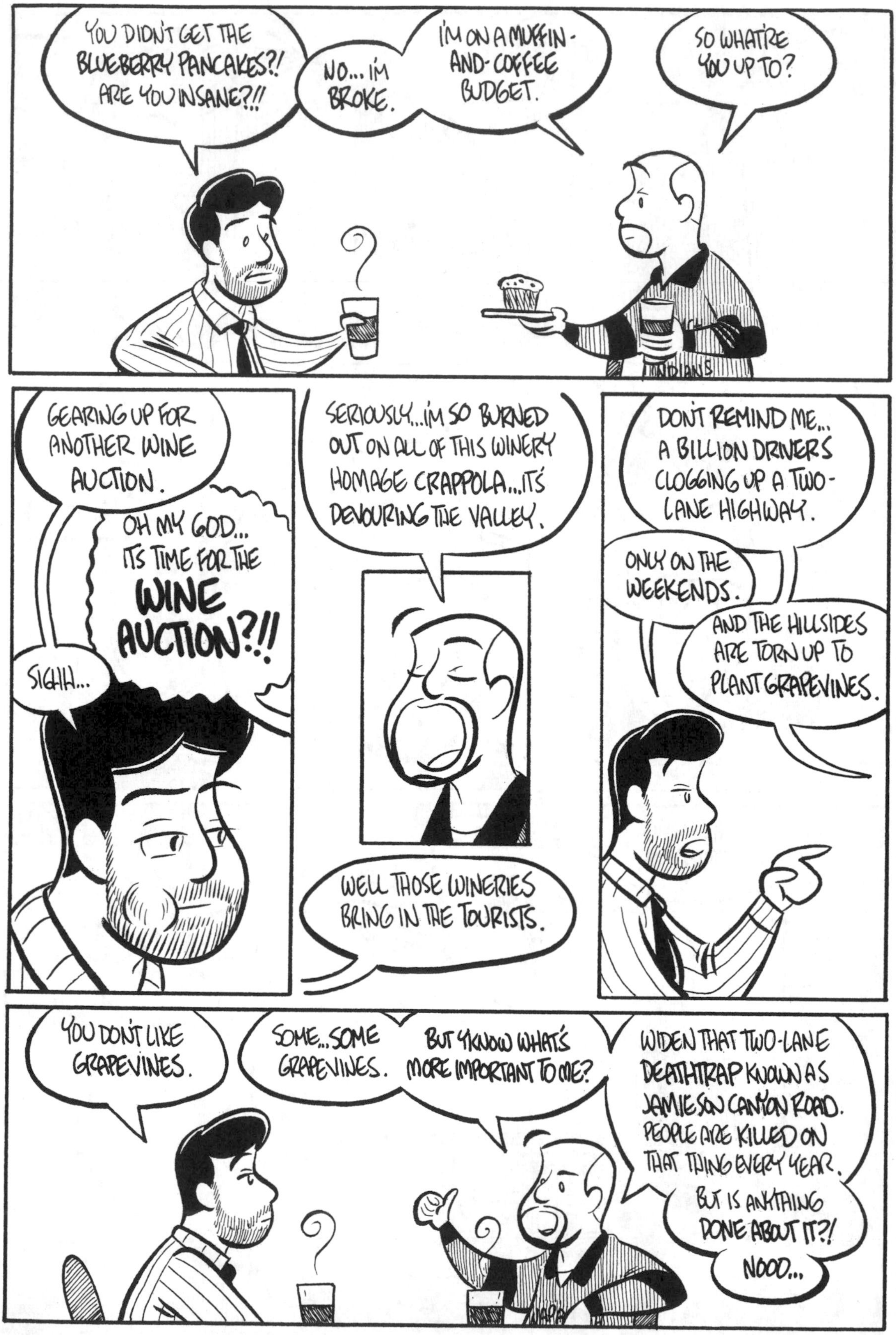
YOU DIDN'T GET THE BLUEBERRY PANCAKES?! ARE YOU INSANE?!!
NO... I'M BROKE.
I'M ON A MUFFIN-AND-COFFEE BUDGET.
SO WHAT'RE YOU UP TO?
INDIANS
GEARING UP FOR ANOTHER WINE AUCTION.
OH MY GOD... IT'S TIME FOR THE WINE AUCTION?!!
SIGHH...
SERIOUSLY...I'M SO BURNED OUT ON ALL OF THIS WINERY HOMAGE CRAPPOLA...IT'S DEVOURING THE VALLEY.
WELL THOSE WINERIES BRING IN THE TOURISTS.
DON'T REMIND ME... A BILLION DRIVERS CLOGGING UP A TWO-LANE HIGHWAY.
ONLY ON THE WEEKENDS.
AND THE HILLSIDES ARE TORN UP TO PLANT GRAPEVINES.
YOU DON'T LIKE GRAPEVINES.
SOME...SOME GRAPEVINES.
BUT Y'KNOW WHAT'S MORE IMPORTANT TO ME?
WIDEN THAT TWO-LANE DEATHTRAP KNOWN AS JAMIESON CANYON ROAD. PEOPLE ARE KILLED ON THAT THING EVERY YEAR.
BUT IS ANYTHING DONE ABOUT IT?!
NOOO...

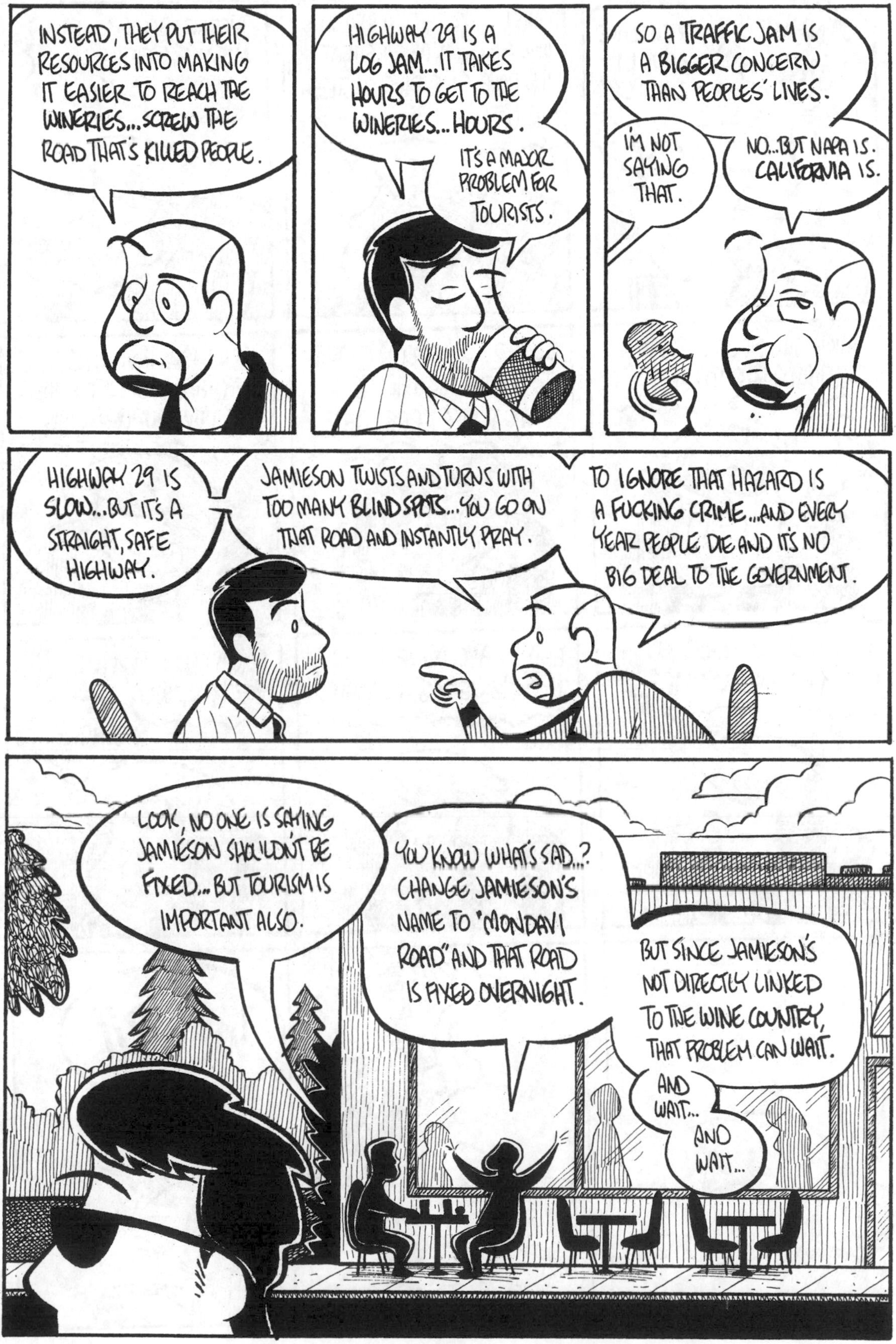
INSTEAD, THEY PUT THEIR RESOURCES INTO MAKING IT EASIER TO REACH THE WINERIES...SCREW THE ROAD THAT'S KILLED PEOPLE.
HIGHWAY 29 IS A LOG JAM...IT TAKES HOURS TO GET TO THE WINERIES...HOURS.
IT'S A MAJOR PROBLEM FOR TOURISTS.
SO A TRAFFIC JAM IS A BIGGER CONCERN THAN PEOPLES' LIVES.
I'M NOT SAYING THAT.
NO...BUT NAPA IS. CALIFORNIA IS.
HIGHWAY 29 IS SLOW...BUT IT'S A STRAIGHT, SAFE HIGHWAY.
JAMIESON TWISTS AND TURNS WITH TOO MANY BLIND SPOTS...YOU GO ON THAT ROAD AND INSTANTLY PRAY.
TO IGNORE THAT HAZARD IS A FUCKING CRIME...AND EVERY YEAR PEOPLE DIE AND IT'S NO BIG DEAL TO THE GOVERNMENT.
LOOK, NO ONE IS SAYING JAMIESON SHOULDN'T BE FIXED...BUT TOURISM IS IMPORTANT ALSO.
YOU KNOW WHAT'S SAD...? CHANGE JAMIESON'S NAME TO "MONDAVI ROAD" AND THAT ROAD IS FIXED OVERNIGHT.
BUT SINCE JAMIESON'S NOT DIRECTLY LINKED TO THE WINE COUNTRY, THAT PROBLEM CAN WAIT.
AND WAIT...
AND WAIT...

PING... PING...
WHEN DO WE LAND IN DALLAS?!!
?!
"THIS IS YOUR CAPTAIN SPEAKING. WELL FOLKS... IT APPEARS THAT WE HAVE SOME DIFFICULTIES IN DALLAS."
"THEY'RE FACING SOME INTENSE WEATHER CONDITIONS THERE...."
"WHICH WILL MAKE IT PRETTY MUCH IMPOSSIBLE TO LAND."
?
"SOOOO... WE'VE BEEN ADVISED TO LAND ELSEWHERE... UNTIL THINGS GET BETTER."
"I'M NOT SURE HOW LONG THIS MAY TAKE... BUT WE'D RATHER SIDE WITH CAUTION ON THIS."
"WE'LL KEEP YOU INFORMED OF ANY AND ALL UPDATES..."
"AND WE APOLOGIZE FOR ANY INCONVENIENCE FROM THIS."
"FLIGHT CREW... PREPARE FOR LANDING."
WHAT...?!
WHAT?!!

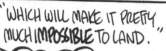

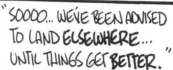

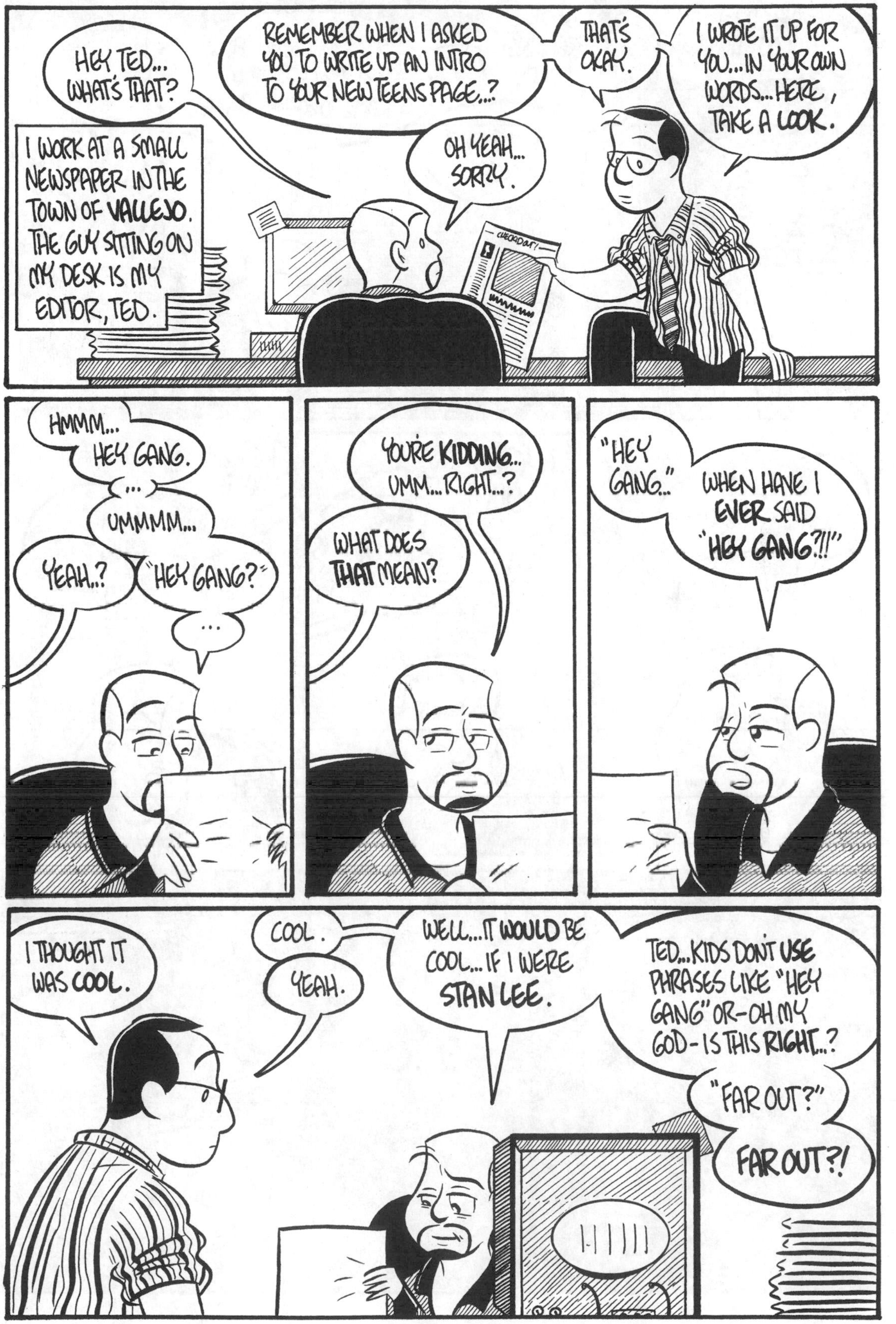
HEY TED... WHAT'S THAT?
REMEMBER WHEN I ASKED YOU TO WRITE UP AN INTRO TO YOUR NEW TEENS PAGE...?
THAT'S OKAY.
I WROTE IT UP FOR YOU... IN YOUR OWN WORDS... HERE, TAKE A LOOK.
I WORK AT A SMALL NEWSPAPER IN THE TOWN OF VALLEJO. THE GUY SITTING ON MY DESK IS MY EDITOR, TED.
OH YEAH... SORRY.
HMMM...
HEY GANG.
...
UMMMM...
YEAH..?
"HEY GANG?"
...
YOU'RE KIDDING... UMM... RIGHT...?
WHAT DOES THAT MEAN?
"HEY GANG."
WHEN HAVE I EVER SAID "HEY GANG?!!"
I THOUGHT IT WAS COOL.
COOL.
YEAH.
WELL... IT WOULD BE COOL... IF I WERE STAN LEE.
TED... KIDS DON'T USE PHRASES LIKE "HEY GANG" OR-OH MY GOD-IS THIS RIGHT...?
"FAR OUT?"
FAR OUT?!

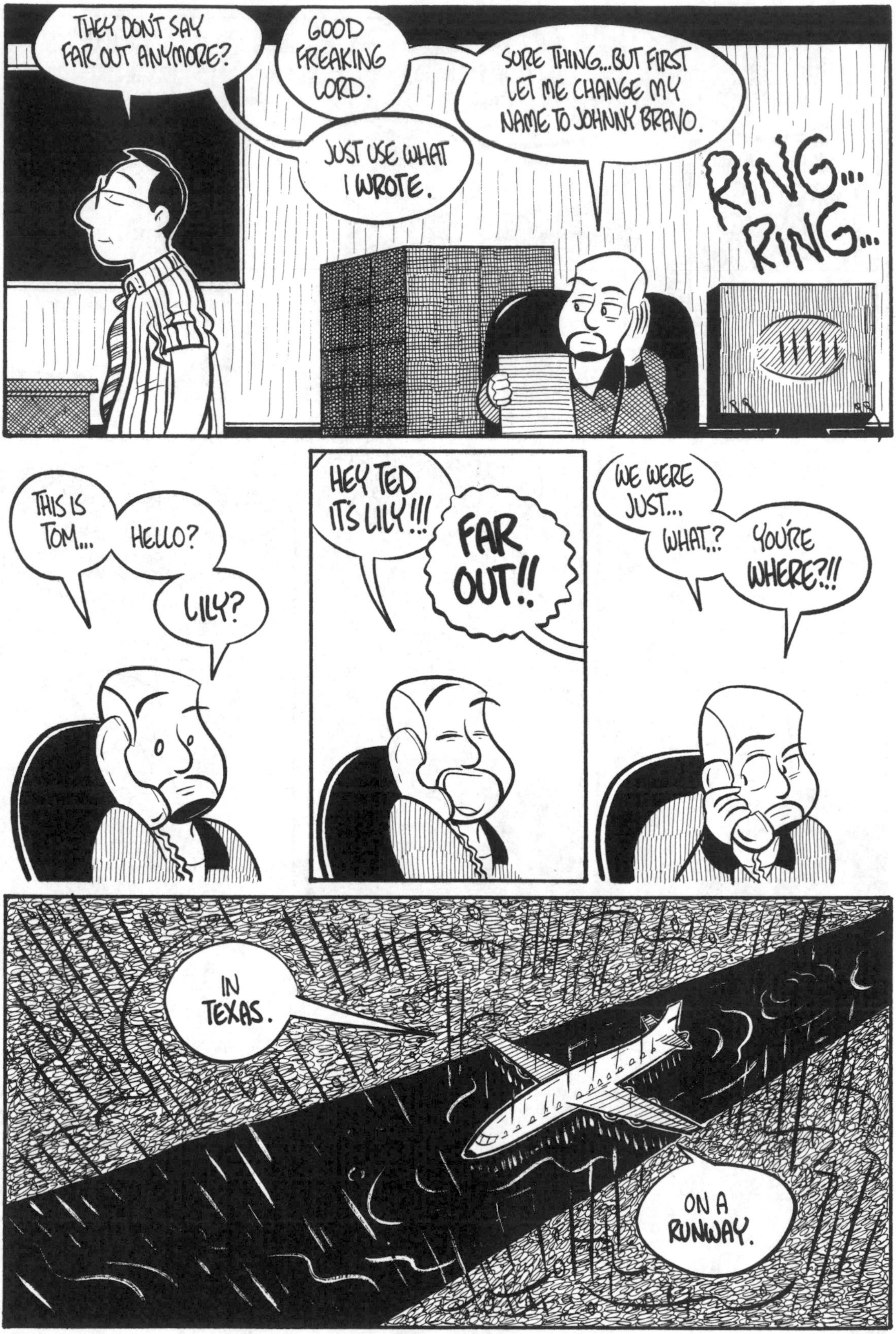
THEY DON'T SAY FAR OUT ANYMORE?
GOOD FREAKING LORD.
JUST USE WHAT I WROTE.
SURE THING...BUT FIRST LET ME CHANGE MY NAME TO JOHNNY BRAVO.
RING... RING...
THIS IS TOM...
HELLO?
LILY?
HEY TED IT'S LILY!!!
FAR OUT!!
WE WERE JUST...
WHAT..?
YOU'RE WHERE?!!
IN TEXAS.
ON A RUNWAY.

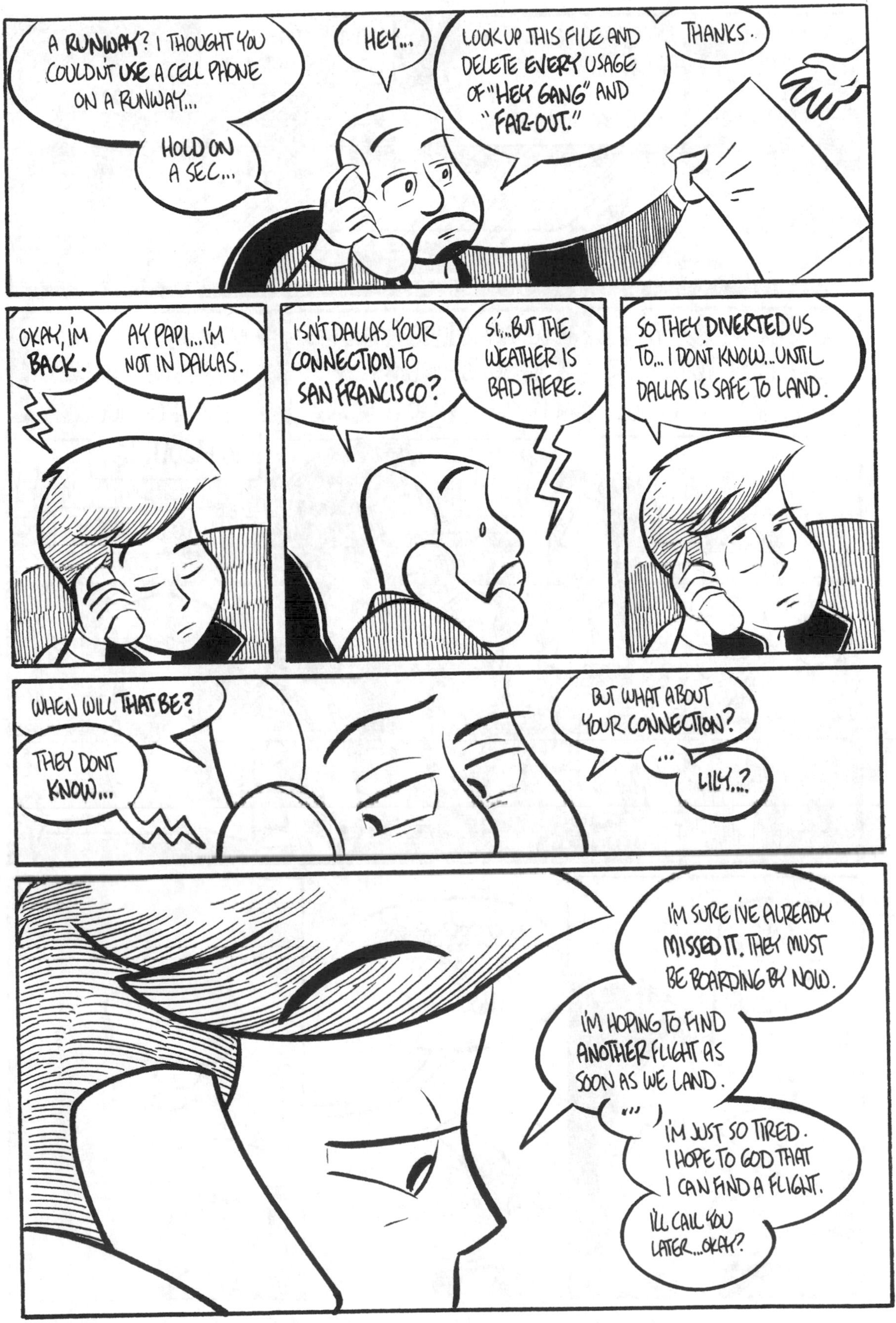

A RUNWAY? I THOUGHT YOU COULDN'T USE A CELL PHONE ON A RUNWAY...
HOLD ON A SEC...
HEY...
LOOK UP THIS FILE AND DELETE EVERY USAGE OF "HEY GANG" AND "FAR-OUT."
THANKS.
OKAY, I'M BACK.
AY PAPI... I'M NOT IN DALLAS.
ISN'T DALLAS YOUR CONNECTION TO SAN FRANCISCO?
SÍ...BUT THE WEATHER IS BAD THERE.
SO THEY DIVERTED US TO... I DONT KNOW...UNTIL DALLAS IS SAFE TO LAND.
WHEN WILL THAT BE?
THEY DONT KNOW...
BUT WHAT ABOUT YOUR CONNECTION?
...
LILY..?
I'M SURE I'VE ALREADY MISSED IT. THEY MUST BE BOARDING BY NOW.
I'M HOPING TO FIND ANOTHER FLIGHT AS SOON AS WE LAND.
...
I'M JUST SO TIRED. I HOPE TO GOD THAT I CAN FIND A FLIGHT.
I'LL CALL YOU LATER...OKAY?

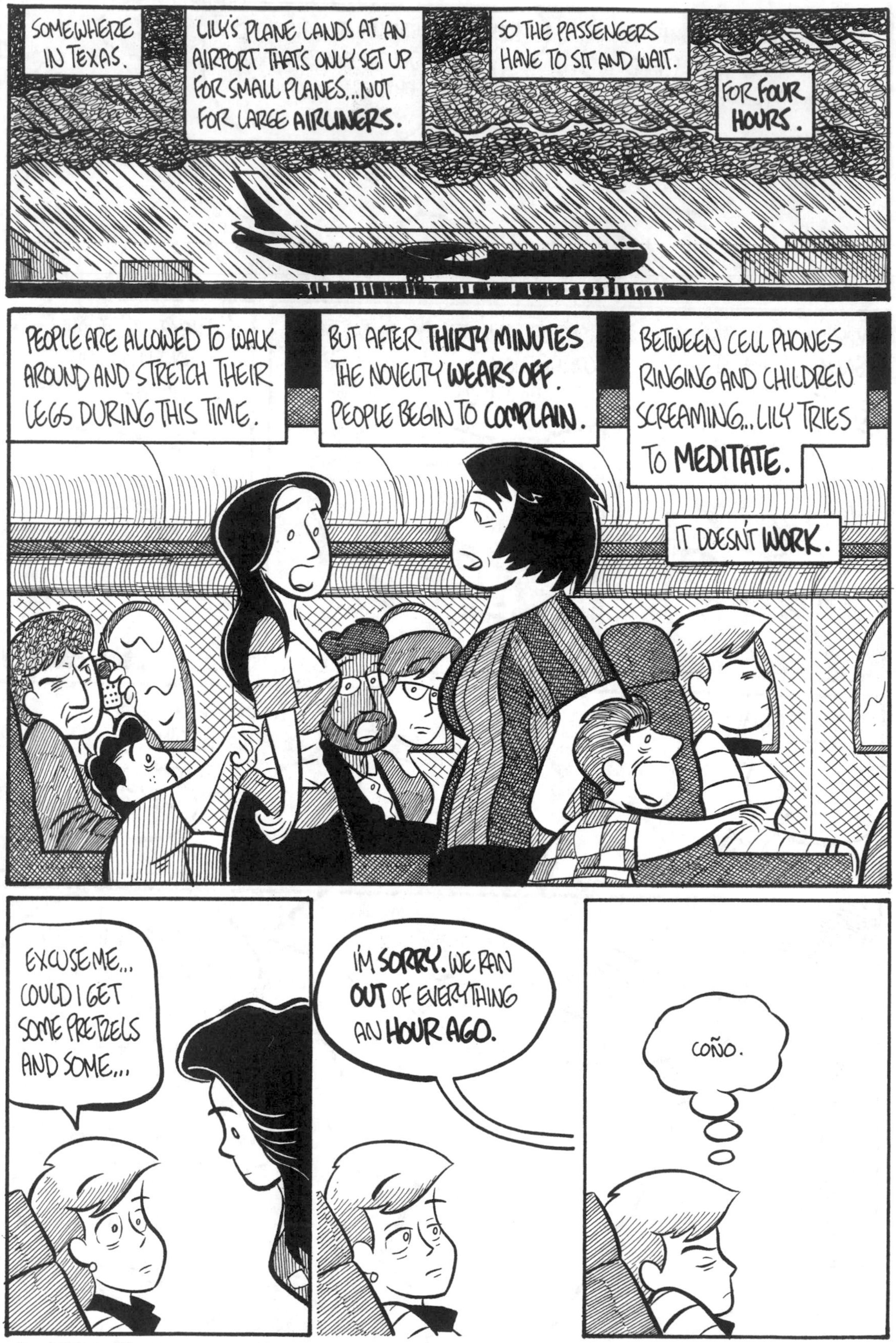
SOMEWHERE IN TEXAS.
LILY'S PLANE LANDS AT AN AIRPORT THAT'S ONLY SET UP FOR SMALL PLANES... NOT FOR LARGE AIRLINERS.
SO THE PASSENGERS HAVE TO SIT AND WAIT.
FOR FOUR HOURS.
PEOPLE ARE ALLOWED TO WALK AROUND AND STRETCH THEIR LEGS DURING THIS TIME.
BUT AFTER THIRTY MINUTES THE NOVELTY WEARS OFF. PEOPLE BEGIN TO COMPLAIN.
BETWEEN CELL PHONES RINGING AND CHILDREN SCREAMING... LILY TRIES TO MEDITATE.
IT DOESN'T WORK.
EXCUSE ME... COULD I GET SOME PRETZELS AND SOME...
I'M SORRY. WE RAN OUT OF EVERYTHING AN HOUR AGO.
COÑO.

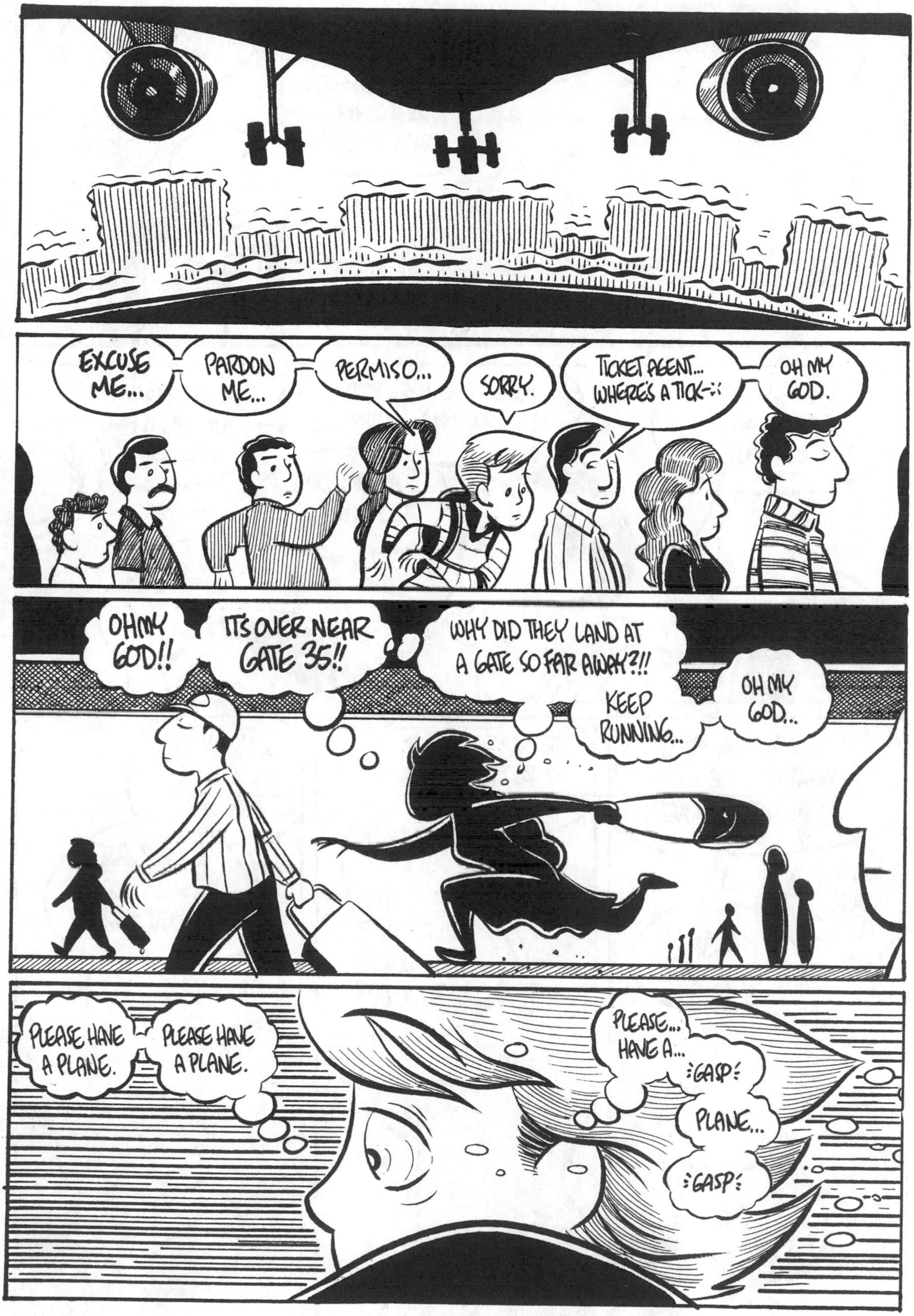
EXCUSE ME...
PARDON ME...
PERMISO...
SORRY.
TICKET AGENT... WHERE'S A TICK-
OH MY GOD.
OHMY GOD!!
IT'S OVER NEAR GATE 35!!
WHY DID THEY LAND AT A GATE SO FAR AWAY?!!
KEEP RUNNING...
OH MY GOD...
PLEASE HAVE A PLANE.
PLEASE HAVE A PLANE.
PLEASE... HAVE A...
GASP
PLANE...
GASP

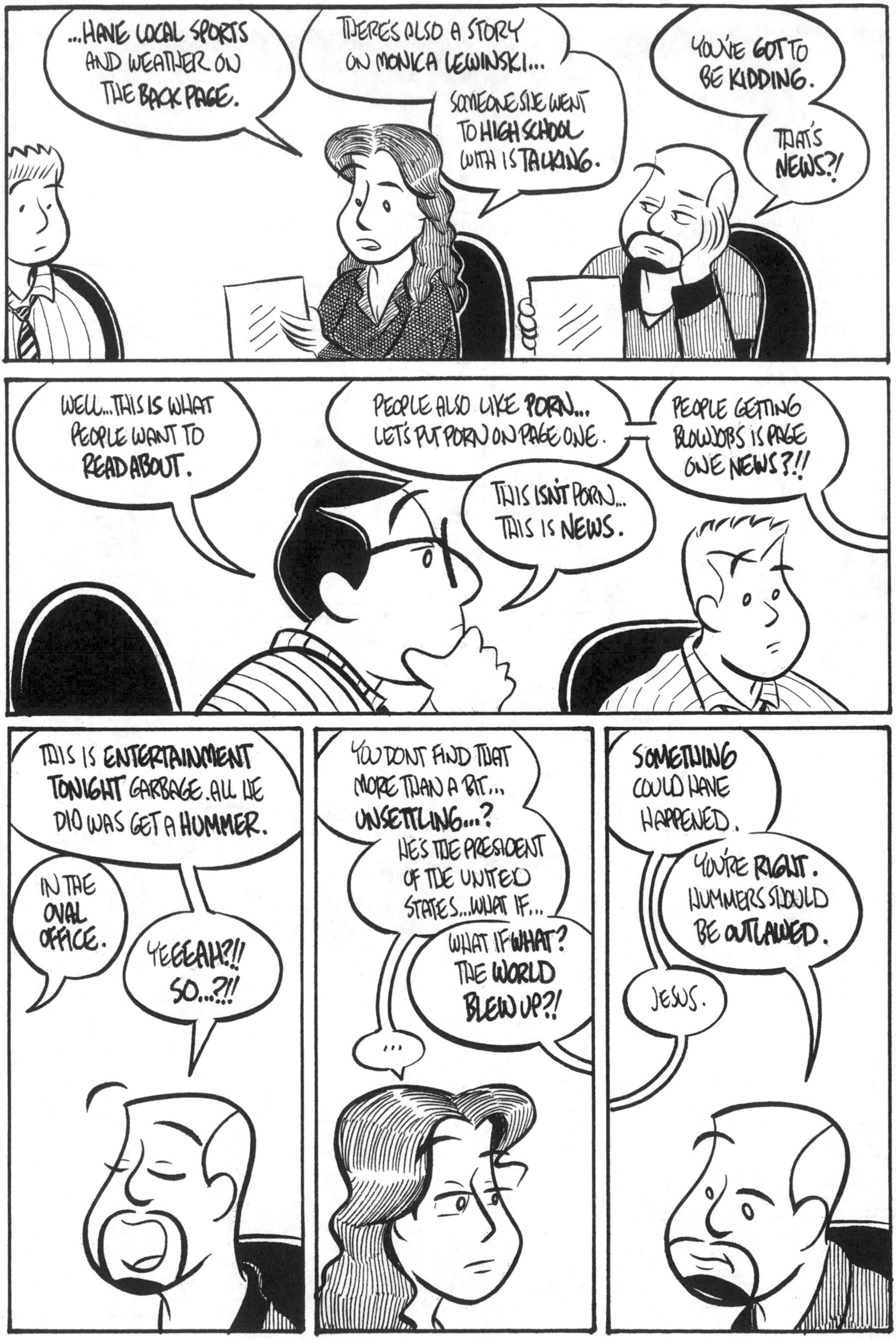
...HAVE LOCAL SPORTS AND WEATHER ON THE BACK PAGE.
THERE'S ALSO A STORY ON MONICA LEWINSKI...
SOMEONE SHE WENT TO HIGH SCHOOL WITH IS TALKING.
YOU'VE GOT TO BE KIDDING.
THAT'S NEWS?!
WELL...THIS IS WHAT PEOPLE WANT TO READ ABOUT.
PEOPLE ALSO LIKE PORN... LET'S PUT PORN ON PAGE ONE.
PEOPLE GETTING BLOWJOBS IS PAGE ONE NEWS?!!
THIS ISN'T PORN... THIS IS NEWS.
THIS IS ENTERTAINMENT TONIGHT GARBAGE. ALL HE DID WAS GET A HUMMER.
IN THE OVAL OFFICE.
YEEEAH?!! SO...?!!
YOU DONT FIND THAT MORE THAN A BIT... UNSETTLING...?
HE'S THE PRESIDENT OF THE UNITED STATES...WHAT IF...
WHAT IF WHAT? THE WORLD BLEW UP?!
...
SOMETHING COULD HAVE HAPPENED.
YOU'RE RIGHT. HUMMERS SHOULD BE OUTLAWED.
JESUS.

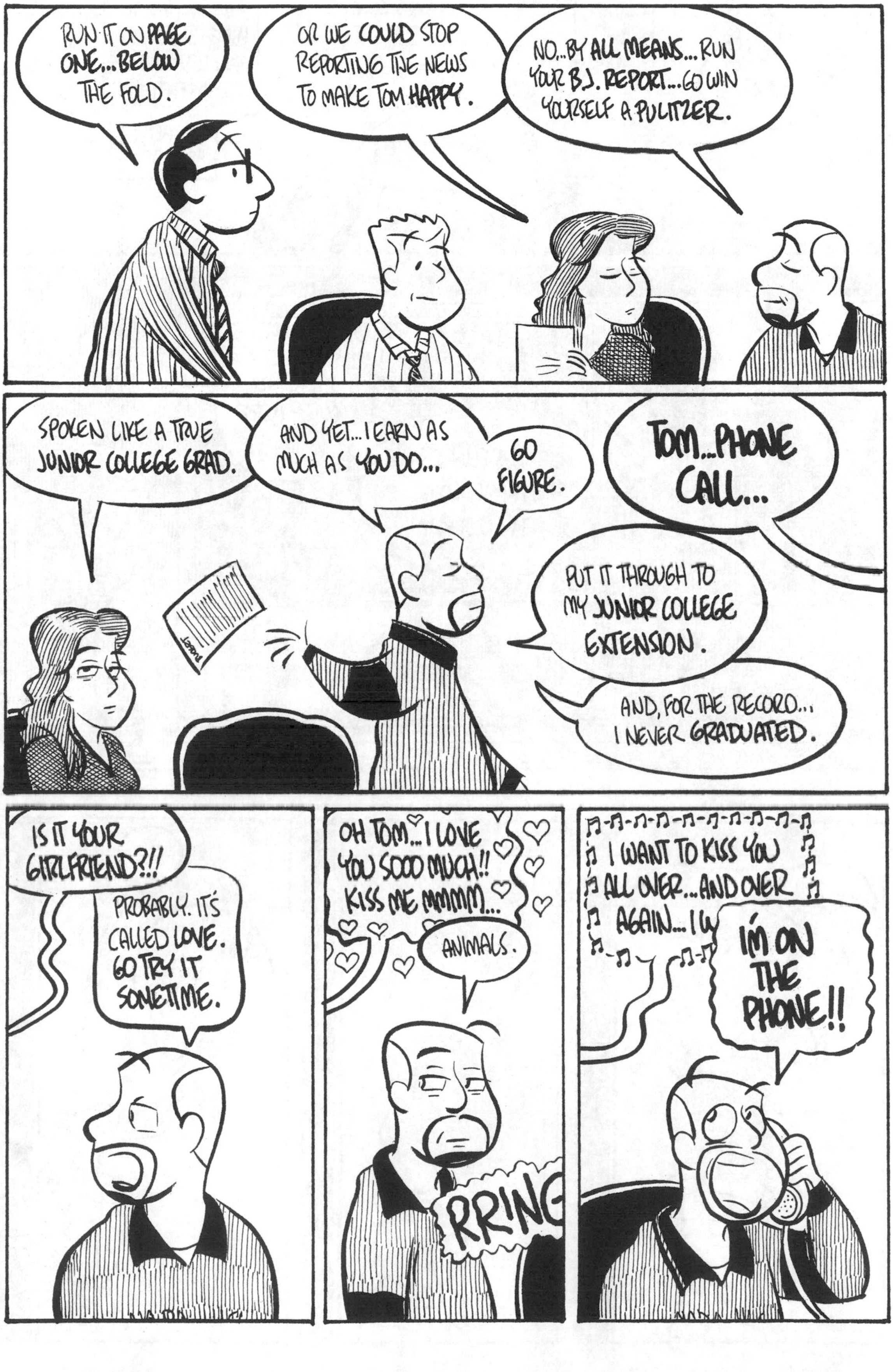
RUN IT ON PAGE ONE... BELOW THE FOLD.
OR WE COULD STOP REPORTING THE NEWS TO MAKE TOM HAPPY.
NO... BY ALL MEANS... RUN YOUR B.J. REPORT... GO WIN YOURSELF A PULITZER.
SPOKEN LIKE A TRUE JUNIOR COLLEGE GRAD.
AND YET... I EARN AS MUCH AS YOU DO...
GO FIGURE.
TOM... PHONE CALL...
PUT IT THROUGH TO MY JUNIOR COLLEGE EXTENSION.
AND, FOR THE RECORD... I NEVER GRADUATED.
IS IT YOUR GIRLFRIEND?!!
PROBABLY. IT'S CALLED LOVE. GO TRY IT SOMETIME.
OH TOM... I LOVE YOU SOOO MUCH!! KISS ME MMMM...
ANIMALS.
RRING
I WANT TO KISS YOU ALL OVER... AND OVER AGAIN... I W
I'M ON THE PHONE!!

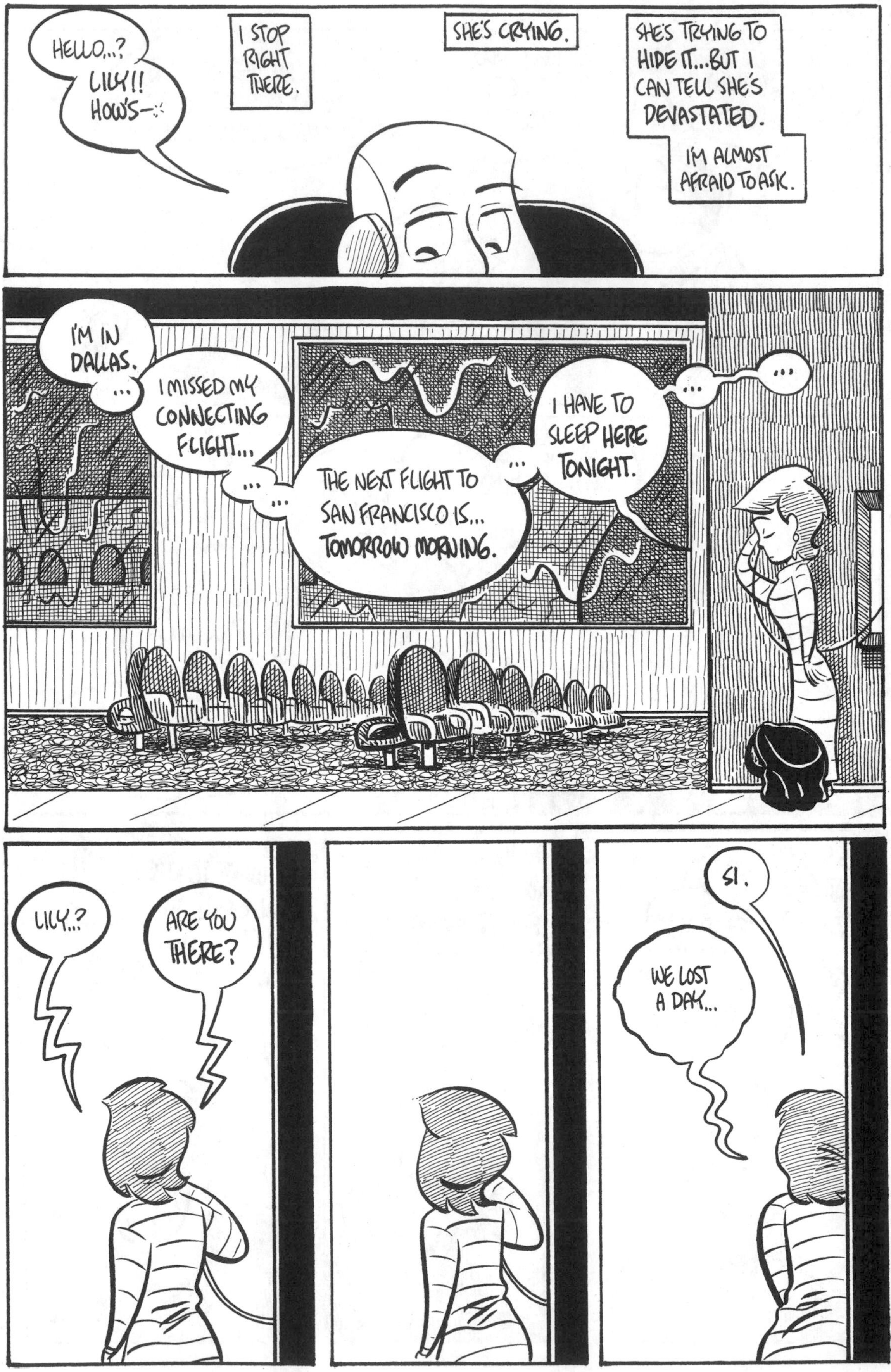
HELLO...?
LILY!! HOW'S—
I STOP RIGHT THERE.
SHE'S CRYING.
SHE'S TRYING TO HIDE IT...BUT I CAN TELL SHE'S DEVASTATED.
I'M ALMOST AFRAID TO ASK.
I'M IN DALLAS.
...
I MISSED MY CONNECTING FLIGHT...
...
...
THE NEXT FLIGHT TO SAN FRANCISCO IS... TOMORROW MORNING.
...
I HAVE TO SLEEP HERE TONIGHT.
...
...
LILY...?
ARE YOU THERE?
SI.
WE LOST A DAY...

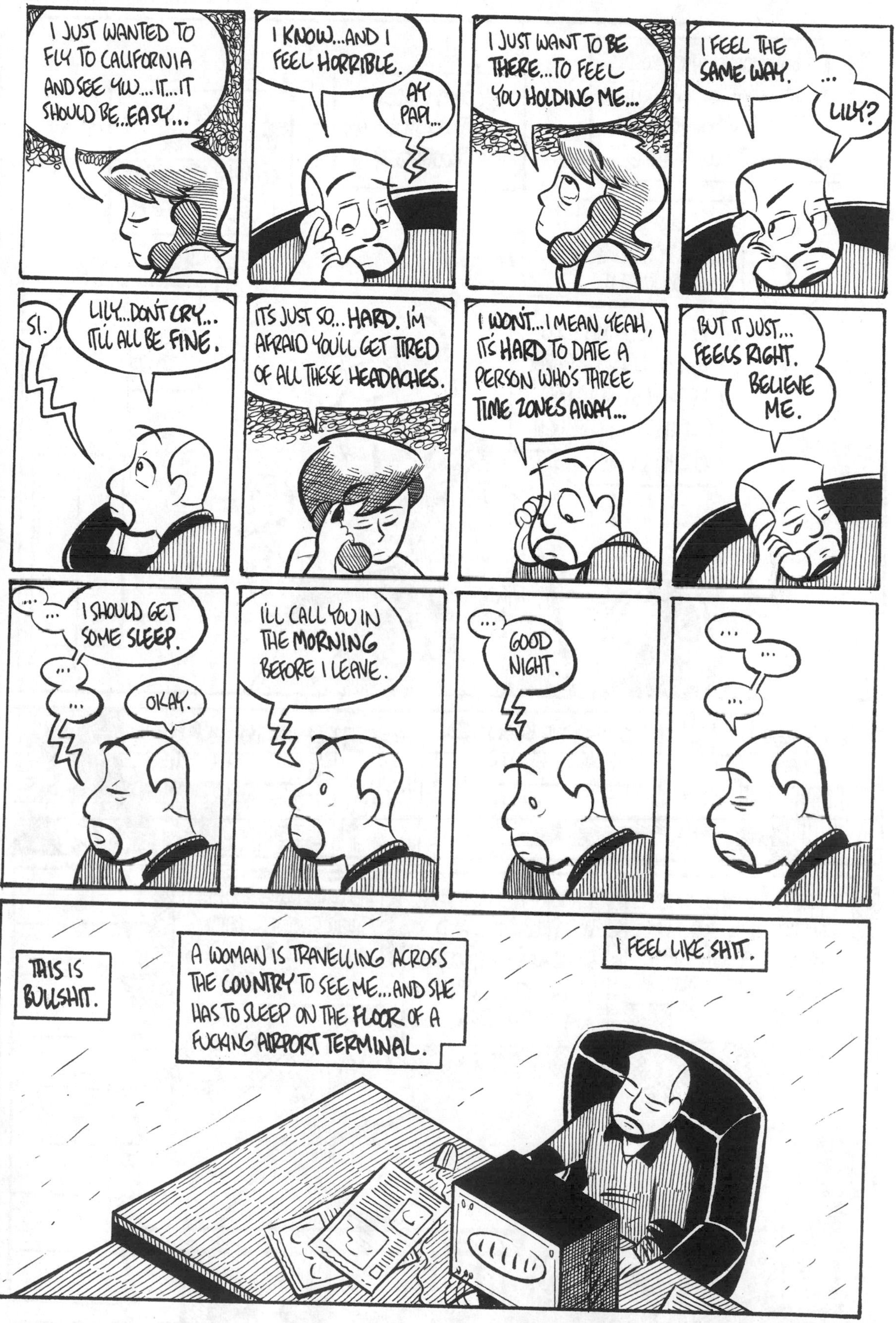
I JUST WANTED TO FLY TO CALIFORNIA AND SEE YOU... IT... IT SHOULD BE... EASY...
I KNOW... AND I FEEL HORRIBLE.
AY PAPI...
I JUST WANT TO BE THERE... TO FEEL YOU HOLDING ME...
I FEEL THE SAME WAY.
...
LILY?
SI.
LILY... DON'T CRY... IT'LL ALL BE FINE.
IT'S JUST SO... HARD. I'M AFRAID YOU'LL GET TIRED OF ALL THESE HEADACHES.
I WON'T... I MEAN, YEAH, IT'S HARD TO DATE A PERSON WHO'S THREE TIME ZONES AWAY...
BUT IT JUST... FEELS RIGHT.
BELIEVE ME.
...
...
I SHOULD GET SOME SLEEP.
...
...
OKAY.
I'LL CALL YOU IN THE MORNING BEFORE I LEAVE.
...
GOOD NIGHT.
...
...
...
THIS IS BULLSHIT.
A WOMAN IS TRAVELLING ACROSS THE COUNTRY TO SEE ME... AND SHE HAS TO SLEEP ON THE FLOOR OF A FUCKING AIRPORT TERMINAL.
I FEEL LIKE SHIT.

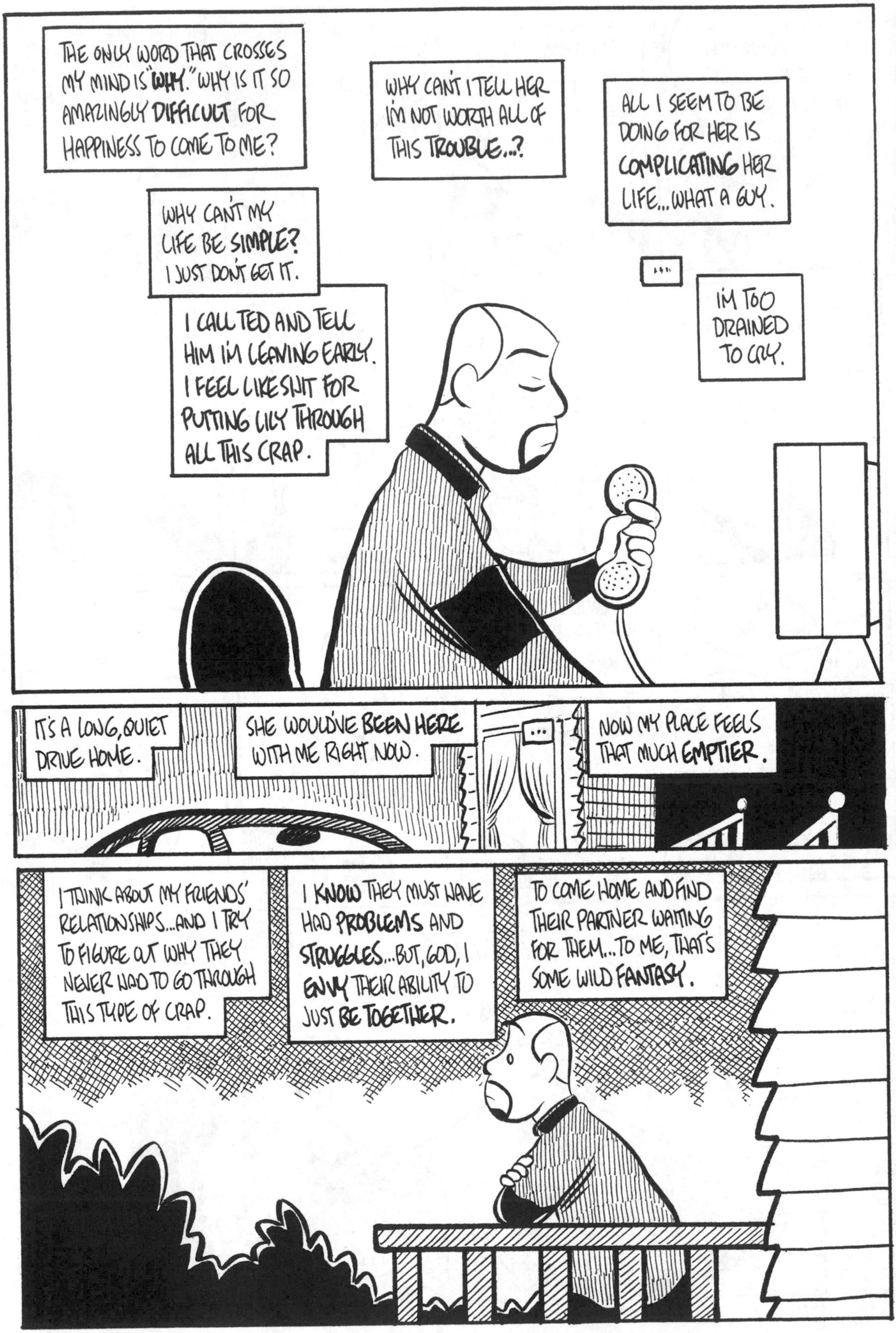
THE ONLY WORD THAT CROSSES MY MIND IS "WHY." WHY IS IT SO AMAZINGLY DIFFICULT FOR HAPPINESS TO COME TO ME?
WHY CAN'T I TELL HER I'M NOT WORTH ALL OF THIS TROUBLE...?
ALL I SEEM TO BE DOING FOR HER IS COMPLICATING HER LIFE... WHAT A GUY.
WHY CAN'T MY LIFE BE SIMPLE? I JUST DON'T GET IT.
I CALL TED AND TELL HIM I'M LEAVING EARLY. I FEEL LIKE SHIT FOR PUTTING LILY THROUGH ALL THIS CRAP.
I'M TOO DRAINED TO CRY.
IT'S A LONG, QUIET DRIVE HOME.
SHE WOULD'VE BEEN HERE WITH ME RIGHT NOW.
NOW MY PLACE FEELS THAT MUCH EMPTIER.
I THINK ABOUT MY FRIENDS' RELATIONSHIPS...AND I TRY TO FIGURE OUT WHY THEY NEVER HAD TO GO THROUGH THIS TYPE OF CRAP.
I KNOW THEY MUST HAVE HAD PROBLEMS AND STRUGGLES...BUT, GOD, I ENVY THEIR ABILITY TO JUST BE TOGETHER.
TO COME HOME AND FIND THEIR PARTNER WAITING FOR THEM...TO ME, THAT'S SOME WILD FANTASY.

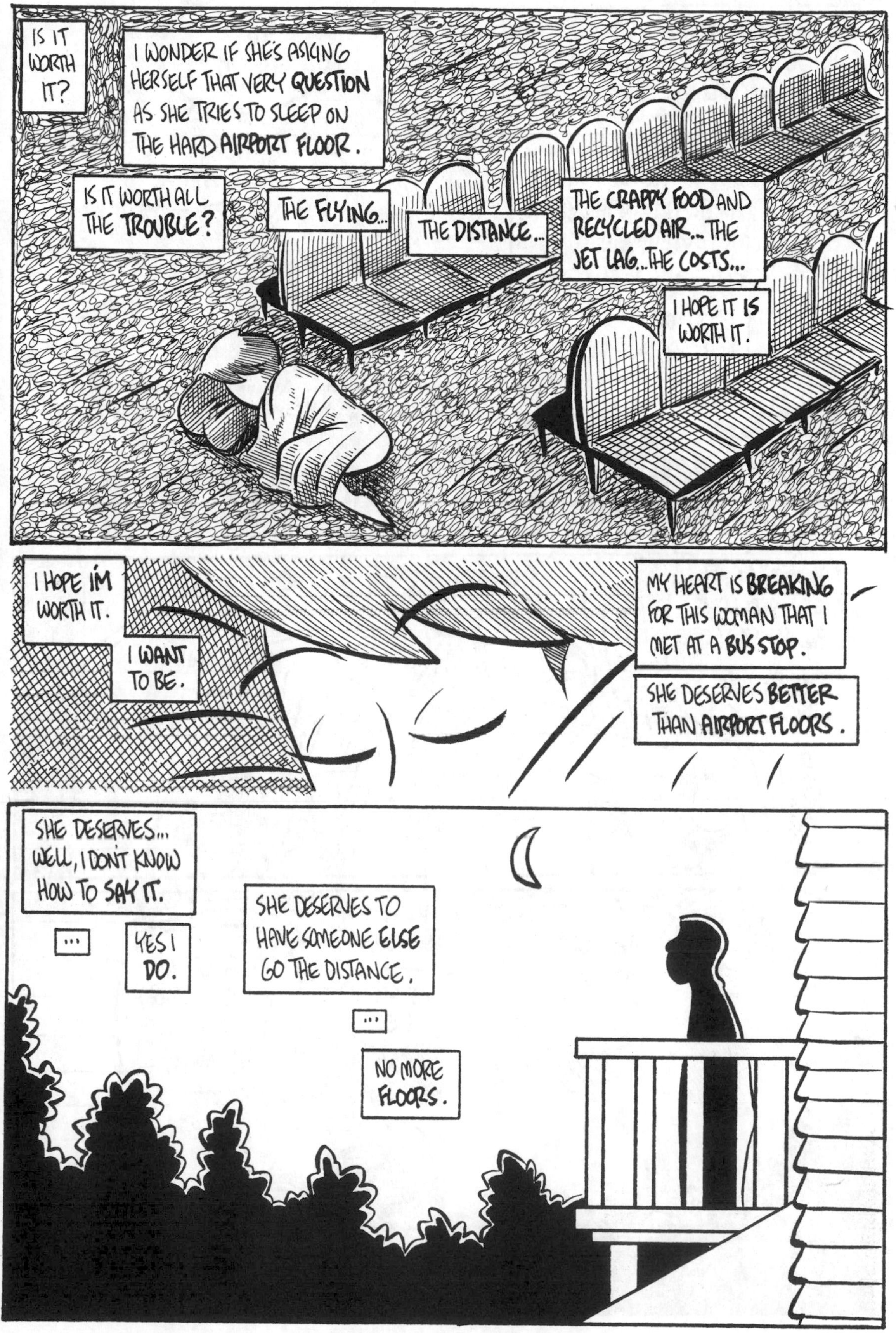
IS IT WORTH IT?
I WONDER IF SHE'S ASKING HERSELF THAT VERY QUESTION AS SHE TRIES TO SLEEP ON THE HARD AIRPORT FLOOR.
IS IT WORTH ALL THE TROUBLE?
THE FLYING...
THE DISTANCE...
THE CRAPPY FOOD AND RECYCLED AIR... THE JET LAG... THE COSTS...
I HOPE IT IS WORTH IT.
I HOPE I'M WORTH IT.
I WANT TO BE.
MY HEART IS BREAKING FOR THIS WOMAN THAT I MET AT A BUS STOP.
SHE DESERVES BETTER THAN AIRPORT FLOORS.
SHE DESERVES... WELL, I DON'T KNOW HOW TO SAY IT.
...
YES I DO.
SHE DESERVES TO HAVE SOMEONE ELSE GO THE DISTANCE.
...
NO MORE FLOORS.

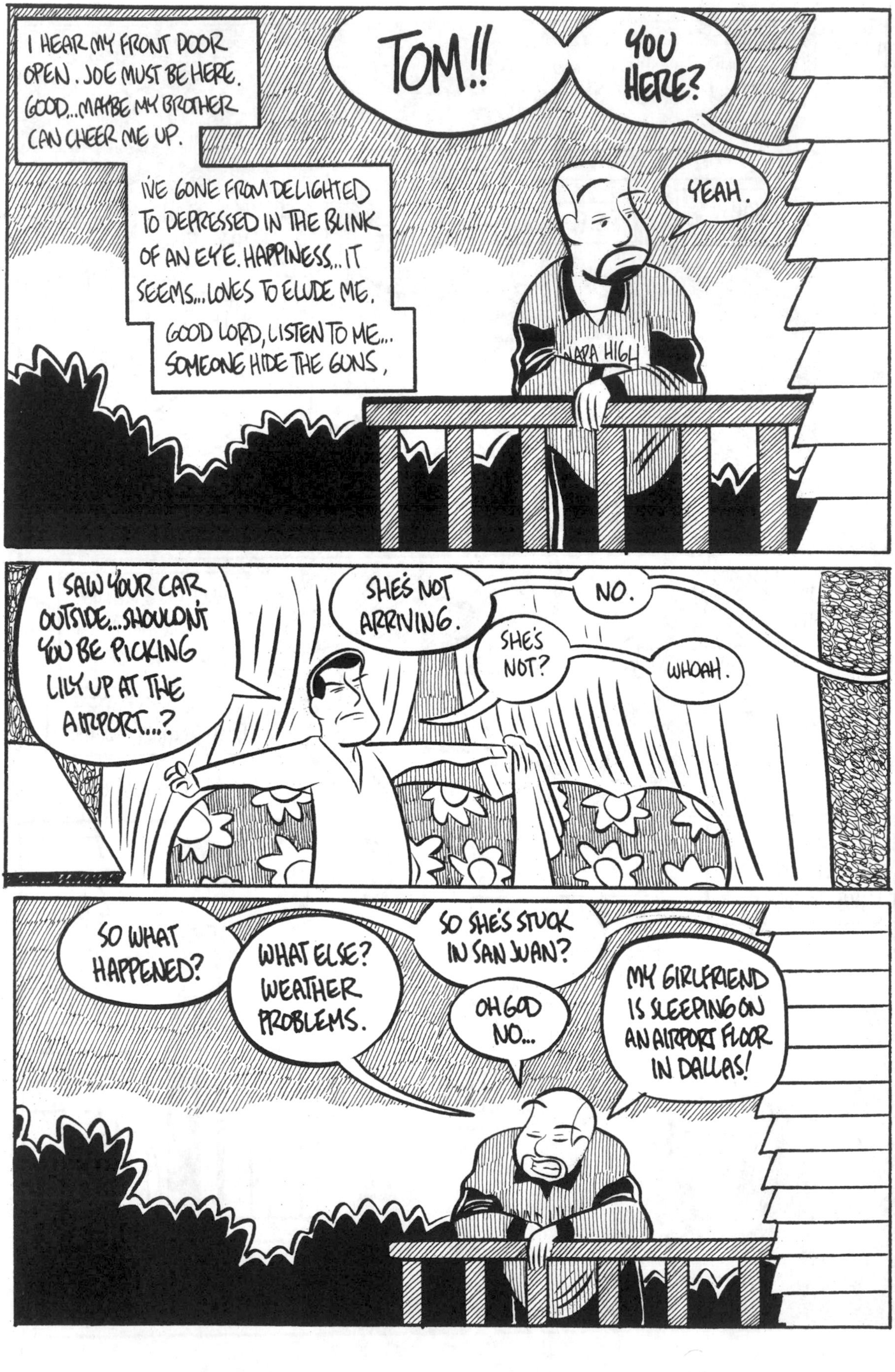
I HEAR MY FRONT DOOR OPEN. JOE MUST BE HERE. GOOD...MAYBE MY BROTHER CAN CHEER ME UP.
I'VE GONE FROM DELIGHTED TO DEPRESSED IN THE BLINK OF AN EYE. HAPPINESS... IT SEEMS... LOVES TO ELUDE ME.
GOOD LORD, LISTEN TO ME... SOMEONE HIDE THE GUNS.
TOM!!
YOU HERE?
YEAH.
NAPA HIGH
I SAW YOUR CAR OUTSIDE...SHOULDN'T YOU BE PICKING LILY UP AT THE AIRPORT...?
SHE'S NOT ARRIVING.
SHE'S NOT?
NO.
WHOAH.
SO WHAT HAPPENED?
WHAT ELSE? WEATHER PROBLEMS.
SO SHE'S STUCK IN SAN JUAN?
OH GOD NO...
MY GIRLFRIEND IS SLEEPING ON AN AIRPORT FLOOR IN DALLAS!

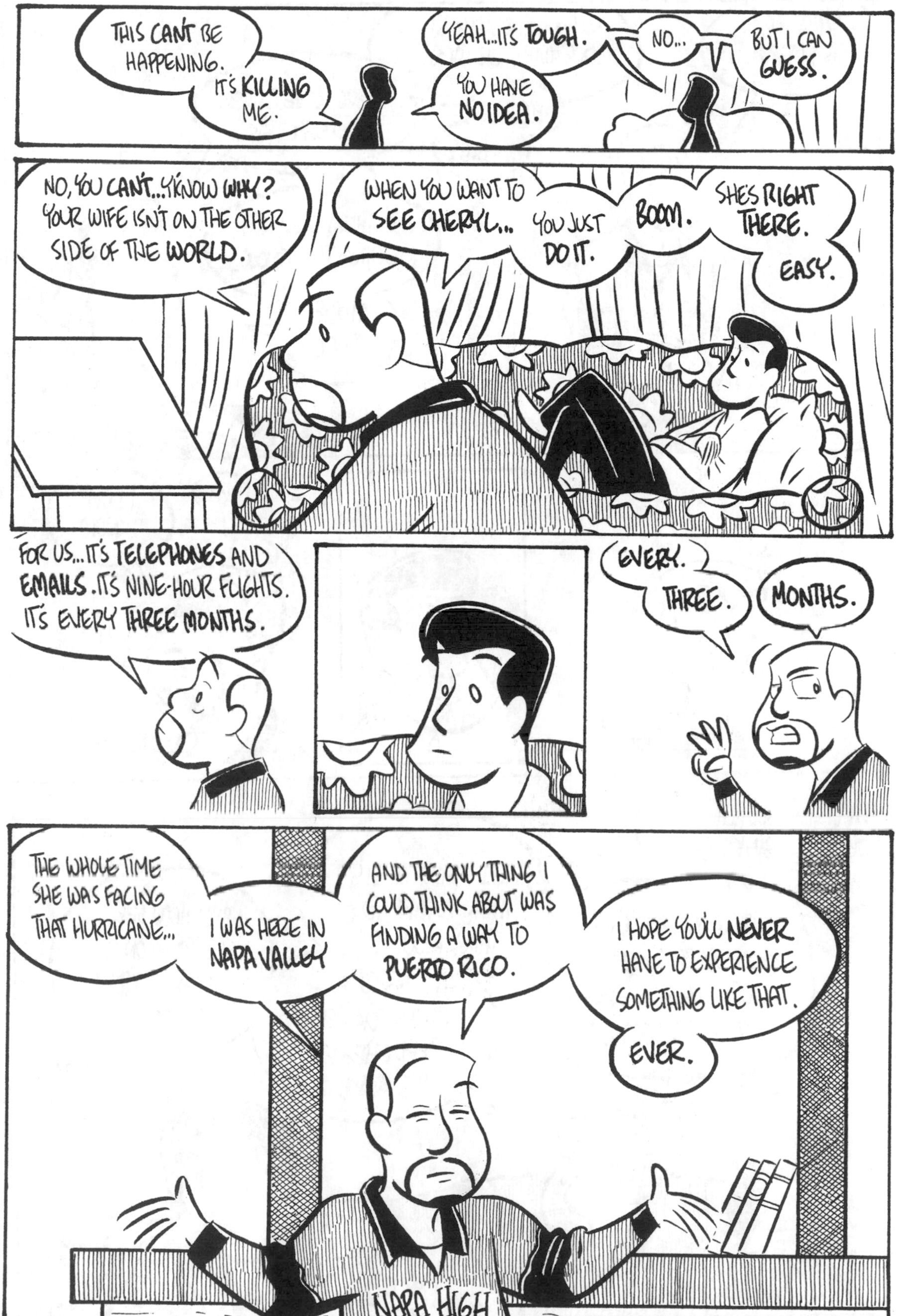
THIS CAN'T BE HAPPENING.
IT'S KILLING ME.
YOU HAVE NO IDEA.
YEAH...IT'S TOUGH.
NO...
BUT I CAN GUESS.
NO, YOU CAN'T...Y'KNOW WHY? YOUR WIFE ISN'T ON THE OTHER SIDE OF THE WORLD.
WHEN YOU WANT TO SEE CHERYL...
YOU JUST DO IT.
BOOM.
SHE'S RIGHT THERE.
EASY.
FOR US...IT'S TELEPHONES AND EMAILS. IT'S NINE-HOUR FLIGHTS. IT'S EVERY THREE MONTHS.
EVERY.
THREE.
MONTHS.
THE WHOLE TIME SHE WAS FACING THAT HURRICANE...
I WAS HERE IN NAPA VALLEY
AND THE ONLY THING I COULD THINK ABOUT WAS FINDING A WAY TO PUERTO RICO.
I HOPE YOU'LL NEVER HAVE TO EXPERIENCE SOMETHING LIKE THAT.
EVER.
NAPA HIGH

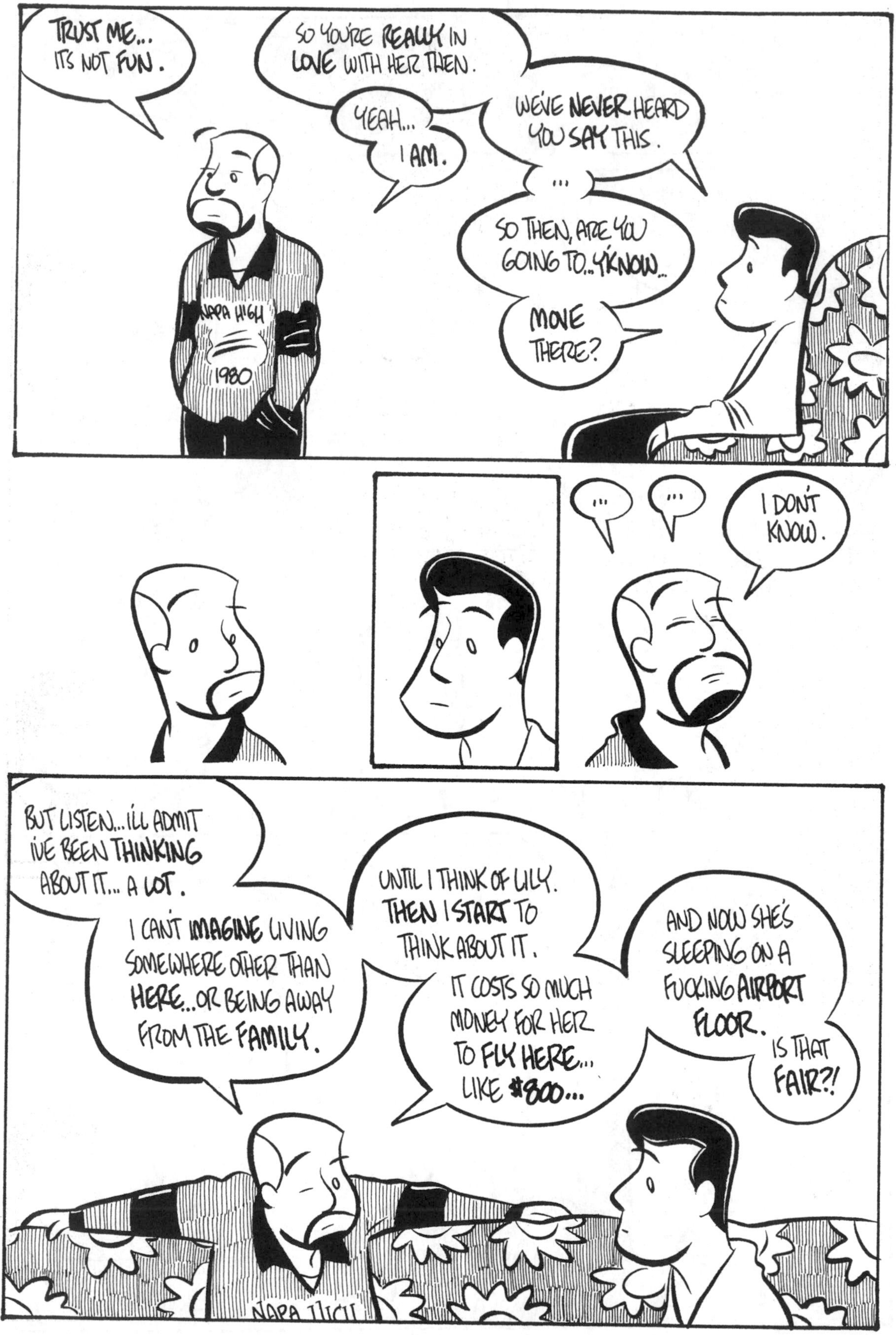
TRUST ME... IT'S NOT FUN.
SO YOU'RE REALLY IN LOVE WITH HER THEN.
YEAH... I AM.
WE'VE NEVER HEARD YOU SAY THIS.
...
SO THEN, ARE YOU GOING TO... Y'KNOW...
MOVE THERE?
NAPA HIGH
1980
...
...
I DON'T KNOW.
BUT LISTEN... I'LL ADMIT I'VE BEEN THINKING ABOUT IT... A LOT.
I CAN'T IMAGINE LIVING SOMEWHERE OTHER THAN HERE... OR BEING AWAY FROM THE FAMILY.
UNTIL I THINK OF LILY. THEN I START TO THINK ABOUT IT.
IT COSTS SO MUCH MONEY FOR HER TO FLY HERE... LIKE $800...
AND NOW SHE'S SLEEPING ON A FUCKING AIRPORT FLOOR.
IS THAT FAIR?!

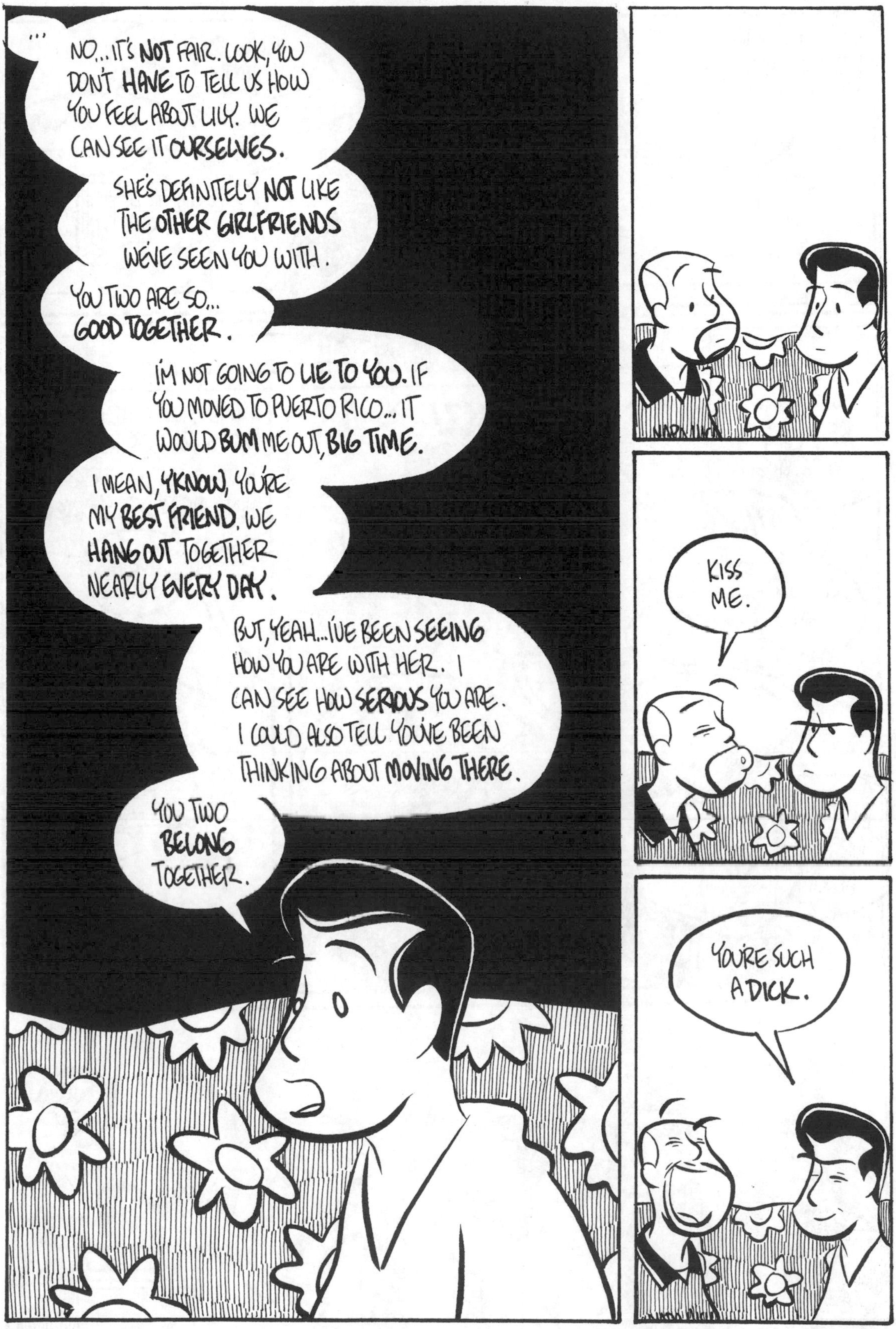
...
NO... IT'S NOT FAIR. LOOK, YOU DON'T HAVE TO TELL US HOW YOU FEEL ABOUT LILY. WE CAN SEE IT OURSELVES.
SHE'S DEFINITELY NOT LIKE THE OTHER GIRLFRIENDS WE'VE SEEN YOU WITH.
YOU TWO ARE SO... GOOD TOGETHER.
I'M NOT GOING TO LIE TO YOU. IF YOU MOVED TO PUERTO RICO... IT WOULD BUM ME OUT, BIG TIME.
I MEAN, Y'KNOW, YOU'RE MY BEST FRIEND. WE HANG OUT TOGETHER NEARLY EVERY DAY.
BUT, YEAH... I'VE BEEN SEEING HOW YOU ARE WITH HER. I CAN SEE HOW SERIOUS YOU ARE. I COULD ALSO TELL YOU'VE BEEN THINKING ABOUT MOVING THERE.
YOU TWO BELONG TOGETHER.
KISS ME.
YOU'RE SUCH A DICK.

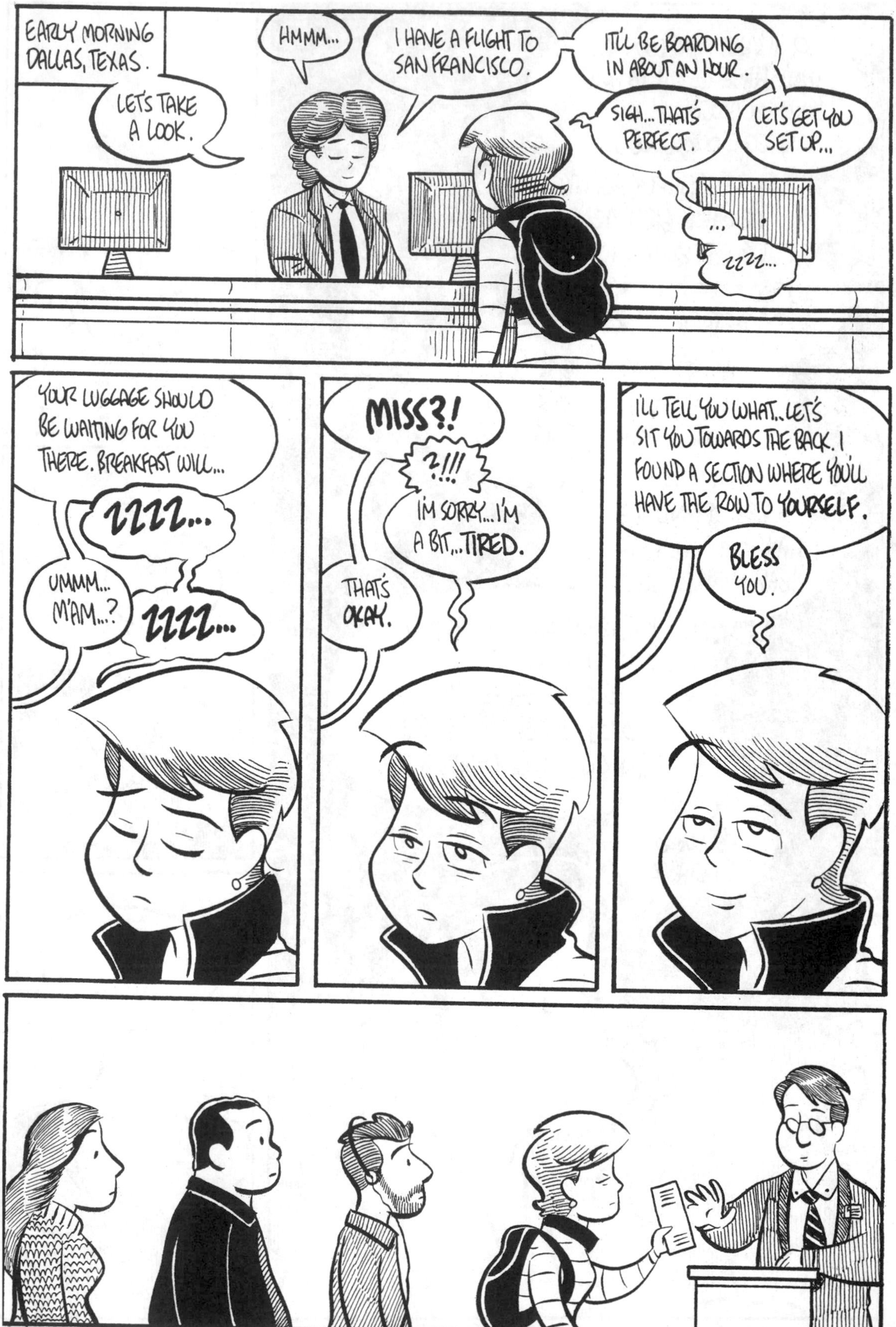
EARLY MORNING
DALLAS, TEXAS.
LET'S TAKE A LOOK.
HMMM...
I HAVE A FLIGHT TO SAN FRANCISCO.
IT'LL BE BOARDING IN ABOUT AN HOUR.
SIGH... THAT'S PERFECT.
LET'S GET YOU SET UP...
...
ZZZZ...
YOUR LUGGAGE SHOULD BE WAITING FOR YOU THERE. BREAKFAST WILL...
ZZZZ...
UMMM... M'AM...?
ZZZZ...
MISS?!
?!!!
I'M SORRY... I'M A BIT... TIRED.
THAT'S OKAY.
I'LL TELL YOU WHAT... LET'S SIT YOU TOWARDS THE BACK. I FOUND A SECTION WHERE YOU'LL HAVE THE ROW TO YOURSELF.
BLESS YOU.

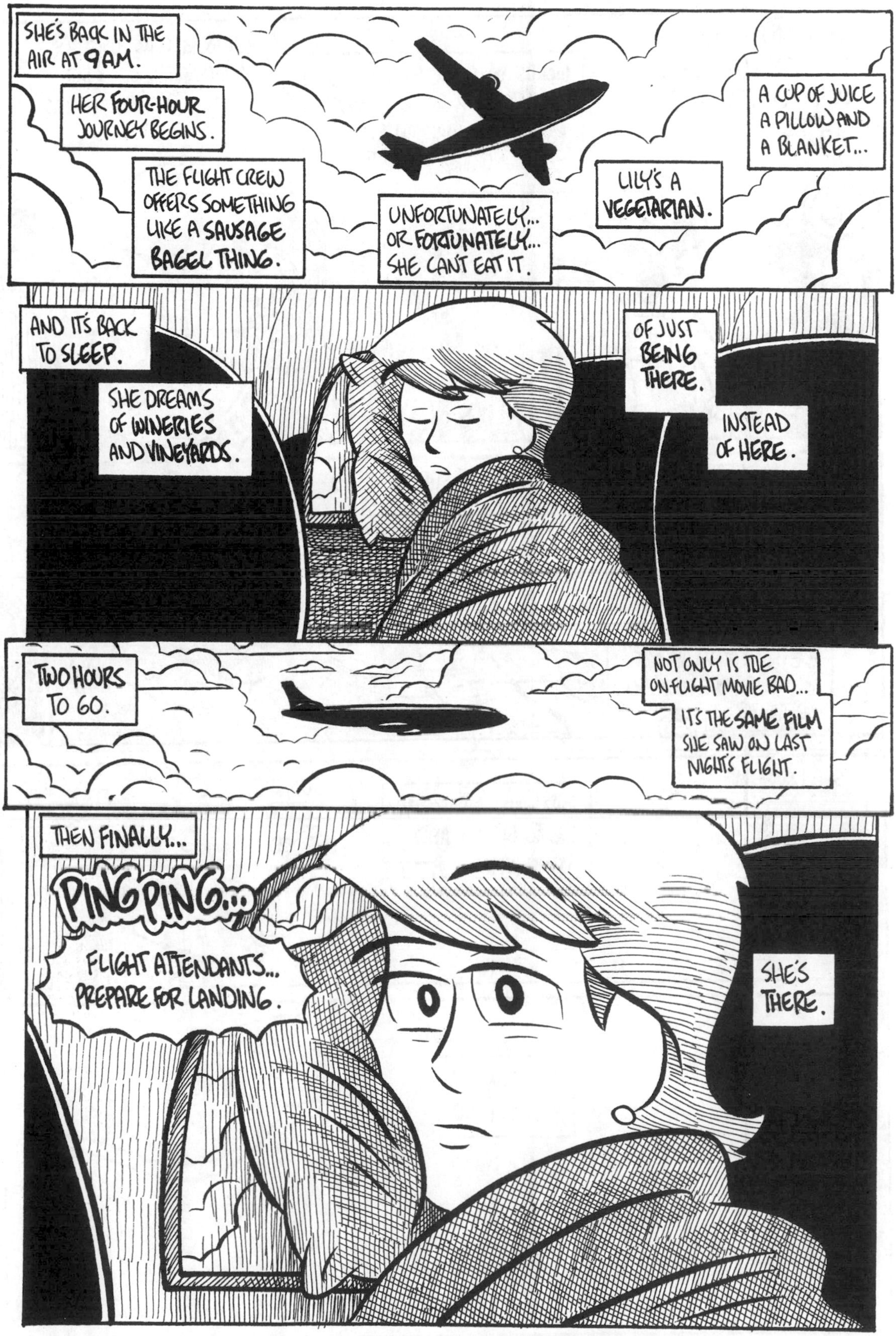
SHE'S BACK IN THE AIR AT 9AM.
HER FOUR-HOUR JOURNEY BEGINS.
THE FLIGHT CREW OFFERS SOMETHING LIKE A SAUSAGE BAGEL THING.
UNFORTUNATELY... OR FORTUNATELY... SHE CAN'T EAT IT.
LILY'S A VEGETARIAN.
A CUP OF JUICE A PILLOW AND A BLANKET...
AND IT'S BACK TO SLEEP.
SHE DREAMS OF WINERIES AND VINEYARDS.
OF JUST BEING THERE.
INSTEAD OF HERE.
TWO HOURS TO GO.
NOT ONLY IS THE ON-FLIGHT MOVIE BAD...
IT'S THE SAME FILM SHE SAW ON LAST NIGHT'S FLIGHT.
THEN FINALLY...
PING PING...
FLIGHT ATTENDANTS... PREPARE FOR LANDING.
SHE'S THERE.

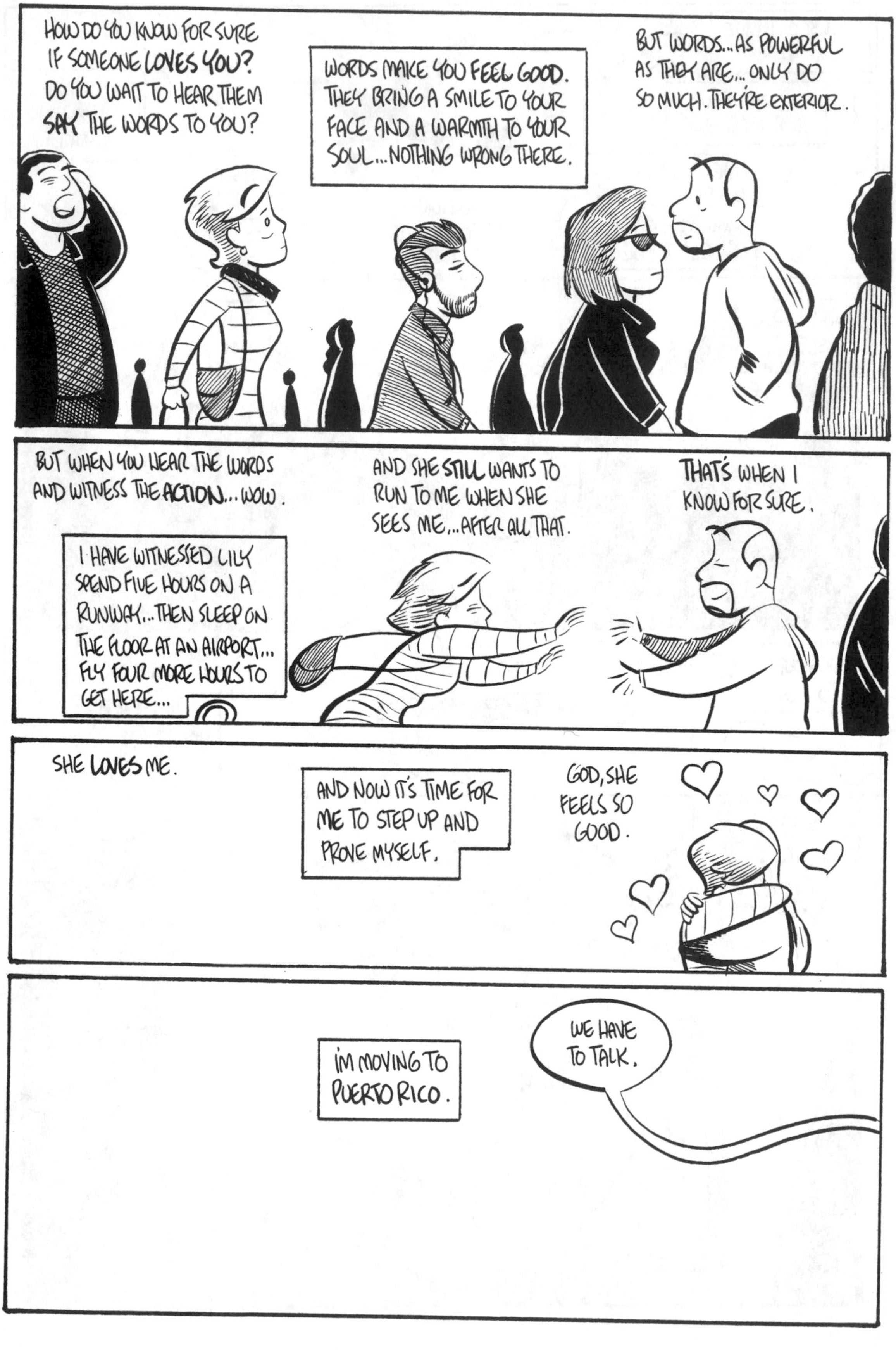
HOW DO YOU KNOW FOR SURE IF SOMEONE LOVES YOU? DO YOU WAIT TO HEAR THEM SAY THE WORDS TO YOU?
WORDS MAKE YOU FEEL GOOD. THEY BRING A SMILE TO YOUR FACE AND A WARMTH TO YOUR SOUL... NOTHING WRONG THERE.
BUT WORDS... AS POWERFUL AS THEY ARE... ONLY DO SO MUCH. THEY'RE EXTERIOR.
BUT WHEN YOU HEAR THE WORDS AND WITNESS THE ACTION... WOW.
I HAVE WITNESSED LILY SPEND FIVE HOURS ON A RUNWAY... THEN SLEEP ON THE FLOOR AT AN AIRPORT... FLY FOUR MORE HOURS TO GET HERE...
AND SHE STILL WANTS TO RUN TO ME WHEN SHE SEES ME... AFTER ALL THAT.
THAT'S WHEN I KNOW FOR SURE.
SHE LOVES ME.
AND NOW IT'S TIME FOR ME TO STEP UP AND PROVE MYSELF.
GOD, SHE FEELS SO GOOD.
I'M MOVING TO PUERTO RICO.
WE HAVE TO TALK.

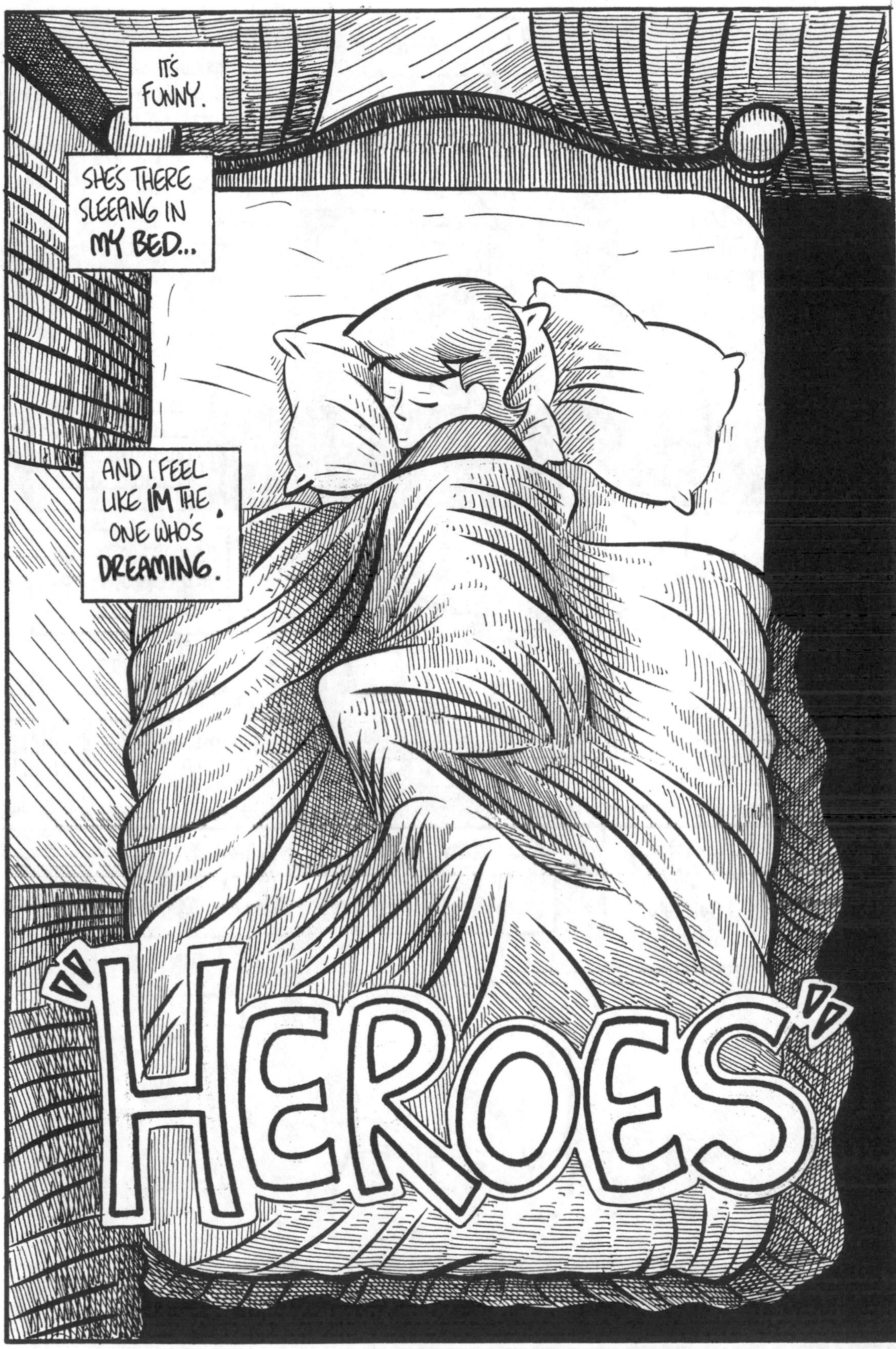
IT'S FUNNY.
SHE'S THERE SLEEPING IN MY BED...
AND I FEEL LIKE I'M THE ONE WHO'S DREAMING.
"HEROES"

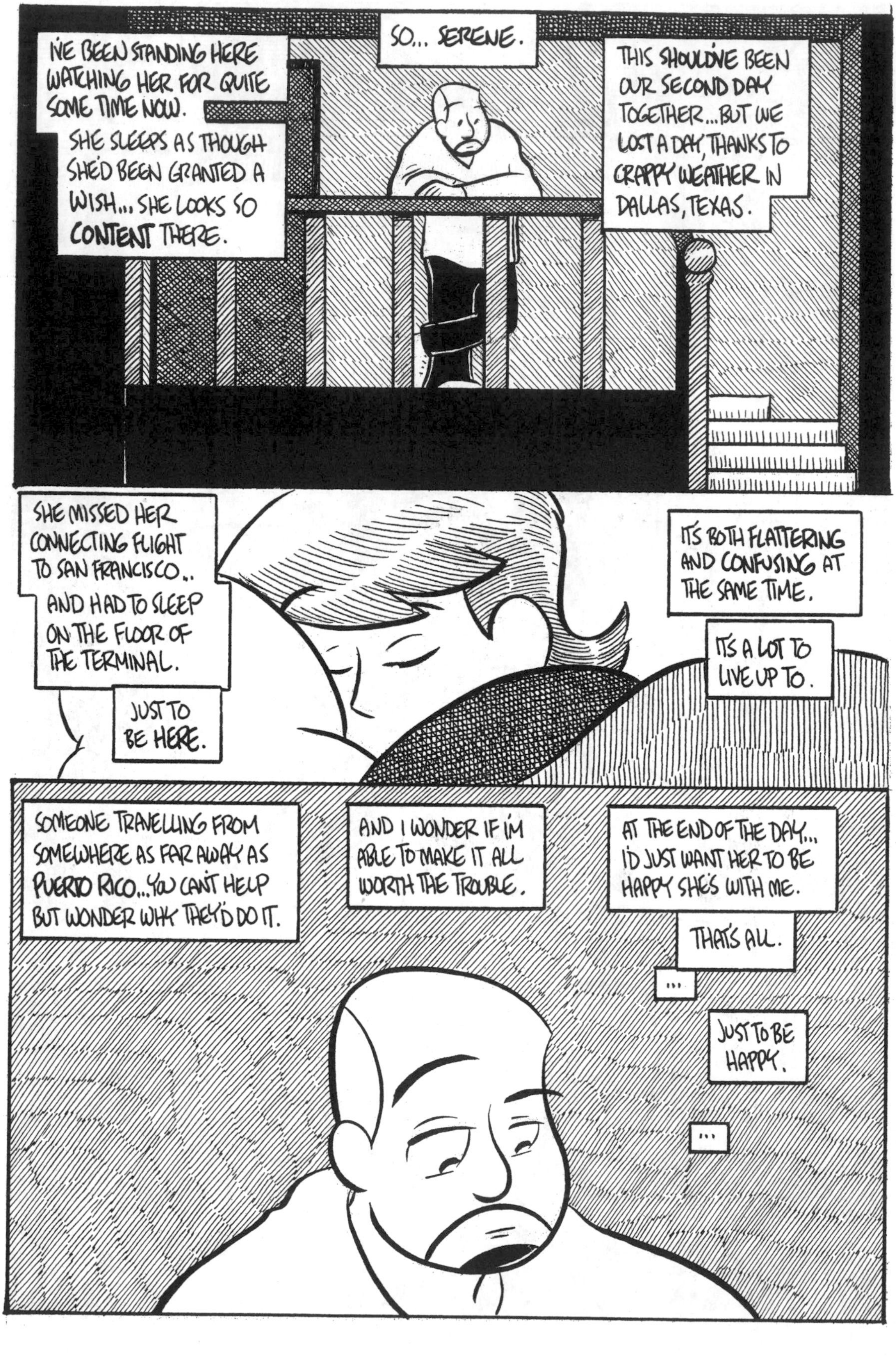

I'VE BEEN STANDING HERE WATCHING HER FOR QUITE SOME TIME NOW.
SHE SLEEPS AS THOUGH SHE'D BEEN GRANTED A WISH... SHE LOOKS SO CONTENT THERE.
SO... SERENE.
THIS SHOULD'VE BEEN OUR SECOND DAY TOGETHER... BUT WE LOST A DAY, THANKS TO CRAPPY WEATHER IN DALLAS, TEXAS.
SHE MISSED HER CONNECTING FLIGHT TO SAN FRANCISCO..
AND HAD TO SLEEP ON THE FLOOR OF THE TERMINAL.
JUST TO BE HERE.
IT'S BOTH FLATTERING AND CONFUSING AT THE SAME TIME.
IT'S A LOT TO LIVE UP TO.
SOMEONE TRAVELLING FROM SOMEWHERE AS FAR AWAY AS PUERTO RICO... YOU CAN'T HELP BUT WONDER WHY THEY'D DO IT.
AND I WONDER IF I'M ABLE TO MAKE IT ALL WORTH THE TROUBLE.
AT THE END OF THE DAY... I'D JUST WANT HER TO BE HAPPY SHE'S WITH ME.
THAT'S ALL.
...
JUST TO BE HAPPY.
...

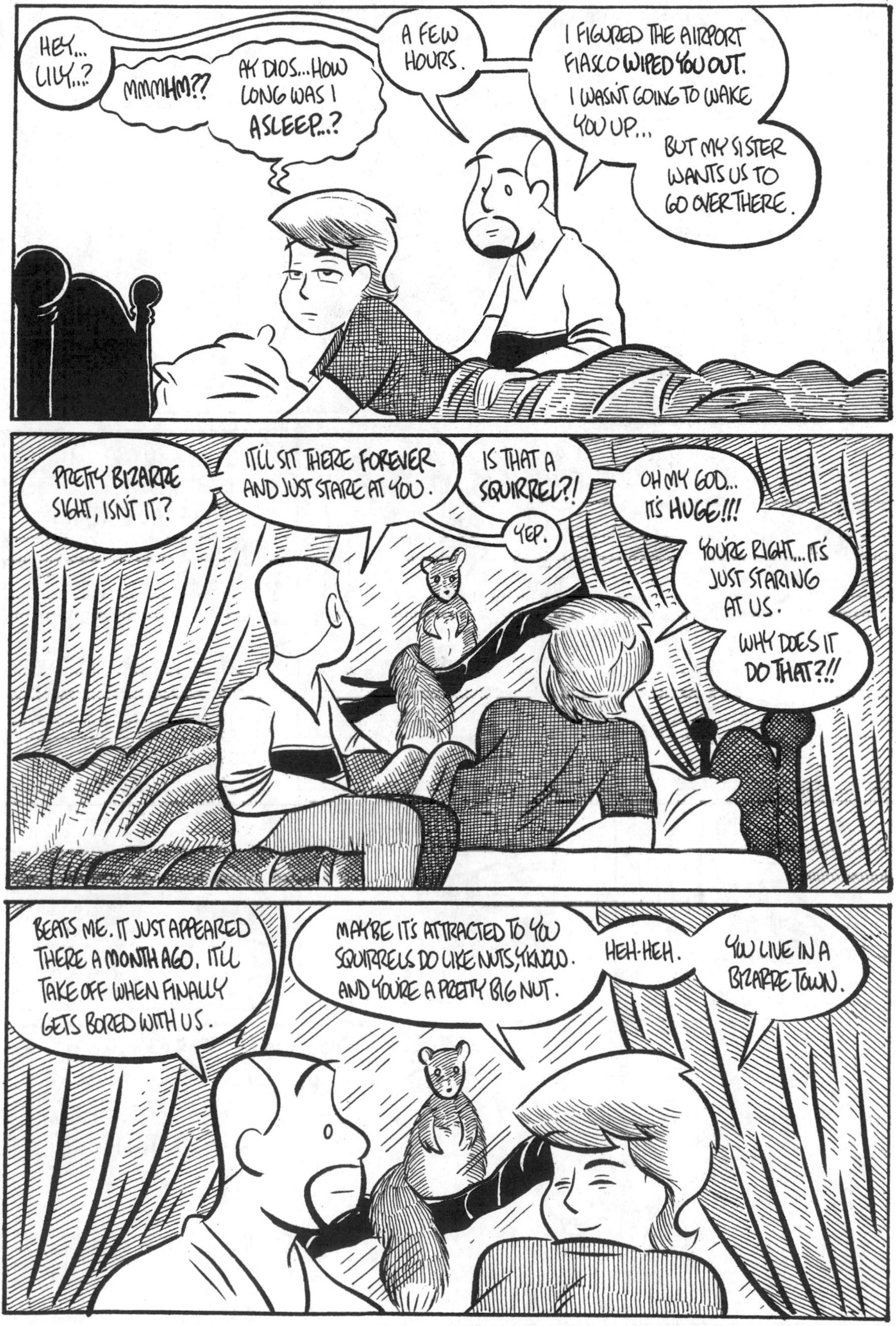
HEY... LILY...?
MMMHM??
AY DIOS...HOW LONG WAS I ASLEEP...?
A FEW HOURS.
I FIGURED THE AIRPORT FIASCO WIPED YOU OUT. I WASN'T GOING TO WAKE YOU UP...
BUT MY SISTER WANTS US TO GO OVER THERE.
PRETTY BIZARRE SIGHT, ISN'T IT?
IT'LL SIT THERE FOREVER AND JUST STARE AT YOU.
IS THAT A SQUIRREL?!
YEP.
OH MY GOD... IT'S HUGE!!!
YOU'RE RIGHT...IT'S JUST STARING AT US.
WHY DOES IT DO THAT?!!
BEATS ME. IT JUST APPEARED THERE A MONTH AGO. IT'LL TAKE OFF WHEN FINALLY GETS BORED WITH US.
MAYBE IT'S ATTRACTED TO YOU SQUIRRELS DO LIKE NUTS, Y'KNOW. AND YOU'RE A PRETTY BIG NUT.
HEH-HEH.
YOU LIVE IN A BIZARRE TOWN.

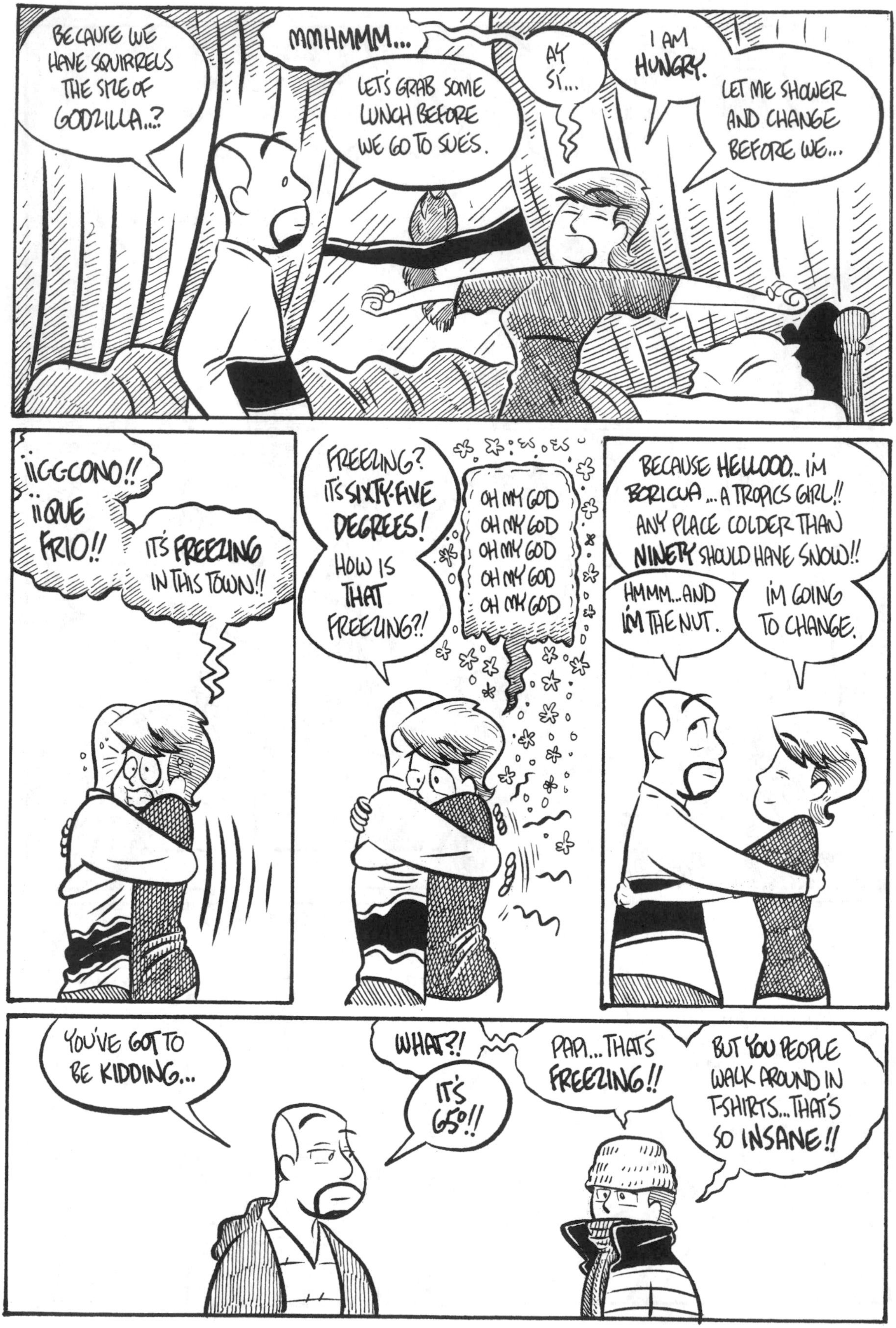

BECAUSE WE HAVE SQUIRRELS THE SIZE OF GODZILLA..?
MMHMMM...
LET'S GRAB SOME LUNCH BEFORE WE GO TO SUE'S.
AY SÍ...
I AM HUNGRY.
LET ME SHOWER AND CHANGE BEFORE WE...
¡¡C-C-CONO!! ¡¡QUE FRIO!!
IT'S FREEZING IN THIS TOWN!!
FREEZING? IT'S SIXTY-FIVE DEGREES! HOW IS THAT FREEZING?!
OH MY GOD OH MY GOD OH MY GOD OH MY GOD OH MY GOD
BECAUSE HELLOOO.. I'M BORICUA... A TROPICS GIRL!! ANY PLACE COLDER THAN NINETY SHOULD HAVE SNOW!!
HMMM...AND I'M THE NUT.
I'M GOING TO CHANGE.
YOU'VE GOT TO BE KIDDING...
WHAT?!
IT'S 65°!!
PAPI... THAT'S FREEZING!!
BUT YOU PEOPLE WALK AROUND IN T-SHIRTS... THAT'S SO INSANE!!

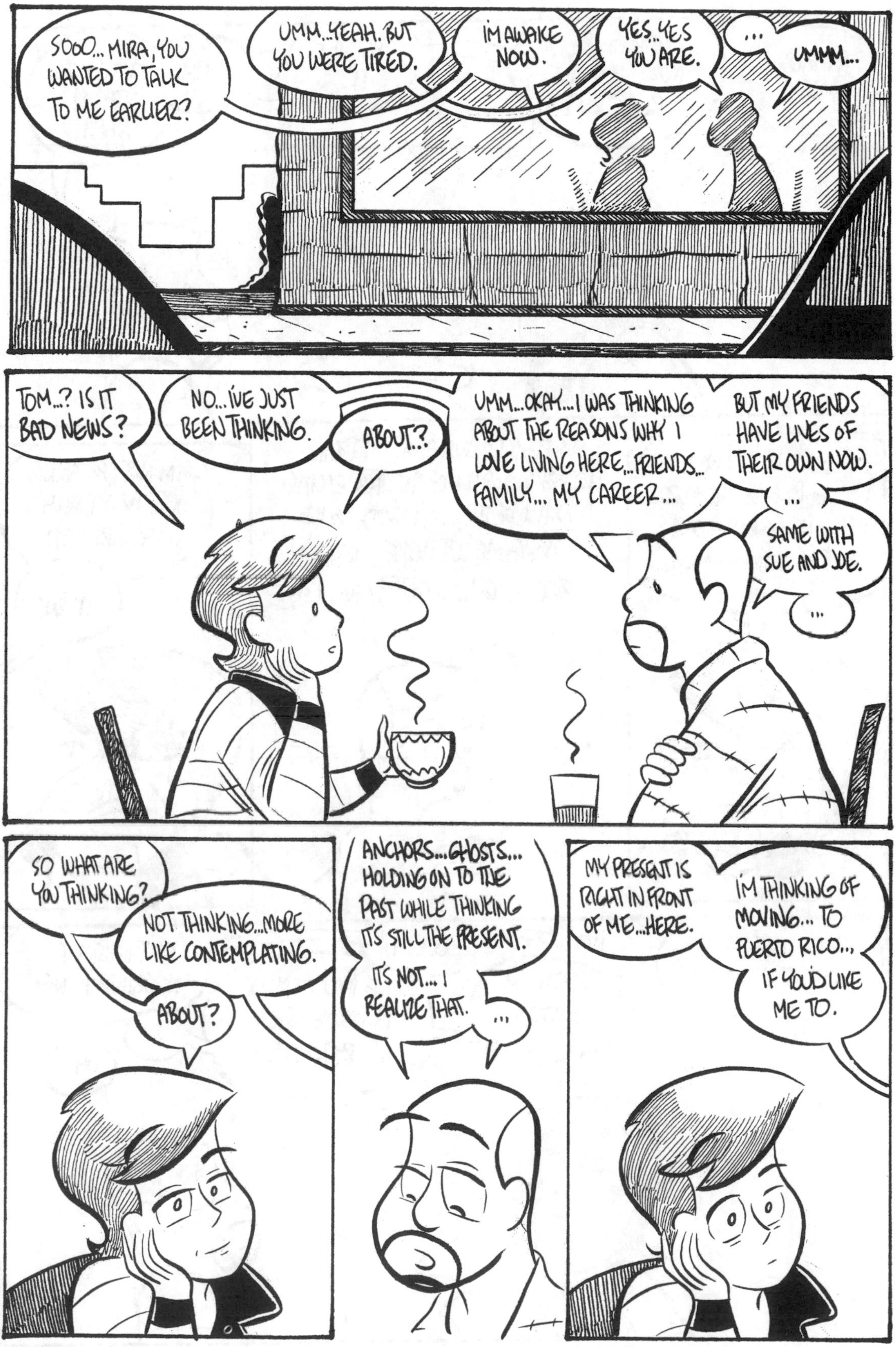
SOOO... MIRA, YOU WANTED TO TALK TO ME EARLIER?
UMM...YEAH. BUT YOU WERE TIRED.
I'M AWAKE NOW.
YES...YES YOU ARE.
...
UMMM...
TOM...? IS IT BAD NEWS?
NO...I'VE JUST BEEN THINKING.
ABOUT...?
UMM...OKAY...I WAS THINKING ABOUT THE REASONS WHY I LOVE LIVING HERE...FRIENDS... FAMILY... MY CAREER...
BUT MY FRIENDS HAVE LIVES OF THEIR OWN NOW.
...
SAME WITH SUE AND JOE.
...
SO WHAT ARE YOU THINKING?
NOT THINKING...MORE LIKE CONTEMPLATING.
ABOUT?
ANCHORS...GHOSTS... HOLDING ON TO THE PAST WHILE THINKING IT'S STILL THE PRESENT.
IT'S NOT... I REALIZE THAT.
...
MY PRESENT IS RIGHT IN FRONT OF ME...HERE.
I'M THINKING OF MOVING... TO PUERTO RICO...
IF YOU'D LIKE ME TO.

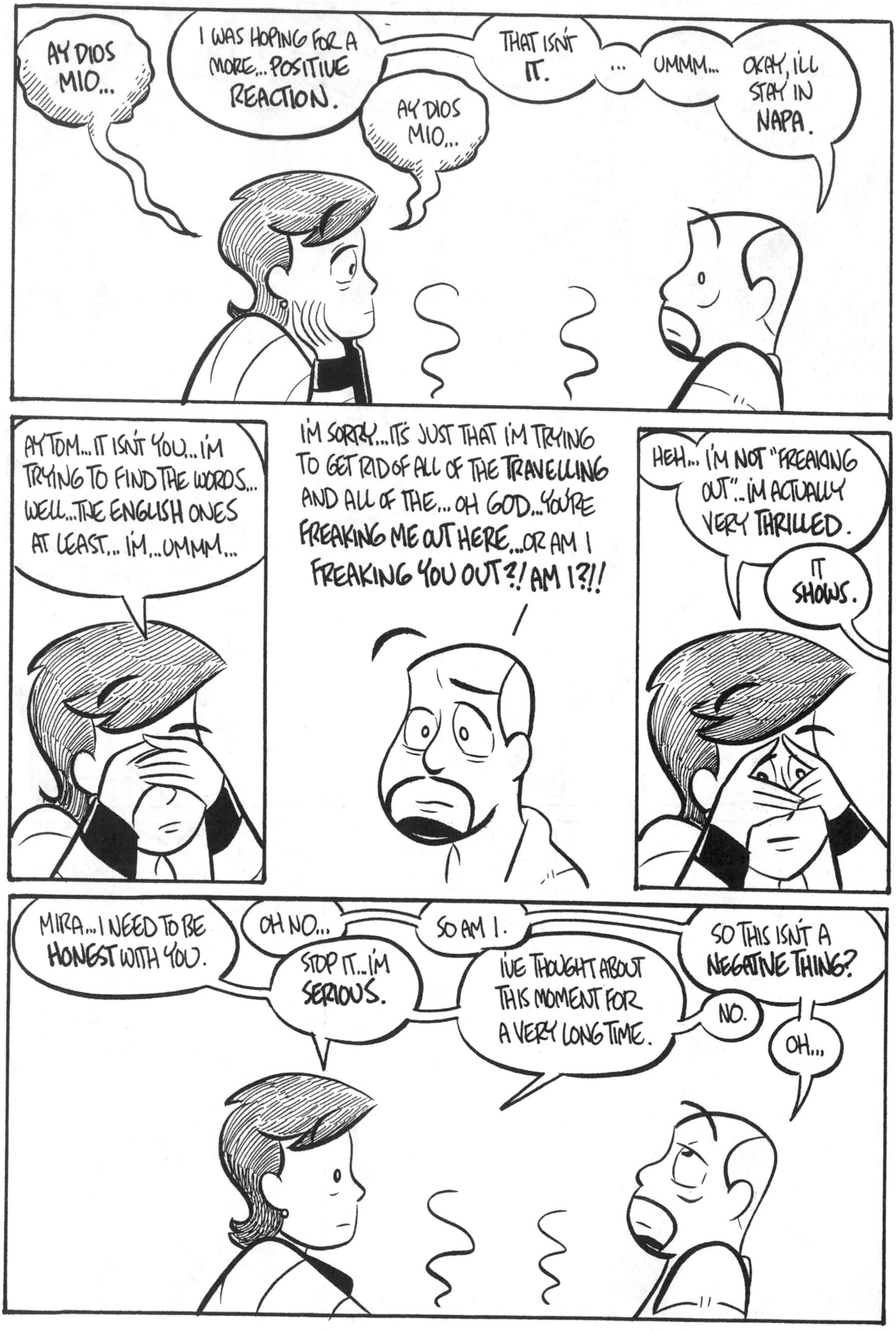
AY DIOS MIO...
I WAS HOPING FOR A MORE... POSITIVE REACTION.
AY DIOS MIO...
THAT ISN'T IT.
...
UMMM...
OKAY, I'LL STAY IN NAPA.
AY TOM... IT ISN'T YOU... I'M TRYING TO FIND THE WORDS... WELL... THE ENGLISH ONES AT LEAST... I'M... UMMM...
I'M SORRY... IT'S JUST THAT I'M TRYING TO GET RID OF ALL OF THE TRAVELLING AND ALL OF THE... OH GOD... YOU'RE FREAKING ME OUT HERE... OR AM I FREAKING YOU OUT?! AM I?!!
HEH... I'M NOT "FREAKING OUT"... I'M ACTUALLY VERY THRILLED.
IT SHOWS.
MIRA... I NEED TO BE HONEST WITH YOU.
OH NO...
STOP IT... I'M SERIOUS.
SO AM I.
I'VE THOUGHT ABOUT THIS MOMENT FOR A VERY LONG TIME.
SO THIS ISN'T A NEGATIVE THING?
NO.
OH...

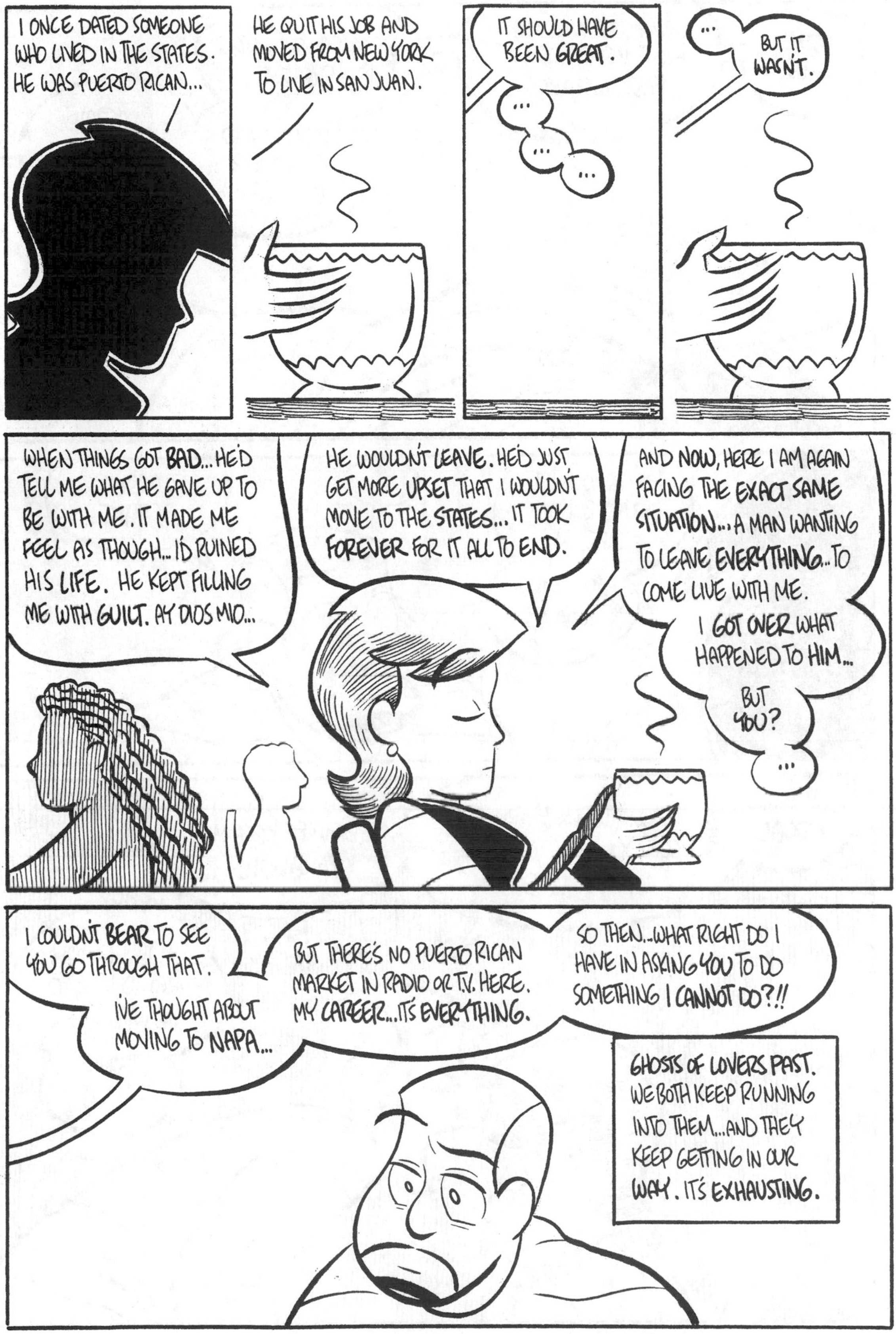
I ONCE DATED SOMEONE WHO LIVED IN THE STATES. HE WAS PUERTO RICAN...
HE QUIT HIS JOB AND MOVED FROM NEW YORK TO LIVE IN SAN JUAN.
IT SHOULD HAVE BEEN GREAT.
...
...
...
...
BUT IT WASN'T.
WHEN THINGS GOT BAD... HE'D TELL ME WHAT HE GAVE UP TO BE WITH ME. IT MADE ME FEEL AS THOUGH... I'D RUINED HIS LIFE. HE KEPT FILLING ME WITH GUILT. AY DIOS MIO...
HE WOULDN'T LEAVE. HE'D JUST GET MORE UPSET THAT I WOULDN'T MOVE TO THE STATES... IT TOOK FOREVER FOR IT ALL TO END.
AND NOW, HERE I AM AGAIN FACING THE EXACT SAME SITUATION... A MAN WANTING TO LEAVE EVERYTHING... TO COME LIVE WITH ME.
I GOT OVER WHAT HAPPENED TO HIM...
BUT YOU?
...
I COULDN'T BEAR TO SEE YOU GO THROUGH THAT.
I'VE THOUGHT ABOUT MOVING TO NAPA...
BUT THERE'S NO PUERTO RICAN MARKET IN RADIO OR T.V. HERE. MY CAREER... IT'S EVERYTHING.
SO THEN... WHAT RIGHT DO I HAVE IN ASKING YOU TO DO SOMETHING I CANNOT DO?!!
GHOSTS OF LOVERS PAST. WE BOTH KEEP RUNNING INTO THEM... AND THEY KEEP GETTING IN OUR WAY. IT'S EXHAUSTING.

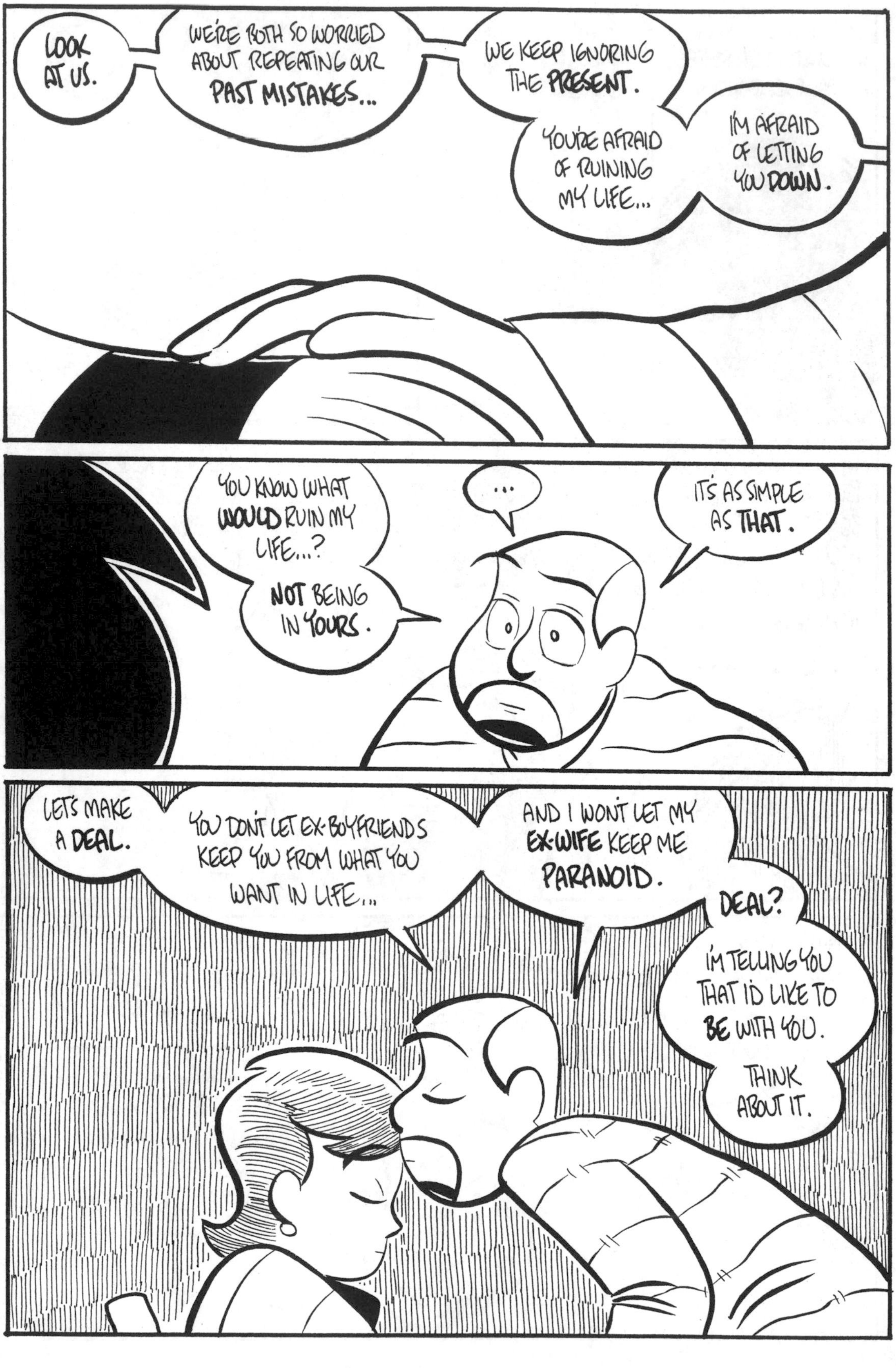
LOOK AT US.
WE'RE BOTH SO WORRIED ABOUT REPEATING OUR PAST MISTAKES...
WE KEEP IGNORING THE PRESENT.
YOU'RE AFRAID OF RUINING MY LIFE...
I'M AFRAID OF LETTING YOU DOWN.
YOU KNOW WHAT WOULD RUIN MY LIFE...?
NOT BEING IN YOURS.
...
IT'S AS SIMPLE AS THAT.
LET'S MAKE A DEAL.
YOU DON'T LET EX-BOYFRIENDS KEEP YOU FROM WHAT YOU WANT IN LIFE...
AND I WON'T LET MY EX-WIFE KEEP ME PARANOID.
DEAL?
I'M TELLING YOU THAT I'D LIKE TO BE WITH YOU.
THINK ABOUT IT.

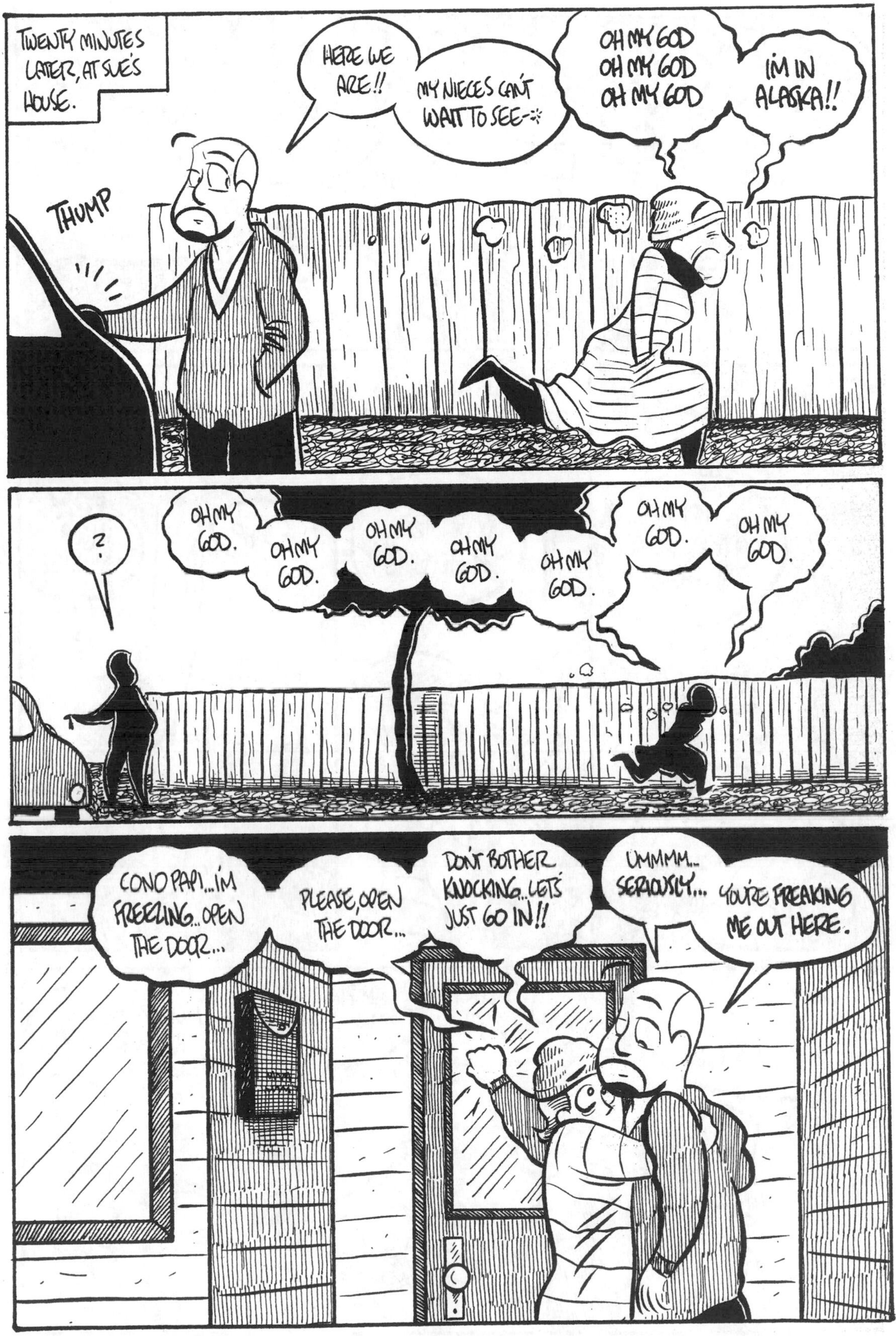
TWENTY MINUTES LATER, AT SUE'S HOUSE.
HERE WE ARE!!
MY NIECES CAN'T WAIT TO SEE-
OH MY GOD OH MY GOD OH MY GOD
I'M IN ALASKA!!
THUMP
?
OH MY GOD.
OH MY GOD.
OH MY GOD.
OH MY GOD.
OH MY GOD.
OH MY GOD.
OH MY GOD.
COÑO PAPI... I'M FREEZING... OPEN THE DOOR...
PLEASE, OPEN THE DOOR...
DON'T BOTHER KNOCKING... LET'S JUST GO IN!!
UMMMM... SERIOUSLY...
YOU'RE FREAKING ME OUT HERE.

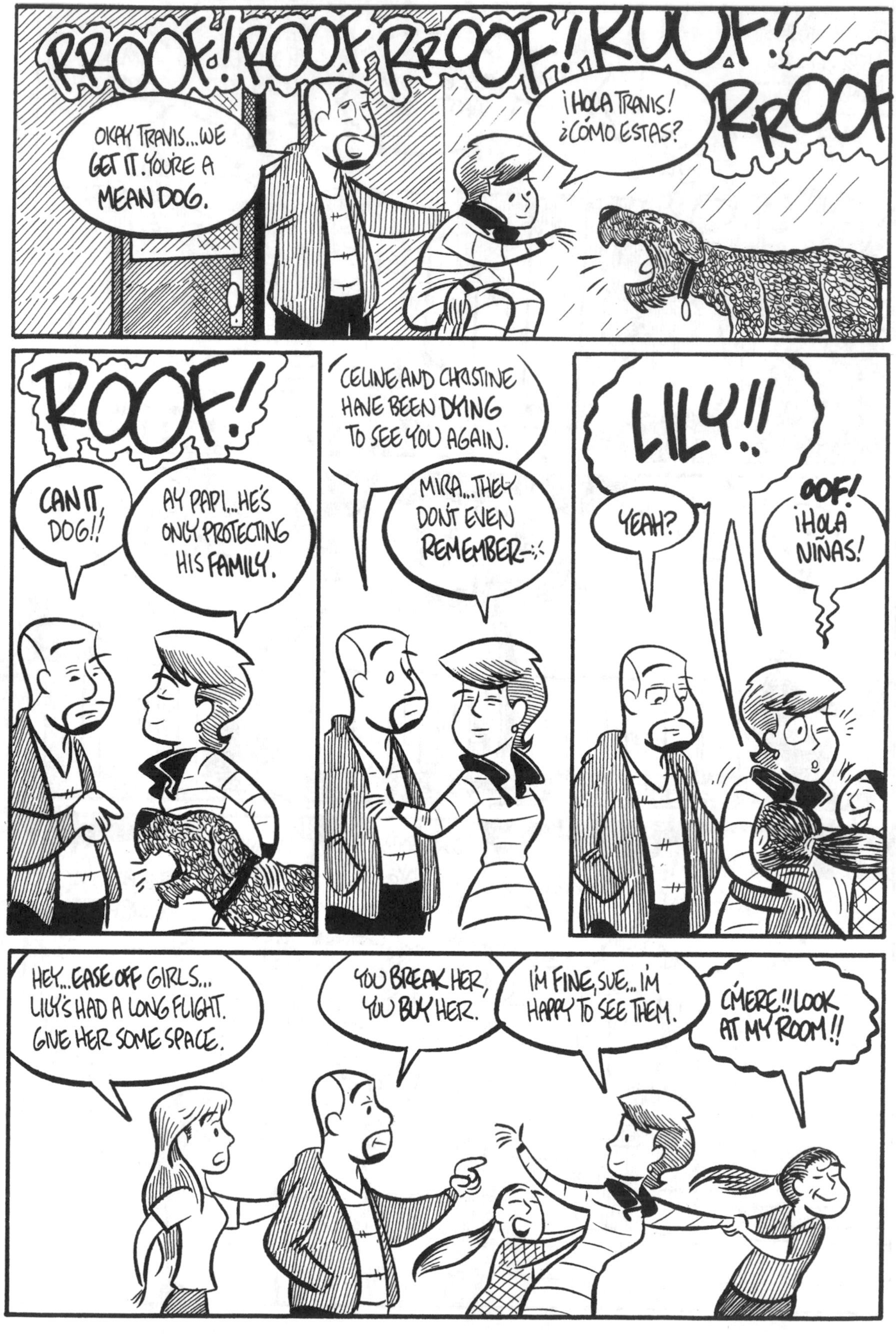
RROOF! ROOF! RROOF! ROOF!
OKAY TRAVIS... WE GET IT. YOU'RE A MEAN DOG.
¡HOLA TRAVIS! ¿CÓMO ESTAS?
RROOF
ROOF!
CAN IT, DOG!!
AY PAPI... HE'S ONLY PROTECTING HIS FAMILY.
CELINE AND CHRISTINE HAVE BEEN DYING TO SEE YOU AGAIN.
MIRA... THEY DON'T EVEN REMEMBER—
LILY!!
YEAH?
OOF! ¡HOLA NIÑAS!
HEY... EASE OFF GIRLS... LILY'S HAD A LONG FLIGHT. GIVE HER SOME SPACE.
YOU BREAK HER, YOU BUY HER.
I'M FINE, SUE... I'M HAPPY TO SEE THEM.
C'MERE!! LOOK AT MY ROOM!!

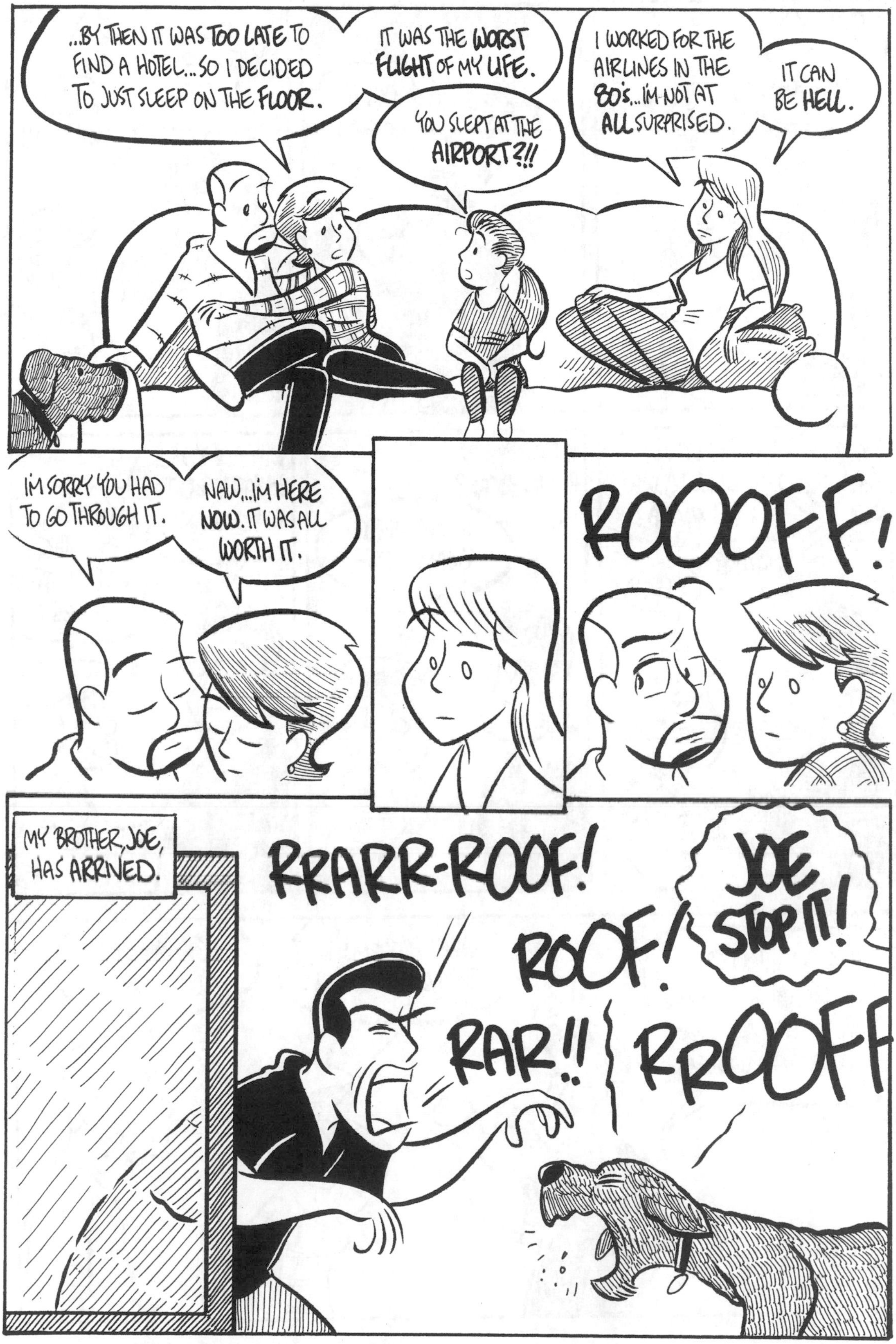

...BY THEN IT WAS TOO LATE TO FIND A HOTEL...SO I DECIDED TO JUST SLEEP ON THE FLOOR.
IT WAS THE WORST FLIGHT OF MY LIFE.
YOU SLEPT AT THE AIRPORT?!!
I WORKED FOR THE AIRLINES IN THE 80's...I'M NOT AT ALL SURPRISED.
IT CAN BE HELL.
I'M SORRY YOU HAD TO GO THROUGH IT.
NAW...I'M HERE NOW. IT WAS ALL WORTH IT.
ROOOFF!
MY BROTHER, JOE, HAS ARRIVED.
RRARR-ROOF!
ROOF!
JOE STOP IT!
RAR!!
RROOFF

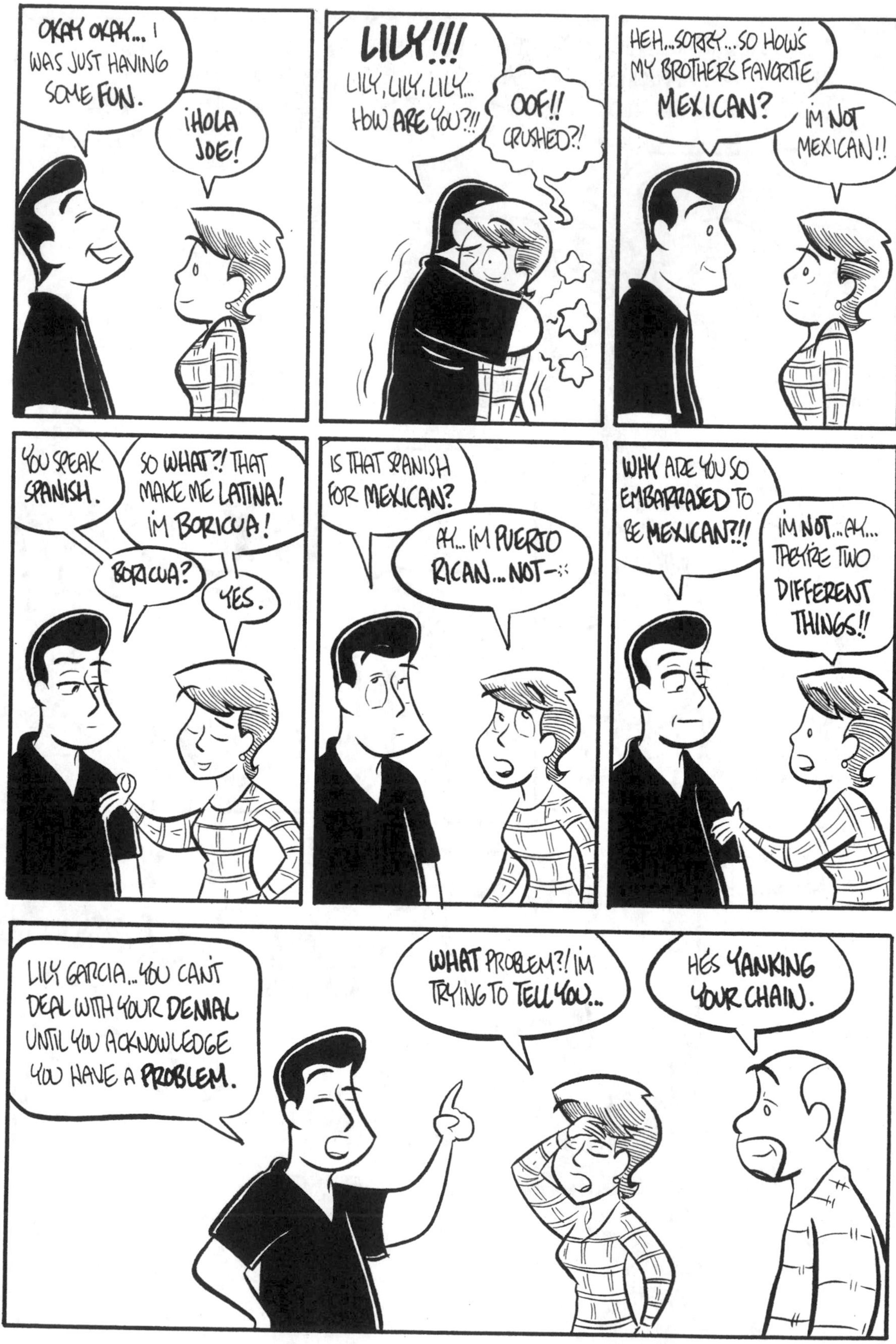
OKAY OKAY... I WAS JUST HAVING SOME FUN.
¡HOLA JOE!
LILY!!!
LILY, LILY, LILY... HOW ARE YOU?!!
OOF!! CRUSHED?!
HEH...SORRY...SO HOW'S MY BROTHER'S FAVORITE MEXICAN?
I'M NOT MEXICAN!!
YOU SPEAK SPANISH.
SO WHAT?! THAT MAKE ME LATINA! I'M BORICUA!
BORICUA?
YES.
IS THAT SPANISH FOR MEXICAN?
AY... I'M PUERTO RICAN...NOT-
WHY ARE YOU SO EMBARRASED TO BE MEXICAN?!!
I'M NOT...AY... THEY'RE TWO DIFFERENT THINGS!!
LILY GARCIA...YOU CAN'T DEAL WITH YOUR DENIAL UNTIL YOU ACKNOWLEDGE YOU HAVE A PROBLEM.
WHAT PROBLEM?! I'M TRYING TO TELL YOU...
HE'S YANKING YOUR CHAIN.

THE DAY HAS GONE BY FAR TOO QUICKLY.

SHE FELL ASLEEP ABOUT AN HOUR AGO. WE DIDN'T HAVE SEX. I COULDN'T... PERFORM.

NOT TOO LONG AGO, IT WOULD TAKE, WELL, NOTHING FOR ME TO HAVE SEX. SOME MUSIC... A PRETTY WOMAN... AND PRESTO. NOW LOOK AT ME.

I HAVE THE GREATEST SEXIEST WOMAN I'VE KNOWN NEXT TO ME... AND NOTHING WORKED.

IT DOESN'T SEEM TO HAVE BOTHERED HER AS SHE HOLDS MY HAND AND SLEEPS WITH HER BODY UP AGAINST MINE.

IT BOTHERS ME, THOUGH. I CAN'T SLEEP. I JUST... LIE HERE... AND TRY TO UNDERSTAND WHY THIS HAS HAPPENED TO ME. MENTALLY, I'VE HAD SEX WITH LILY SIX TIMES... BUT MY BODY... MY BODY HAS SOMEHOW... DISCONNECTED.

I KEEP WONDERING... WHAT IF THIS IS A PERMANENT PROBLEM? I'VE HAD A SEX DRIVE FOR AS LONG AS I CAN REMEMBER. IT WAS AS NATURAL TO ME AS BREATHING.

AND NOW... JESUS.

I MISS IT. I MISS... I... HELL, IT'S IMPOSSIBLE TO PUT INTO WORDS. I JUST MISS THE ABILITY TO PHYSICALLY EXPRESS MY FEELINGS TO THIS AMAZING SEXY WOMAN.
...
I KNOW I'M NOT THE ONLY MAN WITH THIS PROBLEM... BUT I CAN'T HELP FEELING I AM. I DON'T KNOW WHO I COULD TALK TO ABOUT THIS... A SHRINK?
...
"SHRINK" IS THE LAST WORD I WANT TO HEAR.
...
AT LEAST I HAVE HUMOR.
...
I HOPE I CAN FIX THIS.
...
I JUST WANT TO MAKE LOVE TO HER.

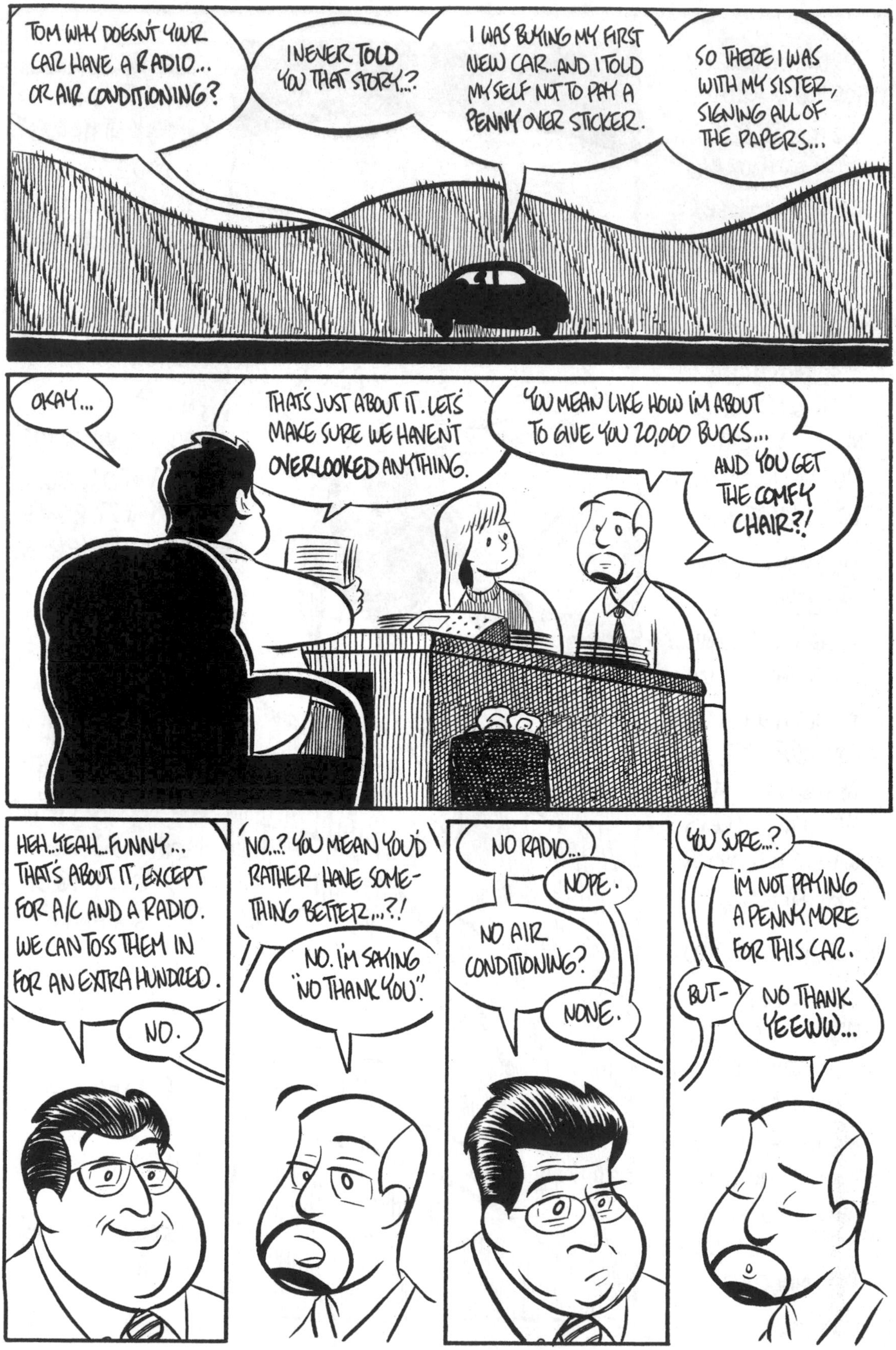
TOM WHY DOESN'T YOUR CAR HAVE A RADIO... OR AIR CONDITIONING?
I NEVER TOLD YOU THAT STORY..?
I WAS BUYING MY FIRST NEW CAR...AND I TOLD MYSELF NOT TO PAY A PENNY OVER STICKER.
SO THERE I WAS WITH MY SISTER, SIGNING ALL OF THE PAPERS...
OKAY...
THAT'S JUST ABOUT IT. LET'S MAKE SURE WE HAVEN'T OVERLOOKED ANYTHING.
YOU MEAN LIKE HOW I'M ABOUT TO GIVE YOU 20,000 BUCKS...
AND YOU GET THE COMFY CHAIR?!
HEH...YEAH...FUNNY... THAT'S ABOUT IT, EXCEPT FOR A/C AND A RADIO. WE CAN TOSS THEM IN FOR AN EXTRA HUNDRED.
NO.
NO..? YOU MEAN YOU'D RATHER HAVE SOME-THING BETTER...?!
NO. I'M SAYING "NO THANK YOU".
NO RADIO...
NOPE.
NO AIR CONDITIONING?
NONE.
YOU SURE...?
I'M NOT PAYING A PENNY MORE FOR THIS CAR.
BUT-
NO THANK YEEWW...

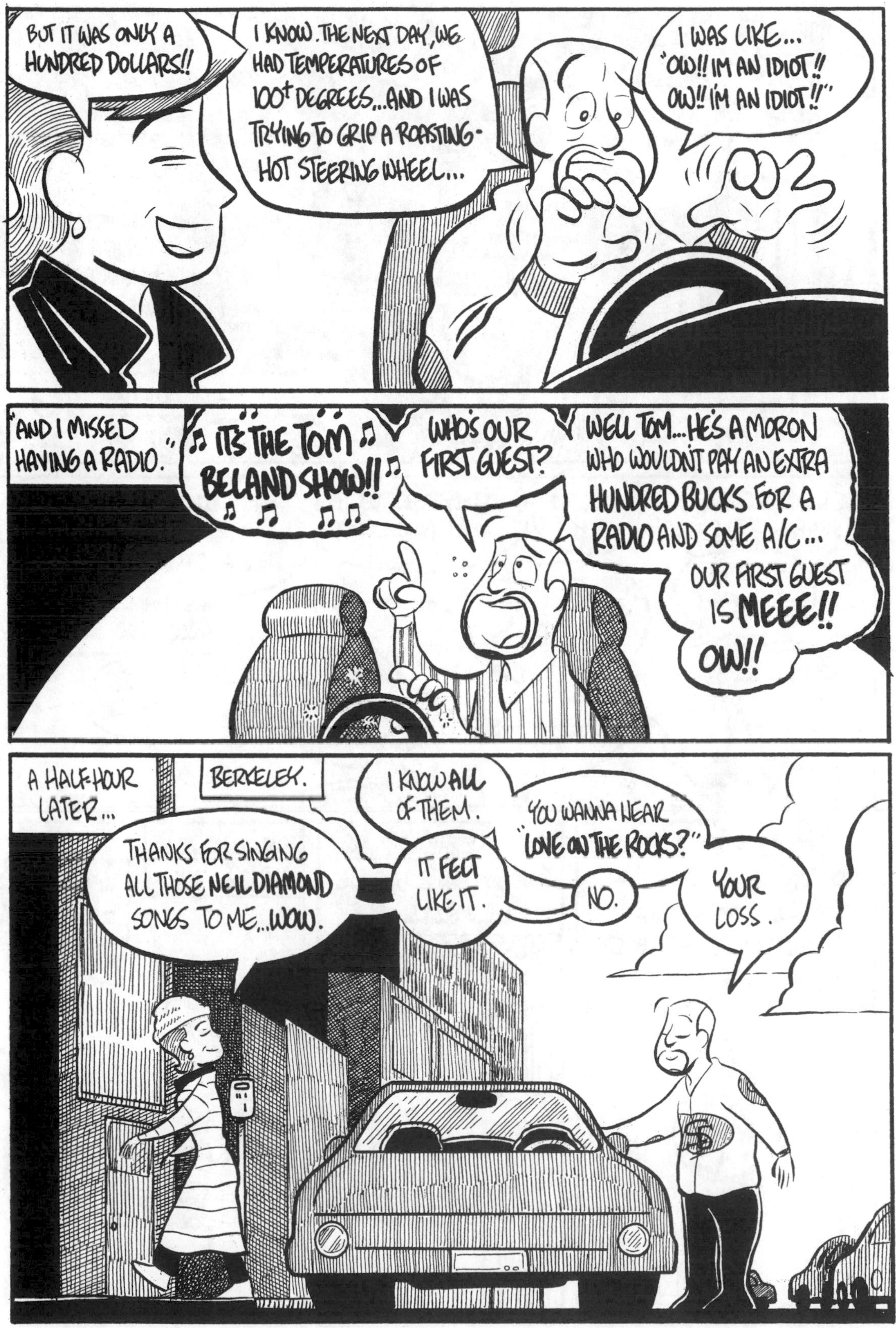
BUT IT WAS ONLY A HUNDRED DOLLARS!!
I KNOW. THE NEXT DAY, WE HAD TEMPERATURES OF 100+ DEGREES... AND I WAS TRYING TO GRIP A ROASTING-HOT STEERING WHEEL...
I WAS LIKE... "OW!! I'M AN IDIOT!! OW!! I'M AN IDIOT!!"
"AND I MISSED HAVING A RADIO."
IT'S THE TOM BELAND SHOW!!
WHO'S OUR FIRST GUEST?
WELL TOM... HE'S A MORON WHO WOULDN'T PAY AN EXTRA HUNDRED BUCKS FOR A RADIO AND SOME A/C... OUR FIRST GUEST IS MEEE!! OW!!
A HALF-HOUR LATER...
BERKELEY.
THANKS FOR SINGING ALL THOSE NEIL DIAMOND SONGS TO ME... WOW.
IT FELT LIKE IT.
I KNOW ALL OF THEM.
YOU WANNA HEAR "LOVE ON THE ROCKS?"
NO.
YOUR LOSS.

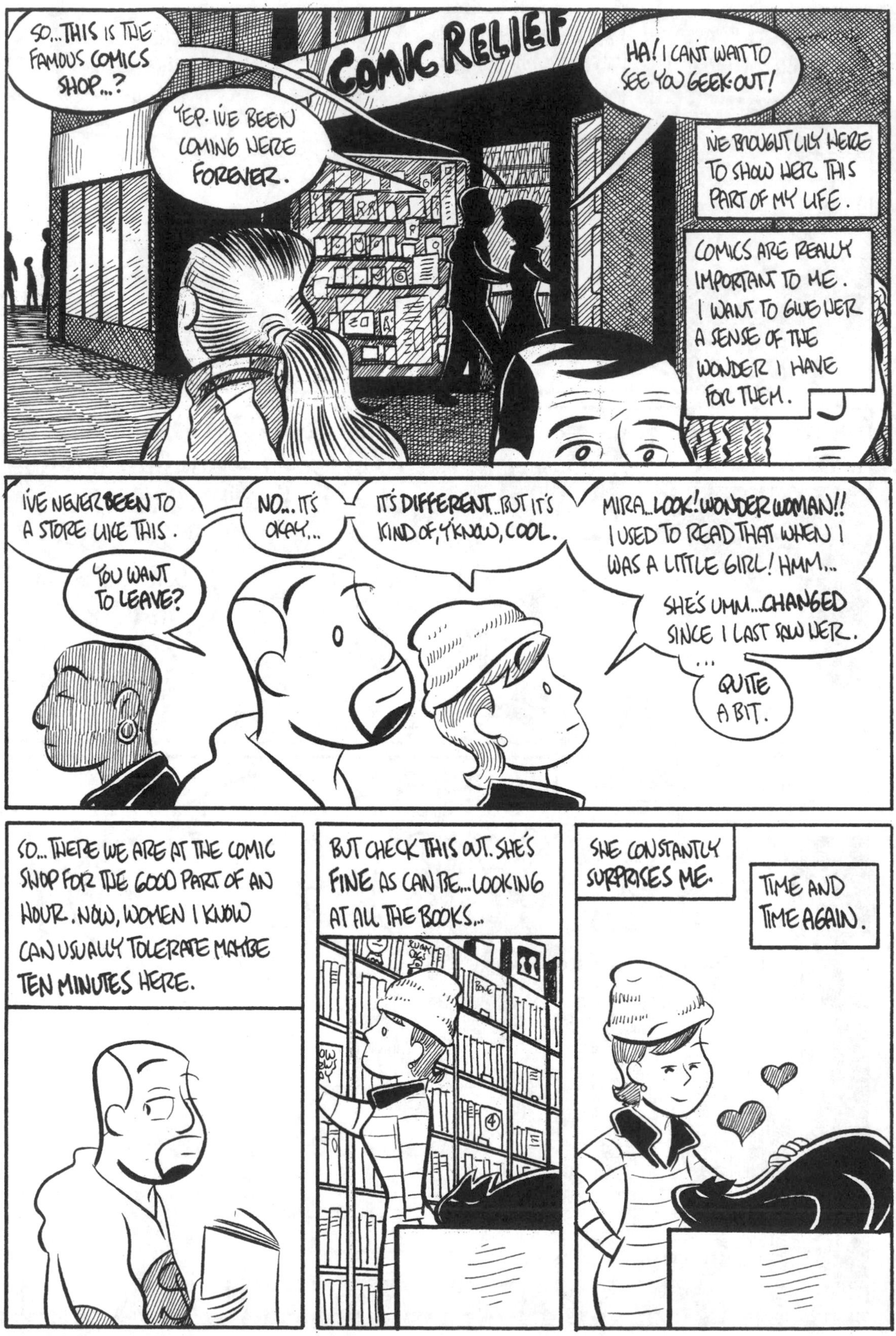

SO... THIS IS THE FAMOUS COMICS SHOP...?
COMIC RELIEF
YEP. I'VE BEEN COMING HERE FOREVER.
HA! I CAN'T WAIT TO SEE YOU GEEK-OUT!
I'VE BROUGHT LILY HERE TO SHOW HER THIS PART OF MY LIFE.
COMICS ARE REALLY IMPORTANT TO ME. I WANT TO GIVE HER A SENSE OF THE WONDER I HAVE FOR THEM.
I'VE NEVER BEEN TO A STORE LIKE THIS.
YOU WANT TO LEAVE?
NO... IT'S OKAY...
IT'S DIFFERENT... BUT IT'S KIND OF, Y'KNOW, COOL.
MIRA... LOOK! WONDER WOMAN!! I USED TO READ THAT WHEN I WAS A LITTLE GIRL! HMM...
SHE'S UMM... CHANGED SINCE I LAST SAW HER.
...
QUITE A BIT.
SO... THERE WE ARE AT THE COMIC SHOP FOR THE GOOD PART OF AN HOUR. NOW, WOMEN I KNOW CAN USUALLY TOLERATE MAYBE TEN MINUTES HERE.
BUT CHECK THIS OUT. SHE'S FINE AS CAN BE... LOOKING AT ALL THE BOOKS...
SHE CONSTANTLY SURPRISES ME.
TIME AND TIME AGAIN.

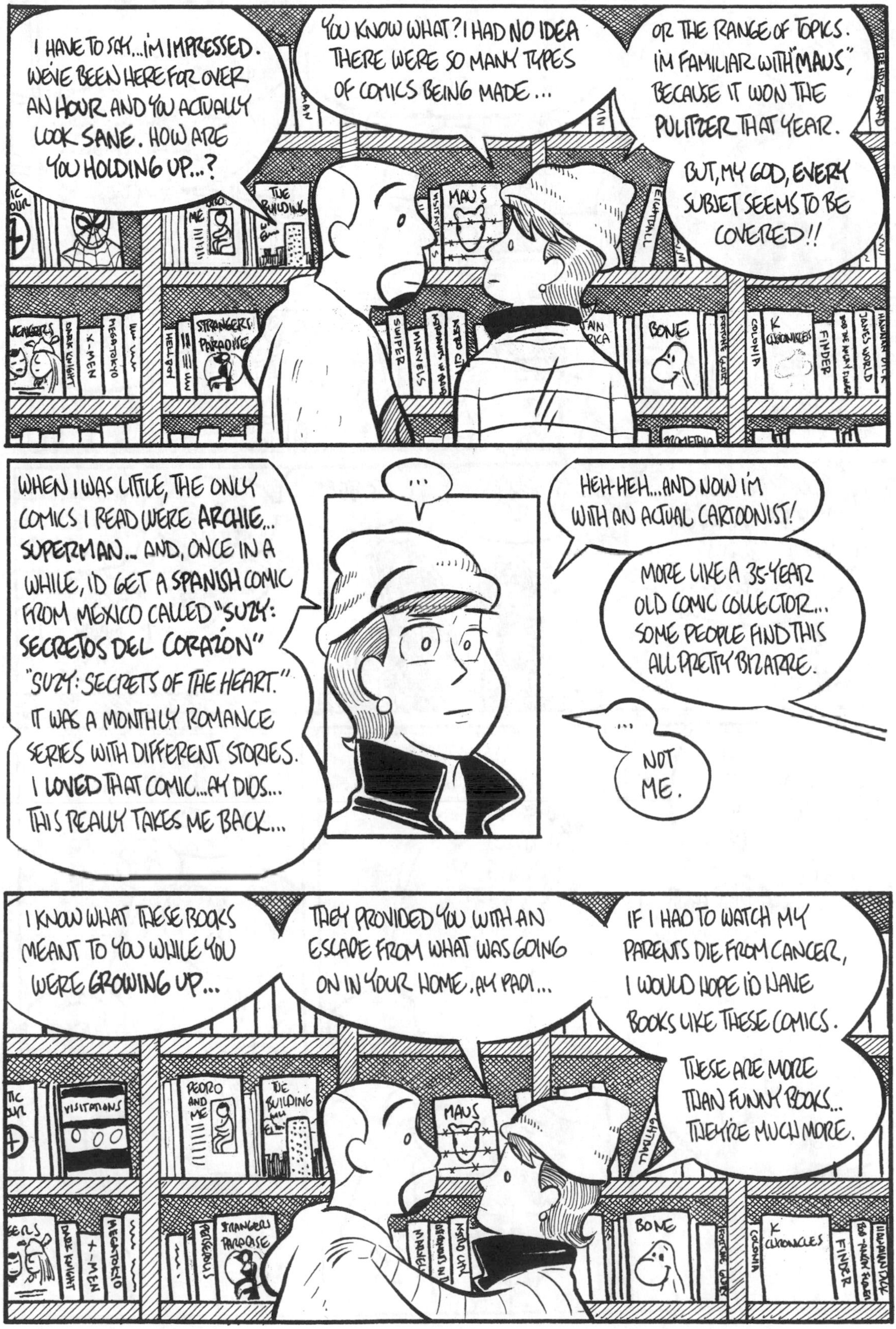
I HAVE TO SAY...I'M IMPRESSED. WE'VE BEEN HERE FOR OVER AN HOUR AND YOU ACTUALLY LOOK SANE. HOW ARE YOU HOLDING UP...?
YOU KNOW WHAT? I HAD NO IDEA THERE WERE SO MANY TYPES OF COMICS BEING MADE...
OR THE RANGE OF TOPICS. I'M FAMILIAR WITH "MAUS," BECAUSE IT WON THE PULITZER THAT YEAR.
BUT, MY GOD, EVERY SUBJET SEEMS TO BE COVERED!!
WHEN I WAS LITTLE, THE ONLY COMICS I READ WERE ARCHIE... SUPERMAN... AND, ONCE IN A WHILE, I'D GET A SPANISH COMIC FROM MEXICO CALLED "SUZY: SECRETOS DEL CORAZÓN" "SUZY: SECRETS OF THE HEART." IT WAS A MONTHLY ROMANCE SERIES WITH DIFFERENT STORIES. I LOVED THAT COMIC...AY DIOS... THIS REALLY TAKES ME BACK...
...
HEH-HEH...AND NOW I'M WITH AN ACTUAL CARTOONIST!
MORE LIKE A 35-YEAR OLD COMIC COLLECTOR... SOME PEOPLE FIND THIS ALL PRETTY BIZARRE.
... NOT ME.
I KNOW WHAT THESE BOOKS MEANT TO YOU WHILE YOU WERE GROWING UP...
THEY PROVIDED YOU WITH AN ESCAPE FROM WHAT WAS GOING ON IN YOUR HOME, AY PAPI...
IF I HAD TO WATCH MY PARENTS DIE FROM CANCER, I WOULD HOPE I'D HAVE BOOKS LIKE THESE COMICS.
THESE ARE MORE THAN FUNNY BOOKS... THEY'RE MUCH MORE.

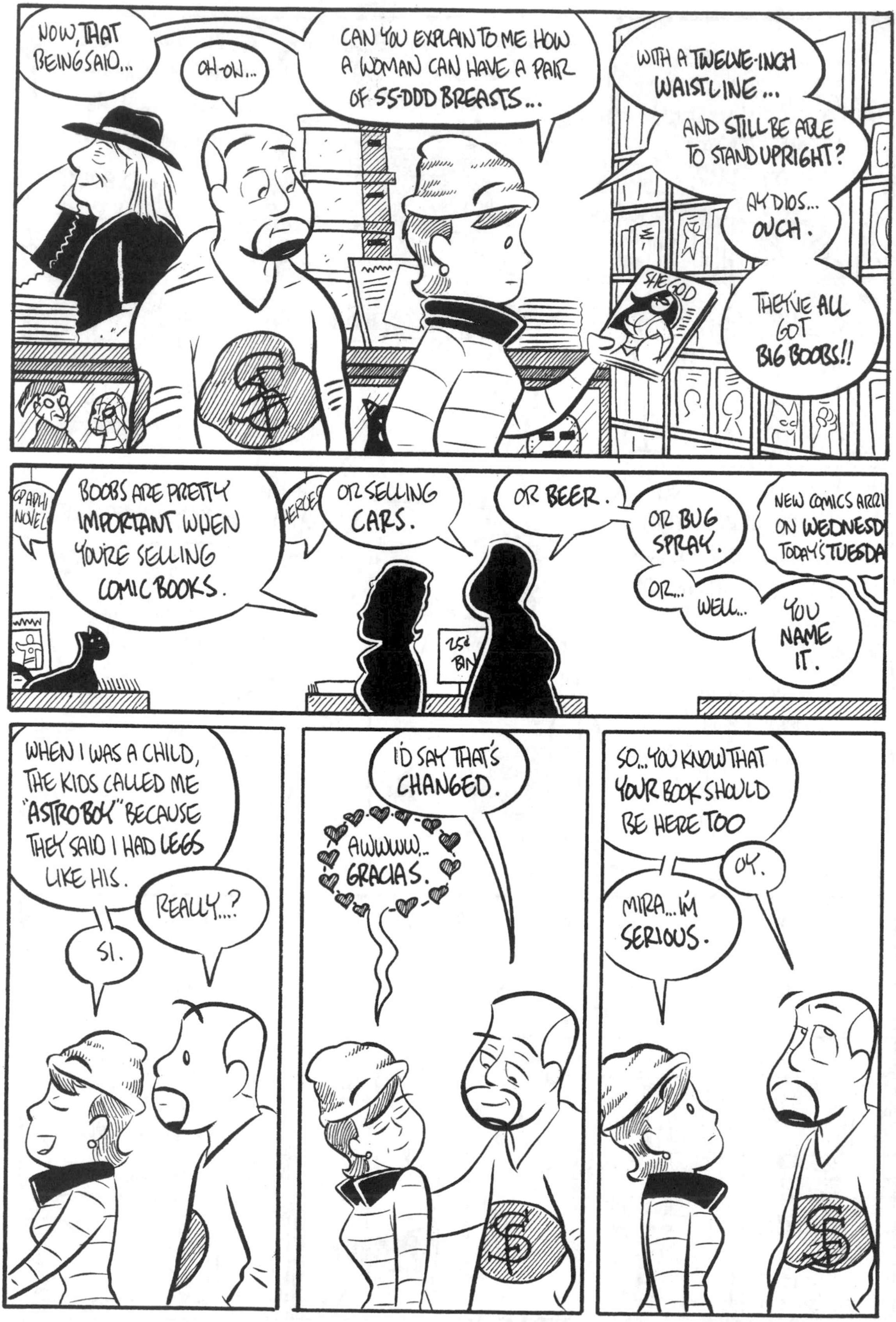
NOW, THAT BEING SAID...
OH-OH...
CAN YOU EXPLAIN TO ME HOW A WOMAN CAN HAVE A PAIR OF 55-DDD BREASTS...
WITH A TWELVE-INCH WAISTLINE...
AND STILL BE ABLE TO STAND UPRIGHT?
AY DIOS... OUCH.
THEY'VE ALL GOT BIG BOOBS!!
SHE GOD
BOOBS ARE PRETTY IMPORTANT WHEN YOU'RE SELLING COMIC BOOKS.
OR SELLING CARS.
OR BEER.
OR BUG SPRAY.
OR...
WELL...
YOU NAME IT.
NEW COMICS ARRI
ON WEDNESD
TODAY'S TUESDA
WHEN I WAS A CHILD, THE KIDS CALLED ME "ASTRO BOY" BECAUSE THEY SAID I HAD LEGS LIKE HIS.
REALLY...?
SI.
I'D SAY THAT'S CHANGED.
AWWWW... GRACIAS.
SO... YOU KNOW THAT YOUR BOOK SHOULD BE HERE TOO
OY.
MIRA... I'M SERIOUS.

HEY, LET'S GET SOME LUNCH. THERE'S A MONGOLIAN BBQ DOWN THE STREET.
TOM... WHY DO YOU CHANGE THE SUBJECT WHEN I TALK ABOUT YOU PRINTING A BOOK OF YOUR OWN?
...
...
SIGH...
I HAVE NO IDEA.
WOULD YOU LIKE TO DO THAT SOME DAY...?
SURE. I'VE DREAMT OF IT.
WELL, LIFE IS ABOUT TAKING CHANCES. IF YOU NEVER TOOK A CHANCE OF SAYING "HELLO" AT THAT BUS STOP... I WOULDN'T BE HERE. SOMETIMES YOU JUST HAVE TO... DO IT.
IT'S THE SAME HERE. COMICS ARE WAITING FOR YOU, TOM... YOU'RE READY. WHY DON'T YOU TAKE A CHANCE AND TRY IT.
YOU HAVE TO ADMIT... IT WOULD BE SO COOL TO WALK IN HERE AND SEE A BOOK YOU'VE PUBLISHED RIGHT NEXT TO SPIDER-MAN!!!
OKAY... YES IT WOULD BE PRETTY AMAZING.
YAY!! I THOUGHT SO!!
YOU'RE NEVER GOING TO GIVE UP ON ME, ARE YOU?
NOPE.
HAH.
CON
21-24

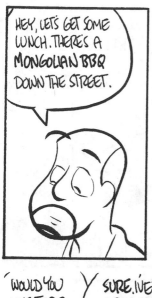

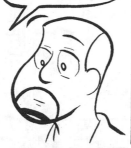

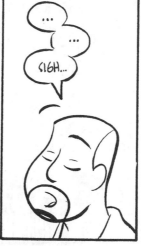

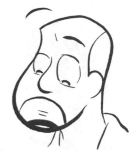

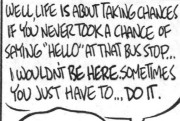

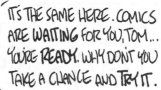

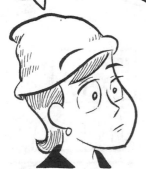

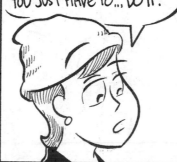

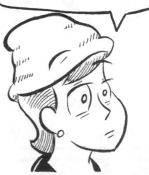

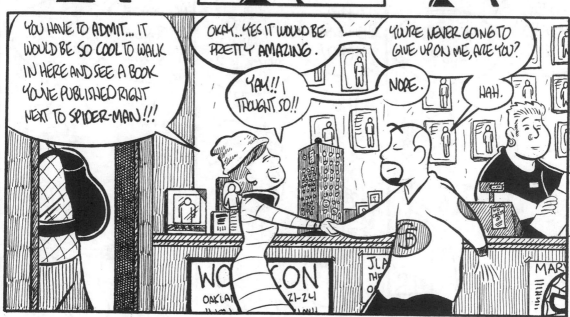

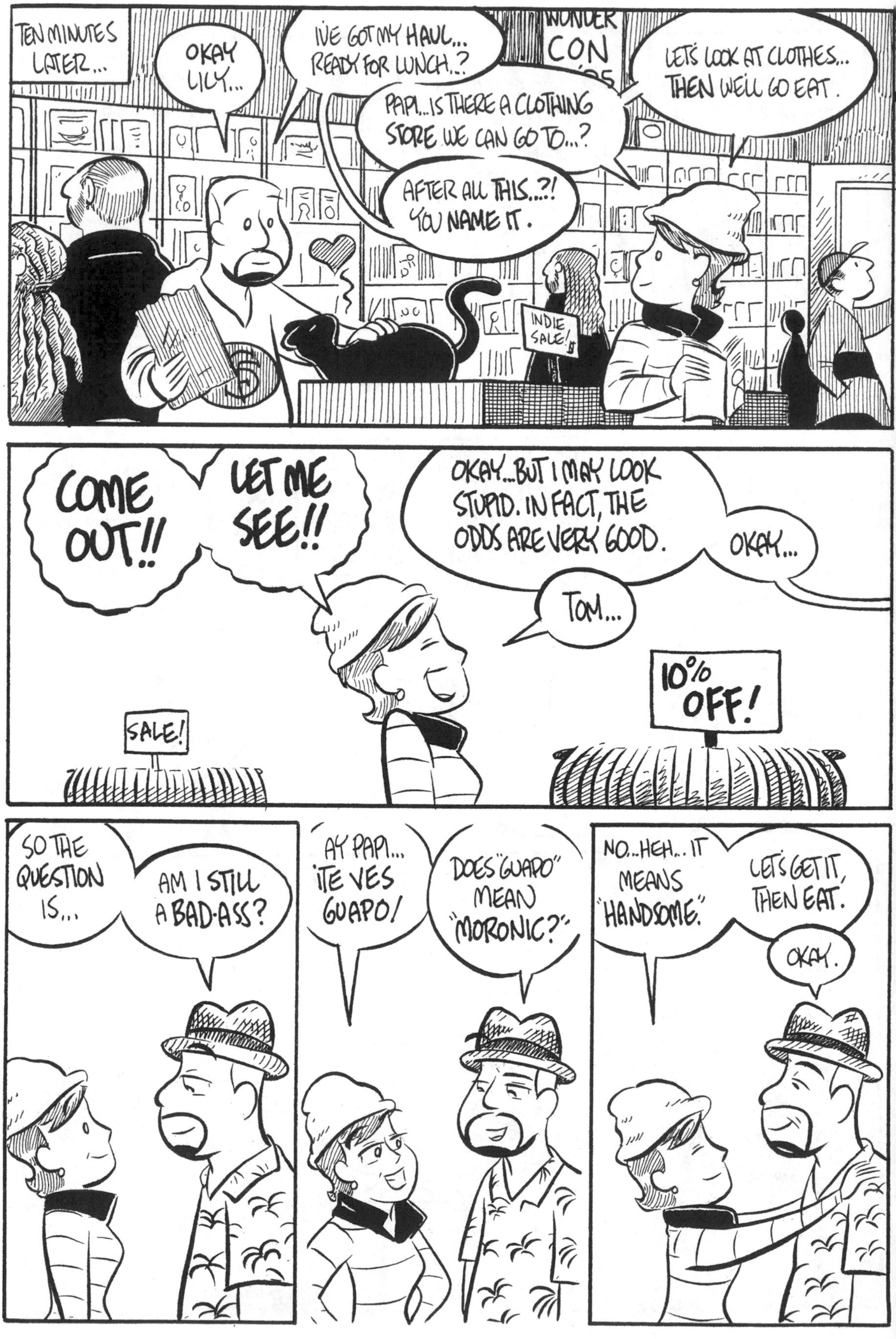
TEN MINUTES LATER...
OKAY LILY...
I'VE GOT MY HAUL... READY FOR LUNCH..?
WONDER CON
PAPI...IS THERE A CLOTHING STORE WE CAN GO TO...?
AFTER ALL THIS...?! YOU NAME IT.
LET'S LOOK AT CLOTHES... THEN WE'LL GO EAT.
INDIE SALE!
COME OUT!!
LET ME SEE!!
OKAY...BUT I MAY LOOK STUPID. IN FACT, THE ODDS ARE VERY GOOD.
OKAY...
TOM...
SALE!
10% OFF!
SO THE QUESTION IS...
AM I STILL A BAD-ASS?
AY PAPI... ¡TE VES GUAPO!
DOES "GUAPO" MEAN "MORONIC?"
NO...HEH... IT MEANS "HANDSOME."
LET'S GET IT, THEN EAT.
OKAY.

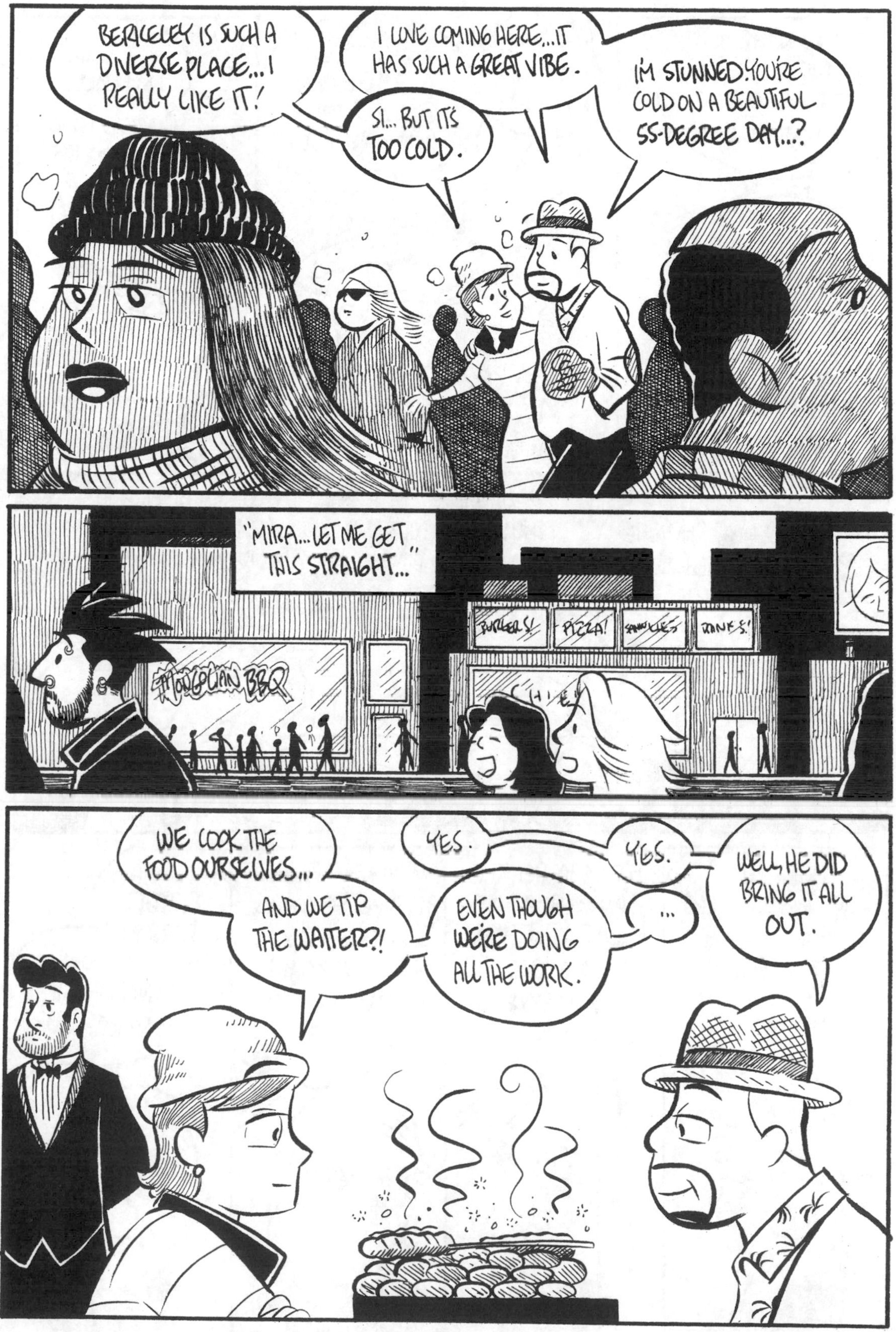
BERKELEY IS SUCH A DIVERSE PLACE... I REALLY LIKE IT!
SI... BUT IT'S TOO COLD.
I LOVE COMING HERE... IT HAS SUCH A GREAT VIBE.
I'M STUNNED. YOU'RE COLD ON A BEAUTIFUL 55-DEGREE DAY...?
"MIRA... LET ME GET THIS STRAIGHT..."
MONGOLIAN BBQ
BURGERS!
PIZZA!
WE COOK THE FOOD OURSELVES...
YES.
AND WE TIP THE WAITER?!
YES.
EVEN THOUGH WE'RE DOING ALL THE WORK.
...
WELL, HE DID BRING IT ALL OUT.

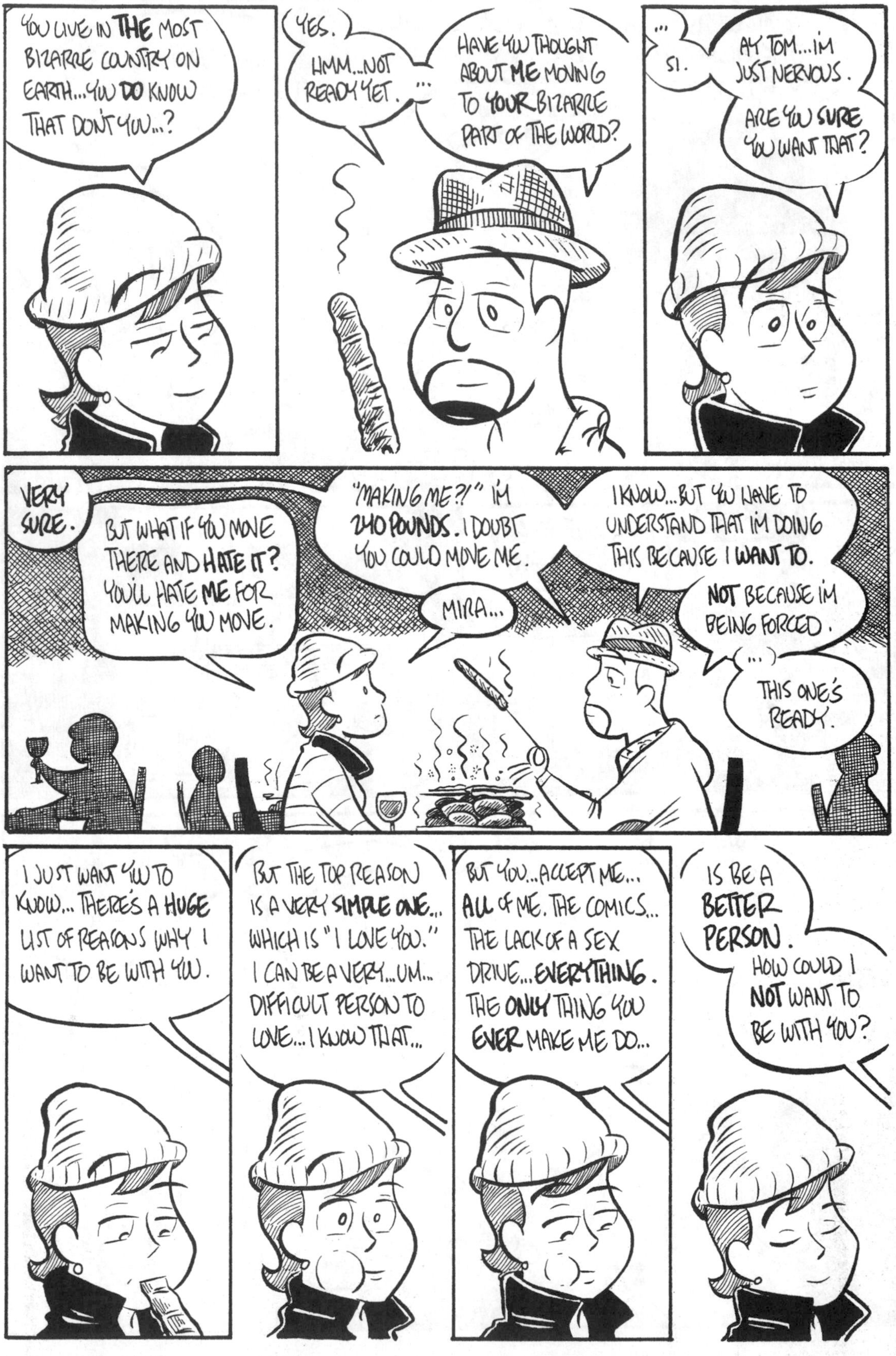
YOU LIVE IN THE MOST BIZARRE COUNTRY ON EARTH... YOU DO KNOW THAT DON'T YOU...?
YES.
HMM... NOT READY YET.
...
HAVE YOU THOUGHT ABOUT ME MOVING TO YOUR BIZARRE PART OF THE WORLD?
...
SI.
AY TOM... I'M JUST NERVOUS.
ARE YOU SURE YOU WANT THAT?
VERY SURE.
BUT WHAT IF YOU MOVE THERE AND HATE IT? YOU'LL HATE ME FOR MAKING YOU MOVE.
"MAKING ME?!" I'M 240 POUNDS. I DOUBT YOU COULD MOVE ME.
MIRA...
I KNOW... BUT YOU HAVE TO UNDERSTAND THAT I'M DOING THIS BECAUSE I WANT TO.
NOT BECAUSE I'M BEING FORCED.
...
THIS ONE'S READY.
I JUST WANT YOU TO KNOW... THERE'S A HUGE LIST OF REASONS WHY I WANT TO BE WITH YOU.
BUT THE TOP REASON IS A VERY SIMPLE ONE... WHICH IS "I LOVE YOU." I CAN BE A VERY... UM... DIFFICULT PERSON TO LOVE... I KNOW THAT...
BUT YOU... ACCEPT ME... ALL OF ME. THE COMICS... THE LACK OF A SEX DRIVE... EVERYTHING. THE ONLY THING YOU EVER MAKE ME DO...
IS BE A BETTER PERSON.
HOW COULD I NOT WANT TO BE WITH YOU?

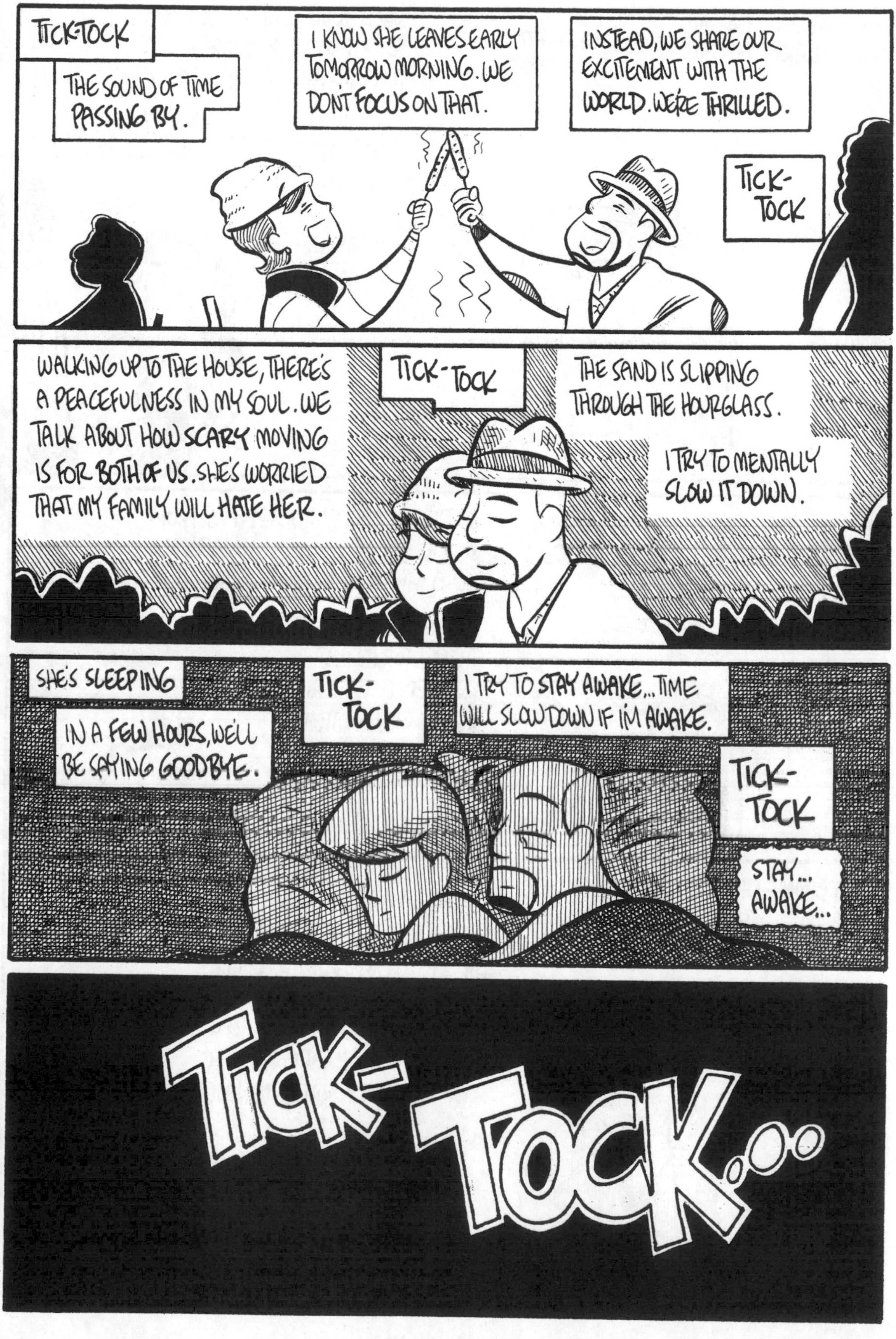
TICK-TOCK
THE SOUND OF TIME PASSING BY.
I KNOW SHE LEAVES EARLY TOMORROW MORNING. WE DON'T FOCUS ON THAT.
INSTEAD, WE SHARE OUR EXCITEMENT WITH THE WORLD. WE'RE THRILLED.
TICK-TOCK
WALKING UP TO THE HOUSE, THERE'S A PEACEFULNESS IN MY SOUL. WE TALK ABOUT HOW SCARY MOVING IS FOR BOTH OF US. SHE'S WORRIED THAT MY FAMILY WILL HATE HER.
TICK-TOCK
THE SAND IS SLIPPING THROUGH THE HOURGLASS.
I TRY TO MENTALLY SLOW IT DOWN.
SHE'S SLEEPING
IN A FEW HOURS, WE'LL BE SAYING GOODBYE.
TICK-TOCK
I TRY TO STAY AWAKE... TIME WILL SLOW DOWN IF I'M AWAKE.
TICK-TOCK
STAY... AWAKE...
TICK-TOCK...

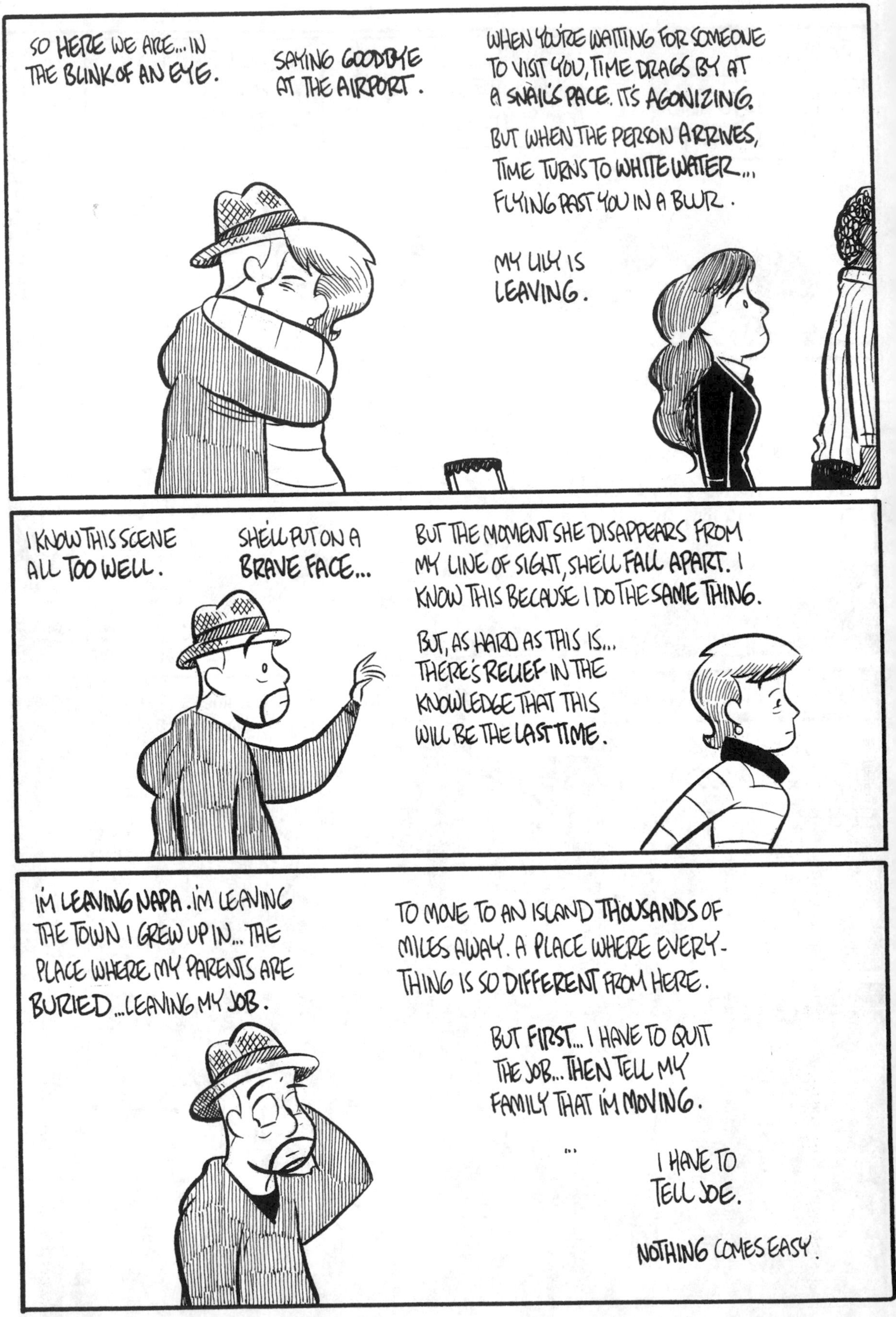
SO HERE WE ARE... IN THE BLINK OF AN EYE.
SAYING GOODBYE AT THE AIRPORT.
WHEN YOU'RE WAITING FOR SOMEONE TO VISIT YOU, TIME DRAGS BY AT A SNAIL'S PACE. IT'S AGONIZING.
BUT WHEN THE PERSON ARRIVES, TIME TURNS TO WHITE WATER... FLYING PAST YOU IN A BLUR.
MY LILY IS LEAVING.
I KNOW THIS SCENE ALL TOO WELL.
SHE'LL PUT ON A BRAVE FACE...
BUT THE MOMENT SHE DISAPPEARS FROM MY LINE OF SIGHT, SHE'LL FALL APART. I KNOW THIS BECAUSE I DO THE SAME THING.
BUT, AS HARD AS THIS IS... THERE'S RELIEF IN THE KNOWLEDGE THAT THIS WILL BE THE LAST TIME.
I'M LEAVING NAPA. I'M LEAVING THE TOWN I GREW UP IN... THE PLACE WHERE MY PARENTS ARE BURIED... LEAVING MY JOB.
TO MOVE TO AN ISLAND THOUSANDS OF MILES AWAY. A PLACE WHERE EVERYTHING IS SO DIFFERENT FROM HERE.
BUT FIRST... I HAVE TO QUIT THE JOB... THEN TELL MY FAMILY THAT I'M MOVING.
...
I HAVE TO TELL JOE.
NOTHING COMES EASY.

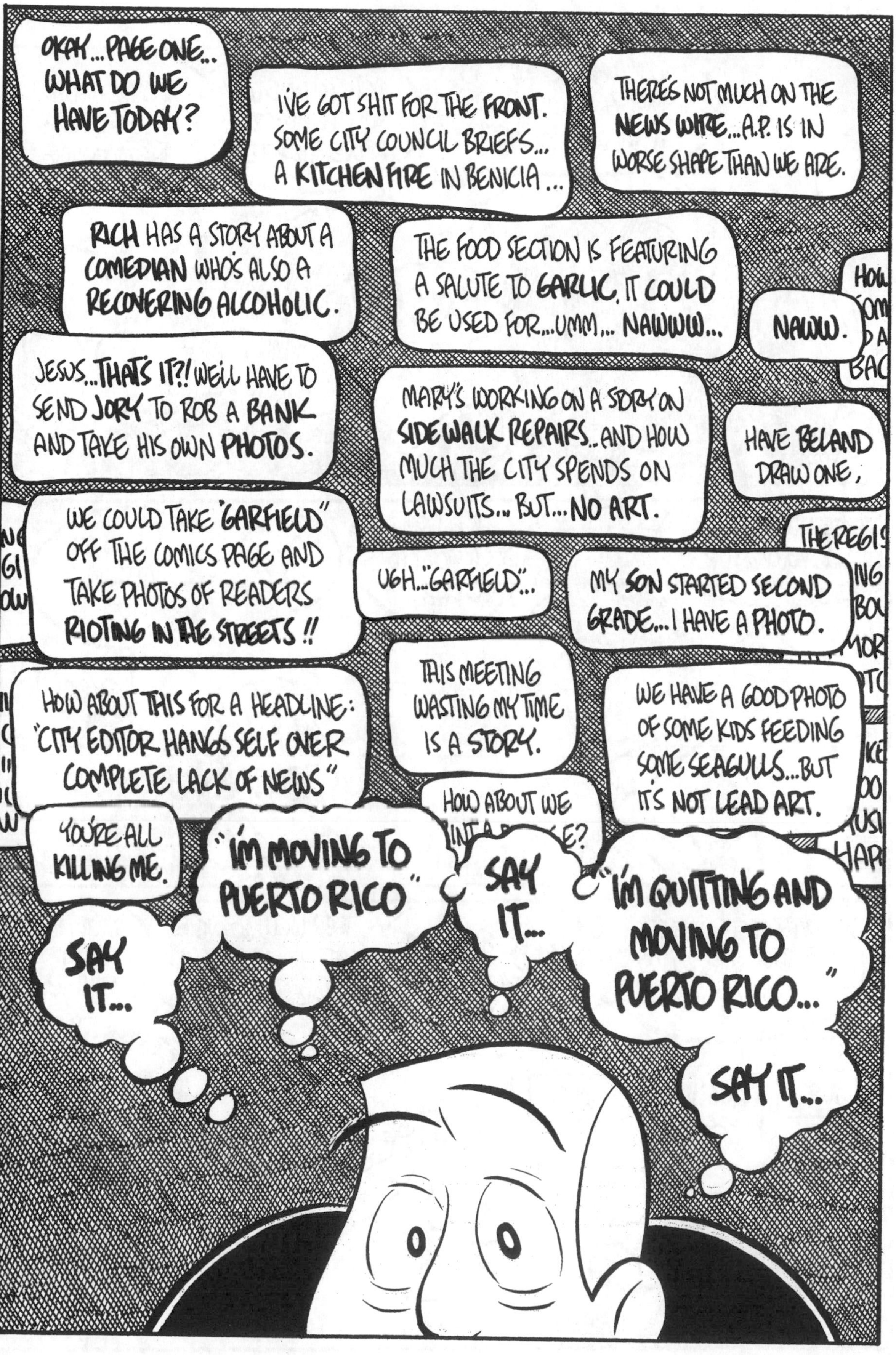
OKAY...PAGE ONE... WHAT DO WE HAVE TODAY?
I'VE GOT SHIT FOR THE FRONT. SOME CITY COUNCIL BRIEFS... A KITCHEN FIRE IN BENICIA...
THERE'S NOT MUCH ON THE NEWS WIRE...A.P. IS IN WORSE SHAPE THAN WE ARE.
RICH HAS A STORY ABOUT A COMEDIAN WHO'S ALSO A RECOVERING ALCOHOLIC.
THE FOOD SECTION IS FEATURING A SALUTE TO GARLIC. IT COULD BE USED FOR...UMM... NAWWW...
NAWW.
JESUS...THAT'S IT?! WE'LL HAVE TO SEND JORY TO ROB A BANK AND TAKE HIS OWN PHOTOS.
MARY'S WORKING ON A STORY ON SIDEWALK REPAIRS...AND HOW MUCH THE CITY SPENDS ON LAWSUITS... BUT...NO ART.
HAVE BELAND DRAW ONE.
WE COULD TAKE "GARFIELD" OFF THE COMICS PAGE AND TAKE PHOTOS OF READERS RIOTING IN THE STREETS!!
UGH..."GARFIELD"...
MY SON STARTED SECOND GRADE...I HAVE A PHOTO.
HOW ABOUT THIS FOR A HEADLINE: "CITY EDITOR HANGS SELF OVER COMPLETE LACK OF NEWS"
THIS MEETING WASTING MY TIME IS A STORY.
WE HAVE A GOOD PHOTO OF SOME KIDS FEEDING SOME SEAGULLS...BUT IT'S NOT LEAD ART.
YOU'RE ALL KILLING ME.
HOW ABOUT WE
"I'M MOVING TO PUERTO RICO"
SAY IT...
"I'M QUITTING AND MOVING TO PUERTO RICO..."
SAY IT...
SAY IT...

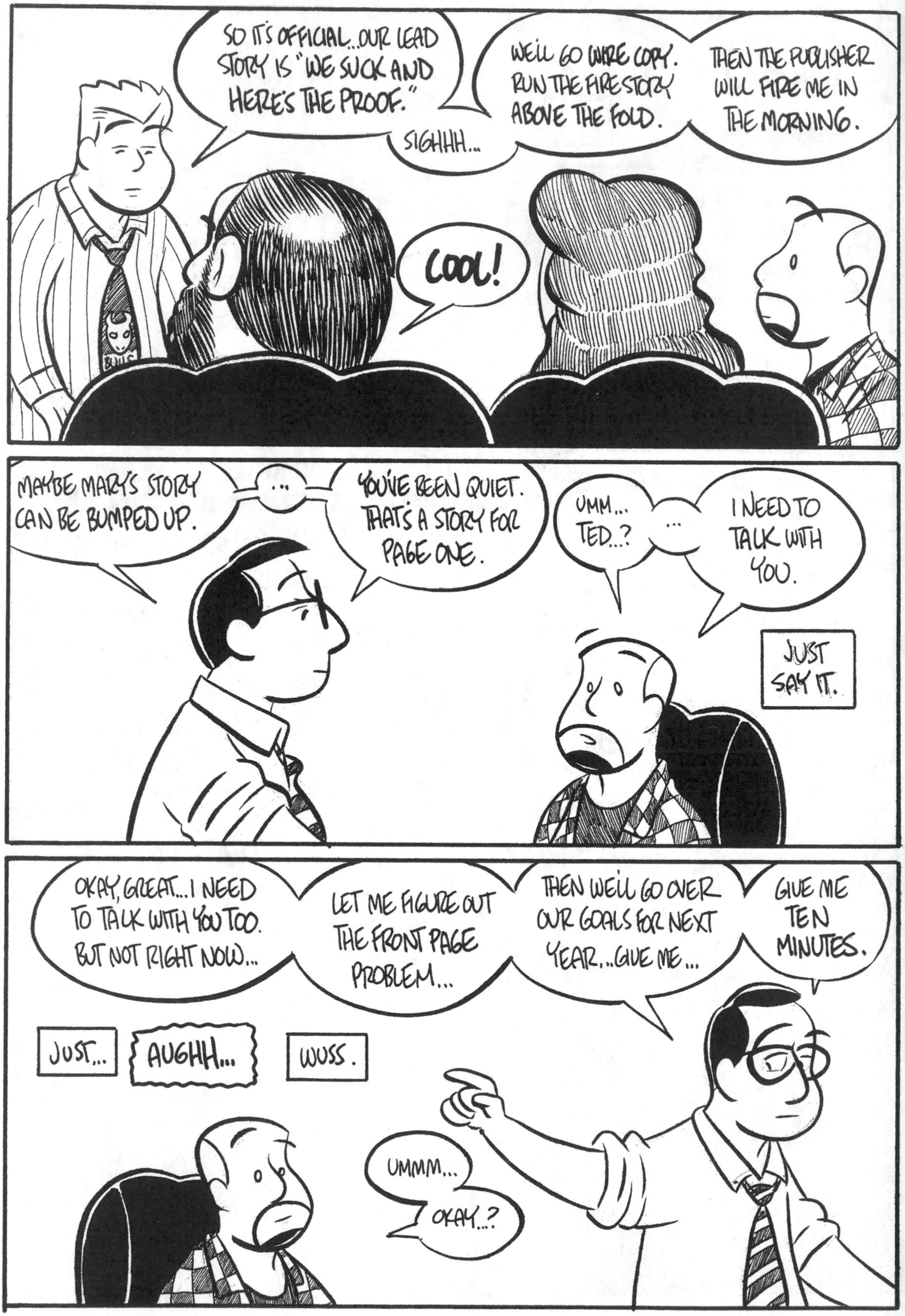
SO IT'S OFFICIAL...OUR LEAD STORY IS "WE SUCK AND HERE'S THE PROOF."
SIGHHH...
WE'LL GO WIRE COPY. RUN THE FIRE STORY ABOVE THE FOLD.
THEN THE PUBLISHER WILL FIRE ME IN THE MORNING.
COOL!
MAYBE MARY'S STORY CAN BE BUMPED UP.
...
YOU'VE BEEN QUIET. THAT'S A STORY FOR PAGE ONE.
UMM... TED...?
...
I NEED TO TALK WITH YOU.
JUST SAY IT.
OKAY, GREAT...I NEED TO TALK WITH YOU TOO. BUT NOT RIGHT NOW...
LET ME FIGURE OUT THE FRONT PAGE PROBLEM...
THEN WE'LL GO OVER OUR GOALS FOR NEXT YEAR...GIVE ME...
GIVE ME TEN MINUTES.
JUST...
AUGHH...
WUSS.
UMMM...
OKAY...?

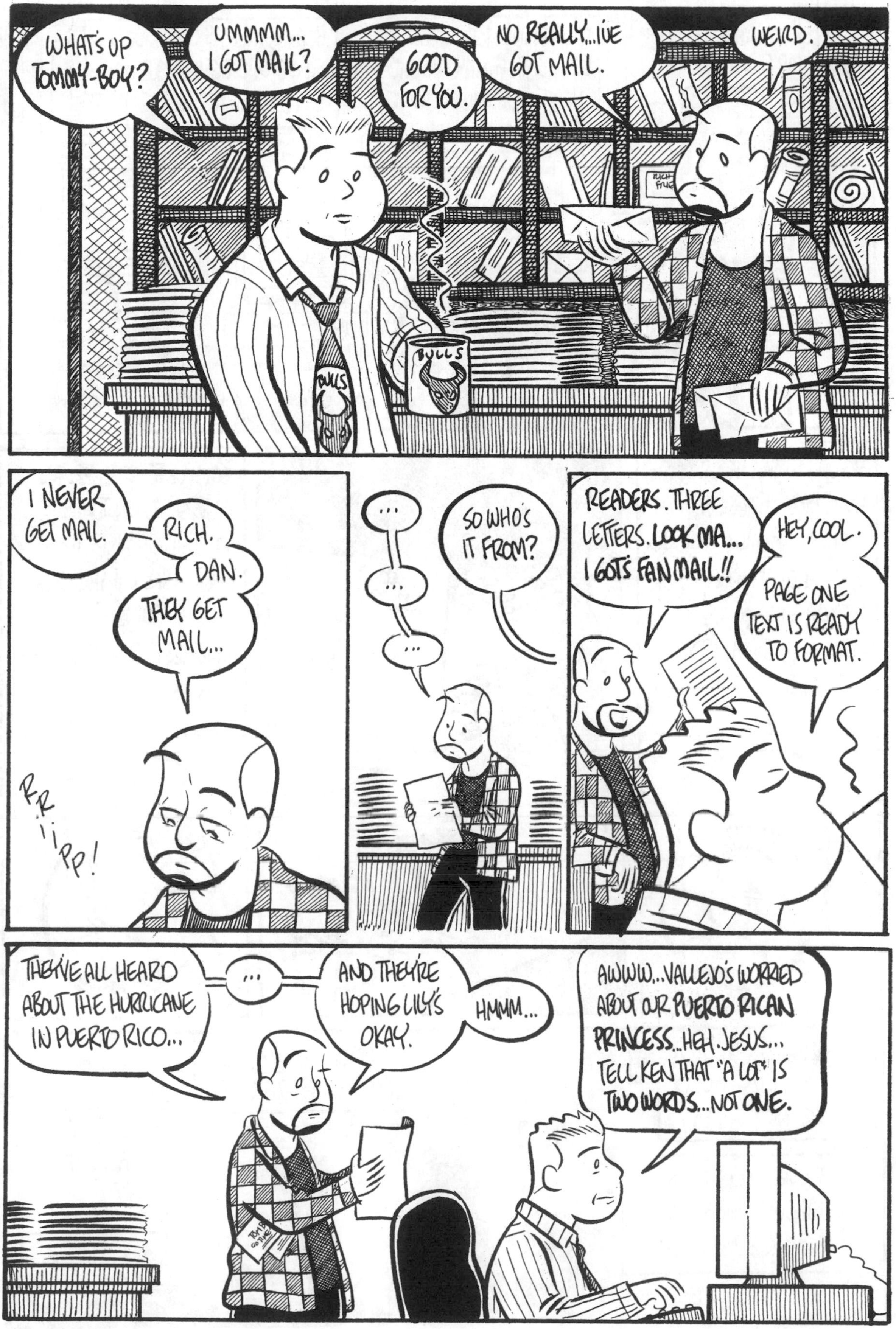
WHAT'S UP TOMMY-BOY?
UMMMM... I GOT MAIL?
GOOD FOR YOU.
NO REALLY...I'VE GOT MAIL.
WEIRD.
I NEVER GET MAIL.
RICH.
DAN.
THEY GET MAIL...
RRiiPP!
...
...
...
SO WHO'S IT FROM?
READERS. THREE LETTERS. LOOK MA... I GOT'S FAN MAIL!!
HEY, COOL.
PAGE ONE TEXT IS READY TO FORMAT.
THEY'VE ALL HEARD ABOUT THE HURRICANE IN PUERTO RICO...
...
AND THEY'RE HOPING LILY'S OKAY.
HMMM...
AWWW... VALLEJO'S WORRIED ABOUT OUR PUERTO RICAN PRINCESS... HEH. JESUS... TELL KEN THAT "A LOT" IS TWO WORDS... NOT ONE.

I'VE BEEN MAKING THIS COMIC STRIP FOR ABOUT FIVE YEARS.

IT CONTAINS STORIES ABOUT MY LIFE...BOTH FUNNY AND SAD. THE STORIES NOW INCLUDE MY RELATIONSHIP WITH LILY.

BEFORE THIS... I'D RECEIVED MAYBE ONE LETTER, BUT NOW I'M LOOKING AT THREE.

THREE IN ONE DAY.

NO ONE IN THIS NEWSROOM... NONE OF MY FRIENDS... EVEN MY FAMILY MEMBERS, THEY HAVE NO IDEA HOW AMAZING THIS FEELS. I'M LITTERALLY STUNNED.

KELLY RODGERS

TIM BROWN

TOM BE %0 VAN

TOM BEL %0 TIME

JON ADAMS

TOM Beland %0 Times Heral

COMPLETE STRANGERS HAVE SAT DOWN TO WRITE SOMETHING TO ME. THEY WANT TO KNOW IF SHES OKAY... IF WE'RE GOING TO GET MARRIED...OR JUST SAYING THEY ENJOY THE STRIP.

IF I WERE TO STAY HERE... THREE LETTERS COULD EVOLVE INTO THIRTY.

JEEZE...I CAN'T EVEN IMAGINE THIRTY PEOPLE READING MY STUFF.

BUT WHAT IF I STAY...AND THESE THREE ARE IT...?!

...

WHY DID THEY HAVE TO ARRIVE TODAY?!!

...

I'M STILL QUITTING.

I LOVE THIS JOB. IT'S THE FIRST PLACE I'VE EVER FELT...WELL... I GUESS "RESPECTED" IS THE WORD I'M LOOKING FOR.

THINK ABOUT THAT FOR A MOMENT...GETTING RESPECT FOR SOMETHING YOU DO.

I NEVER THOUGHT I'D HAVE THAT.

IF EVER I AM A WHOLE PERSON, IT'S HERE IN THIS NEWSROOM.

THERE'S MARK, THE FOOD EDITOR AND HUGE CLEVELAND SPORTS FAN.

AND JACK, THE CITY EDITOR. BEING A CHICAGO BULLS FAN, HE LOVES TO PLAY THE AUDIO OF JORDAN'S GAME-WINNING SHOT AGAINST CLEVELAND ON HIS COMPUTER, TO DRIVE MARK NUTS.

IT WORKS EVERY TIME.

AND THERE'S RICH, WRITER OF A BILLION STORIES. IF NOT FOR RICH, I'D HAVE NEVER FLOWN TO ORLANDO WHERE I MET LILY.

THERE'S MATTHIAS, THE REPORTER WHO LOOKS LIKE A BACKSTREET BOY...WHICH HE CONSIDERS A CURSE.

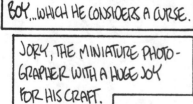

JORY, THE MINIATURE PHOTO-GRAPHER WITH A HUGE JOY FOR HIS CRAFT.

JIM, THE COMPUTER GUY.

JIM TOLD ME THAT IF I GOT THE CHANCE TO LIVE IN THE TROPICS WITH THE WOMAN I LOVE, TO TAKE IT.

ALL THESE PEOPLE HAVE NO IDEA WHAT THEY MEAN TO ME. IT'S SO HARD TO LEAVE HERE...

BUT I'M ABOUT TO.

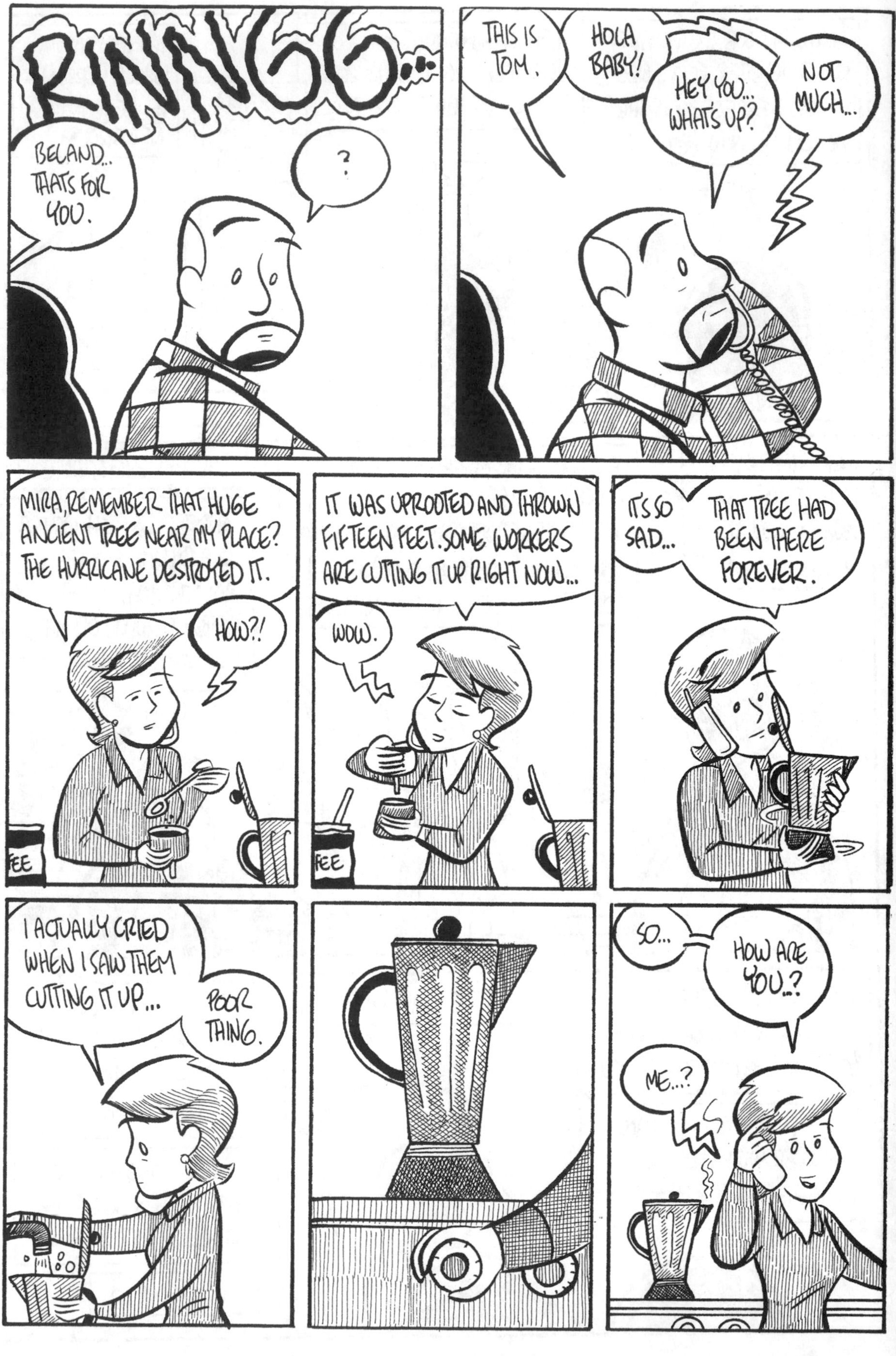
RINNGG...
BELAND... THATS FOR YOU.
?
THIS IS TOM.
HOLA BABY!
HEY YOU... WHAT'S UP?
NOT MUCH...
MIRA, REMEMBER THAT HUGE ANCIENT TREE NEAR MY PLACE? THE HURRICANE DESTROYED IT.
HOW?!
IT WAS UPROOTED AND THROWN FIFTEEN FEET. SOME WORKERS ARE CUTTING IT UP RIGHT NOW...
WOW.
IT'S SO SAD...
THAT TREE HAD BEEN THERE FOREVER.
I ACTUALLY CRIED WHEN I SAW THEM CUTTING IT UP...
POOR THING.
SO...
HOW ARE YOU..?
ME..?

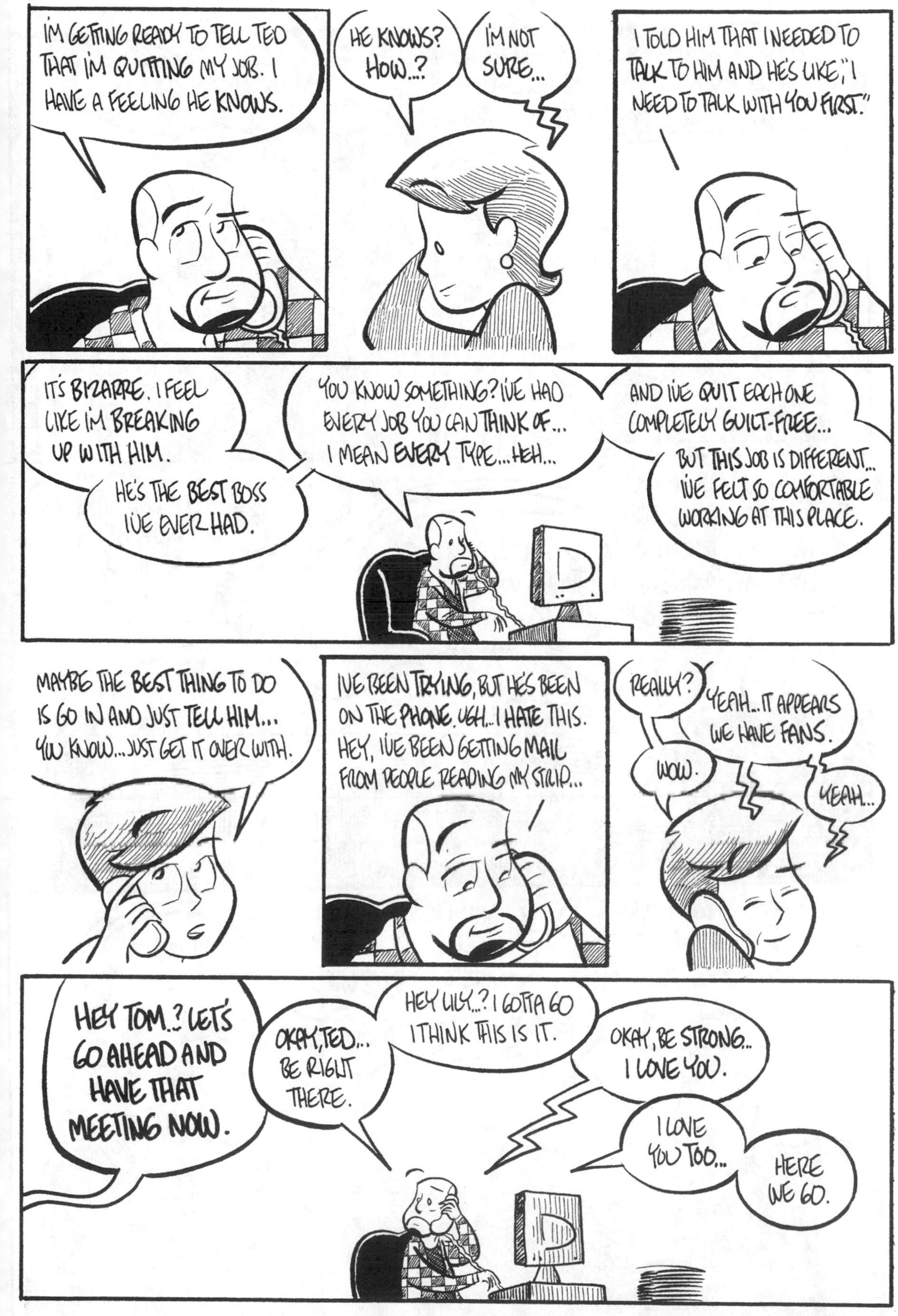
I'M GETTING READY TO TELL TED THAT I'M QUITTING MY JOB. I HAVE A FEELING HE KNOWS.
HE KNOWS? HOW..?
I'M NOT SURE...
I TOLD HIM THAT I NEEDED TO TALK TO HIM AND HE'S LIKE, "I NEED TO TALK WITH YOU FIRST."
IT'S BIZARRE. I FEEL LIKE I'M BREAKING UP WITH HIM.
HE'S THE BEST BOSS I'VE EVER HAD.
YOU KNOW SOMETHING? I'VE HAD EVERY JOB YOU CAN THINK OF... I MEAN EVERY TYPE...HEH...
AND I'VE QUIT EACH ONE COMPLETELY GUILT-FREE...
BUT THIS JOB IS DIFFERENT... I'VE FELT SO COMFORTABLE WORKING AT THIS PLACE.
MAYBE THE BEST THING TO DO IS GO IN AND JUST TELL HIM... YOU KNOW...JUST GET IT OVER WITH.
I'VE BEEN TRYING, BUT HE'S BEEN ON THE PHONE. UGH...I HATE THIS. HEY, I'VE BEEN GETTING MAIL FROM PEOPLE READING MY STRIP...
REALLY?
YEAH...IT APPEARS WE HAVE FANS.
WOW.
YEAH...
HEY TOM..? LET'S GO AHEAD AND HAVE THAT MEETING NOW.
OKAY, TED... BE RIGHT THERE.
HEY LILY..? I GOTTA GO I THINK THIS IS IT.
OKAY, BE STRONG... I LOVE YOU.
I LOVE YOU TOO...
HERE WE GO.

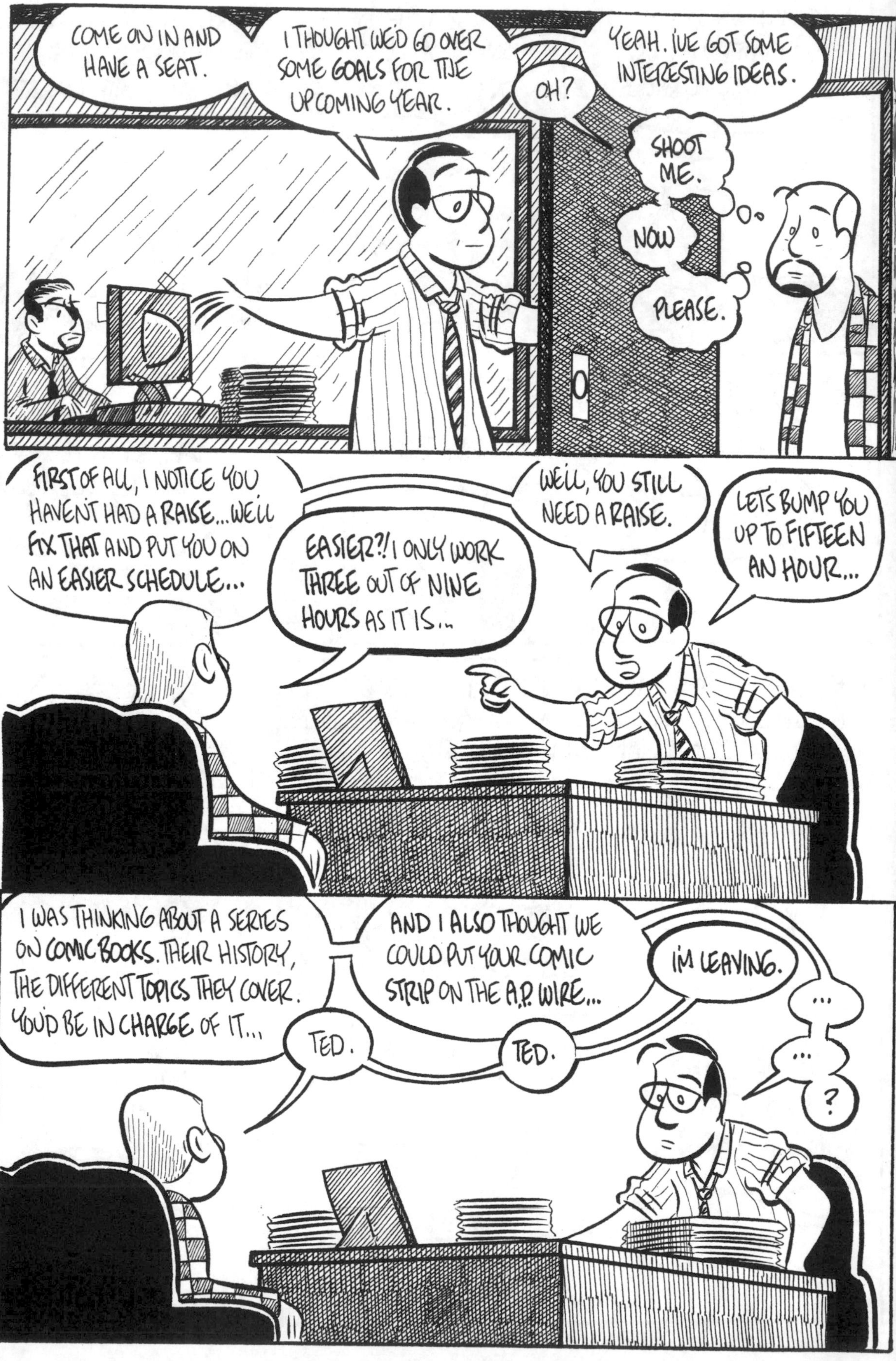
COME ON IN AND HAVE A SEAT.
I THOUGHT WE'D GO OVER SOME GOALS FOR THE UPCOMING YEAR.
OH?
YEAH. I'VE GOT SOME INTERESTING IDEAS.
SHOOT ME.
NOW
PLEASE.
FIRST OF ALL, I NOTICE YOU HAVEN'T HAD A RAISE... WE'LL FIX THAT AND PUT YOU ON AN EASIER SCHEDULE...
EASIER?! I ONLY WORK THREE OUT OF NINE HOURS AS IT IS...
WELL, YOU STILL NEED A RAISE.
LET'S BUMP YOU UP TO FIFTEEN AN HOUR...
I WAS THINKING ABOUT A SERIES ON COMIC BOOKS. THEIR HISTORY, THE DIFFERENT TOPICS THEY COVER. YOU'D BE IN CHARGE OF IT...
TED.
AND I ALSO THOUGHT WE COULD PUT YOUR COMIC STRIP ON THE A.P. WIRE...
TED.
I'M LEAVING.
...
...
?

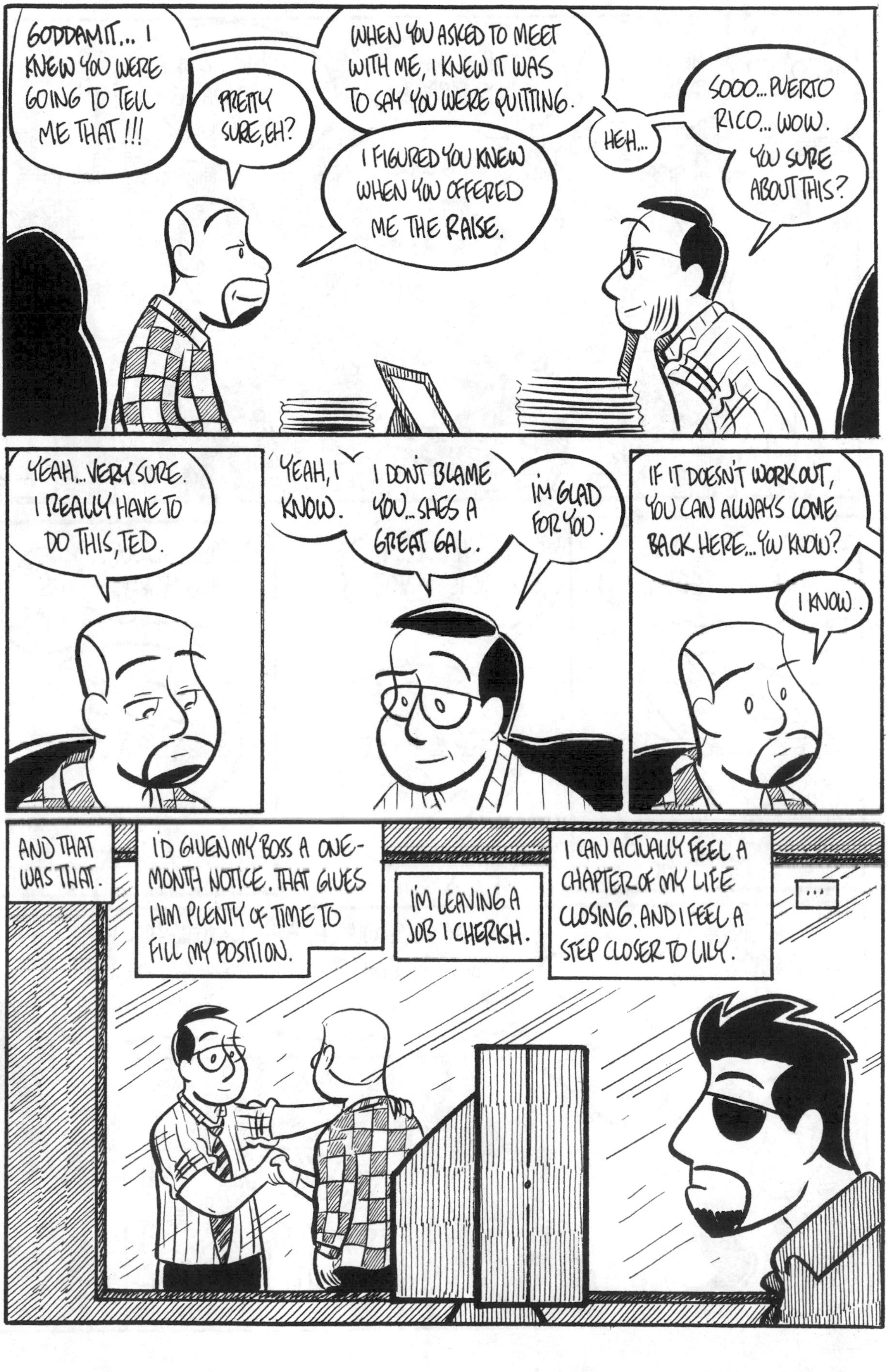
GODDAMIT... I KNEW YOU WERE GOING TO TELL ME THAT!!!
WHEN YOU ASKED TO MEET WITH ME, I KNEW IT WAS TO SAY YOU WERE QUITTING.
PRETTY SURE, EH?
I FIGURED YOU KNEW WHEN YOU OFFERED ME THE RAISE.
HEH...
SOOO... PUERTO RICO... WOW. YOU SURE ABOUT THIS?
YEAH... VERY SURE. I REALLY HAVE TO DO THIS, TED.
YEAH, I KNOW.
I DON'T BLAME YOU... SHE'S A GREAT GAL.
I'M GLAD FOR YOU.
IF IT DOESN'T WORK OUT, YOU CAN ALWAYS COME BACK HERE... YOU KNOW?
I KNOW.
AND THAT WAS THAT.
I'D GIVEN MY BOSS A ONE-MONTH NOTICE. THAT GIVES HIM PLENTY OF TIME TO FILL MY POSITION.
I'M LEAVING A JOB I CHERISH.
I CAN ACTUALLY FEEL A CHAPTER OF MY LIFE CLOSING. AND I FEEL A STEP CLOSER TO LILY.
...

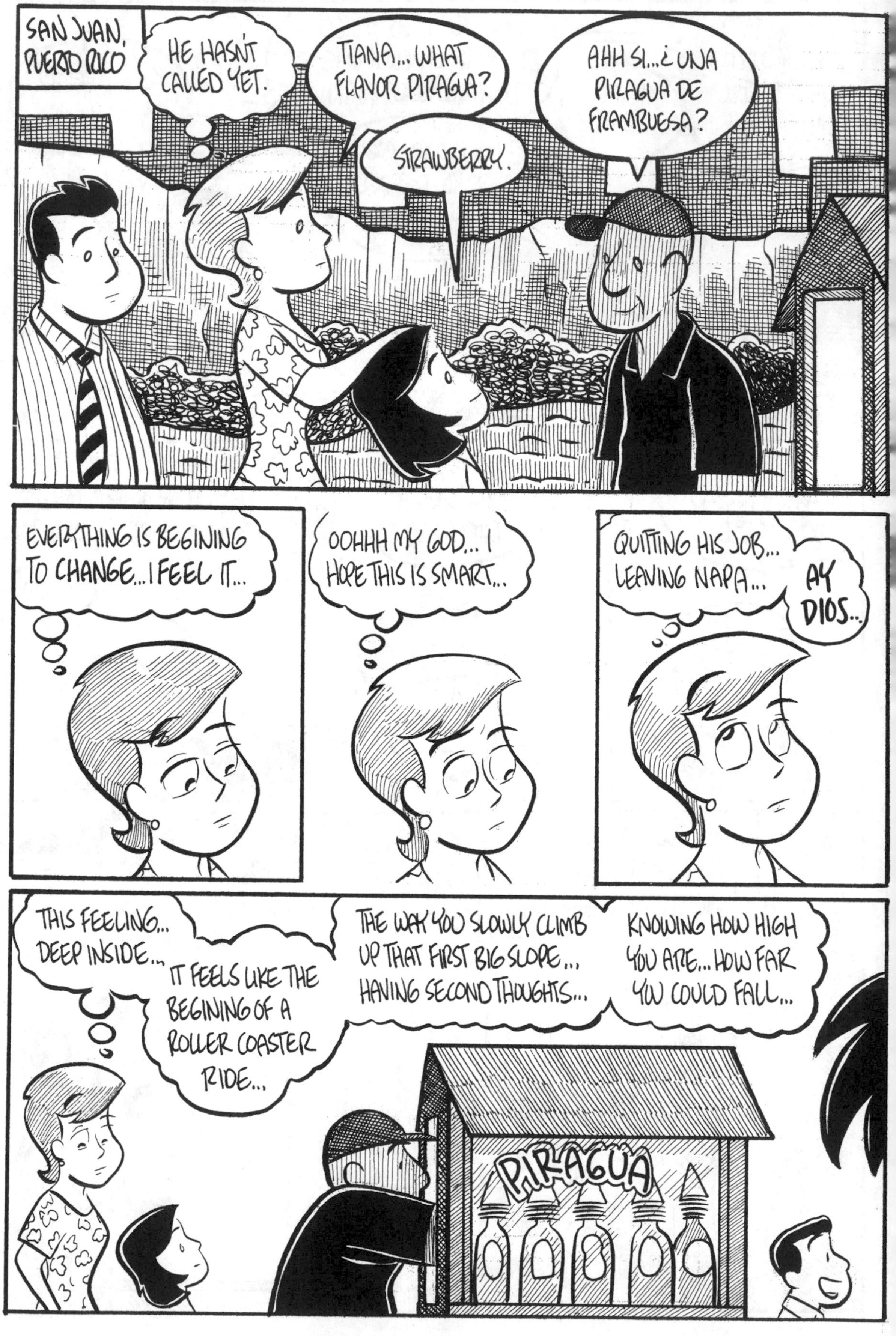
SAN JUAN, PUERTO RICO
HE HASN'T CALLED YET.
TIANA... WHAT FLAVOR PIRAGUA?
STRAWBERRY.
AHH SI...¿UNA PIRAGUA DE FRAMBUESA?
EVERYTHING IS BEGINING TO CHANGE...I FEEL IT...
OOHHH MY GOD... I HOPE THIS IS SMART...
QUITTING HIS JOB... LEAVING NAPA...
AY DIOS...
THIS FEELING... DEEP INSIDE...
IT FEELS LIKE THE BEGINING OF A ROLLER COASTER RIDE...
THE WAY YOU SLOWLY CLIMB UP THAT FIRST BIG SLOPE... HAVING SECOND THOUGHTS...
KNOWING HOW HIGH YOU ARE... HOW FAR YOU COULD FALL...
PIRAGUA

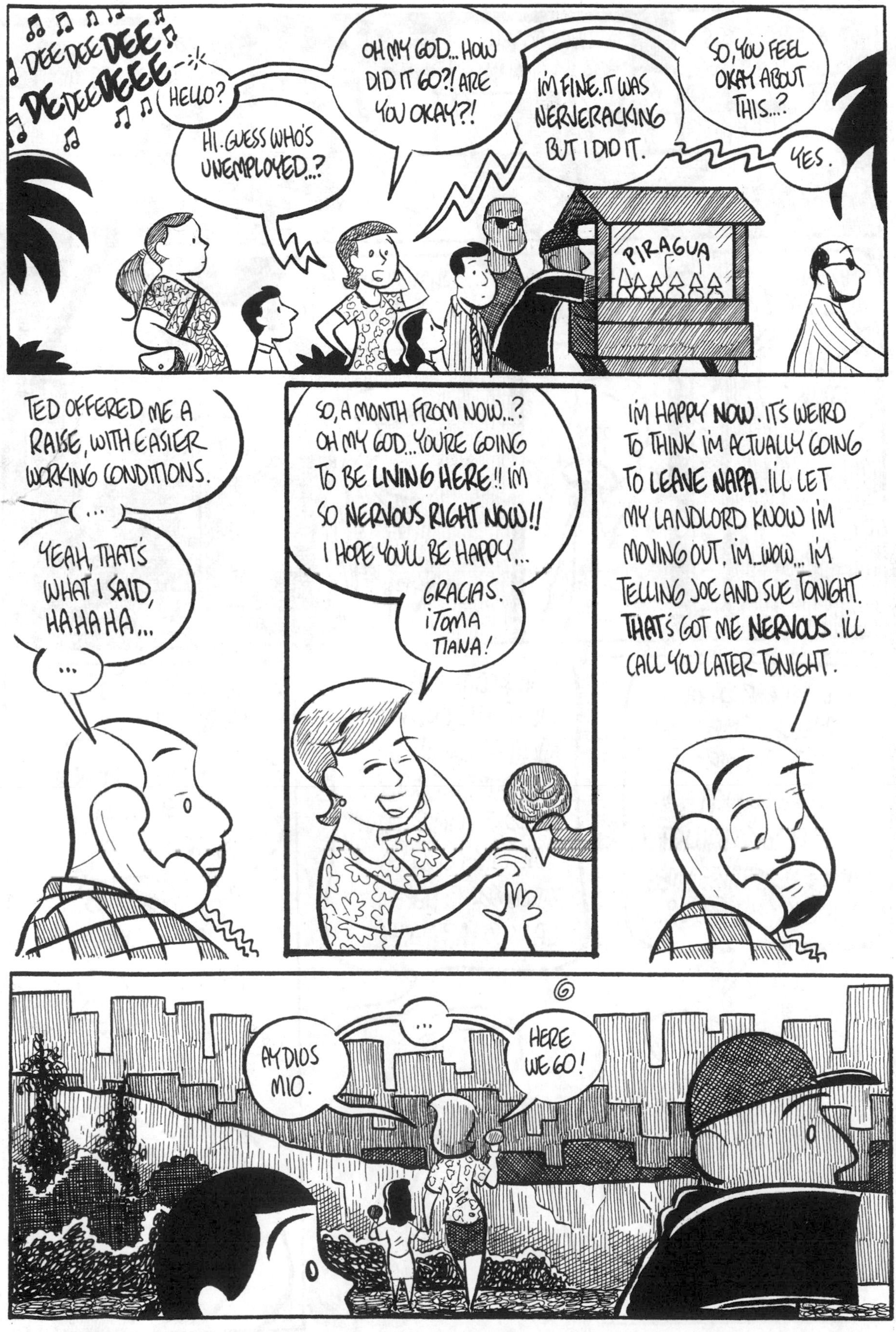

DEE DEE DEE DE DEE DEEE
HELLO?
HI. GUESS WHO'S UNEMPLOYED...?
OH MY GOD... HOW DID IT GO?! ARE YOU OKAY?!
I'M FINE. IT WAS NERVERACKING BUT I DID IT.
SO, YOU FEEL OKAY ABOUT THIS...?
YES.
PIRAGUA
TED OFFERED ME A RAISE, WITH EASIER WORKING CONDITIONS.
...
YEAH, THAT'S WHAT I SAID, HA HA HA...
...
SO, A MONTH FROM NOW...? OH MY GOD... YOU'RE GOING TO BE LIVING HERE!! I'M SO NERVOUS RIGHT NOW!! I HOPE YOU'LL BE HAPPY...
GRACIAS. ¡TOMA TIANA!
I'M HAPPY NOW. IT'S WEIRD TO THINK I'M ACTUALLY GOING TO LEAVE NAPA. I'LL LET MY LANDLORD KNOW I'M MOVING OUT. I'M...WOW... I'M TELLING JOE AND SUE TONIGHT. THAT'S GOT ME NERVOUS. I'LL CALL YOU LATER TONIGHT.
6
...
AY DIOS MIO.
HERE WE GO!

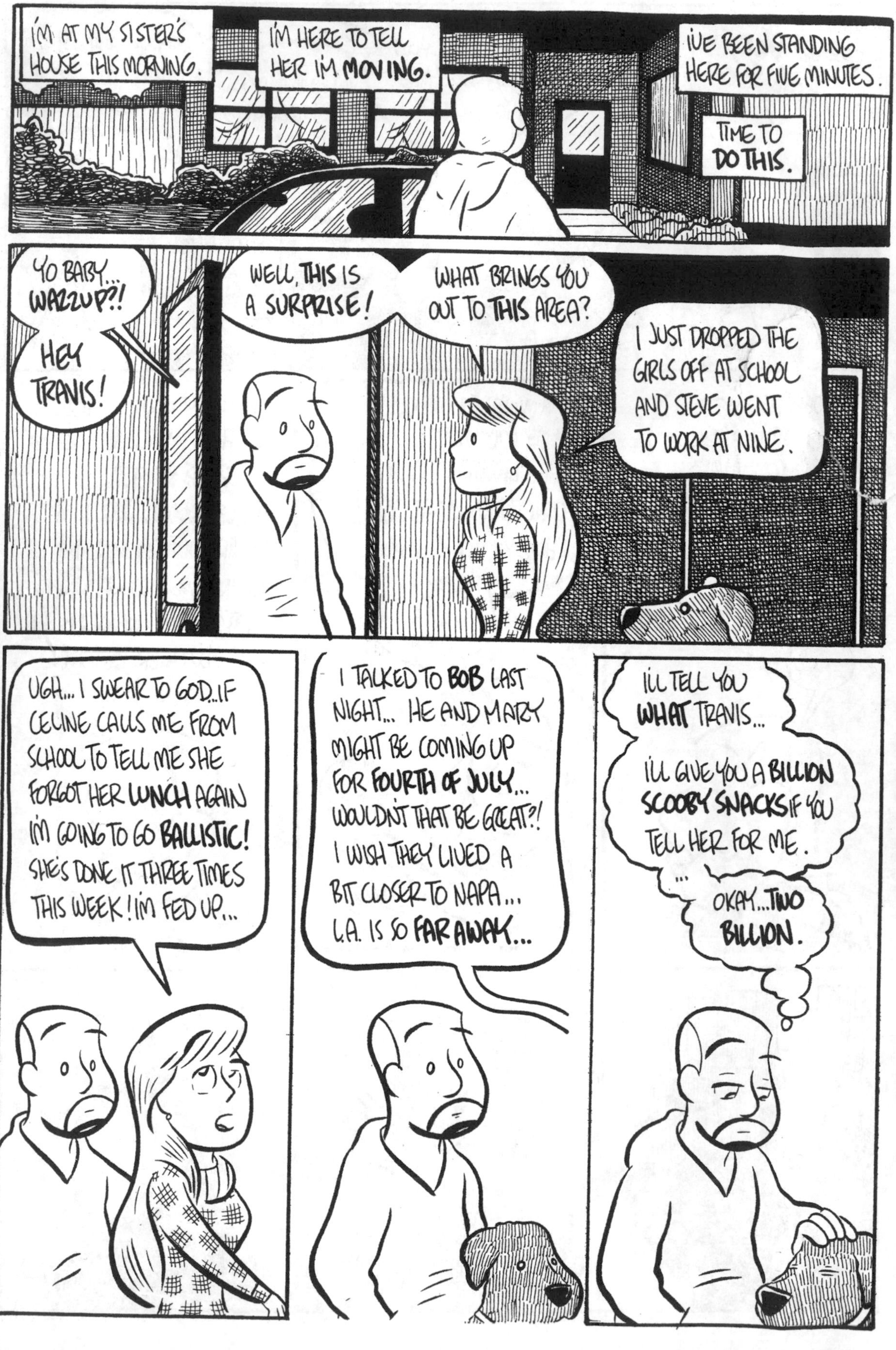

I'M AT MY SISTER'S HOUSE THIS MORNING.
I'M HERE TO TELL HER I'M MOVING.
I'VE BEEN STANDING HERE FOR FIVE MINUTES.
TIME TO DO THIS.
YO BABY... WAZZUP?!
HEY TRAVIS!
WELL, THIS IS A SURPRISE!
WHAT BRINGS YOU OUT TO THIS AREA?
I JUST DROPPED THE GIRLS OFF AT SCHOOL AND STEVE WENT TO WORK AT NINE.
UGH... I SWEAR TO GOD...IF CELINE CALLS ME FROM SCHOOL TO TELL ME SHE FORGOT HER LUNCH AGAIN I'M GOING TO GO BALLISTIC! SHE'S DONE IT THREE TIMES THIS WEEK! I'M FED UP...
I TALKED TO BOB LAST NIGHT... HE AND MARY MIGHT BE COMING UP FOR FOURTH OF JULY... WOULDN'T THAT BE GREAT?! I WISH THEY LIVED A BIT CLOSER TO NAPA... L.A. IS SO FAR AWAY...
I'LL TELL YOU WHAT TRAVIS...
I'LL GIVE YOU A BILLION SCOOBY SNACKS IF YOU TELL HER FOR ME.
... OKAY...TWO BILLION.

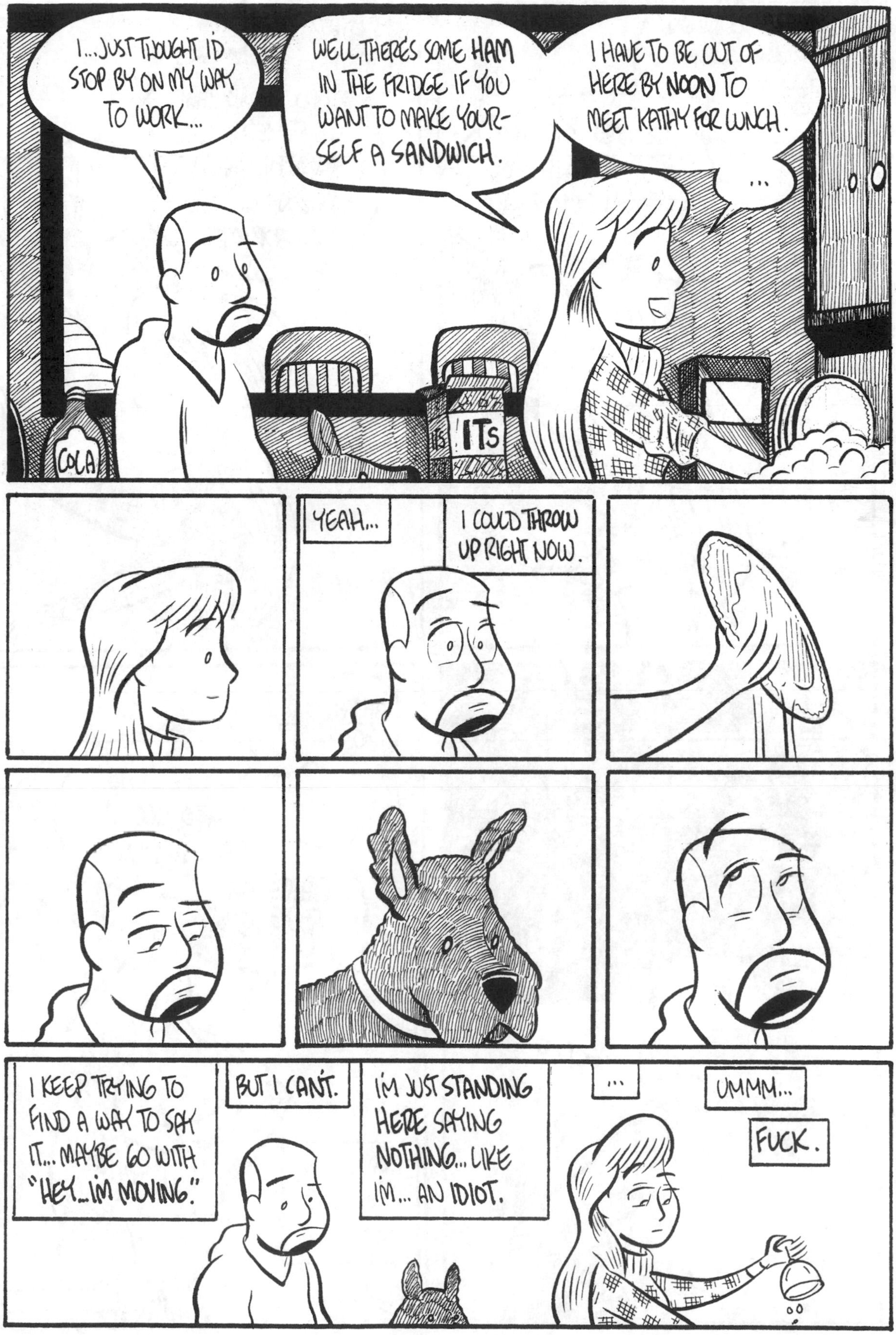

I...JUST THOUGHT I'D STOP BY ON MY WAY TO WORK...
WELL, THERE'S SOME HAM IN THE FRIDGE IF YOU WANT TO MAKE YOURSELF A SANDWICH.
I HAVE TO BE OUT OF HERE BY NOON TO MEET KATHY FOR LUNCH.
...
COLA
ITS
YEAH...
I COULD THROW UP RIGHT NOW.
I KEEP TRYING TO FIND A WAY TO SAY IT... MAYBE GO WITH "HEY...I'M MOVING."
BUT I CAN'T.
I'M JUST STANDING HERE SAYING NOTHING... LIKE I'M... AN IDIOT.
...
UMMM...
FUCK.

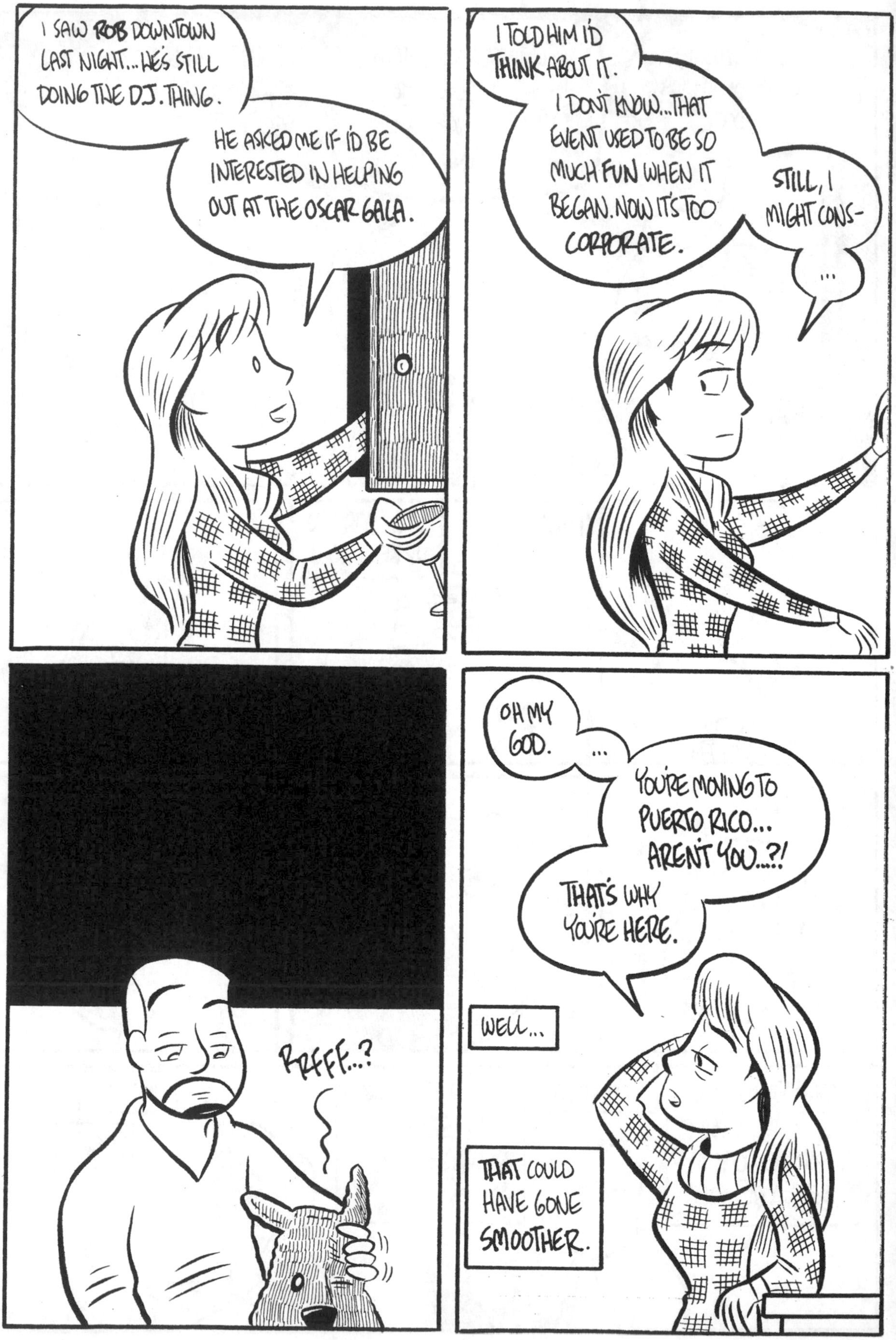
I SAW ROB DOWNTOWN LAST NIGHT... HE'S STILL DOING THE D.J. THING.
HE ASKED ME IF I'D BE INTERESTED IN HELPING OUT AT THE OSCAR GALA.
I TOLD HIM I'D THINK ABOUT IT.
I DON'T KNOW... THAT EVENT USED TO BE SO MUCH FUN WHEN IT BEGAN. NOW IT'S TOO CORPORATE.
STILL, I MIGHT CONS-
...
RRFFF..?
OH MY GOD.
...
YOU'RE MOVING TO PUERTO RICO... AREN'T YOU..?!
THAT'S WHY YOU'RE HERE.
WELL...
THAT COULD HAVE GONE SMOOTHER.

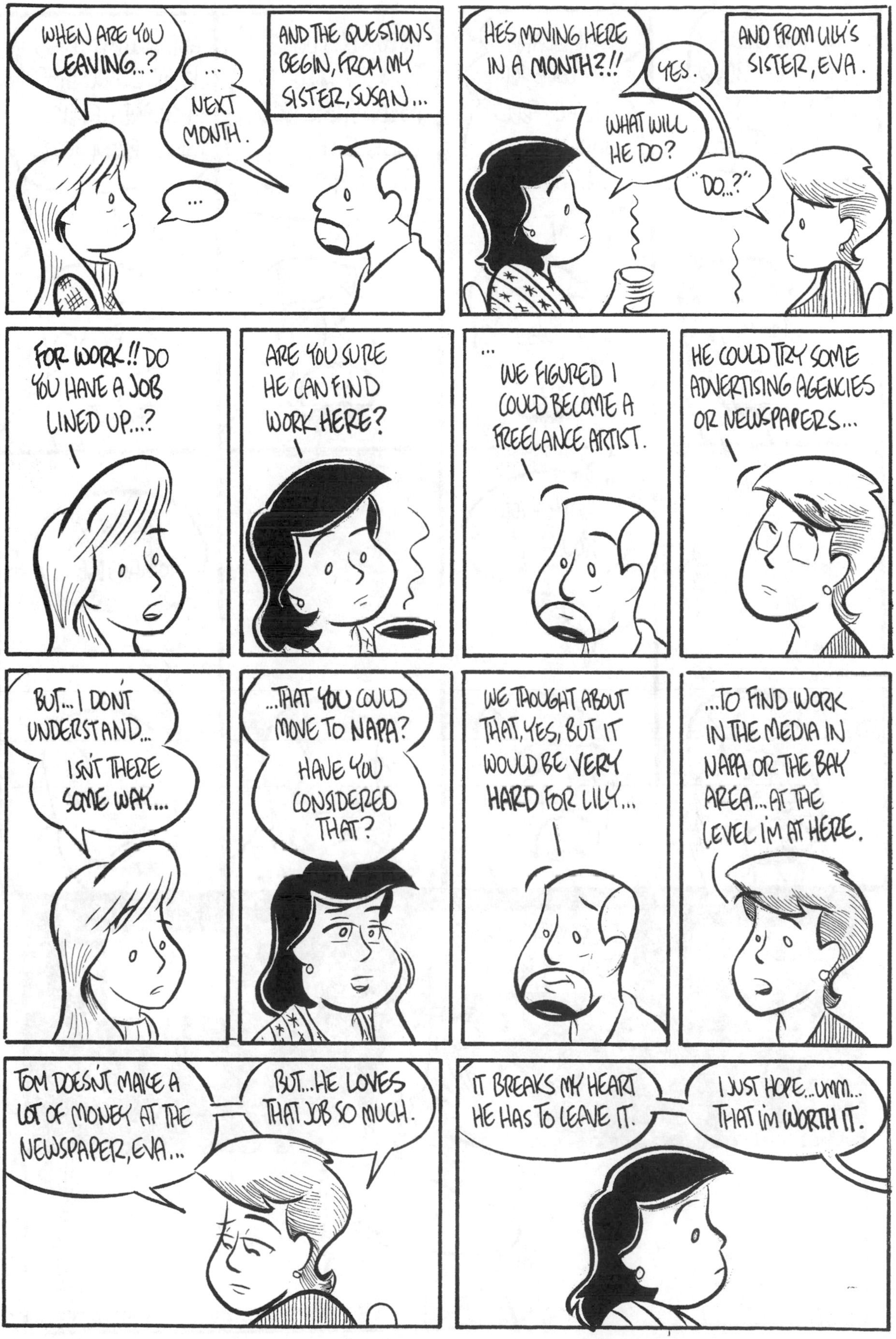
WHEN ARE YOU LEAVING...?
AND THE QUESTIONS BEGIN, FROM MY SISTER, SUSAN...
...
NEXT MONTH.
...
HE'S MOVING HERE IN A MONTH?!!
YES.
AND FROM LILY'S SISTER, EVA.
WHAT WILL HE DO?
"DO...?"
FOR WORK!! DO YOU HAVE A JOB LINED UP...?
ARE YOU SURE HE CAN FIND WORK HERE?
...
WE FIGURED I COULD BECOME A FREELANCE ARTIST.
HE COULD TRY SOME ADVERTISING AGENCIES OR NEWSPAPERS...
BUT... I DON'T UNDERSTAND...
ISN'T THERE SOME WAY...
...THAT YOU COULD MOVE TO NAPA?
HAVE YOU CONSIDERED THAT?
WE THOUGHT ABOUT THAT, YES, BUT IT WOULD BE VERY HARD FOR LILY...
...TO FIND WORK IN THE MEDIA IN NAPA OR THE BAY AREA... AT THE LEVEL I'M AT HERE.
TOM DOESN'T MAKE A LOT OF MONEY AT THE NEWSPAPER, EVA...
BUT... HE LOVES THAT JOB SO MUCH.
IT BREAKS MY HEART HE HAS TO LEAVE IT.
I JUST HOPE... UMM... THAT I'M WORTH IT.

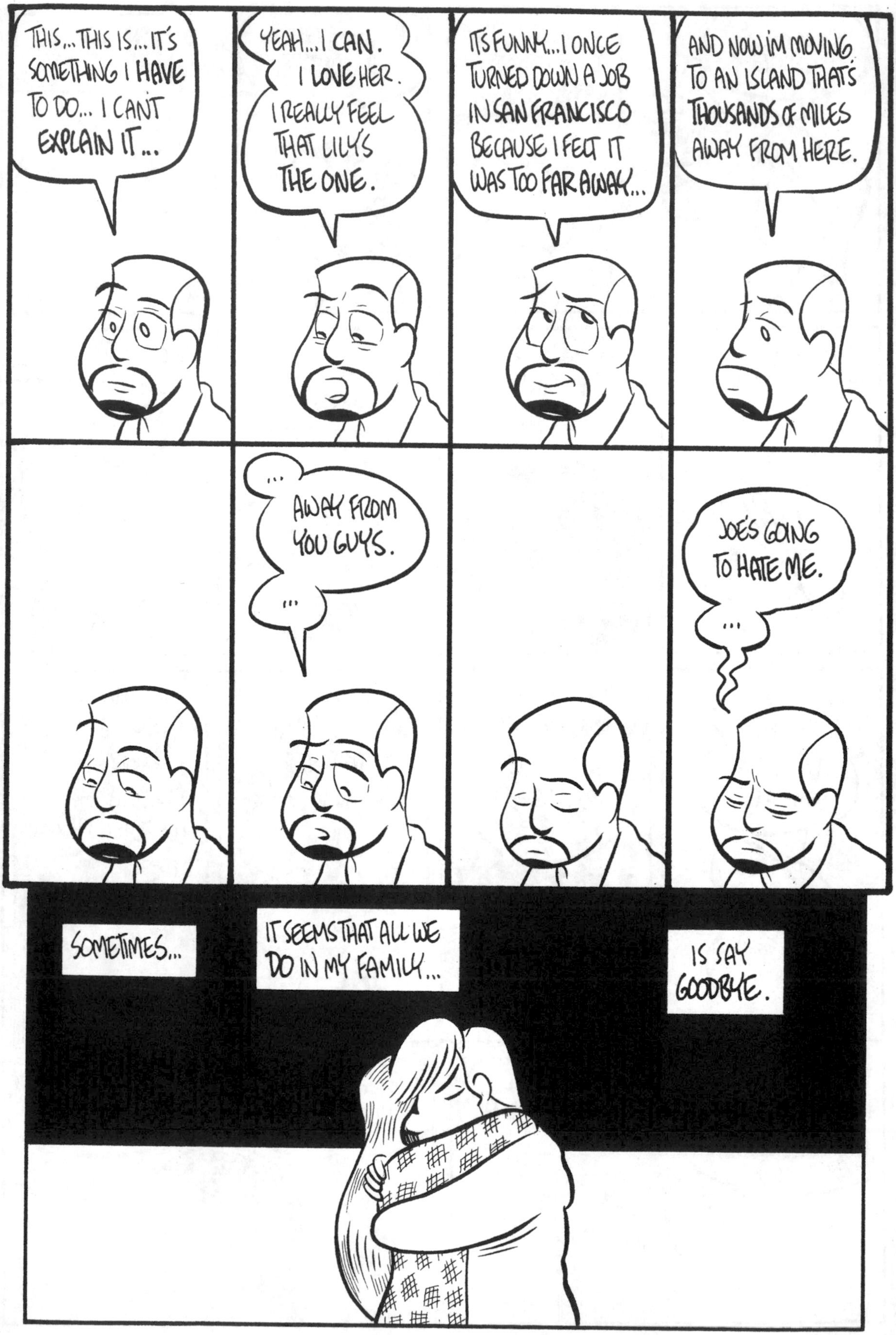
THIS... THIS IS... IT'S SOMETHING I HAVE TO DO... I CAN'T EXPLAIN IT...
YEAH... I CAN. I LOVE HER. I REALLY FEEL THAT LILY'S THE ONE.
ITS FUNNY... I ONCE TURNED DOWN A JOB IN SAN FRANCISCO BECAUSE I FELT IT WAS TOO FAR AWAY...
AND NOW IM MOVING TO AN ISLAND THAT'S THOUSANDS OF MILES AWAY FROM HERE.
...
AWAY FROM YOU GUYS.
...
JOE'S GOING TO HATE ME.
...
SOMETIMES...
IT SEEMS THAT ALL WE DO IN MY FAMILY...
IS SAY GOODBYE.

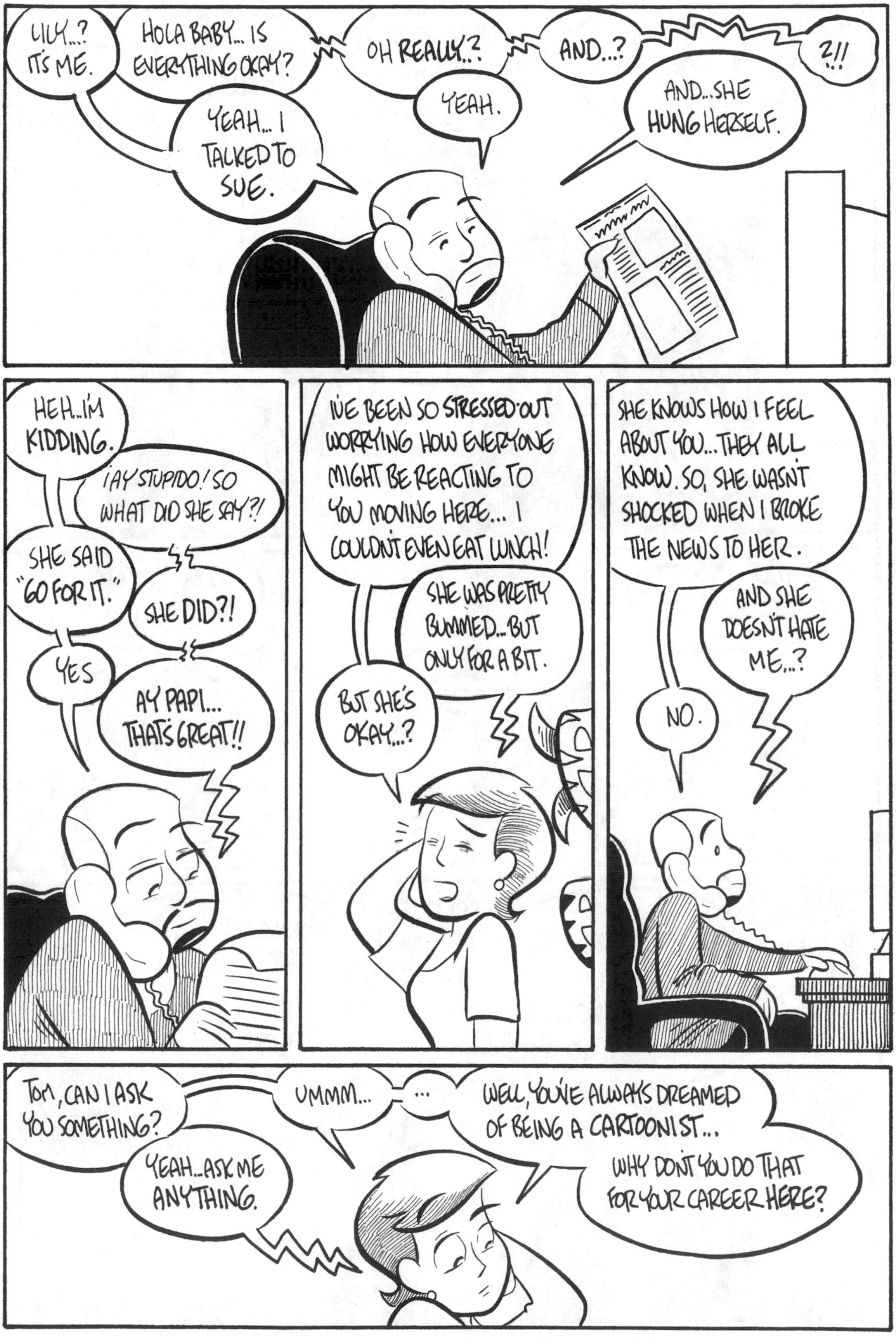
LILY...? IT'S ME.
HOLA BABY... IS EVERYTHING OKAY?
YEAH... I TALKED TO SUE.
OH REALLY..?
YEAH.
AND...?
AND...SHE HUNG HERSELF.
?!!
HEH..I'M KIDDING.
¡AY STUPIDO! SO WHAT DID SHE SAY?!
SHE SAID "GO FOR IT."
SHE DID?!
YES
AY PAPI... THAT'S GREAT!!
I'VE BEEN SO STRESSED-OUT WORRYING HOW EVERYONE MIGHT BE REACTING TO YOU MOVING HERE... I COULDN'T EVEN EAT LUNCH!
SHE WAS PRETTY BUMMED...BUT ONLY FOR A BIT.
BUT SHE'S OKAY...?
SHE KNOWS HOW I FEEL ABOUT YOU...THEY ALL KNOW. SO, SHE WASN'T SHOCKED WHEN I BROKE THE NEWS TO HER.
AND SHE DOESN'T HATE ME...?
NO.
TOM, CAN I ASK YOU SOMETHING?
YEAH...ASK ME ANYTHING.
UMMM...
...
WELL, YOU'VE ALWAYS DREAMED OF BEING A CARTOONIST...
WHY DON'T YOU DO THAT FOR YOUR CAREER HERE?

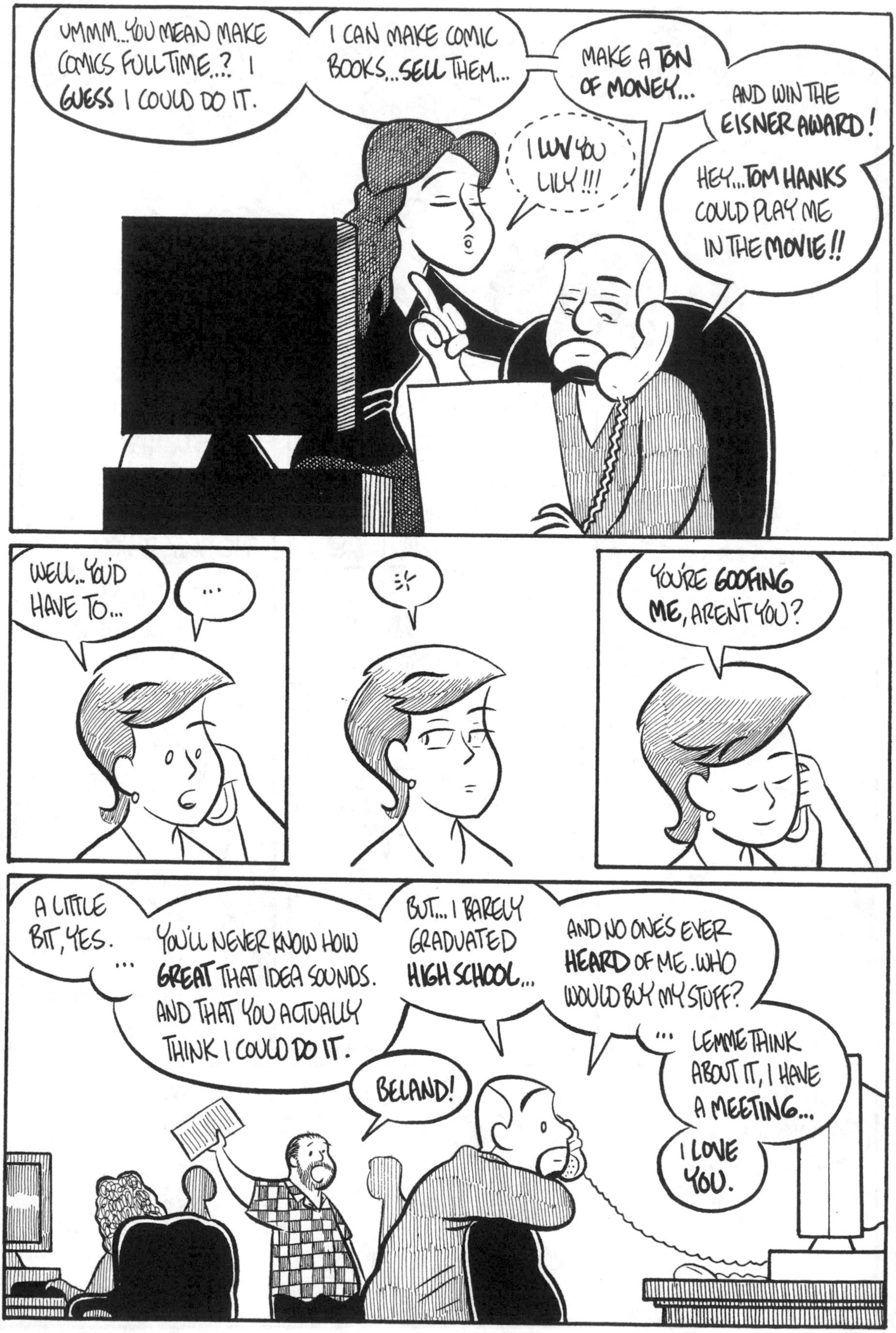

UMMM...YOU MEAN MAKE COMICS FULLTIME..? I GUESS I COULD DO IT.
I CAN MAKE COMIC BOOKS...SELL THEM...
MAKE A TON OF MONEY...
AND WIN THE EISNER AWARD!
HEY...TOM HANKS COULD PLAY ME IN THE MOVIE!!
I LUV YOU LILY!!!
WELL..YOU'D HAVE TO...
...
YOU'RE GOOFING ME, AREN'T YOU?
A LITTLE BIT, YES.
... YOU'LL NEVER KNOW HOW GREAT THAT IDEA SOUNDS. AND THAT YOU ACTUALLY THINK I COULD DO IT.
BUT... I BARELY GRADUATED HIGH SCHOOL...
AND NO ONE'S EVER HEARD OF ME. WHO WOULD BUY MY STUFF?
... LEMME THINK ABOUT IT, I HAVE A MEETING...
I LOVE YOU.
BELAND!

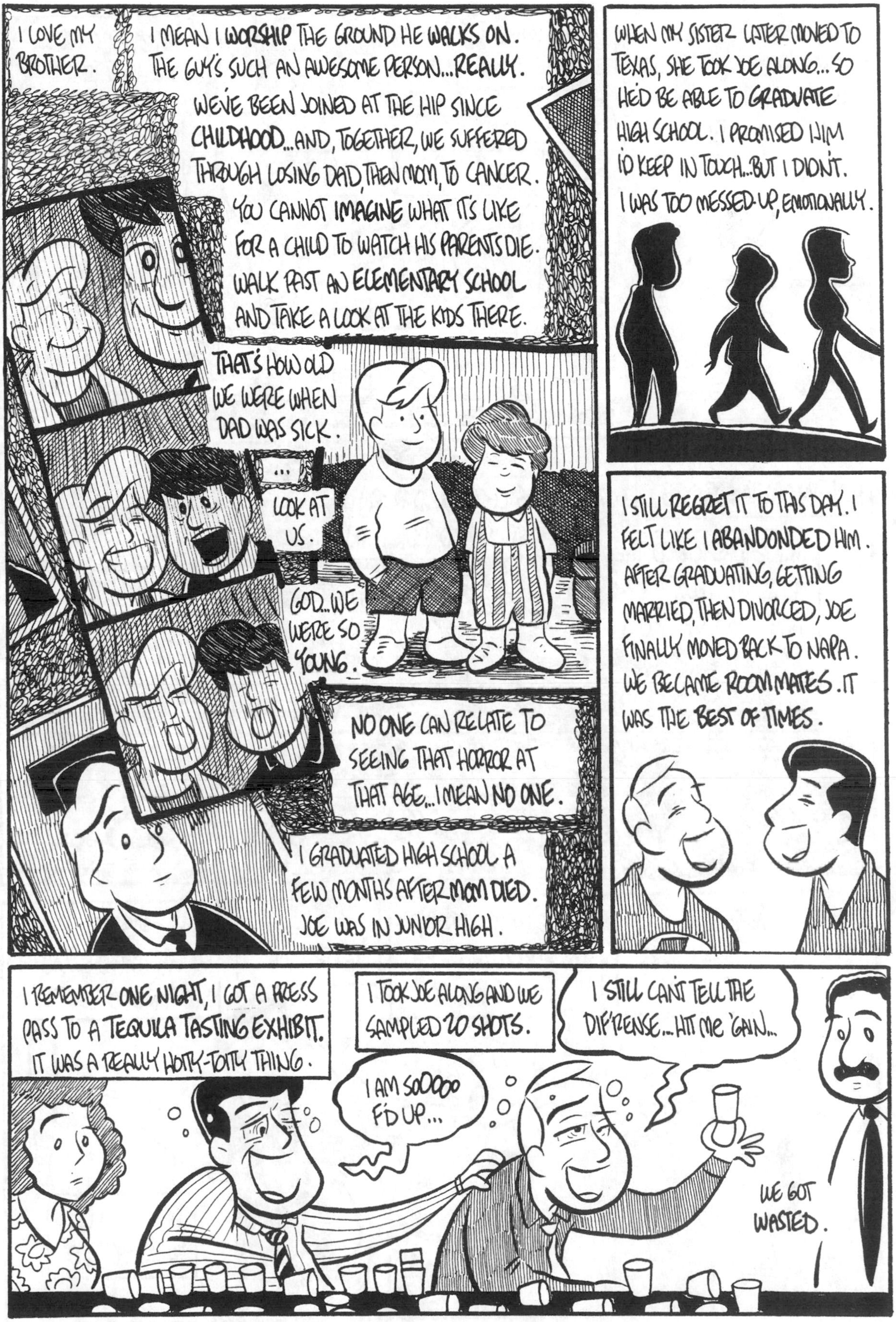
I LOVE MY BROTHER.
I MEAN I WORSHIP THE GROUND HE WALKS ON. THE GUY'S SUCH AN AWESOME PERSON...REALLY.
WE'VE BEEN JOINED AT THE HIP SINCE CHILDHOOD...AND, TOGETHER, WE SUFFERED THROUGH LOSING DAD, THEN MOM, TO CANCER.
YOU CANNOT IMAGINE WHAT IT'S LIKE FOR A CHILD TO WATCH HIS PARENTS DIE. WALK PAST AN ELEMENTARY SCHOOL AND TAKE A LOOK AT THE KIDS THERE.
THAT'S HOW OLD WE WERE WHEN DAD WAS SICK.
...
LOOK AT US.
GOD...WE WERE SO YOUNG.
NO ONE CAN RELATE TO SEEING THAT HORROR AT THAT AGE...I MEAN NO ONE.
I GRADUATED HIGH SCHOOL A FEW MONTHS AFTER MOM DIED. JOE WAS IN JUNIOR HIGH.
WHEN MY SISTER LATER MOVED TO TEXAS, SHE TOOK JOE ALONG...SO HE'D BE ABLE TO GRADUATE HIGH SCHOOL. I PROMISED HIM TO KEEP IN TOUCH...BUT I DIDN'T. I WAS TOO MESSED-UP, EMOTIONALLY.
I STILL REGRET IT TO THIS DAY. I FELT LIKE I ABANDONDED HIM. AFTER GRADUATING, GETTING MARRIED, THEN DIVORCED, JOE FINALLY MOVED BACK TO NAPA. WE BECAME ROOMMATES. IT WAS THE BEST OF TIMES.
I REMEMBER ONE NIGHT, I GOT A PRESS PASS TO A TEQUILA TASTING EXHIBIT. IT WAS A REALLY HOITY-TOITY THING.
I TOOK JOE ALONG AND WE SAMPLED 20 SHOTS.
I STILL CAN'T TELL THE DIF'RENSE...HIT ME 'GAIN...
I AM SOOOOO F'D UP...
WE GOT WASTED.

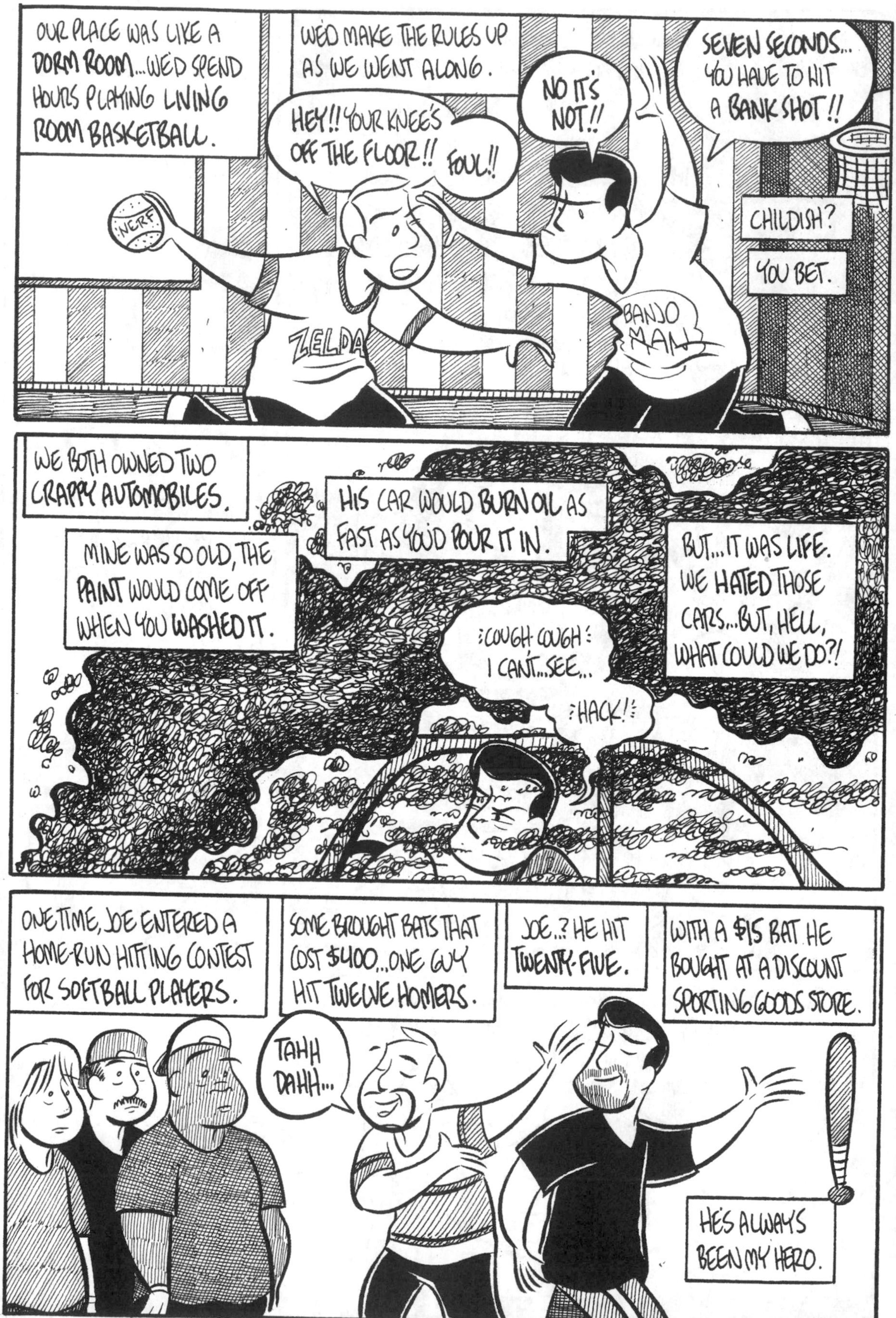
OUR PLACE WAS LIKE A DORM ROOM... WE'D SPEND HOURS PLAYING LIVING ROOM BASKETBALL.
WE'D MAKE THE RULES UP AS WE WENT ALONG.
HEY!! YOUR KNEE'S OFF THE FLOOR!! FOUL!!
NO IT'S NOT!!
SEVEN SECONDS... YOU HAVE TO HIT A BANK SHOT!!
NERF
ZELDA
BANJO MAN
CHILDISH?
YOU BET.
WE BOTH OWNED TWO CRAPPY AUTOMOBILES.
HIS CAR WOULD BURN OIL AS FAST AS YOU'D POUR IT IN.
MINE WAS SO OLD, THE PAINT WOULD COME OFF WHEN YOU WASHED IT.
BUT... IT WAS LIFE. WE HATED THOSE CARS... BUT, HELL, WHAT COULD WE DO?!
COUGH COUGH I CAN'T... SEE...
HACK!
ONE TIME, JOE ENTERED A HOME-RUN HITTING CONTEST FOR SOFTBALL PLAYERS.
SOME BROUGHT BATS THAT COST $400... ONE GUY HIT TWELVE HOMERS.
JOE..? HE HIT TWENTY-FIVE.
WITH A $15 BAT HE BOUGHT AT A DISCOUNT SPORTING GOODS STORE.
TAHH DAHH...
HE'S ALWAYS BEEN MY HERO.

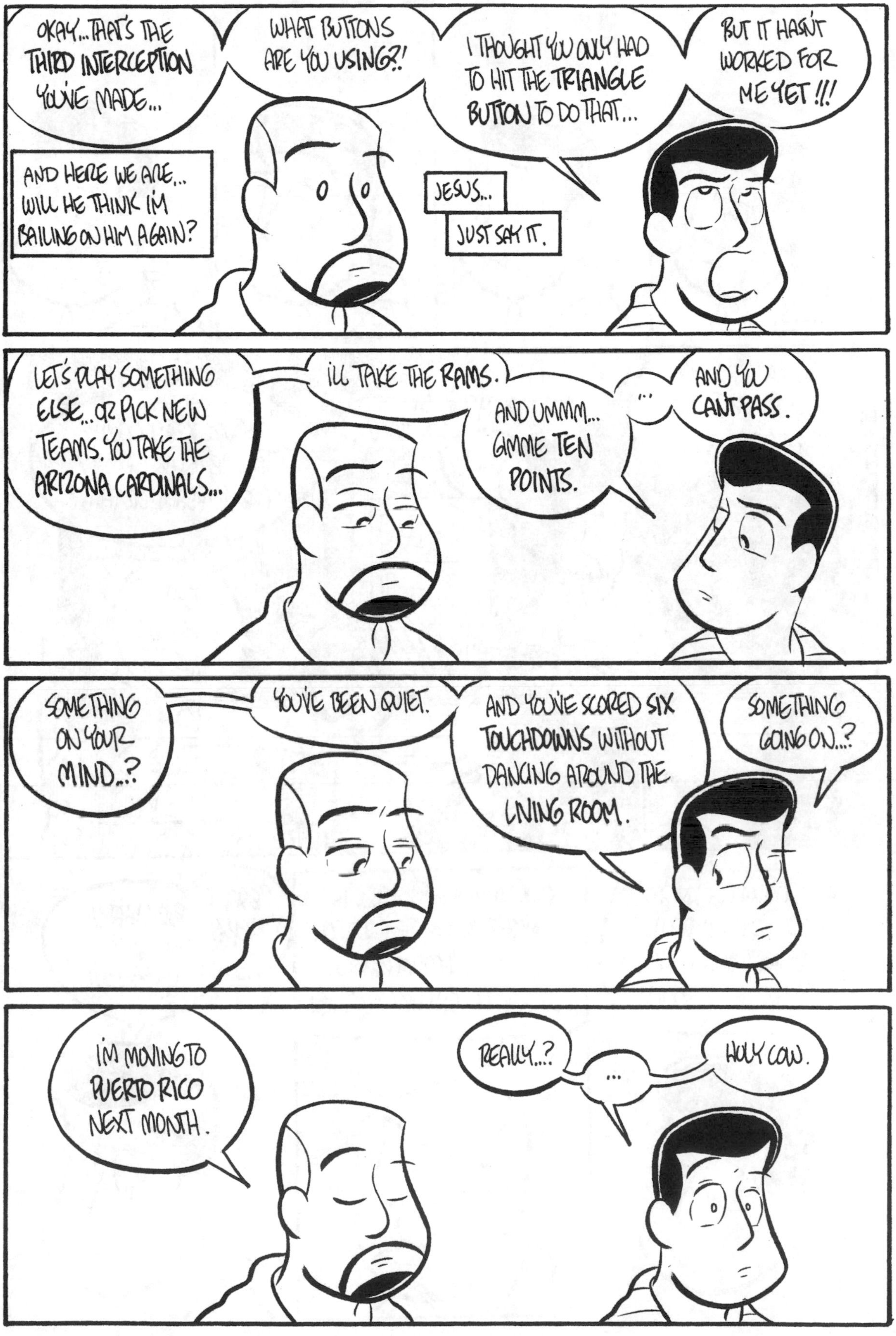
OKAY...THAT'S THE THIRD INTERCEPTION YOU'VE MADE...
WHAT BUTTONS ARE YOU USING?!
I THOUGHT YOU ONLY HAD TO HIT THE TRIANGLE BUTTON TO DO THAT...
BUT IT HASN'T WORKED FOR ME YET!!!
AND HERE WE ARE... WILL HE THINK I'M BAILING ON HIM AGAIN?
JESUS...
JUST SAY IT.
LET'S PLAY SOMETHING ELSE...OR PICK NEW TEAMS. YOU TAKE THE ARIZONA CARDINALS...
I'LL TAKE THE RAMS.
AND UMMM... GIMME TEN POINTS.
...
AND YOU CAN'T PASS.
SOMETHING ON YOUR MIND..?
YOU'VE BEEN QUIET.
AND YOU'VE SCORED SIX TOUCHDOWNS WITHOUT DANCING AROUND THE LIVING ROOM.
SOMETHING GOING ON...?
I'M MOVING TO PUERTO RICO NEXT MONTH.
REALLY..?
...
HOLY COW.

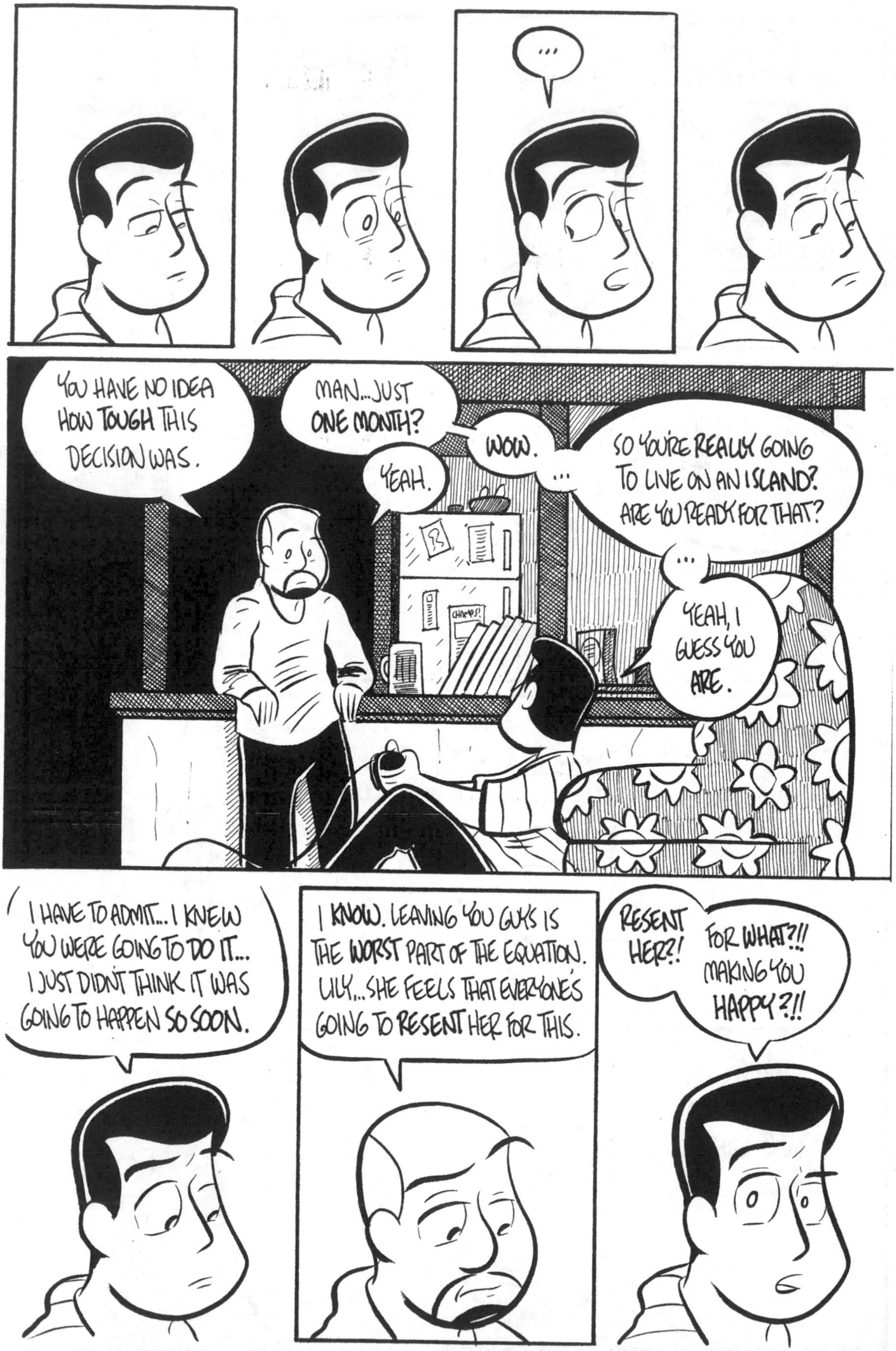
...
YOU HAVE NO IDEA HOW TOUGH THIS DECISION WAS.
MAN...JUST ONE MONTH?
YEAH.
WOW.
...
SO YOU'RE REALLY GOING TO LIVE ON AN ISLAND? ARE YOU READY FOR THAT?
...
YEAH, I GUESS YOU ARE.
I HAVE TO ADMIT... I KNEW YOU WERE GOING TO DO IT... I JUST DIDN'T THINK IT WAS GOING TO HAPPEN SO SOON.
I KNOW. LEAVING YOU GUYS IS THE WORST PART OF THE EQUATION. LILY... SHE FEELS THAT EVERYONE'S GOING TO RESENT HER FOR THIS.
RESENT HER?!
FOR WHAT?!! MAKING YOU HAPPY?!!

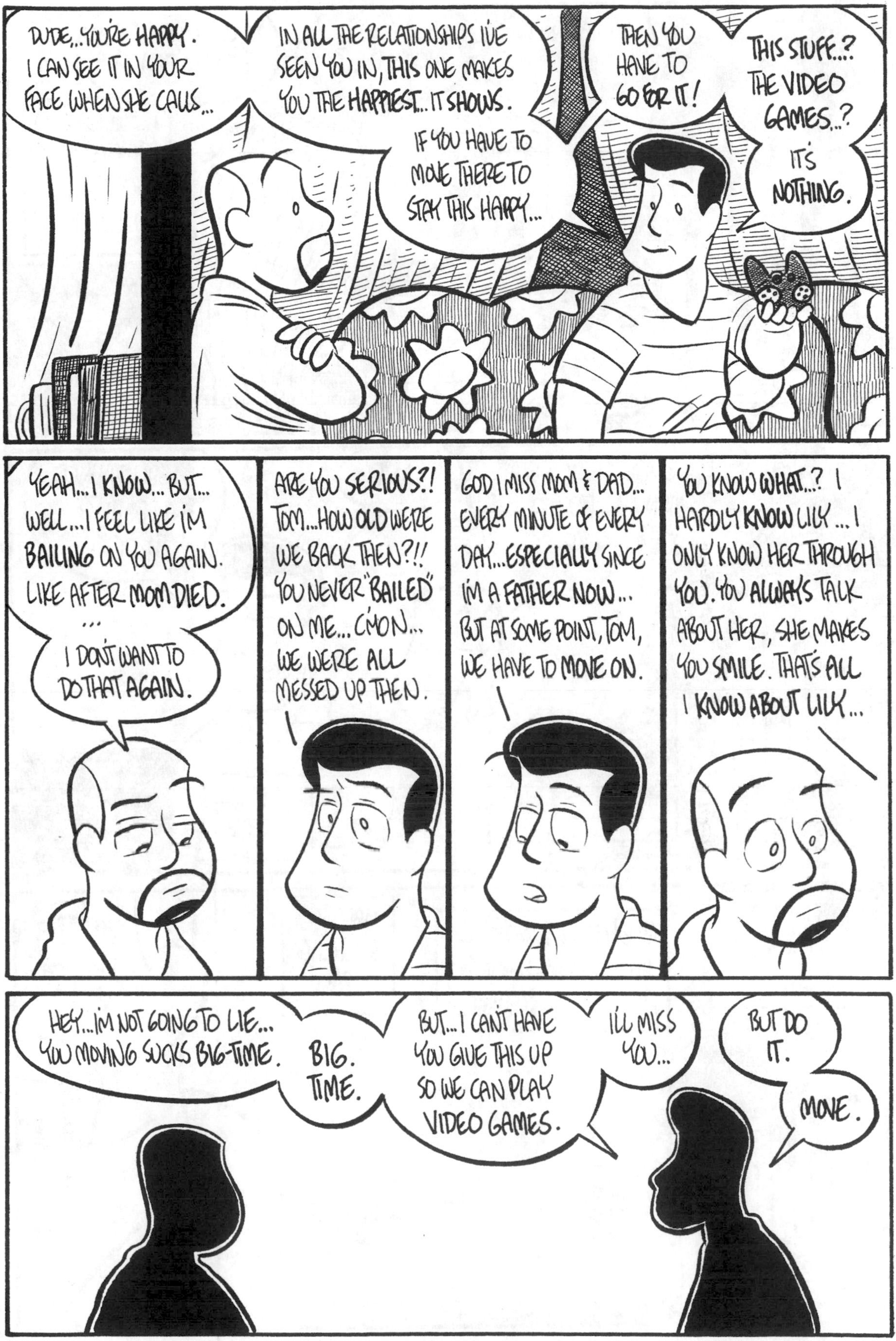
DUDE... YOU'RE HAPPY. I CAN SEE IT IN YOUR FACE WHEN SHE CALLS...
IN ALL THE RELATIONSHIPS I'VE SEEN YOU IN, THIS ONE MAKES YOU THE HAPPIEST... IT SHOWS.
IF YOU HAVE TO MOVE THERE TO STAY THIS HAPPY...
THEN YOU HAVE TO GO FOR IT!
THIS STUFF...? THE VIDEO GAMES...?
IT'S NOTHING.
YEAH... I KNOW... BUT... WELL... I FEEL LIKE I'M BAILING ON YOU AGAIN. LIKE AFTER MOM DIED.
...
I DON'T WANT TO DO THAT AGAIN.
ARE YOU SERIOUS?! TOM... HOW OLD WERE WE BACK THEN?!! YOU NEVER "BAILED" ON ME... C'MON... WE WERE ALL MESSED UP THEN.
GOD I MISS MOM & DAD... EVERY MINUTE OF EVERY DAY... ESPECIALLY SINCE I'M A FATHER NOW... BUT AT SOME POINT, TOM, WE HAVE TO MOVE ON.
YOU KNOW WHAT...? I HARDLY KNOW LILY... I ONLY KNOW HER THROUGH YOU. YOU ALWAYS TALK ABOUT HER, SHE MAKES YOU SMILE. THAT'S ALL I KNOW ABOUT LILY...
HEY... I'M NOT GOING TO LIE... YOU MOVING SUCKS BIG-TIME.
BIG. TIME.
BUT... I CAN'T HAVE YOU GIVE THIS UP SO WE CAN PLAY VIDEO GAMES.
I'LL MISS YOU...
BUT DO IT.
MOVE.

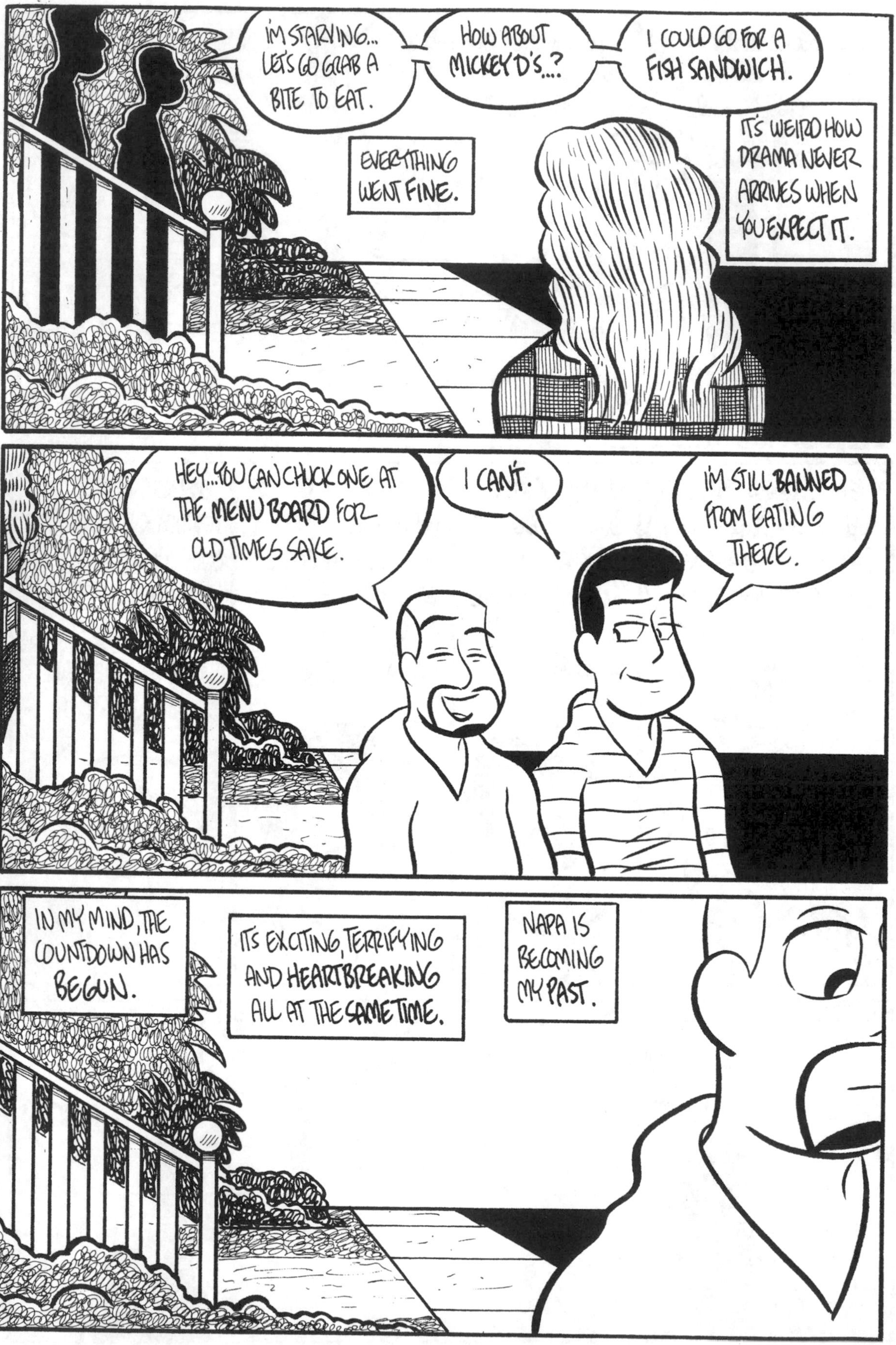
I'M STARVING... LET'S GO GRAB A BITE TO EAT.
HOW ABOUT MICKEY D'S...?
I COULD GO FOR A FISH SANDWICH.
EVERYTHING WENT FINE.
IT'S WEIRD HOW DRAMA NEVER ARRIVES WHEN YOU EXPECT IT.
HEY...YOU CAN CHUCK ONE AT THE MENU BOARD FOR OLD TIMES SAKE.
I CAN'T.
I'M STILL BANNED FROM EATING THERE.
IN MY MIND, THE COUNTDOWN HAS BEGUN.
IT'S EXCITING, TERRIFYING AND HEARTBREAKING ALL AT THE SAME TIME.
NAPA IS BECOMING MY PAST.

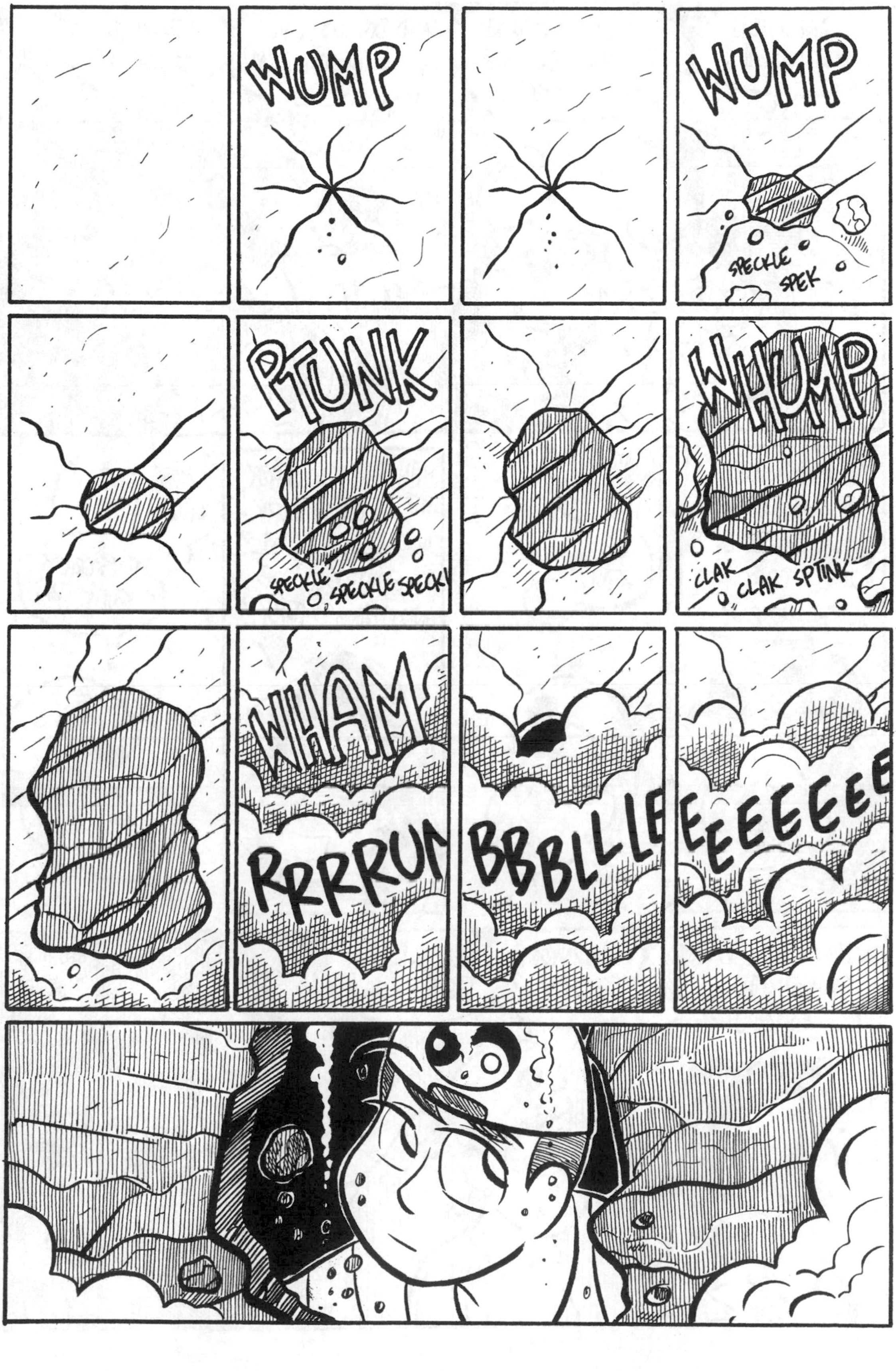
WUMP
WUMP
SPECKLE
SPEK
PTUNK
SPECKLE
SPECKLE
SPECK
WHUMP
CLAK
CLAK
SPTINK
WHAM
RRRRUMBBBLLLEEEEEEEE

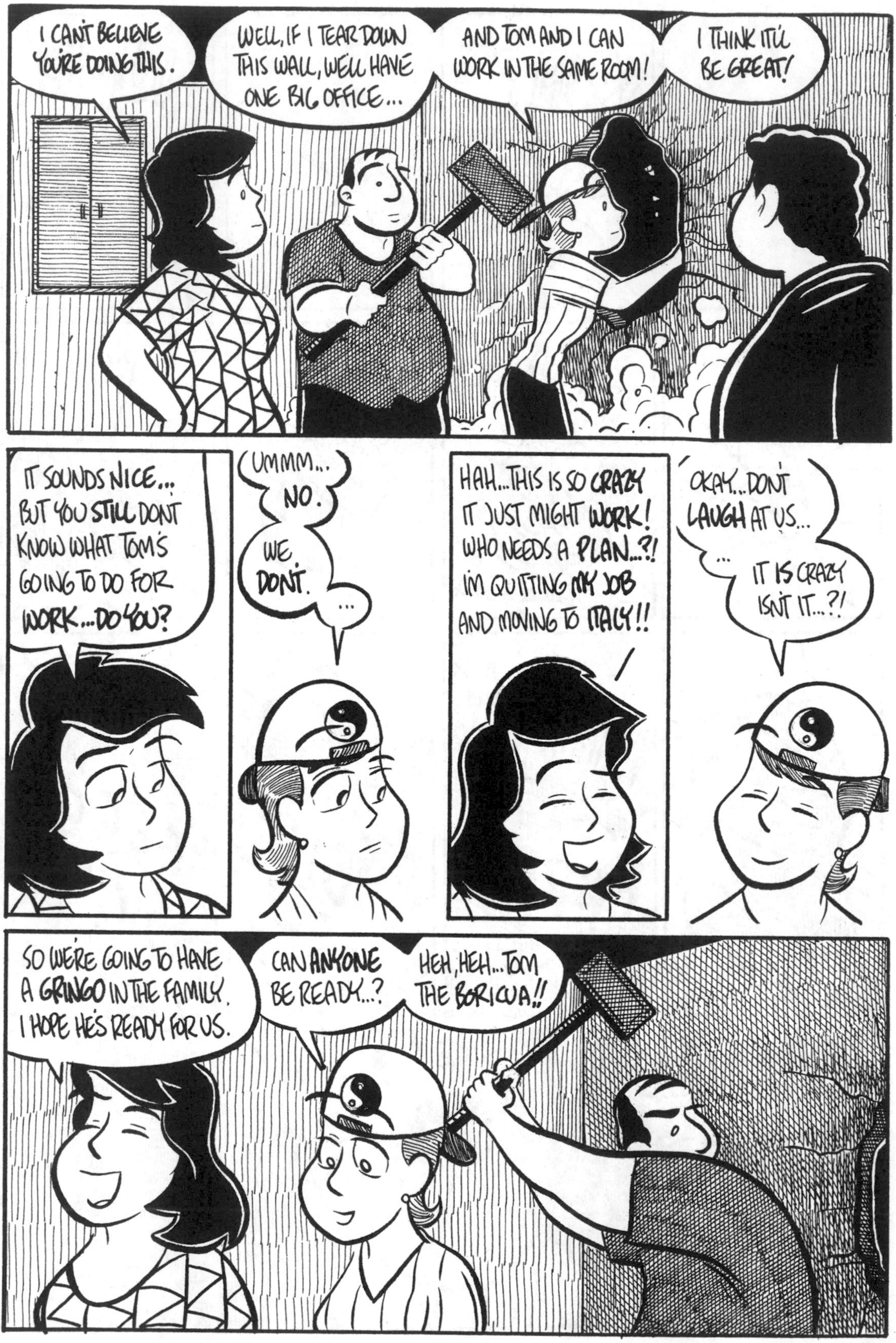

I CAN'T BELIEVE YOU'RE DOING THIS.
WELL, IF I TEAR DOWN THIS WALL, WE'LL HAVE ONE BIG OFFICE...
AND TOM AND I CAN WORK IN THE SAME ROOM!
I THINK IT'LL BE GREAT!
IT SOUNDS NICE... BUT YOU STILL DON'T KNOW WHAT TOM'S GOING TO DO FOR WORK... DO YOU?
UMMM... NO.
WE DON'T.
...
HAH... THIS IS SO CRAZY IT JUST MIGHT WORK! WHO NEEDS A PLAN...?! I'M QUITTING MY JOB AND MOVING TO ITALY!!
OKAY... DON'T LAUGH AT US...
...
IT IS CRAZY ISN'T IT...?!
SO WE'RE GOING TO HAVE A GRINGO IN THE FAMILY. I HOPE HE'S READY FOR US.
CAN ANYONE BE READY...?
HEH, HEH... TOM THE BORICUA!!

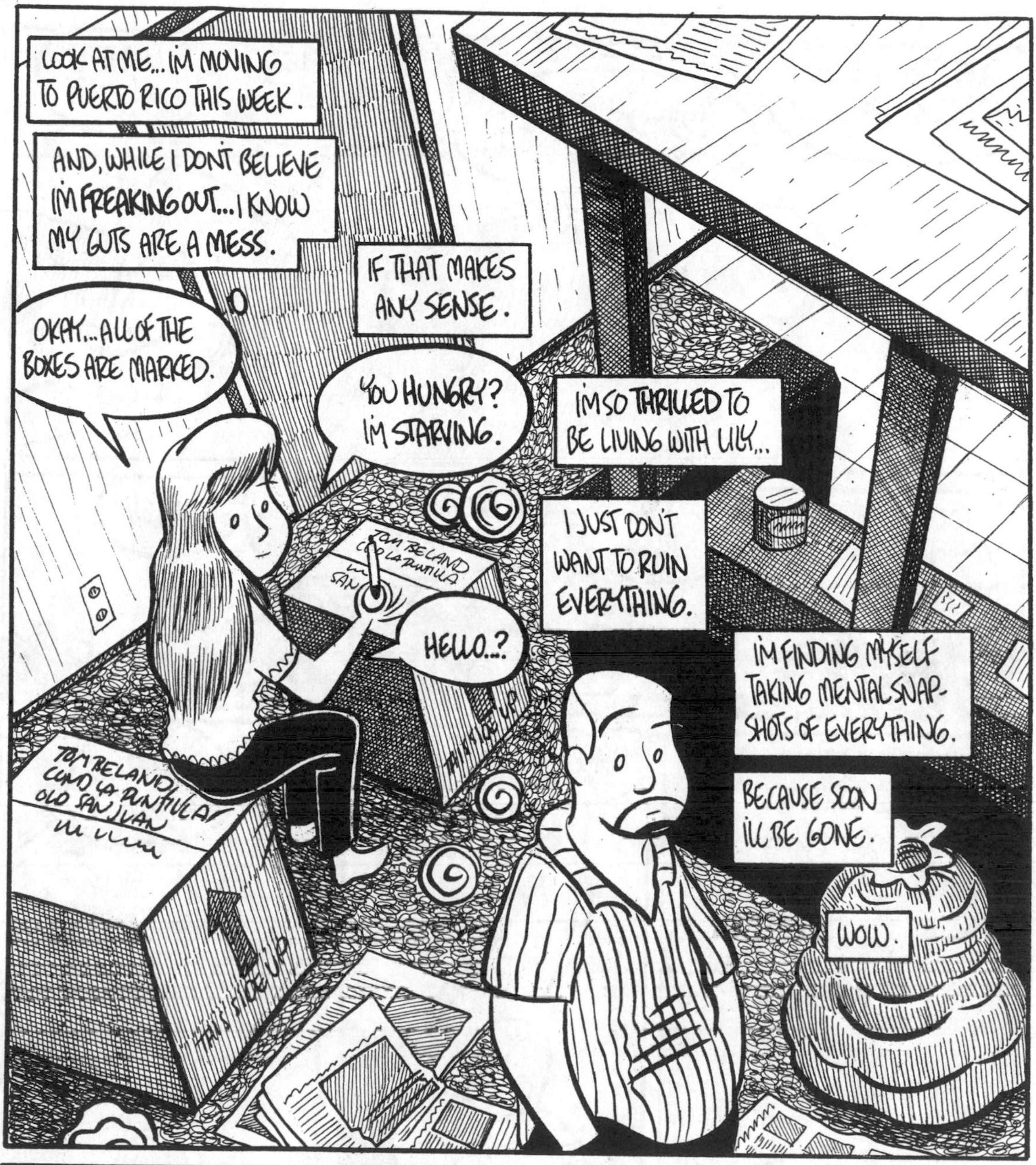
LOOK AT ME... I'M MOVING TO PUERTO RICO THIS WEEK.
AND, WHILE I DON'T BELIEVE I'M FREAKING OUT... I KNOW MY GUTS ARE A MESS.
IF THAT MAKES ANY SENSE.
OKAY... ALL OF THE BOXES ARE MARKED.
YOU HUNGRY? I'M STARVING.
I'M SO THRILLED TO BE LIVING WITH LILY...
I JUST DON'T WANT TO RUIN EVERYTHING.
HELLO..?
I'M FINDING MYSELF TAKING MENTAL SNAPSHOTS OF EVERYTHING.
BECAUSE SOON I'LL BE GONE.
WOW.
TOM BELAND
OLD SAN JUAN
THIS SIDE UP

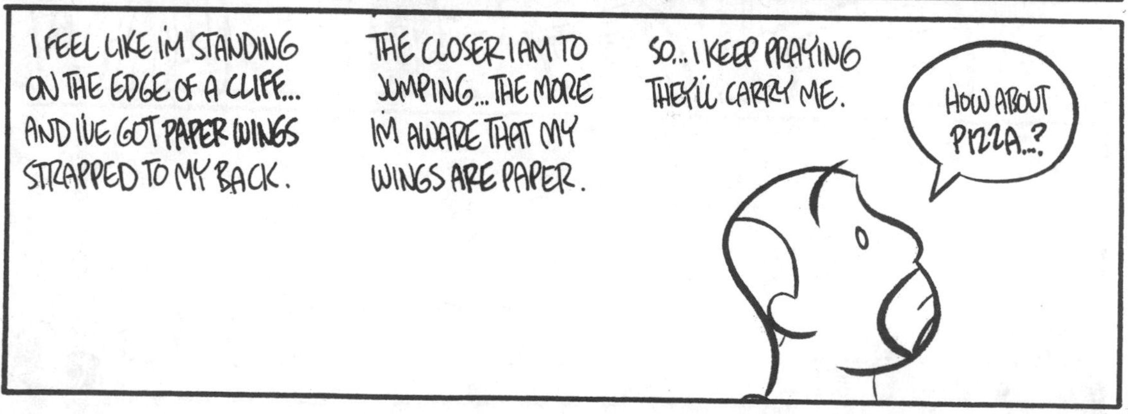
I FEEL LIKE I'M STANDING ON THE EDGE OF A CLIFF... AND I'VE GOT PAPER WINGS STRAPPED TO MY BACK.
THE CLOSER I AM TO JUMPING... THE MORE I'M AWARE THAT MY WINGS ARE PAPER.
SO... I KEEP PRAYING THEY'LL CARRY ME.
HOW ABOUT PIZZA..?

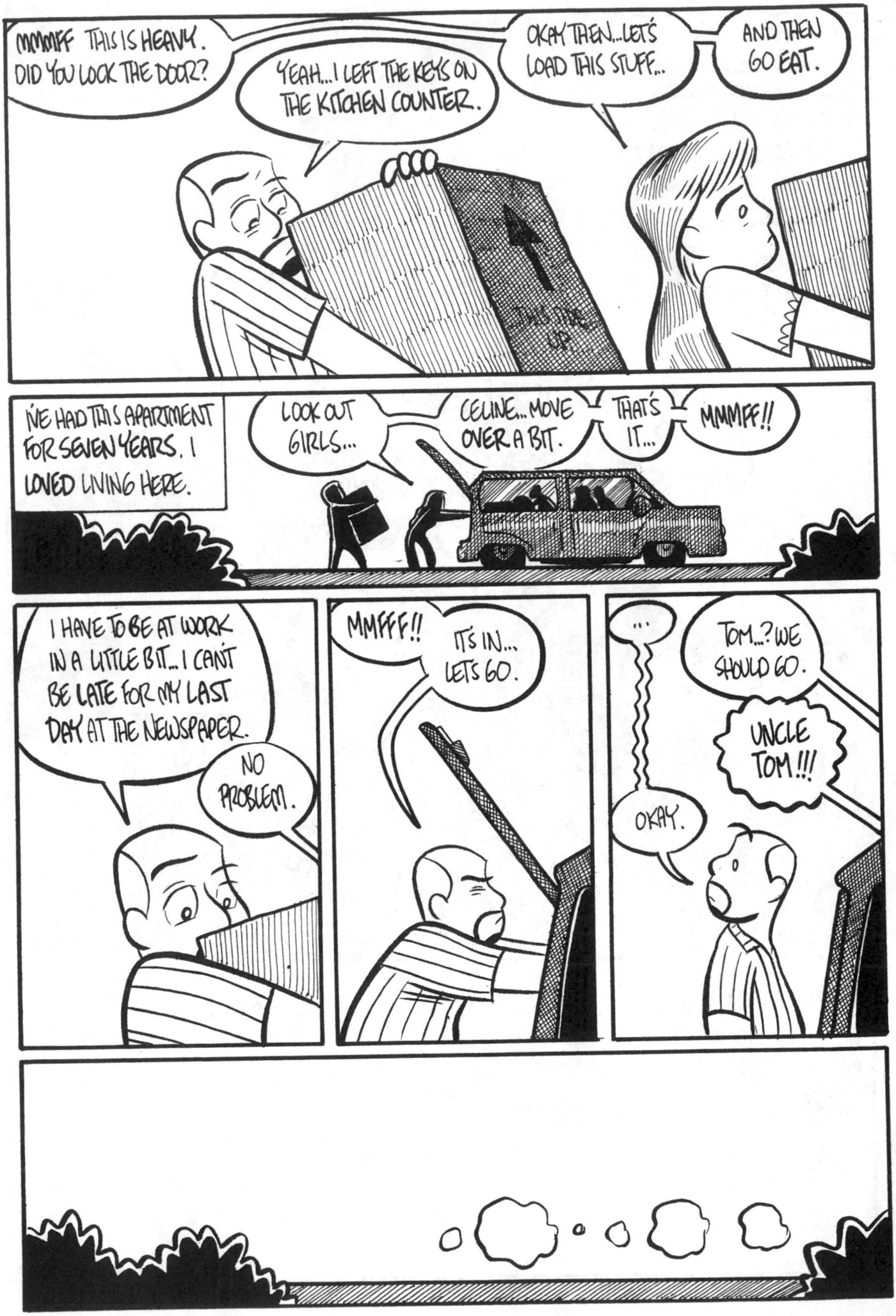

MMMFF THIS IS HEAVY. DID YOU LOCK THE DOOR?
YEAH... I LEFT THE KEYS ON THE KITCHEN COUNTER.
OKAY THEN... LET'S LOAD THIS STUFF...
AND THEN GO EAT.
THIS SIDE UP
I'VE HAD THIS APARTMENT FOR SEVEN YEARS. I LOVED LIVING HERE.
LOOK OUT GIRLS...
CELINE... MOVE OVER A BIT.
THAT'S IT...
MMMFF!!
I HAVE TO BE AT WORK IN A LITTLE BIT... I CAN'T BE LATE FOR MY LAST DAY AT THE NEWSPAPER.
NO PROBLEM.
MMFFF!!
IT'S IN... LET'S GO.
...
TOM...? WE SHOULD GO.
UNCLE TOM!!!
OKAY.

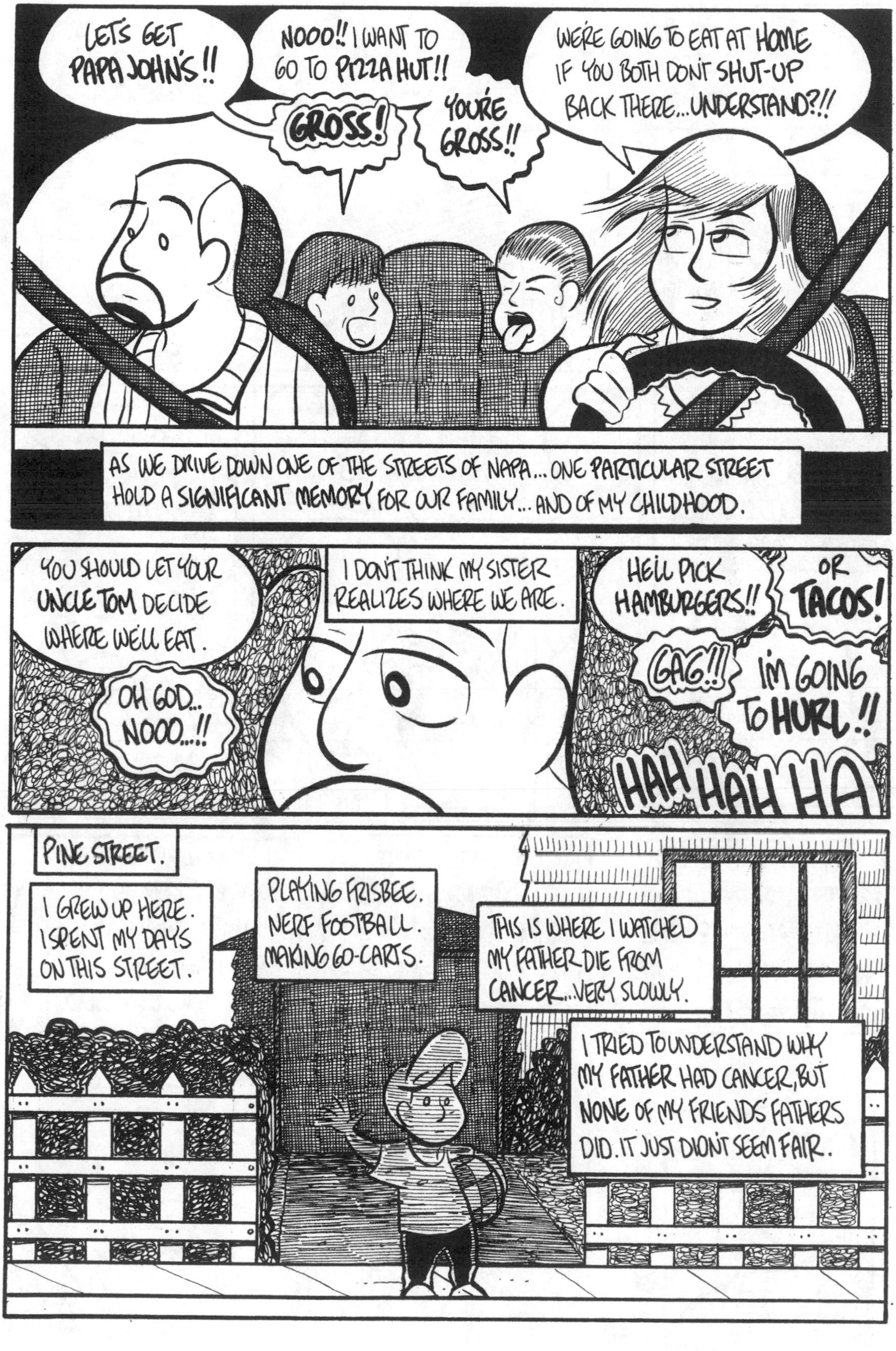
LET'S GET PAPA JOHN'S!!
NOOO!! I WANT TO GO TO PIZZA HUT!!
GROSS!
YOU'RE GROSS!!
WE'RE GOING TO EAT AT HOME IF YOU BOTH DON'T SHUT-UP BACK THERE...UNDERSTAND?!!
AS WE DRIVE DOWN ONE OF THE STREETS OF NAPA... ONE PARTICULAR STREET HOLD A SIGNIFICANT MEMORY FOR OUR FAMILY... AND OF MY CHILDHOOD.
YOU SHOULD LET YOUR UNCLE TOM DECIDE WHERE WE'LL EAT.
OH GOD... NOOO...!!
I DON'T THINK MY SISTER REALIZES WHERE WE ARE.
HE'LL PICK HAMBURGERS!!
OR TACOS!
GAG!!
I'M GOING TO HURL!!
HAH HAH HA
PINE STREET.
I GREW UP HERE. I SPENT MY DAYS ON THIS STREET.
PLAYING FRISBEE. NERF FOOTBALL. MAKING GO-CARTS.
THIS IS WHERE I WATCHED MY FATHER DIE FROM CANCER...VERY SLOWLY.
I TRIED TO UNDERSTAND WHY MY FATHER HAD CANCER, BUT NONE OF MY FRIENDS' FATHERS DID. IT JUST DIDN'T SEEM FAIR.

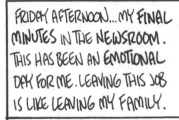

FRIDAY AFTERNOON... MY FINAL MINUTES IN THE NEWSROOM. THIS HAS BEEN AN EMOTIONAL DAY FOR ME. LEAVING THIS JOB IS LIKE LEAVING MY FAMILY.

I'VE BEEN A BANK TELLER, A HOTEL CLERK, A FRY COOK, EVEN A PRINTER...

DONE YET...?

ALMOST. ONE SEC.

THIS WAS THE FIRST JOB I HAD WHERE I REALLY FELT RESPECTED.

DONE.

MY THOUGHTS MATTERED. MY SENSE OF HUMOR WAS **APPRECIATED**... AND THEY MADE ME FEEL **SPECIAL**. THAT'S SO **RARE** TODAY.

PUERTO RICO...

I STILL CAN'T BELIEVE YOU'LL BE LIVING ON AN ISLAND... YOU.

HEH... I KNOW.

SO DO THEY HAVE ESPN IN PUERTO RICO?

YES... I MADE SURE THEY DID.

COOL.

I'M GOING TO MISS THIS... THE **NEWSROOM**. IT'S ONE OF MY FAVORITE PLACES ON **EARTH**. THE VIBE... THE PEOPLE... I LOVE EVERYTHING ABOUT IT.

WELL BELAND... I CAN'T WAIT TO HAVE AN ACTUAL EDITORS MEETING WITHOUT ALL OF THE DICK JOKES.

I WISH I COULD STAY HERE JUSTINE, IF ONLY TO SEE YOU BITCH ABOUT HAVING TO DESIGN MY PAGES. BELIEVE ME... I WILL BE MISSED... YOU... WILL MISS... ME...!

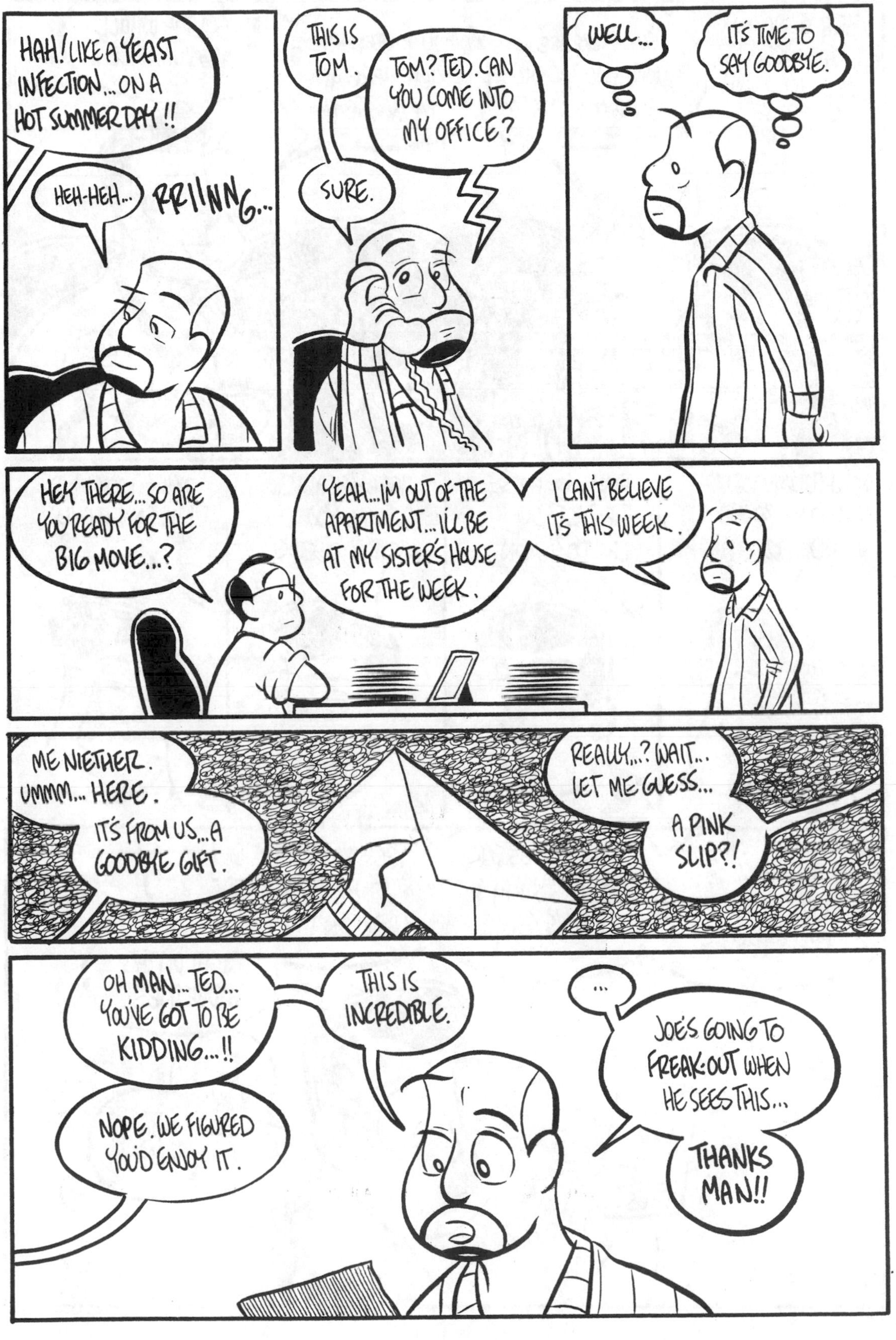
HAH! LIKE A YEAST INFECTION... ON A HOT SUMMER DAY!!
HEH-HEH...
RRIINNG...
THIS IS TOM.
TOM? TED. CAN YOU COME INTO MY OFFICE?
SURE.
WELL...
IT'S TIME TO SAY GOODBYE.
HEY THERE... SO ARE YOU READY FOR THE BIG MOVE...?
YEAH... I'M OUT OF THE APARTMENT... I'LL BE AT MY SISTER'S HOUSE FOR THE WEEK.
I CAN'T BELIEVE IT'S THIS WEEK.
ME NIETHER. UMMM... HERE.
IT'S FROM US... A GOODBYE GIFT.
REALLY...? WAIT... LET ME GUESS...
A PINK SLIP?!
OH MAN... TED... YOU'VE GOT TO BE KIDDING...!!
THIS IS INCREDIBLE.
NOPE. WE FIGURED YOU'D ENJOY IT.
...
JOE'S GOING TO FREAK-OUT WHEN HE SEES THIS...
THANKS MAN!!

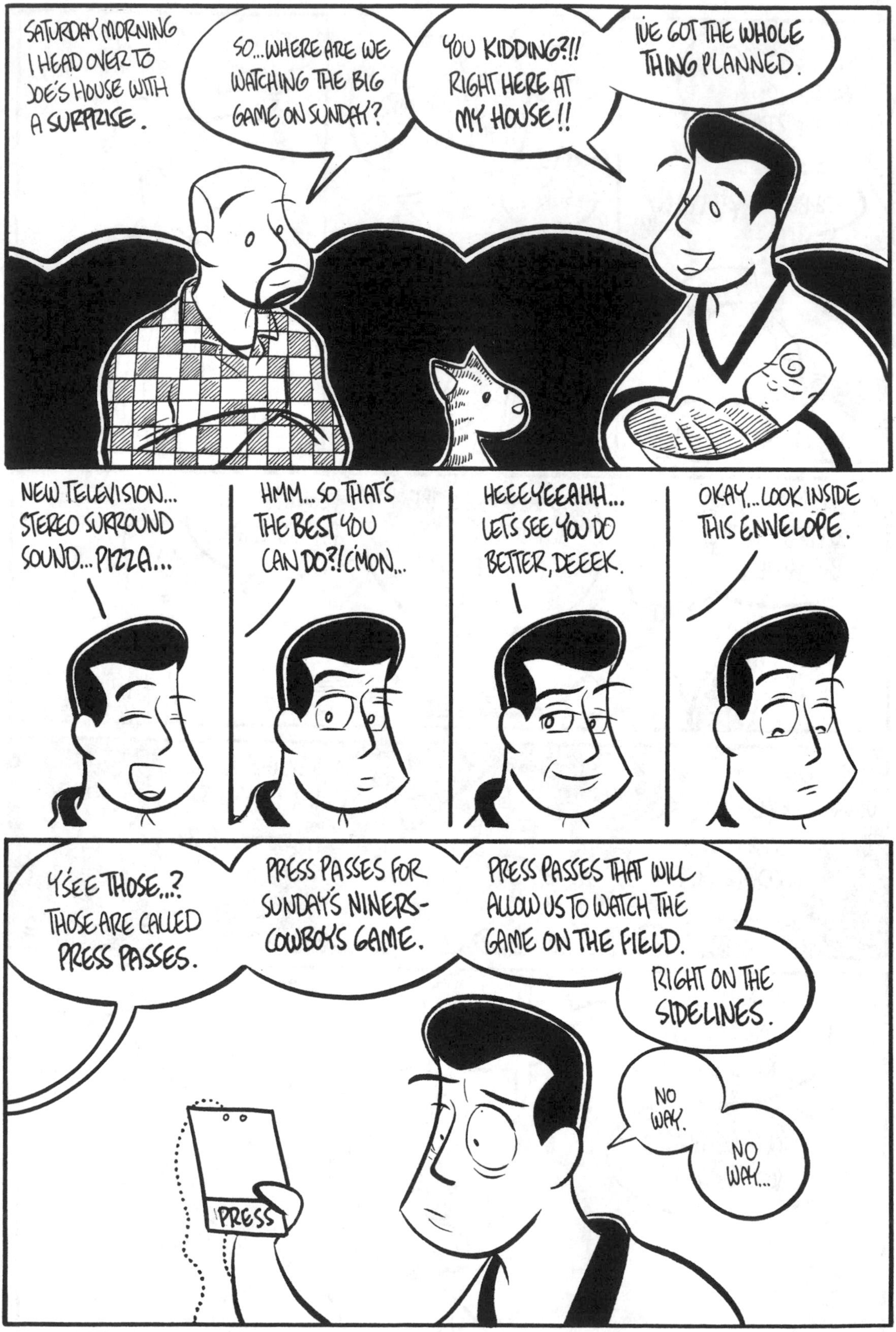
SATURDAY MORNING I HEAD OVER TO JOE'S HOUSE WITH A SURPRISE.
SO...WHERE ARE WE WATCHING THE BIG GAME ON SUNDAY?
YOU KIDDING?!! RIGHT HERE AT MY HOUSE!!
I'VE GOT THE WHOLE THING PLANNED.
NEW TELEVISION... STEREO SURROUND SOUND...PIZZA...
HMM...SO THAT'S THE BEST YOU CAN DO?! C'MON...
HEEEYEEAHH... LET'S SEE YOU DO BETTER, DEEEK.
OKAY...LOOK INSIDE THIS ENVELOPE.
Y'SEE THOSE...? THOSE ARE CALLED PRESS PASSES.
PRESS PASSES FOR SUNDAY'S NINERS-COWBOYS GAME.
PRESS PASSES THAT WILL ALLOW US TO WATCH THE GAME ON THE FIELD.
RIGHT ON THE SIDELINES.
NO WAY.
NO WAY...
PRESS

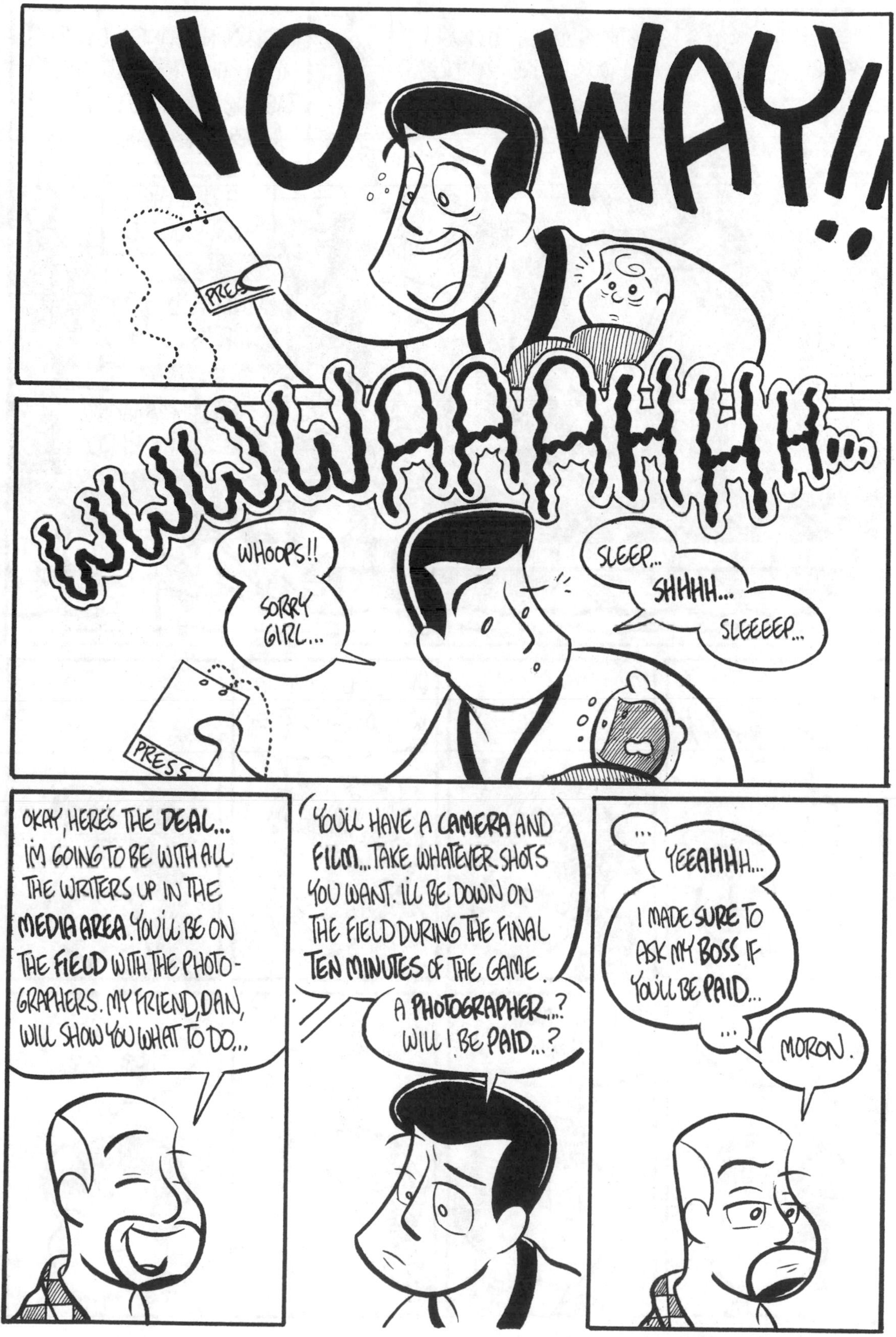
NO WAY!!
PRESS
WWWWAAAAHHHH...
WHOOPS!! SORRY GIRL...
SLEEP... SHHHH... SLEEEEP...
PRESS
OKAY, HERE'S THE DEAL... I'M GOING TO BE WITH ALL THE WRITERS UP IN THE MEDIA AREA. YOU'LL BE ON THE FIELD WITH THE PHOTOGRAPHERS. MY FRIEND, DAN, WILL SHOW YOU WHAT TO DO...
YOU'LL HAVE A CAMERA AND FILM... TAKE WHATEVER SHOTS YOU WANT. I'LL BE DOWN ON THE FIELD DURING THE FINAL TEN MINUTES OF THE GAME.
A PHOTOGRAPHER...? WILL I BE PAID...?
...
YEEAHHH...
I MADE SURE TO ASK MY BOSS IF YOU'LL BE PAID...
...
MORON.

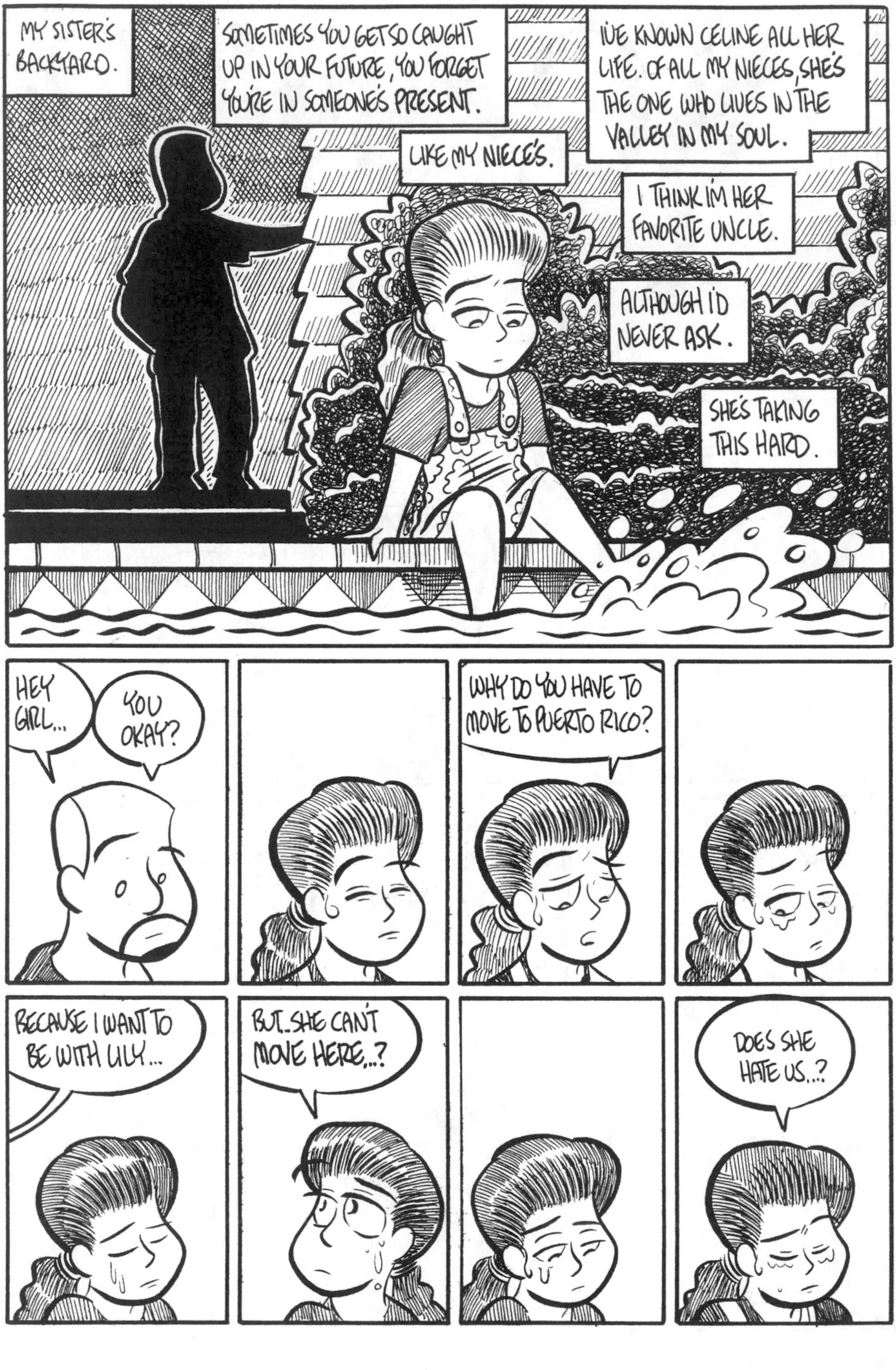
MY SISTER'S BACKYARD.
SOMETIMES YOU GET SO CAUGHT UP IN YOUR FUTURE, YOU FORGET YOU'RE IN SOMEONE'S PRESENT.
LIKE MY NIECE'S.
I'VE KNOWN CELINE ALL HER LIFE. OF ALL MY NIECES, SHE'S THE ONE WHO LIVES IN THE VALLEY IN MY SOUL.
I THINK I'M HER FAVORITE UNCLE.
ALTHOUGH I'D NEVER ASK.
SHE'S TAKING THIS HARD.
HEY GIRL...
YOU OKAY?
WHY DO YOU HAVE TO MOVE TO PUERTO RICO?
BECAUSE I WANT TO BE WITH LILY...
BUT...SHE CAN'T MOVE HERE...?
DOES SHE HATE US...?

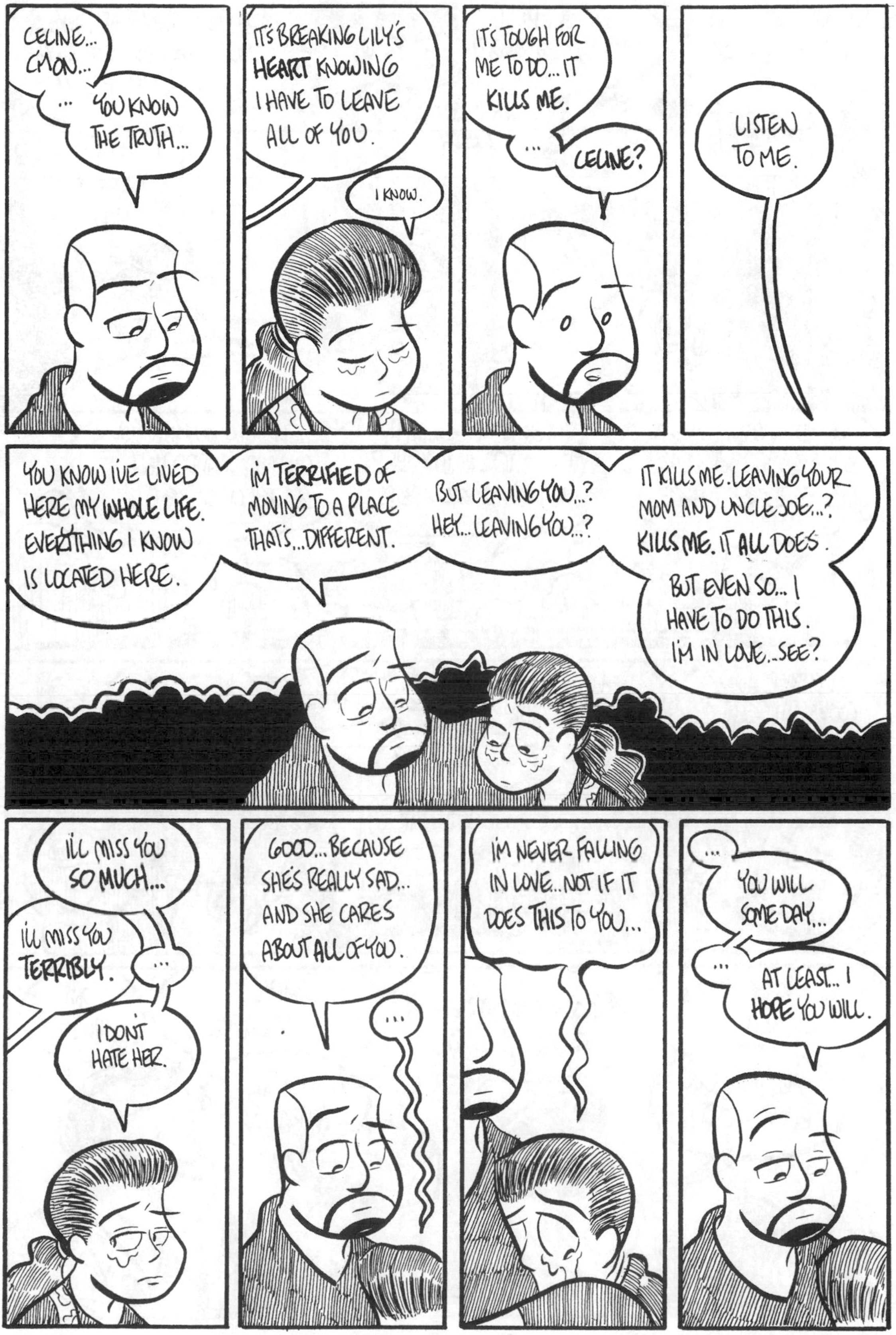

CELINE... C'MON...
... YOU KNOW THE TRUTH...
IT'S BREAKING LILY'S HEART KNOWING I HAVE TO LEAVE ALL OF YOU.
I KNOW.
IT'S TOUGH FOR ME TO DO... IT KILLS ME.
... CELINE?
LISTEN TO ME.
YOU KNOW I'VE LIVED HERE MY WHOLE LIFE. EVERYTHING I KNOW IS LOCATED HERE.
I'M TERRIFIED OF MOVING TO A PLACE THAT'S... DIFFERENT.
BUT LEAVING YOU...? HEY... LEAVING YOU...?
IT KILLS ME. LEAVING YOUR MOM AND UNCLE JOE...? KILLS ME. IT ALL DOES.
BUT EVEN SO... I HAVE TO DO THIS. I'M IN LOVE... SEE?
I'LL MISS YOU SO MUCH...
I'LL MISS YOU TERRIBLY.
...
I DON'T HATE HER.
GOOD... BECAUSE SHE'S REALLY SAD... AND SHE CARES ABOUT ALL OF YOU.
...
I'M NEVER FALLING IN LOVE... NOT IF IT DOES THIS TO YOU...
...
YOU WILL SOME DAY...
...
AT LEAST... I HOPE YOU WILL.

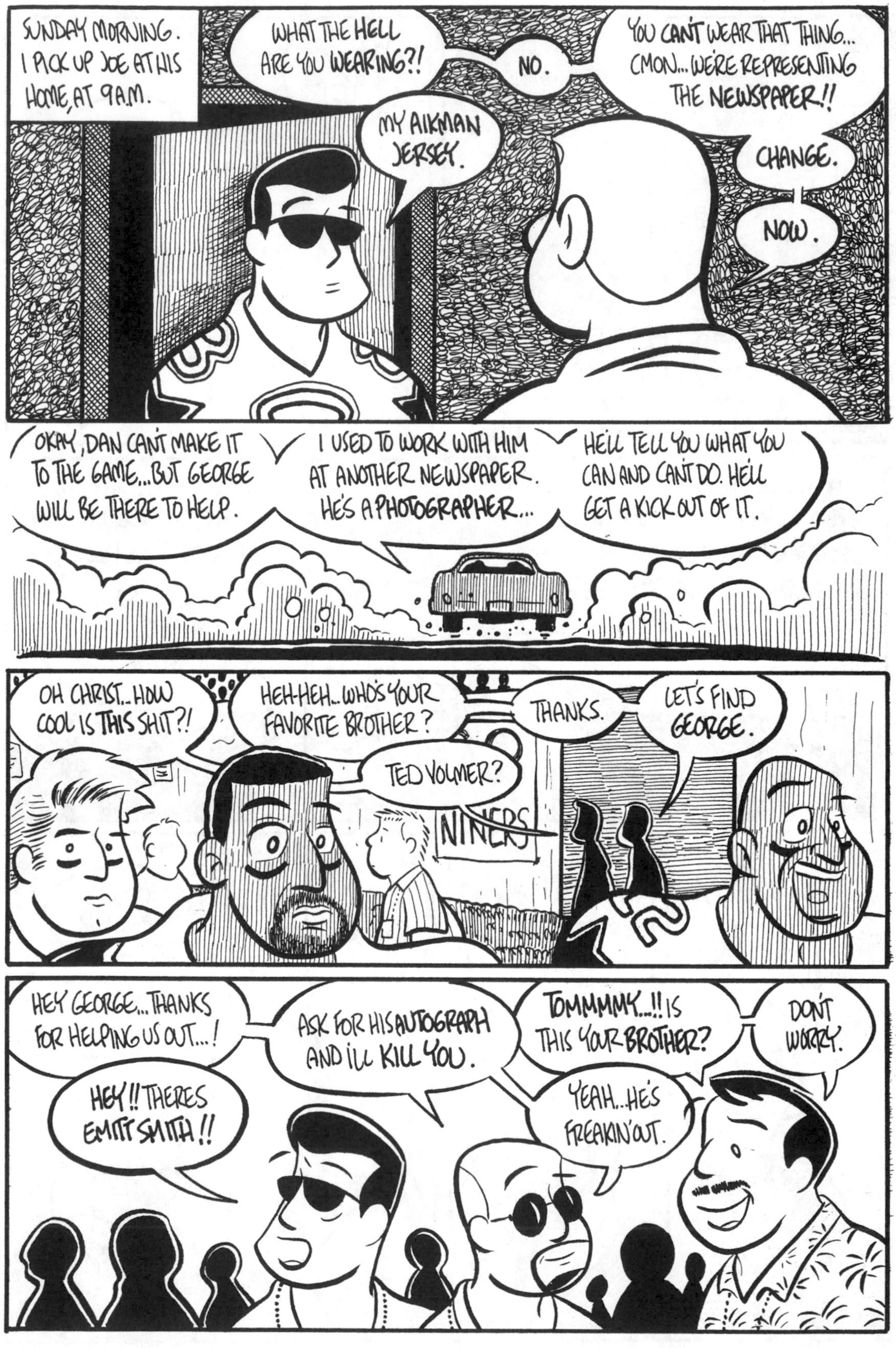
SUNDAY MORNING. I PICK UP JOE AT HIS HOME, AT 9 A.M.
WHAT THE HELL ARE YOU WEARING?!
MY AIKMAN JERSEY.
NO.
YOU CAN'T WEAR THAT THING... C'MON... WE'RE REPRESENTING THE NEWSPAPER!!
CHANGE.
NOW.
OKAY, DAN CAN'T MAKE IT TO THE GAME... BUT GEORGE WILL BE THERE TO HELP.
I USED TO WORK WITH HIM AT ANOTHER NEWSPAPER. HE'S A PHOTOGRAPHER...
HE'LL TELL YOU WHAT YOU CAN AND CAN'T DO. HE'LL GET A KICK OUT OF IT.
OH CHRIST... HOW COOL IS THIS SHIT?!
HEH-HEH... WHO'S YOUR FAVORITE BROTHER?
TED VOLMER?
THANKS.
LET'S FIND GEORGE.
NINERS
HEY GEORGE... THANKS FOR HELPING US OUT...!
ASK FOR HIS AUTOGRAPH AND I'LL KILL YOU.
TOMMMMY...!! IS THIS YOUR BROTHER?
DON'T WORRY.
HEY!! THERES EMITT SMITH!!
YEAH... HE'S FREAKIN' OUT.

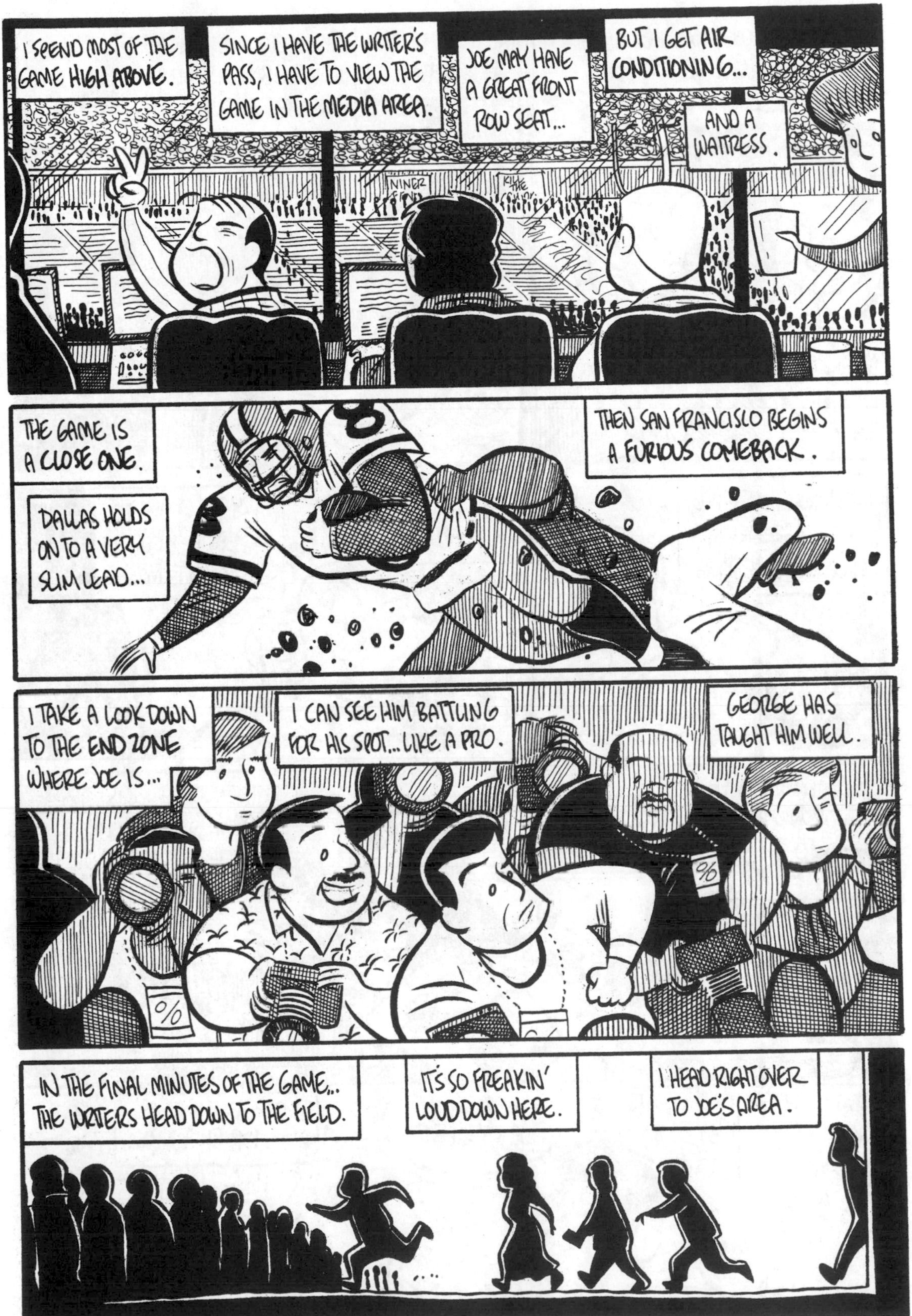
I SPEND MOST OF THE GAME HIGH ABOVE.
SINCE I HAVE THE WRITER'S PASS, I HAVE TO VIEW THE GAME IN THE MEDIA AREA.
JOE MAY HAVE A GREAT FRONT ROW SEAT...
BUT I GET AIR CONDITIONING...
AND A WAITRESS.
NINER
SAN FRANCISCO
THE GAME IS A CLOSE ONE.
DALLAS HOLDS ON TO A VERY SLIM LEAD...
THEN SAN FRANCISCO BEGINS A FURIOUS COMEBACK.
I TAKE A LOOK DOWN TO THE END ZONE WHERE JOE IS...
I CAN SEE HIM BATTLING FOR HIS SPOT... LIKE A PRO.
GEORGE HAS TAUGHT HIM WELL.
IN THE FINAL MINUTES OF THE GAME... THE WRITERS HEAD DOWN TO THE FIELD.
IT'S SO FREAKIN' LOUD DOWN HERE.
I HEAD RIGHT OVER TO JOE'S AREA.

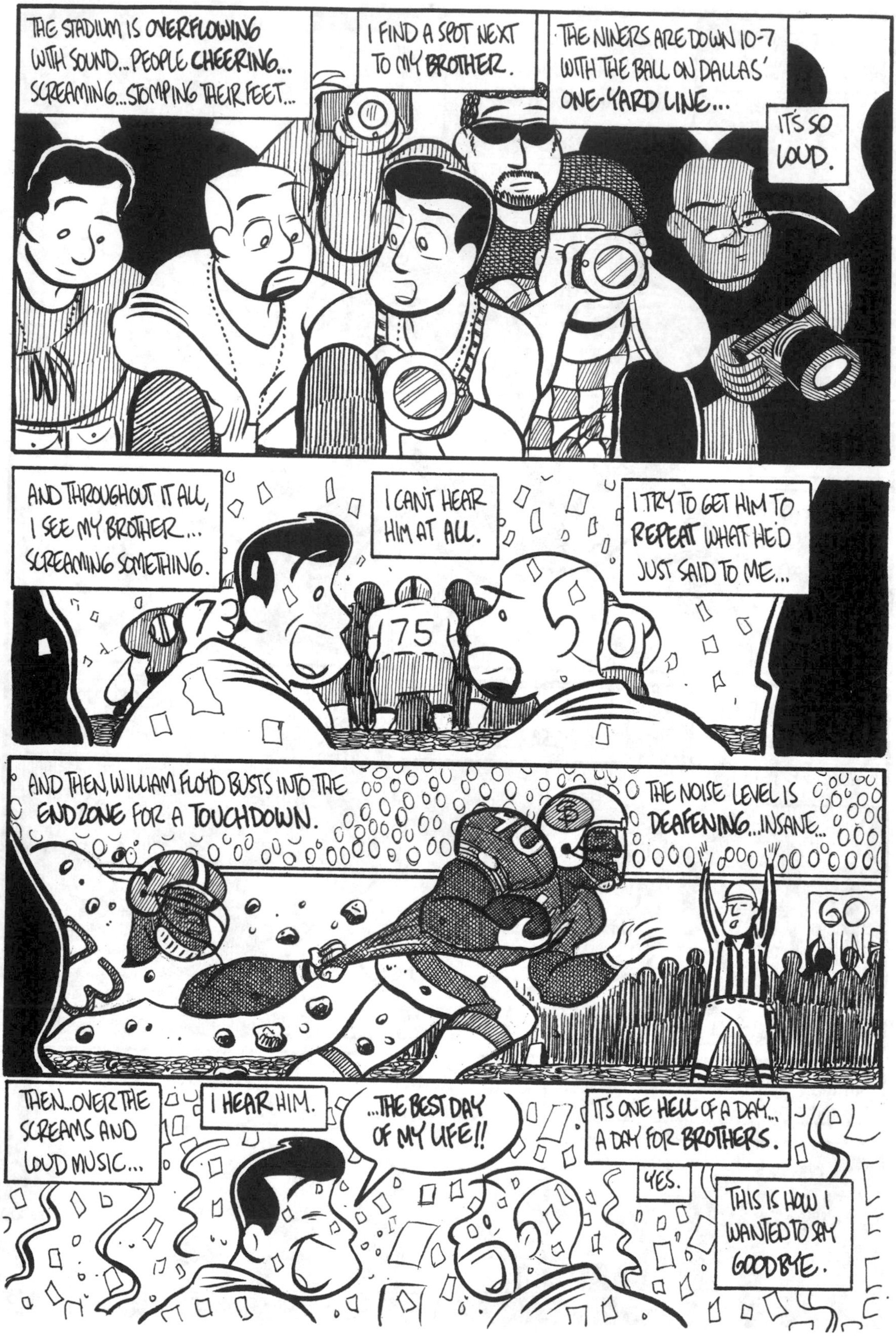
THE STADIUM IS OVERFLOWING WITH SOUND... PEOPLE CHEERING... SCREAMING... STOMPING THEIR FEET...
I FIND A SPOT NEXT TO MY BROTHER.
THE NINERS ARE DOWN 10-7 WITH THE BALL ON DALLAS' ONE-YARD LINE...
IT'S SO LOUD.
AND THROUGHOUT IT ALL, I SEE MY BROTHER... SCREAMING SOMETHING.
I CAN'T HEAR HIM AT ALL.
I TRY TO GET HIM TO REPEAT WHAT HE'D JUST SAID TO ME...
73
75
AND THEN, WILLIAM FLOYD BUSTS INTO THE END ZONE FOR A TOUCHDOWN.
THE NOISE LEVEL IS DEAFENING... INSANE...
GO
THEN... OVER THE SCREAMS AND LOUD MUSIC...
I HEAR HIM.
...THE BEST DAY OF MY LIFE!!
IT'S ONE HELL OF A DAY... A DAY FOR BROTHERS.
YES.
THIS IS HOW I WANTED TO SAY GOODBYE.

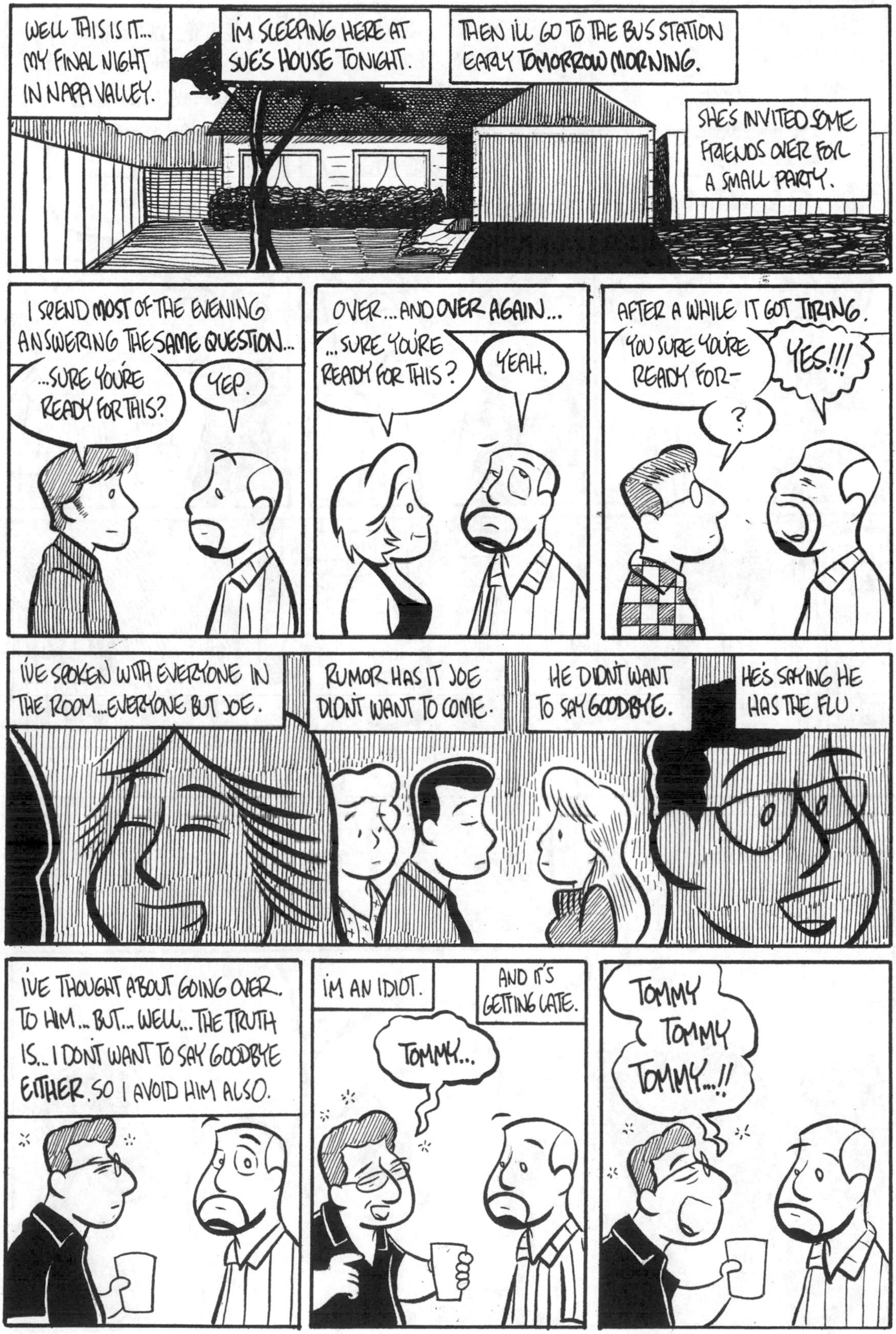

WELL THIS IS IT... MY FINAL NIGHT IN NAPA VALLEY.
I'M SLEEPING HERE AT SUE'S HOUSE TONIGHT.
THEN I'LL GO TO THE BUS STATION EARLY TOMORROW MORNING.
SHE'S INVITED SOME FRIENDS OVER FOR A SMALL PARTY.
I SPEND MOST OF THE EVENING ANSWERING THE SAME QUESTION...
...SURE YOU'RE READY FOR THIS?
YEP.
OVER... AND OVER AGAIN...
...SURE YOU'RE READY FOR THIS?
YEAH.
AFTER A WHILE IT GOT TIRING.
YOU SURE YOU'RE READY FOR-
YES!!!
?
I'VE SPOKEN WITH EVERYONE IN THE ROOM... EVERYONE BUT JOE.
RUMOR HAS IT JOE DIDN'T WANT TO COME.
HE DIDN'T WANT TO SAY GOODBYE.
HE'S SAYING HE HAS THE FLU.
I'VE THOUGHT ABOUT GOING OVER TO HIM... BUT... WELL... THE TRUTH IS... I DON'T WANT TO SAY GOODBYE EITHER. SO I AVOID HIM ALSO.
I'M AN IDIOT.
AND IT'S GETTING LATE.
TOMMY...
TOMMY TOMMY TOMMY...!!

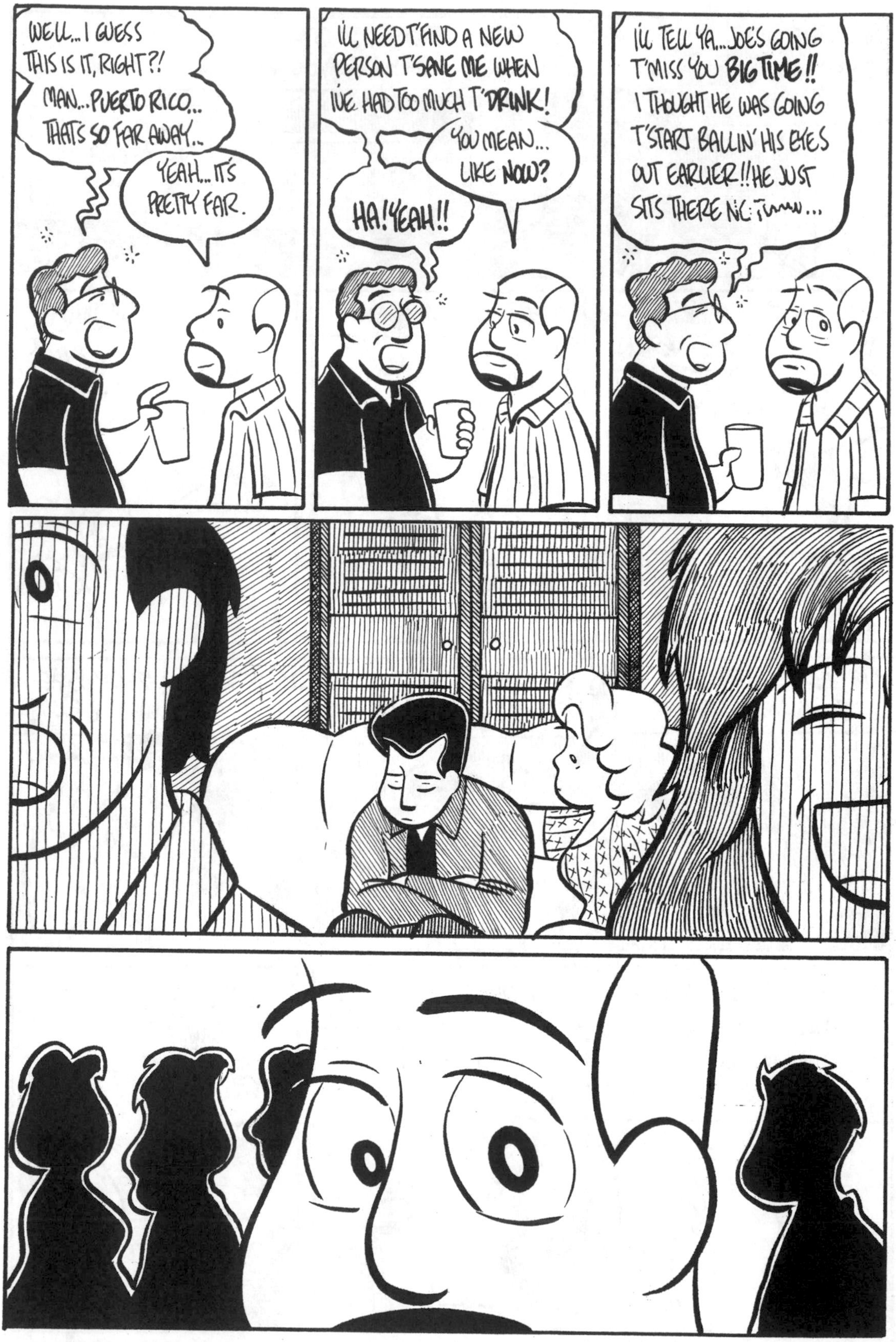
WELL... I GUESS THIS IS IT, RIGHT?! MAN... PUERTO RICO... THAT'S SO FAR AWAY...
YEAH... IT'S PRETTY FAR.
I'LL NEED T'FIND A NEW PERSON T'SAVE ME WHEN I'VE HAD TOO MUCH T'DRINK!
YOU MEAN... LIKE NOW?
HA! YEAH!!
I'LL TELL YA... JOE'S GOING T'MISS YOU BIG TIME!! I THOUGHT HE WAS GOING T'START BALLIN' HIS EYES OUT EARLIER!! HE JUST SITS THERE N...

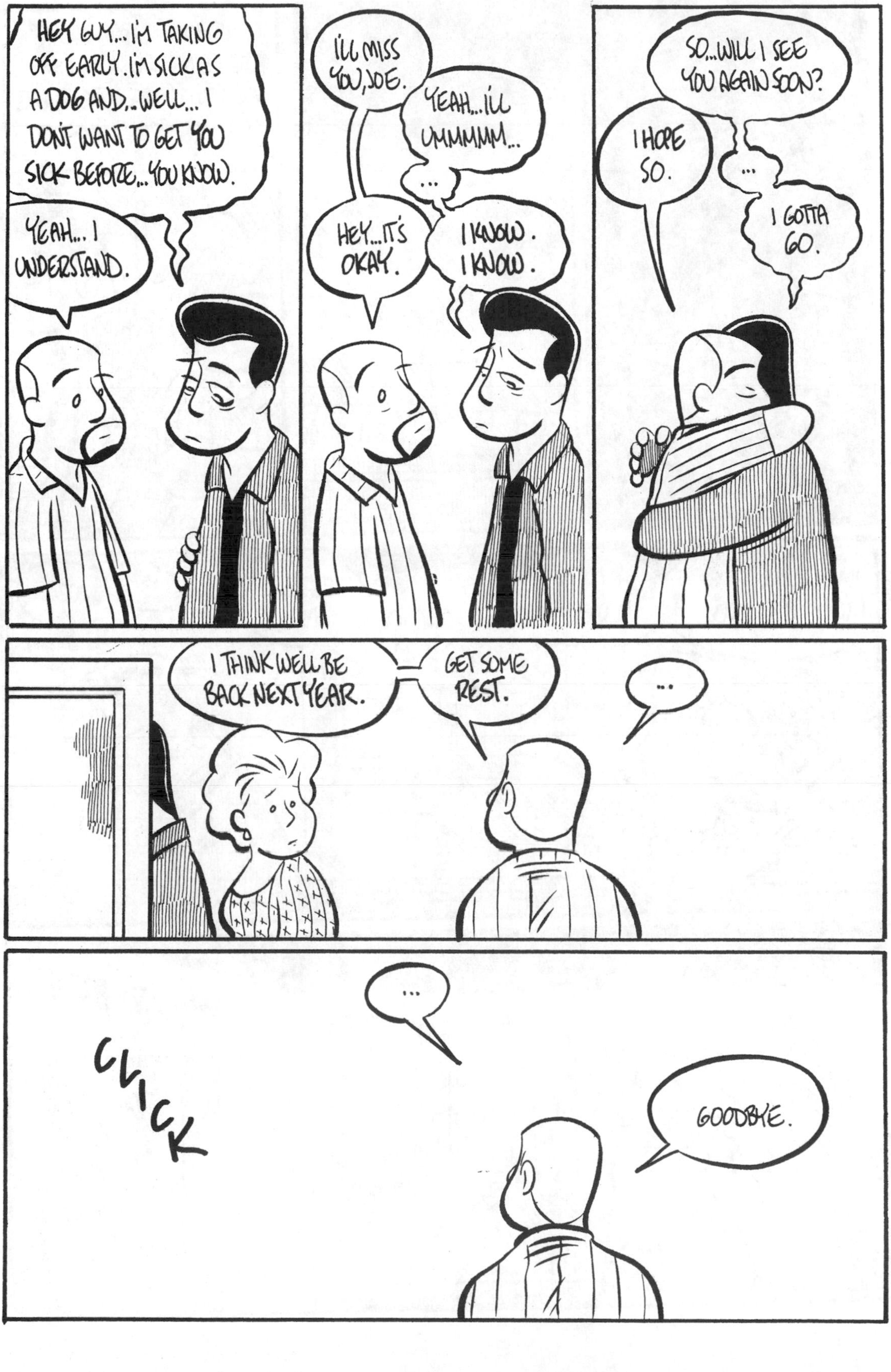
HEY GUY... I'M TAKING OFF EARLY. I'M SICK AS A DOG AND.. WELL... I DON'T WANT TO GET YOU SICK BEFORE... YOU KNOW.
YEAH... I UNDERSTAND.
I'LL MISS YOU, JOE.
YEAH... I'LL UMMMMM...
...
HEY... IT'S OKAY.
I KNOW. I KNOW.
SO... WILL I SEE YOU AGAIN SOON?
I HOPE SO.
...
I GOTTA GO.
I THINK WE'LL BE BACK NEXT YEAR.
GET SOME REST.
..
...
CLICK
GOODBYE.

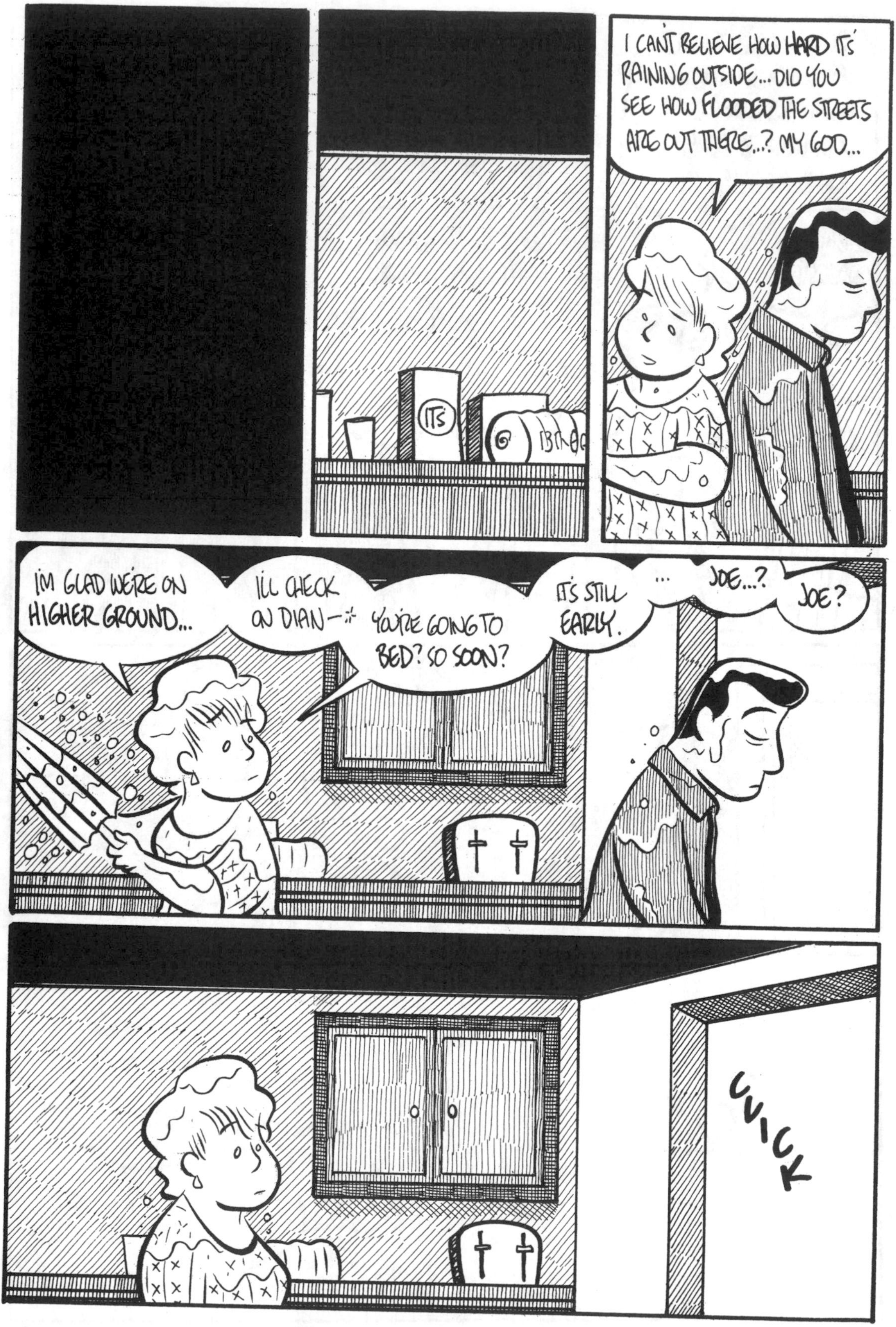

I CAN'T BELIEVE HOW HARD IT'S RAINING OUTSIDE... DID YOU SEE HOW FLOODED THE STREETS ARE OUT THERE...? MY GOD...
I'M GLAD WE'RE ON HIGHER GROUND...
I'LL CHECK ON DIAN—
YOU'RE GOING TO BED? SO SOON?
IT'S STILL EARLY.
...
JOE...?
JOE?
CLICK

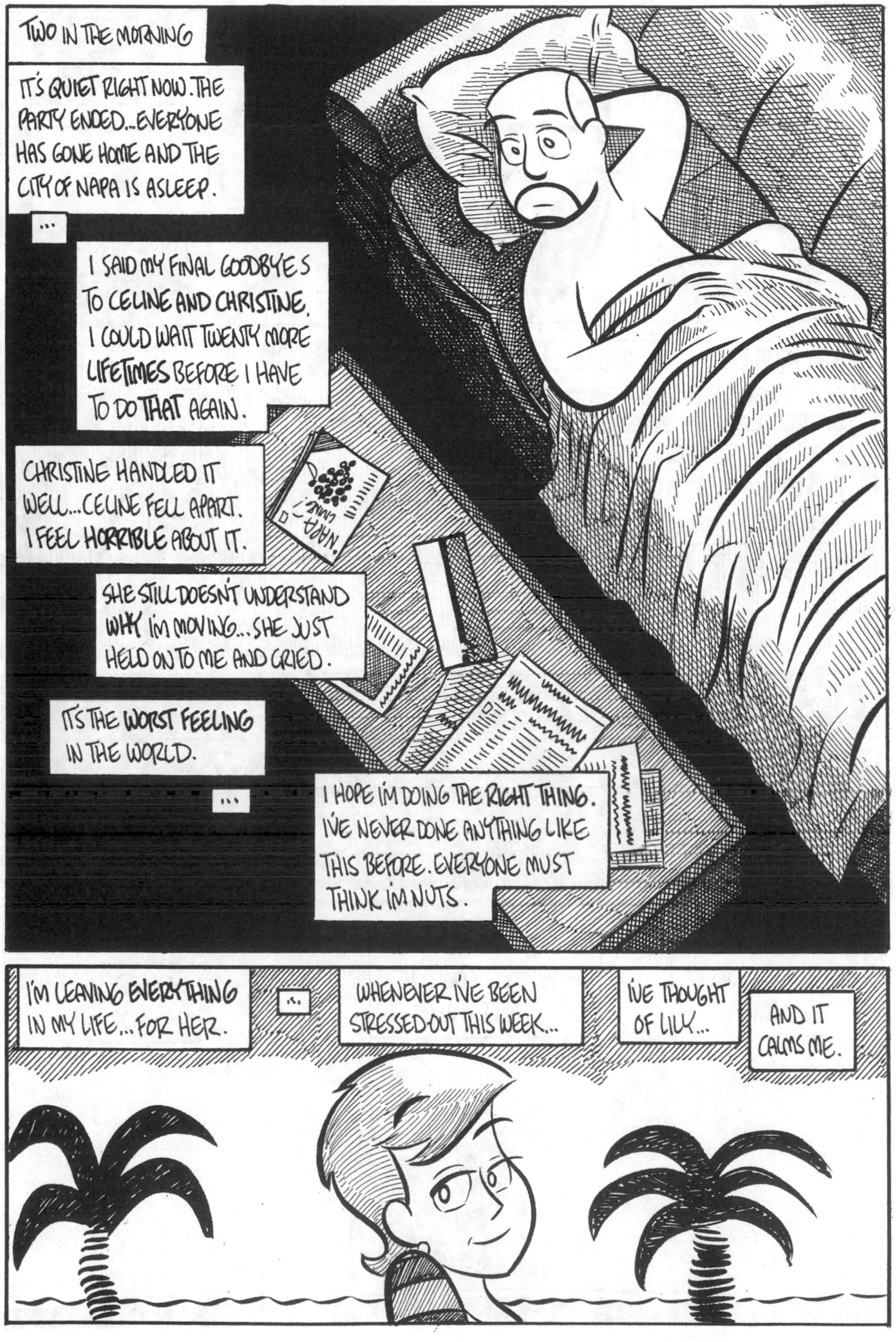
TWO IN THE MORNING
IT'S QUIET RIGHT NOW. THE PARTY ENDED... EVERYONE HAS GONE HOME AND THE CITY OF NAPA IS ASLEEP.
...
I SAID MY FINAL GOODBYES TO CELINE AND CHRISTINE. I COULD WAIT TWENTY MORE LIFETIMES BEFORE I HAVE TO DO THAT AGAIN.
CHRISTINE HANDLED IT WELL... CELINE FELL APART. I FEEL HORRIBLE ABOUT IT.
SHE STILL DOESN'T UNDERSTAND WHY I'M MOVING... SHE JUST HELD ON TO ME AND CRIED.
IT'S THE WORST FEELING IN THE WORLD.
...
I HOPE I'M DOING THE RIGHT THING. I'VE NEVER DONE ANYTHING LIKE THIS BEFORE. EVERYONE MUST THINK I'M NUTS.
I'M LEAVING EVERYTHING IN MY LIFE... FOR HER.
...
WHENEVER I'VE BEEN STRESSED-OUT THIS WEEK...
I'VE THOUGHT OF LILY...
AND IT CALMS ME.

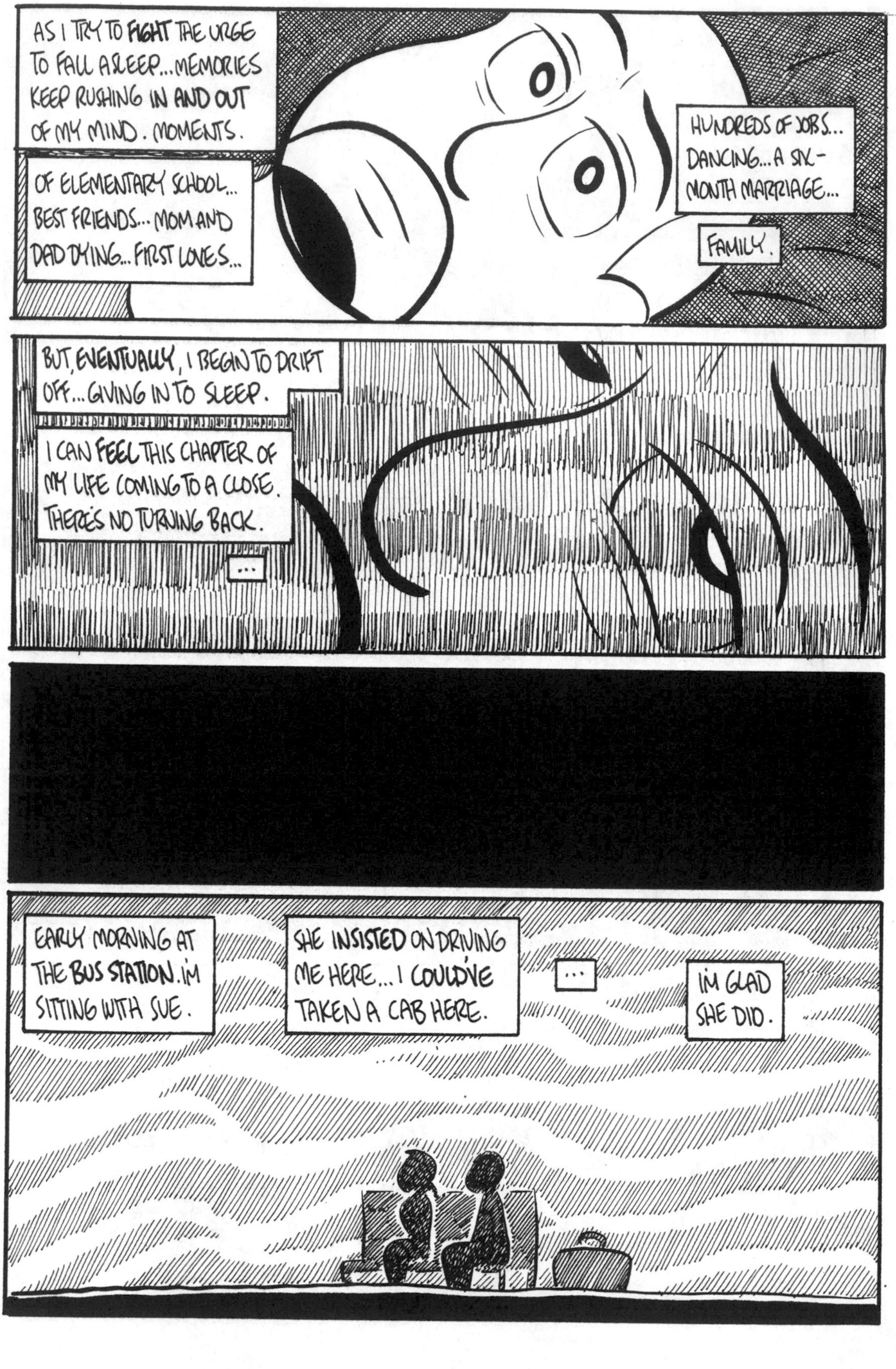
AS I TRY TO FIGHT THE URGE TO FALL ASLEEP... MEMORIES KEEP RUSHING IN AND OUT OF MY MIND. MOMENTS.
OF ELEMENTARY SCHOOL... BEST FRIENDS... MOM AND DAD DYING... FIRST LOVES...
HUNDREDS OF JOBS... DANCING... A SIX-MONTH MARRIAGE...
FAMILY.
BUT, EVENTUALLY, I BEGIN TO DRIFT OFF... GIVING IN TO SLEEP.
I CAN FEEL THIS CHAPTER OF MY LIFE COMING TO A CLOSE. THERE'S NO TURNING BACK.
...
EARLY MORNING AT THE BUS STATION. I'M SITTING WITH SUE.
SHE INSISTED ON DRIVING ME HERE... I COULD'VE TAKEN A CAB HERE.
...
I'M GLAD SHE DID.

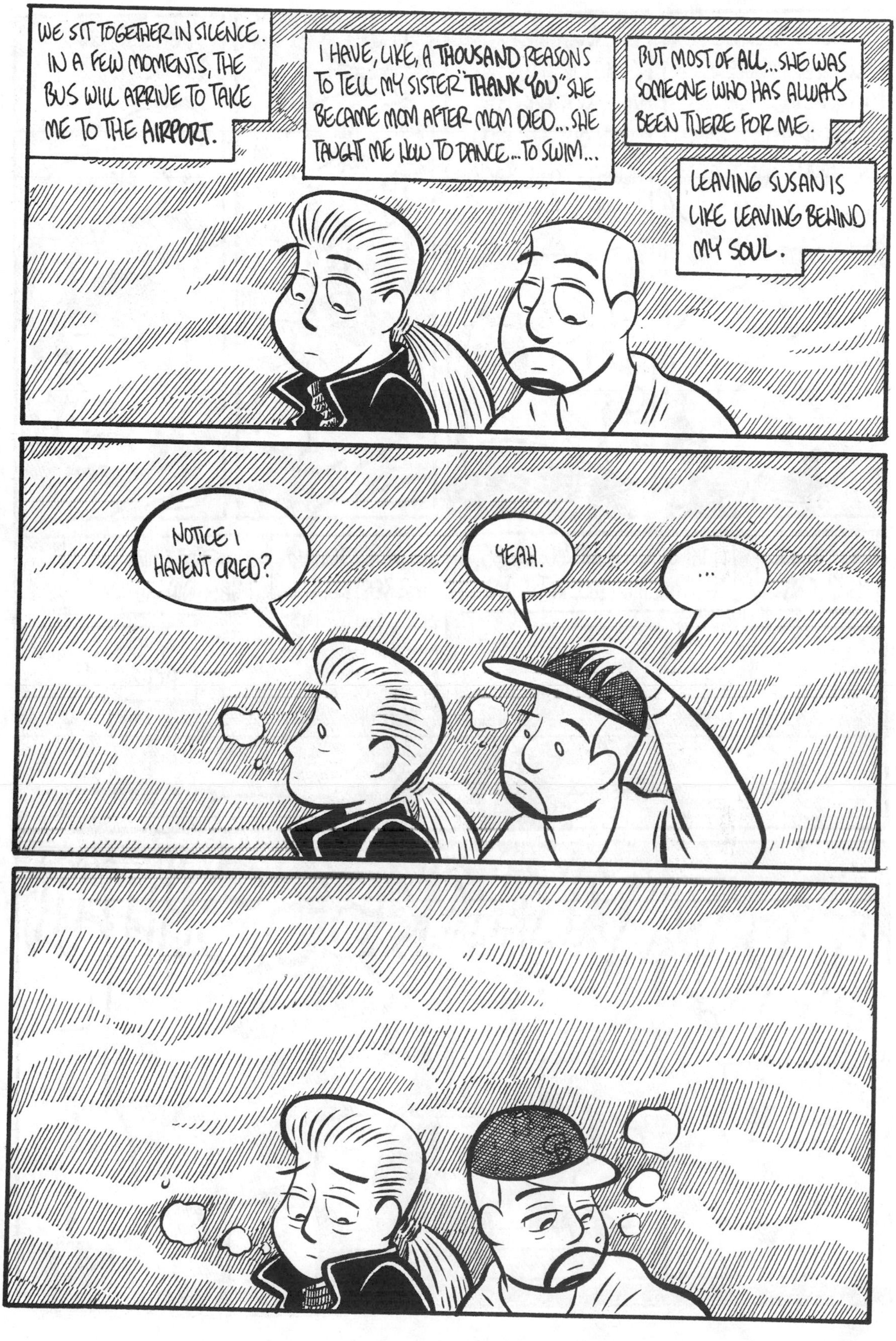
WE SIT TOGETHER IN SILENCE. IN A FEW MOMENTS, THE BUS WILL ARRIVE TO TAKE ME TO THE AIRPORT.
I HAVE, LIKE, A THOUSAND REASONS TO TELL MY SISTER "THANK YOU." SHE BECAME MOM AFTER MOM DIED... SHE TAUGHT ME HOW TO DANCE... TO SWIM...
BUT MOST OF ALL... SHE WAS SOMEONE WHO HAS ALWAYS BEEN THERE FOR ME.
LEAVING SUSAN IS LIKE LEAVING BEHIND MY SOUL.
NOTICE I HAVEN'T CRIED?
YEAH.
...

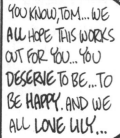

YOU KNOW, TOM... WE ALL HOPE THIS WORKS OUT FOR YOU... YOU DESERVE TO BE... TO BE HAPPY. AND WE ALL LOVE LILY...

BUT, YOU HAVE TO KNOW... IF, FOR SOME REASON, IT DOESN'T WORK OUT... YOU CAN ALWAYS COME BACK HOME... TO NAPA.

I KNOW.
...
IT'LL WORK.
...

BUT...
...
UMMM...
THANKS.

EVERYTHING IS SILENT.

I DRINK IN MY SURROUNDINGS. THE FOG... THE CHILL IN THE AIR...

MY SISTER, TRYING HER BEST NOT TO CRY IN FRONT OF ME.

THE BIRDS ARE JUST BEGINNING TO CHIRP.

MY HEART ACHES.

VRRMMMMKSSSHHHH

TIME FOR GOODBYES.

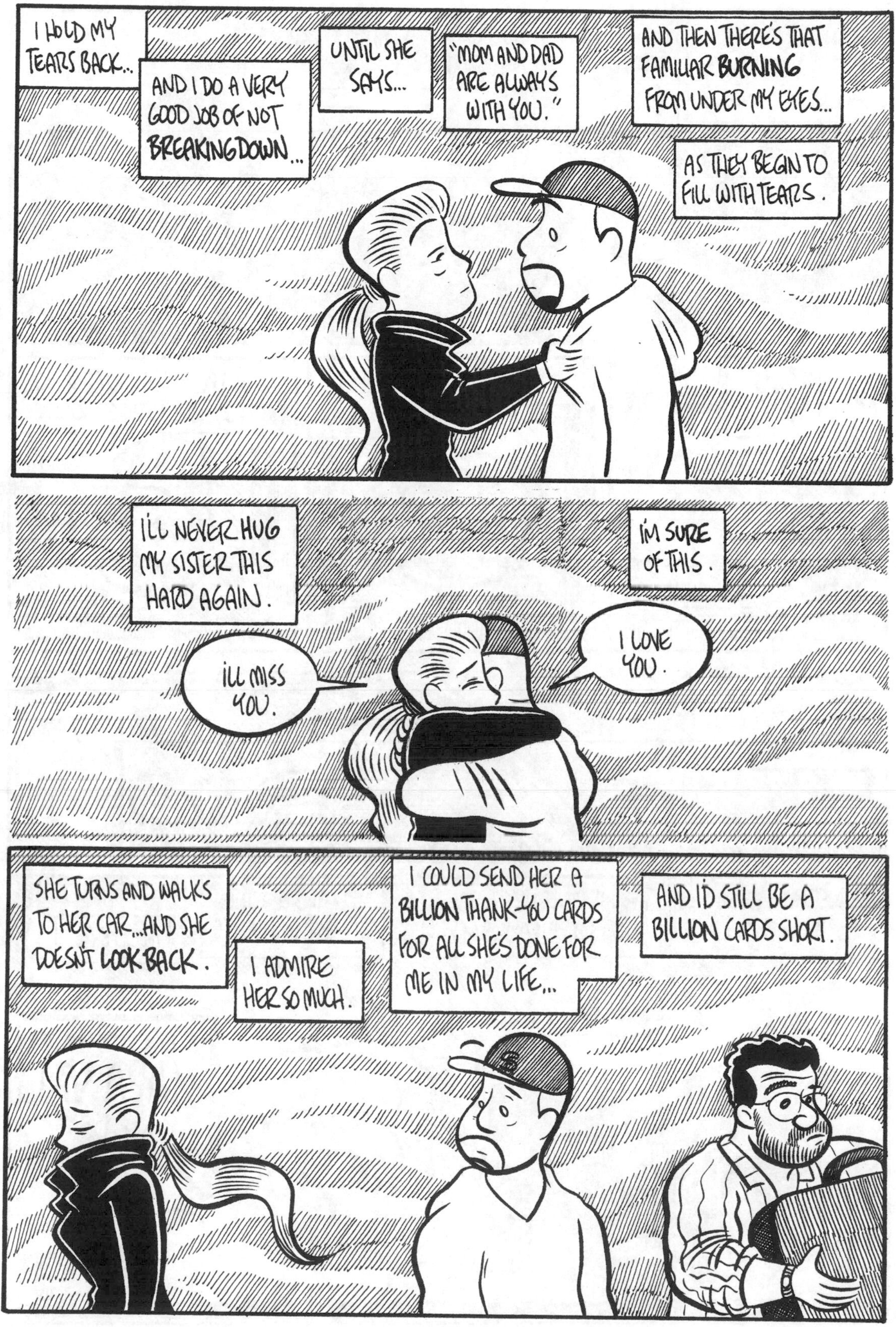

I HOLD MY TEARS BACK...
AND I DO A VERY GOOD JOB OF NOT BREAKING DOWN...
UNTIL SHE SAYS...
"MOM AND DAD ARE ALWAYS WITH YOU."
AND THEN THERE'S THAT FAMILIAR BURNING FROM UNDER MY EYES...
AS THEY BEGIN TO FILL WITH TEARS.
I'LL NEVER HUG MY SISTER THIS HARD AGAIN.
I'M SURE OF THIS.
I'LL MISS YOU.
I LOVE YOU.
SHE TURNS AND WALKS TO HER CAR...AND SHE DOESN'T LOOK BACK.
I ADMIRE HER SO MUCH.
I COULD SEND HER A BILLION THANK-YOU CARDS FOR ALL SHE'S DONE FOR ME IN MY LIFE...
AND I'D STILL BE A BILLION CARDS SHORT.

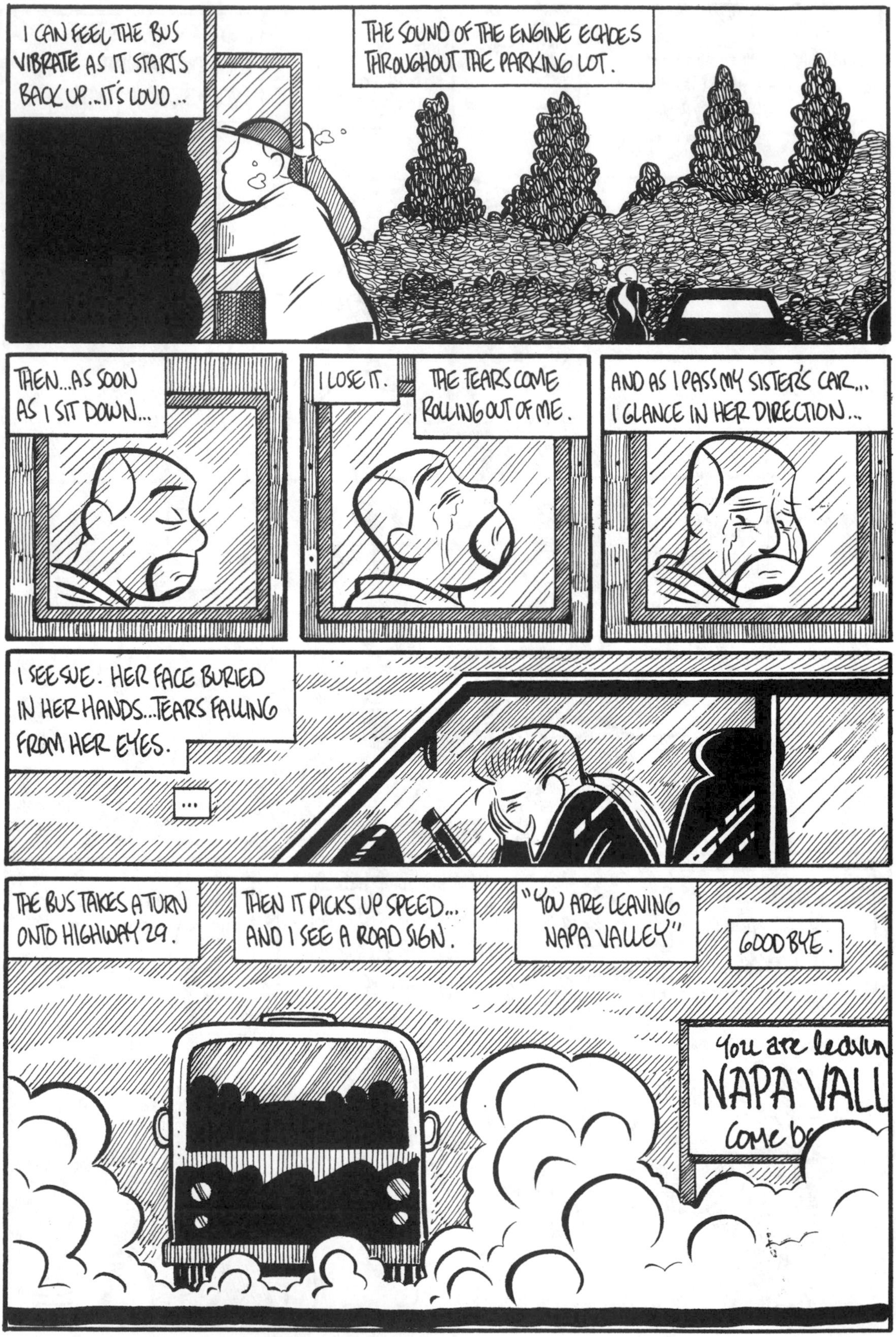
I CAN FEEL THE BUS VIBRATE AS IT STARTS BACK UP...IT'S LOUD...
THE SOUND OF THE ENGINE ECHOES THROUGHOUT THE PARKING LOT.
THEN...AS SOON AS I SIT DOWN...
I LOSE IT.
THE TEARS COME ROLLING OUT OF ME.
AND AS I PASS MY SISTER'S CAR... I GLANCE IN HER DIRECTION...
I SEE SUE. HER FACE BURIED IN HER HANDS...TEARS FALLING FROM HER EYES.
...
THE BUS TAKES A TURN ONTO HIGHWAY 29.
THEN IT PICKS UP SPEED... AND I SEE A ROAD SIGN.
"YOU ARE LEAVING NAPA VALLEY"
GOODBYE.